THE PIVOTAL PROBLEMS

OF EDUCATION

THE MACMILLAN COMPANY
NEW YORK · BOSTON · CHICAGO · DALLAS
ATLANTA · SAN FRANCISCO

MACMILLAN AND CO., Limited
LONDON · BOMBAY · CALCUTTA · MADRAS
MELBOURNE

THE MACMILLAN COMPANY
OF CANADA, Limited
TORONTO

The Pivotal Problems
OF EDUCATION

An Introduction to the
Christian Philosophy
of Education

BY WILLIAM F. CUNNINGHAM, C. S. C., Ph. D.
Professor of Education at the University of Notre Dame

New York

THE MACMILLAN COMPANY

1940

Imprimi Potest

THOMAS A. STEINER, C.S.C.
Provincial

Nihil Obstat

ARTHUR J. SCANLAN, S.T.D.
Censor librorum

Imprimatur

✠FRANCIS J. SPELLMAN, D.D.
Archbishop of New York

– Printed in the United States of America –
Published, October, 1940

To

My mother and father

PREFACE

Anyone familiar with the educational literature of the last two decades is aware that there has been a very decided shift from emphasis upon educational devices to discussion of the deeper problems underlying educational procedure on all levels of the educational ladder. Fundamentally these problems are concerned with ends rather than means and as such they are peculiarly the province of educational philosophy. The philosopher concerns himself with means but only after he has determined the ends to be striven for. As a philosopher, his function is to evaluate means in terms of their contribution to the attainment of ends already determined. This task of determining ends and evaluating means is the most difficult problem confronting the educator. It calls for constant and continued reflective thinking upon the experience of all mankind throughout the centuries and in addition, it must supplement this with the special light scientific investigation has added for the improvement of means.

It is the hope of the author that this book will aid both the beginning student, as well as the student who has already read deeply in the philosophical literature dealing with education as one of the great social problems of the day. This is an ambitious project. If the book is simple enough to be understood by beginning students, will it be of any value to advanced students? On the other hand, if it is difficult enough to challenge the attention of advanced students, can it be meaningful to those beginning their study of education? Though the author has had primarily in mind the graduate student making an overview of the main problems in this field, use of the text for four years in planographed form with students in undergraduate courses leads him to believe that it is not too difficult for the beginning student who can read understandingly and who is not adverse to carrying on reflective thinking. After all, the junior classman in college has been experiencing life for twenty years and fourteen of these have been devoted to schooling. This experience should furnish an adequate foundation for intelligent thinking concerning the purposes of the school and profitable study of procedures to be followed in the achievement of these purposes. This is philosophizing about education.

If the author has been successful in his endeavor, although the organization of the seventeen chapters into which the work is divided, is best adapted to a graduate course in "The Philosophy of Education" covering all four of the "pivotal problems," nevertheless he feels it may be adapted to such undergraduate courses as "Principles of Education," either secondary or elementary, if these courses, as their name implies, are truly courses in *principles* of education. Principles are generalizations made to give guidance for putting into operation practical school procedures. When first studied by the undergraduate student, principles often lack meaning because of his limited experience. But the graduate student, particularly if he has had some years of teaching, should find them more meaningful because of this experience. All students must add the "vicarious experience" of wide reading, if they expect to deepen their understanding of these problems.

In a course in "Principles of Secondary Education" the three chapters of Problem 3, "The Teacher (Method)" would be omitted, leaving the topics which they discuss to be covered in the course commonly called "Principles and Technique of Teaching," the old name for which was "General Methods." In place of these three chapters three units should be introduced, one dealing with "The Psychology of the Secondary School Pupil" (the psychology of adolescence) immediately following Chapter V, "Theories of Learning"; the other two are "Foreign Secondary Schools" and "The History of the High School." Both of these topics are treated briefly in Section 1 of Chapter XI, "The Dilemma of Democratic Education." Whatever time remains may well be spent on Chapter XII, "The American Educational Ladder," developing the interrelationships of the several levels of the ladder, with expanded treatment of the secondary school curriculum. A similar adjustment can be made for courses in "Principles of Elementary Education." The concluding chapter, XVII, "The Philosophy of Catholic Education" is merely an attempt to give from a fresh point of view a summary statement of the general theory running throughout the book.

When an author has worked for years over one book rethinking, rewriting and refining, it is impossible to hold in mind all those who have contributed in a greater or less degree to the production of the work in its finished form. He wishes, therefore, to thank both his undergraduate and graduate students of the past years for the many helpful suggestions they have given him. He is indebted particularly to three of his graduate students without whose help the book might never have been completed. They are Sister Mary Loyole, S.N.D., of Notre Dame College, Cleveland; Sister Mary Eunicia, B.V.M., of Clarke College, Dubuque; and Sister M. Noreen, S.S.N.D., of St. Alphonsus Ligori High School, St. Louis. Miss Grace Lushbaugh of Riley High School, South Bend, Indiana, read and carefully annotated the 1936 and 1937 planographed editions and Rev. Charles Miltner, C.S.C.,

President of Portland University, Portland, Oregon, has read the entire manuscript. I am deeply indebted to both for many helpful suggestions. Two student secretaries, Joseph Krupa, 1936–38, and John Julian, 1938–40, have done the typing. To all these I express my sincere thanks for the assistance they have given me. For whatever mistakes or errors may have crept into the work in spite of careful revision, I carry full responsibility.

As an aid towards introducing students to and arousing their interest in the literature of the field, I have made generous use of quotations. Some of these are introduced for purposes of criticism; others as confirming the point of view presented here. For courteous permission to use these copyrighted materials without charge, I wish to thank the following publishers:

American Book Company, D. Appleton-Century Co., American Council on Education, the Atlantic Monthly Co., Benziger Brothers, Bookman Publishing Co., the Carnegie Foundation for the Advancement of Teaching, Catholic Education Press, Cokesbury Press, Commonweal Publishing Co., The Curtis Publishing Co., Dartmouth College Press, John Day Co., Doubleday, Doran and Co., Farrar and Rinehart, Harcourt, Brace & Co., B. Herder Book Co., Henry Holt and Co., Houghton Mifflin Co., International Catholic Truth Society, Lawrence College Press, J. B. Lippincott Co., Loyola University Press, J. W. Luce Co., the Macmillan Co., A. C. McClurg Co., McGraw-Hill Book Co., The New Republic, the North Central Association of Colleges and Secondary Schools, W. W. Norton Co., Ohio State University Press, Ronald Press Co., Charles Scribner's Sons, Sheed & Ward, Teachers College Bureau of Publications, United States Office of Education, University of Chicago Press, Yale University Press and Mr. Will Durant.

The following publishers have granted permission to reproduce here the materials named: W. B. Saunders Co., Figure

4, "The Reflex" from C. Judson Herrick's *Introduction to Neurology;* The Macmillan Co., Figure 11, "The Normal Distribution Curve" from Thorndike and Gates' *Elementary Principles of Education;* and the Bureau of Publications, Teachers College, Columbia University, Table II, "Average Amounts in Minutes per Week and Percentages of Time in Each Grade Allotted to the Subjects by Forty-Four Cities in 1926" from C. H. Mann's *How Schools Use Their Time.* To these I extend special thanks. In each case when material is used, full acknowledgment is made.

W. F. C.

University of Notre Dame,
August, 1940

THE PIVOTAL PROBLEMS OF EDUCATION

The function of the administration
of education is

		The Problems
		I
"to enable the right pupils	—	The Pupil
		II
to receive the right education	—	The Curriculum
		III
from the right teachers, . . .	—	The Teacher
		IV
under conditions which will enable	—	The Institution

under conditions which will enable
the pupils best to profit by their
training."

Sir Graham Balfour, *Educational Administration*,
Oxford University Press, 1921, p. 38.

TABLE OF CONTENTS

Introduction: The Philosophy of Education

Part I. Ends in Education

Problem 1. The Pupil, His Nature and Needs (Objectives)

Section A. Biological and Psychological Foundations

Conclusion to Part I

Part II. Means in Education

Section A. Problem 2. The Curriculum (Materials)

Section B. Problem 3. The Teacher (Method)

Section C. Problem 4. The Institution (Administration)

Conclusion

APPENDIX

DIAGRAMS

FIGURES

TABLES

THE PIVOTAL PROBLEMS
OF EDUCATION

THE PHILOSOPHY OF EDUCATION

The Philosophy of Education is the basic element in the professional training of the teacher. In this science the teacher seeks for the meaning of the educative process as it takes place in the mind of the pupil and for the goal towards which it should be directed. He must turn to the same source for the fundamental principles which should guide in the selection and arrangement of the materials of the curriculum in the various stages of the educative process and for the educative values of the different disciplines to be employed.

The philosophy of education, as a branch of applied science, is not concerned directly with the establishment of fundamental principles in any department of philosophy. Its business is to apply the truths and principles established by pure philosophy to the practical conduct of the educative process. It seeks to lift into consciousness and to make rational and deliberate, as well as more immediate and effective, the relation between the philosophical truth and the life and conduct of the pupil, and endeavors to guide the teacher in the manifold relations which he sustains towards his pupils in the imparting of knowledge, in the building of habits, and in the gaining of power and insight into the purposes and meanings of life.

Thomas Edward Shields, *Philosophy of Education*, Catholic Education Press, 1917, pp. 21–23.

THE SCIENCE AND PHILOSOPHY OF EDUCATION

The science and philosophy of education can and should work together in overcoming the split between knowledge and action, between theory and practice, which now affects both education and society so seriously and harmfully. Indeed, it is not too much to say that institution of a happy marriage between theory and practice is in the end the chief meaning of a science and a philosophy of education that work together for common ends.

John Dewey, "The Relation of Science and Philosophy as the Basis of Education," *School and Society*, April 9, 1938, pp. 471–473.

CHAPTER I

WHAT IS THE PHILOSOPHY OF EDUCATION?

The word "philosophy" like the word "psychology" is suffering from overuse by many educators who have no accurate idea of its real meaning. We have the "philosophy of this" and the "philosophy of that," but most of the presentations which carry such titles reveal that they have little relationship with philosophy in its traditional significance. In fact, one wonders whether the authors who use this phrase ever had any training in philosophy, either formally in school or informally through reading the great classics of philosophy which have come down to us through the ages.

Our purpose in this chapter, therefore, is to make clear what we mean by the Philosophy of Education. The easiest approach to this problem is first to answer the question, "What is education?"; second, to analyze and define what is meant by the term "philosophy"; then we will be in a position to answer the question which forms the title of this chapter, "What Is the Philosophy of Education?"

1. WHAT IS EDUCATION?

Definitions of education are commonly descriptive or normative. Descriptive definitions deal with the process of education; normative definitions, with the aims it is hoped that the

3

process will realize. Our purpose will be to work out a definition which shall be both descriptive and normative.

As a process, education may be looked at from two points of view; from that of society and from that of the individual. Society seeks to perpetuate itself by handing on its cultural acquisitions to each succeeding generation. Here is the process, social, through society, and also the aim, transmission. Putting the two together we have one view of education which has played and still plays a great part in the history of the race, namely, social transmission. This view has been characteristic of Oriental peoples. The caste system of India is a striking illustration of its effective operation.

As an individual process, education seeks to bring about growth and development within the individual. In history this has been the educational theory of Occidental peoples, notably the Greeks. But the thing to be kept clearly in mind is that these two aspects of education are complementary, not conflicting. *Individual development* is unthinkable (in the beginning at least) except insofar as the individual comes into possession of the social inheritance; and *social transmission* is impossible without bringing about changes within the individual. Not every society would admit that the changes wrought by another society in its younger generation have brought about desirable development, but the society which planned those changes conceived them as desirable and, therefore advancing the development of each succeeding generation.

From both points of view, that of society and of the individual, education is the bringing about of changes. Calling to mind the condition of the newly born human infant "mewling and puking in his nurse's arms" and contrasting this infant with the full-grown cultured adult, we have some idea of how many, how various, and how great are the changes directed and carried forward by society for the purpose of transforming this little animal into a coöperating and contributing member of the social group. An intelligent approach to the problem of directing this educative process necessarily involves some classification of the many changes to be brought about, so that procedures may be planned for the purpose of forwarding those changes. As a first division, one we believe to be primary, we present a classification that is threefold in character.

(A) FROM CAPACITIES TO ABILITIES

Comparing the newly born human infant with the young of the lower animals of the vertebrate kingdom, we see a striking difference. The chick stepping out of the egg in the incubator is able to take care of itself if food is at hand and the proper temperature preserved. Not so, the young of the human species. Apart from the so-called "mass reactions" (random movements of the limbs), about the only things it can do are grasp, suck, and swallow, along with the systemic operations necessary for the preservation of life. These elementary modes of behavior are inherited. That is, they are instinctive. Apart from the maturation process, all else has to be learned. And it is this learning process which demands the long period of dependence, social infancy, characteristic of the young of the human species now extended well into, and, for many, to the close of, the period of adolescence. Among the lower animals instincts take the place of this long period of learning. But instincts mean fixed modes of response, such as the bird building its nest. Since they are fixed, they do not change; hence, in animal life there is no progress. Man, however, although he gets a slow start, through learning goes far beyond the possibilities of the lower animals, each generation standing on the shoulders of the preceding, thus building a civilization.

His period of dependence means plasticity. Plasticity means educability, and educability means the ability to learn. Mature man has no instincts in the strictly scientific meaning of the term, *i.e.*, inherited modes of behavior not modified by learning, but he has a vast number of abilities. At first, however, these abilities are nothing more than capacities. This means they must be developed, and here is the first of the three changes we distinguish in our analysis of the educative process, namely, the change from undeveloped capacities to developed abilities, *e.g.*, the ability to use oral and written language.

(B) FROM IGNORANCE TO KNOWLEDGE

Every ability implies, of course, some knowledge. Yet the word "knowledge" carries a connotation which is not present in the word "ability." Mastery of the three school abilities, the three R's, reading, writing and reckoning, is, if you will, a form of knowledge, but the supreme value of these "tools of learning" is that they are the most important means for growth in further knowledge. [In the case of the supreme human ability, the ability to think, this too is conditioned by the possession of knowledge. No one can think unless he has something to think about. This means ideas, percepts, or concepts derived from experience. Thinking is the use we make of percepts and concepts in our attempts to solve life's problems and, in arriving at solutions, growing in knowledge.] All of our knowledge begins in sense experience (percepts), but as rational beings, our aim is to proceed, through insight into the problems that confront us, to meanings and understandings, and thus arrive at solutions of these problems. This is growth in knowledge. Hence, a second group of changes involved in the process of education is the change from ignorance of the social inheritance, characteristic of the newly born infant, to knowledge thereof, characteristic of the adult.

(c) FROM IMPULSES TO IDEALS

But the acquisition of knowledge and the development of abilities do not exhaust the content of this process we call education. There is another group of changes which must take place within the individual human being as he passes from infancy through childhood and adolescence to adulthood. As an infant his whole being is dominated by the needs of his rapidly growing body, particularly the need for food. Through childhood his *ego* is exerting itself in a way that promises the development of a tyrant in his dealings with others unless he is constantly submitted to the discipline of recognizing the rights of others. With arrival at adolescence, the sex impulse asserts itself. Throughout this whole period of development as soon as the child is capable of recognizing the difference between *meum* and *tuum* he experiences the urge to collect for himself those things of this world which in any way contribute so his comfort or to the exaltation of his *ego*. Certainly from the point of view of society the individual who has grown only in knowledge and ability to satisfy these animal impulses may well be a liability instead of an asset. The graduate of the School of Business who has developed himself in the field of accounting until he can pass with ease the examination which will qualify him as a C.P.A., and who has mastered the intricacies of the field of finance until he is qualified to lecture and write intelligently on corporation finance, this individual is not thereby a proven asset to the society in which he lives. If he uses his knowledge of finance to effect a defalcation of funds from the governmental agency in which he is employed and then uses his ability in accounting to cover it up, no one would deny that there is something fundamentally lacking in the education he has received.

Similarly, the physician or surgeon who, through study and

practice has made himself an expert in the field of obstetrics and by this knowledge develops a lucrative practice specializing in abortion, has missed something in those years of application to what we call getting an education. These are all illustrations of instances where the animal impulses so evidently dominant in the life of the infant and early childhood, have retained this dominance into adulthood instead of being submitted to the rational controls of human conduct characteristic of civilized society. These controls we call ideals. They work from within, but they find their approbation in the approval which society gives to their pursuit. Here then is the third group of changes which take place in the process of education. It is the change from domination by animal impulses to motivation by human ideals. Unless this third change is concomitant with growth in knowledge and the development of ability, it were better for the individual and for the society in which he lives, that these other two changes had not taken place at all.

We are prepared now to formulate our definition of education. We have distinguished three groups of changes, all of which are involved in any process of education that may be called complete. But it is important to keep in mind that these distinctions do not destroy the unity of the educative process. These distinctions are logical. Ability cannot be separated from knowledge nor can ideals, *i.e.*, purposes for which they are going to be used, be separated from either. Man is a unitary organism. We make these distinctions for purposes of study, that is, so that we may understand the nature of these changes and plan procedures for their realization. This is the work of the teacher, and this analysis will be helpful to him. But the process itself is one and it takes place in a unitary organism, the organism called man. With this understanding of how all three types of changes integrate one with another we may define education as *the process of growth and development whereby the individual assimilates a body of knowledge, makes his own a group of life ideals, and develops the ability to use that knowledge in the pursuit of these ideals.* (For definitions by other authors see pp. 18–21.)

2. WHAT IS PHILOSOPHY?

The etymology of the word "philosophy" throws little light on its meaning as it is used today. As a lover (philos) of wisdom (sophia) the philosopher makes no claim of having achieved wisdom. Rather, he is in pursuit of it. Science is knowledge (scientia) but not all knowledge is science, certainly not the unorganized knowledge of the man in the street. Rather, science is systematized knowledge. The purpose of science is investigation and description. The purpose of philosophy is interpretation and unification. The method of science is experimentation. The method of philosophy is reflection. The subject matter of science is the particular; hence we speak of the particular sciences: chemistry, biology, economics, etc. The subject matter of philosophy is the general.

(A) SPECULATIVE PHILOSOPHY

As the general science, anything that exists is subject matter for philosophy. Nevertheless, philosophy considers reality only under its more general aspects. What are the kinds of beings which may become subject matter of the knowledge of man? Philosophy answers that there are three: (1) matter, the physical universe; (2) spirit, the very contrary of matter; and (3) the union of matter and spirit which is man. Hence the three departments of philosophy dealing specifically with these different modes of being are: (1) *cosmology*, the philosophy of the physical universe; (2) *natural theology*, the philosophy of God, pure spirit, commonly called *theodicy*, (to distinguish it from *supernatural theology*, the study of God with the aid of revelation); and (3) *philosophy of mind*, the philosophy of man. In this third discipline the inquiries are into the origin, nature, and destiny of man. The old name for this discipline was *rational psychology*. The Latin manuals use the term *anthropology*. The English dictionary gives as the first meaning of "anthropology," "a: the science of the human organism," (Webster's Secondary School Dictionary) but unhappily the term is now commonly used as the name for the science dealing with the origin, classification, and distribution of races; hence we must use "philosophy of mind." These three departments of philosophy are grouped today in one class, *special metaphysics*.

But there are two other disciplines more fundamental than these three, furnishing the foundation on which they rest. These constitute what is called *general metaphysics*. There is, first of all, the inquiry into the concept *being* in general and following that, the causes of being. This department is called *ontology*, from the Greek word meaning "being." But back of that is a still more fundamental inquiry, namely: Can we know *being?* This is the problem of knowledge, with its name derived from the Greek word meaning "knowledge," *epistemology*.

The inquiries in these five disciplines are far beyond those in which science is interested. Science seeks the immediate, the proximate explanations of things. Philosophy seeks the ultimate. It goes beyond the physical. The Greek word "meta" means after or beyond. *Metaphysics* then, including both *general metaphysics* and *special metaphysics*, gives us five different fields of inquiry. These are presented in Diagram 1., Departments 1 to 5.

DIAGRAM 1.—AN OUTLINE OF PHILOSOPHY

Divisions			Departments	Subject Matter
Pure Philosophy	Speculative (descriptive)	General Metaphysics (metaphysical, beings)	1. Epistemology	Theory of Knowledge
			2. Ontology	Theory of Being
		Special Metaphysics	3. Cosmology	Physical Universe
			4. Philosophy *Psy'* of Mind	Man
			5. Theodicy	God
	Practical (normative)	(psychological, acts)	6. Logic	The True
			7. Aesthetics	The Beautiful
			8. Ethics	The Good
Applied Philosophy		(illustrations)	1. Philosophy of History	
			2. Philosophy of Literature	
			3. Philosophy of Religion	
			4. Philosophy of Education, etc.	

(B) PRACTICAL PHILOSOPHY

The metaphysical aspect of philosophy considers beings as they are and the possibility of our knowing them as such. For this reason it is called speculative philosophy. But, after all, "The proper study of mankind is man." So following the metaphysical inquiry into the origin, nature, and destiny of man, it is proper to turn to the study of man's acts in his efforts to achieve that destiny. This is called *practical philosophy*. It is divided into three fields following the three lines of activity which man carries on in his search for the true, the beautiful, and the good. The first discipline in this group is *logic*. It lays down the rules of right reason, and its objective is to aid man in his search for truth. The second is *aesthetics*. It

formulates the principles which should guide man in his efforts
to enjoy and to create the beautiful. The third is *ethics*. It
formulates the principles which should guide man in his efforts
to realize the good in conduct. Quite evidently these three
disciplines concern themselves with the three fundamental
phases of man's mental life, the cognitive (*knowing*), the
affective (*feeling*) and the conative (*doing*). They stand in
sharp contrast with the five disciplines of speculative philosophy or metaphysics, though resting upon it as their foundation. Speculative philosophy is *descriptive* of being in all its
modes. Practical philosophy is *normative*, that is, it sets up
norms for human living. Such is the outline of what is called
pure philosophy. Diagram 1. shows the eight disciplines with
the subject matter of each indicated insofar as that can be done
by a single word or phrase (p. 11).

With this analysis we are in a position to see the full scope of
this "widely accepted definition of philosophy: *the science of all
things through their ultimate reasons and causes, as discovered by
the unaided light of human reason*. The first part of this definition marks off philosophy from the special sciences, the last
part marks it off from supernatural theology." [1]

(c) APPLIED PHILOSOPHY

There is a broader interpretation of the term philosophy,
however, which is given to it when it is applied to the various
fields of human living. This meaning of the term is stated by
Coffey as follows:

> Man's conduct in life has undoubtedly many determining in-
> fluences, but it will hardly be denied that among them the pre-
> dominant influence is exerted by the views that he holds, the
> things he believes to be true, concerning his own origin, nature
> and destiny, as well as the origin, nature and destiny of the uni-

[1] P. Coffey, *Ontology*, Longmans Green, 1918, p. 5.

verse in which he finds himself. The Germans have an expressive
term for that which, in the absence of a more appropriate term,
we may translate as a man's *world-outlook;* they call it his *Weltanschauung.* Now this world-outlook is formed by each individual
for himself from his interpretation of *his experience as a whole.*
It is not unusual to call this world-outlook a man's *philosophy of
life.* If we use the term *philosophy* in this wide sense it obviously
includes whatever light a man may gather from the special
sciences, and whatever light he may gather from a divinely revealed religion if he believes in such, as well as the light his own
reason may shed upon a special and direct study of those ultimate
questions themselves to which we have just referred.[1]

This is *applied philosophy*, i.e., philosophy applied to man's
conduct of life. In this wider connotation of the term we have
the philosophy of history, of art, etc., and the philosophy of
education.[2]

[1] *Ibid.*, pp. 4–5.

[2] The student's attention is called to the fact that the "Outline of Philosophy"
presented in Diagram 1 on page 11 is not the only outline that may properly
be made of this field. The traditional analysis going back through St. Thomas to
Aristotle is given in diagrammatic form by Jacques Maritain in his *Introduction
to Philosophy*, Longmans Green, 1931, p. 271. The main difference between the
analysis presented by Maritain and the one given in Diagram 1, is found in the
division "Speculative Philosophy." Our analysis is made on the basis of subject
matter or content; Maritain's on the basis of method. His book, *The Degrees of
Knowledge*, Centenary Press, 1937, gives this in great detail distinguishing three
departments in "Speculative Philosophy" on the basis of the *degrees of abstraction* employed by each in arriving at knowledge: (1) philosophy of nature, *ens
mobile,* the study of the being of things in their sensible properties, (2) philosophy
of mathematics, *ens quantum,* the study of the being of things under the sole
property, quantity, and (3) metaphysics, *ens in quantum ens,* the study of the
being of things with the sole property of being. This gives a different alignment
to the five departments distinguished in our two divisions, "General" and
"Special Metaphysics," but all five departments are included. This approach
from the point of view of degrees of abstraction employed, may be more satisfying to one experienced in philosophical inquiry but it is often meaningless to
the beginning student. Today in the undergraduate curriculum in philosophy,
mathematics is not included as one of the departments. Hence the use here of
the other analysis on the basis of content, that is, the subject matter studied in
each department. The distinctions in Diagram 1 are easily grasped by the
student and since they exhaust being in all its modes, the outcome for the student

3. WHAT IS THE PHILOSOPHY OF EDUCATION?

As "applied philosophy," therefore, the Philosophy of Education includes all the light we may gain on the problem of education from the special sciences. The special sciences which have a definite contribution to offer are, first of all, *biology* and *psychology*, which give the answer to our inquiry into the nature of man; hence we have, in our Outline, Part I, Section A, Chapters III to V, biological and psychological foundations. In the second place, *sociology* gives the answer to our inquiry in regard to the nature of society; hence we have, in Part I, Section B, Chapter VI, "The Universal Human Needs," sociological foundations. Further, in the philosophy of supernaturalism, which it is our purpose to present, *revealed religion* will make two distinct contributions. In our inquiry into the nature of man, theology gives us first the doctrine of man's fallen nature; and second, the means at man's disposal to rise above that fallen nature, that means being grace, by which he becomes again an adopted son of God through the redeeming influence of God's Divine Son, Jesus Christ; thus we have, in Part I, Section B, Chapter VII, "The Fourth Factor in Man-making," theological foundations.

The strict definition of pure philosophy is meaningful for us, however, in our effort to clarify the significance of the term

---

is *unification*, the prime purpose of philosophical inquiry. Whether this analysis owes its origin to Aristotle, St. Thomas, or Christian Wolf (its author) is not a matter of great moment for the teacher. The two things that matter are answers to these two questions: (1) Is it valid? and (2) Can it be understood and become meaningful to students? Experience in teaching this analysis to undergraduate students in the course "Introduction to Philosophy" during many years has convinced the author that both these questions are answered in the affirmative. No matter which analysis is preferred, however, both lead to the division called "applied philosophy" within which is located the subject matter of this presentation, the applications of principles from departments of "pure philosophy," notably, philosophy of mind, logic, and ethics, to the problems of education—hence, "The Philosophy of Education."

when applied to education. First, philosophy is the science of "all things"; so the philosophy of education looks at the problem of education in all its main aspects. In our analysis, that large problem divides itself into what we call the four "pivotal problems." The significance of this title lies in the fact that every problem which arises in education may be logically grouped under one of these four headings.

In the second place, philosophy is the science of all things "through their ultimate reasons and causes." So, too, the philosophy of education studies only the deeper problems in the field of education as a whole, leaving to the science of education the study of those problems which are immediate and can best be approached through the scientific method, *e.g.*, the problem of measurement of student ability, etc.

The philosophy of education, as an application of principles formulated within the various philosophical disciplines, seeks guidance in the investigation of its several problems from these disciplines. Four of these disciplines are concerned with man as the immediate center of interest. Philosophy of mind investigates man's origin, nature, and destiny. The three normative disciplines, logic, aesthetics, and ethics, are concerned with his thoughts, feelings, and actions. Keeping this distinction between the descriptive and normative in mind, we see that the principles which arise within these disciplines fall into two classes, *viz.*, those concerned with man's *end*, that is, his perfection as a human being here and now in this life and, as a spiritual, immortal being, his end in the life to come after death (*speculative philosophy*); and second, those concerned with the *means* to that end, namely, those means which are regulative of his thoughts, feelings, and actions (*normative philosophy*). These are the two key words in any philosophical investigation into the life of man, namely, *ends* and *means*. When we use the phrase "a man's philosophy of life" we refer, first of all, to the supreme purpose which actuates him in living, and secondly, to the means which he uses in his efforts to achieve that purpose. Similarly, when we use the phrase "Philosophy of Education" we are referring, first of all, to the purposes of education in the life of man; and secondly, to the procedures which are to be followed in the achievement of those purposes. Again, it is an inquiry into ends and means. In the technical vocabulary of education today, ends are spoken of as "objectives" while means, for the most part, are referred to as "techniques." Thus we have "techniques of curriculum building," "techniques of teaching," and "techniques of administration." These phrases indicate three of the pivotal problems of education which have suggested the title of this treatise. They comprise Part II of the treatment, but we have retained the philosophical terminology in labeling it, namely, "Means in Education." The study of objectives takes up the whole of Part I under the general title, "Ends in Education." This is the more important, the more difficult and, fundamentally, the more philosophical part of our inquiry. Here we are concerned with the pupil, his nature and needs. In order to have insight into his needs we must first inquire into the nature of man. This includes the nature of learning, which makes education possible. Then follows an inquiry into the nature of society which conditions all learning, and finally an inquiry into the nature of God (at least such an inquiry will be included in a philosophy of education which includes the supernatural), insofar as man is related to Him. With this analysis we identify the pivotal problems of education as four, namely:

1. The Pupil:..................... Nature and Needs
2. The Curriculum:............... Materials to be Taught
3. The Teacher:................... Methods to be Employed
4. The Institution as a Whole:...... Administration

THE FOUR PHILOSOPHIES

Ends and means then are the key words for any inquiry that merits the appellation "Philosophy of Education." But the fact is that the end of man is conceived differently by different groups of thinkers. For many in the world today, *e.g.*, in Germany, man ceases to be an end in himself and becomes a means toward another end, the State. The philosophy behind this deification of the State is *idealism*. Others do not go so far as to submit the individual completely to the welfare of the group but do hold that this life is all; therefore, it behooves man to make the most of it. They are *materialists*, and Russia is the striking example. American educators sympathetic with this view hold that man exists to enjoy nature to the fullest and they have adopted as the euphemistic label for themselves "Naturalists." A third group of thinkers admit that man by nature is of the animal kingdom but contend that he is a different kind of animal. This difference is not merely one of complexity. This is the point of view of the materialistic evolutionists who claim that man differs from the animals of the lower orders merely on account of the social life we call civilization. But for the third group man is not merely a social animal. He is, above all, a *rational animal*. In fact, this power of reason is what makes him human; hence the name, *humanism*. A fourth group agrees with this latter group that man is a rational animal differing, not merely in degree but in kind, from all other members of the animal kingdom, but more than this, they hold that *he is a religious animal*. That is, in origin and in destiny he is definitely related to a superior being, the Author of the universe, God. Further, God in His goodness, having created man, has not deserted him. On the contrary, God, through Revelation has promised man eternal life with Him and assures him help to achieve that goal. This reward is far beyond anything due his nature; hence the name, "Supernaturalism." In the next chapter we will analyse in some detail these four views on the nature of man and therefore his end, and the means these views offer for the attainment of their respective ends.

DEFINITIONS OF EDUCATION BY OTHER AUTHORS

ADDISON. What sculpture is to the block of marble, education is to the human soul.

ARISTOTLE. The true aim of education is the attainment of happiness through perfect virtue.

BABBITT. The faculty which is by far the most important of the mind, and which we must earnestly strive to develop and perfect in our pupils, is the faculty of judgment, or the reasoning faculty.

BACON. Education, as science itself, is but a means to an end,— the dominance of man over things; human science and human power coincide.

BAGLEY. Education may be tentatively defined . . . as the process by means of which the individual acquires experiences that will function in rendering more efficient his future action.

BUTLER, NATHANIEL. It has been said that an educated man has a sharp axe in his hand and an uneducated man a dull one. I should say that the purpose of a college education is to sharpen the axe to its keenest edge.

BUTLER, NICHOLAS MURRAY. Education must mean a gradual adjustment to the spiritual possessions of the race. The child is entitled to his scientific, literary, aesthetic, institutional, and religious inheritance.

CHAPMAN AND COUNTS. Adaptation (adjustment) includes not only the changing of the individual to fit the environment, but also the most thoroughgoing attempts on his part to change the conditions under which he lives.

COMENIUS. Education is the development of the whole man.

———. To be acquainted with all things.

DEWEY. Education is the process of remaking experience, giving it a more socialized value through increased individual experi-

ence, by giving the individual better control over his own
powers.

EMERSON. The end of education is to train away all impediment,
and to leave only pure power.

FROEBEL. The object of Education is the realization of a faithful,
pure, inviolate, and hence holy life.

GENTILE. The main purpose of education is the development of an
ever deepening insight, an ever more profound consciousness of
consciousness.

HERBART. The end of education is to produce a well-balanced
many-sidedness of interest. Morality is universally acknowledged as the highest aim of humanity, and consequently of
education.

HUXLEY. Education is the instrument of intellect in the laws of
nature; under which name I include, not merely things and
their forces, but men and their ways; and the fashioning of the
affections and the will into an earnest and living desire to move
in harmony with their laws.

JAMES.* Education is the organization of acquired habits of action,
such as will fit the individual to his physical and social environment.

JEVONS. It is the purpose of education so to exercise the faculties
of the mind that the infinitely varied experiences of after-life
may be observed and reasoned with best effect.

KANT. The purpose of education is to train children, not with reference to their success in the present state of society but to a
better possible state, in accordance with an ideal conception
of humanity.

KEITH. The educational ideal is an adequate participation in the
present life of the race and in the ideals of the race.

LOCKE. The attainment of a sound mind in a sound body is the end
of education. The business of education is not to make the
young perfect in any one of the sciences, but so to open and
dispose their minds as may best make them capable of any,
when they shall apply themselves to it.

LUTHER. The object of education is preparation for more effective
service in state and church.

* Definitions starred emphasize phases of education as defined in this chapter.

MILL. Education includes the culture which each generation purposely gives to those who are to be its successors in order to qualify them for at least keeping up, and if possible, raising the improvement that has been attained.

MILTON. I call a complete and generous education that which fits a man to perform justly, skillfully, and magnanimously all the offices both public and private, of peace and war.

MONTAIGNE. Education is the art of forming men, not specialists.

NEWMAN. Discourse VI. "Knowledge Viewed in Relation to Learning," *Idea of a University*. Education is a high word; it is the preparation for knowledge, and it is the imparting of knowledge in proportion to that preparation.

ORCUTT. Education is not the storing of knowledge, but the development of power.

PACE. *Catholic Encyclopedia*. Education may be defined as that form of social activity whereby, under the direction of mature minds and by the use of adequate means the physical, intellectual and moral powers of the immature human being are so developed as to prepare him for the accomplishment of his life work here and for the attainment of his eternal destiny. Article, "Education."

PAINTER. The function of education is to assist and direct the processes of physical and mental growth during the formation periods of childhood and youth.

PALEY. Education, in the most extensive sense of the word, may comprehend every preparation that is made in our youth for the sequel of our lives.

PALMER.* Teaching may be defined as the awakening of another's mind, and the training of its faculties to a normal self-activity.

PESTALOZZI. Education means a natural, progressive, and systematic development of all the powers.

PLATO. Education consists of giving to the body and the soul all the perfection of which they are susceptible.

POPE PIUS XI., *The Christian Education of Youth*. The true Christian, product of Christian Education, is the supernatural man who thinks, judges and acts constantly and consistently in accordance with right reason illumined by the supernatural light of the example and teaching of Christ.

RABELAIS. The aim of education is the forming of a complete man, skilled in art and industry.

RICHTER. It is the business of education to develop the ideal prize man.

ROSENKRANS. Education is the process by which the individual man elevates himself to the species.

ROUSSEAU. Correct education disposes the child to take the path that will lead him to truth when he has reached the age to understand it, and to goodness when he has acquired the faculty of recognizing and loving it.

——. Education is nothing but the formation of habits.

RUSKIN. The manufacture of souls of good quality.

SHIELDS, *Philosophy of Education.* In one word Christian education aims at transforming a child of the flesh into a child of God. p. 180.

SOCRATES. The aim of education is to dispel error and to discover truth.

SPALDING, *Means and Ends in Education.* The aim and end of education is to bring forth in the individual the divine image of humanity as it exists in the thought of God, as it is revealed in the life of Christ. p. 105.

SPENCER. To prepare us for complete living is the function which education has to discharge.

TATE. One great end of education is to communicate to the pupil that sort of knowledge which is most likely to be useful to him in the sphere of life which Providence has assigned to him.

THIRY.* The end of education is triple: (1) to develop the mental faculties, (2) to communicate knowledge, and (3) to mould character.

THORNDIKE.* The work of education is to make changes in human minds and bodies.

THORNDIKE AND GATES. Education aims at satisfying the wants of all people in order to give each person the fullest realization of his own desires. The chief aim of education is to realize the fullest satisfaction of human wants.

VAN DYKE. Education is to create men who can see clearly, image vividly, think steadily, and will nobly.

WARD. Education means the universal distribution of extant knowledge.

SUGGESTED READINGS

1. WHAT IS EDUCATION?

Definitions by other authors, pp. 18–21; specified references for definitions by Newman, Shields and Spalding are given.

Burton, William H., *Introduction to Education*, Appleton-Century, 1934, Part I., entire "The Function and Aim of Education," pp. 17–116.

Fiske, John, *The Meaning of Infancy*, Houghton Mifflin, 1893 (reprinted as one of the Riverside Educational Monographs) "states the biological function of prolonged infancy in man," p. viii.

Pope Pius, XI, Encyclical, *The Christian Education of Youth*, 1931, any edition.

Thompson, Merritt M., *An Outline of the History of Education*, Burns and Noble, 1933, gives a series of definitions, pp. 141–145.

Thorndike, Edward L. and Arthur I. Gates, *Elementary Principles of Education*, Macmillan, 1929, paragraph title, "Education Concerned with Making Changes," p. 1.

2. WHAT IS PHILOSOPHY?

Catholic Encyclopedia, article "Philosophy," and those on each of the eight departments of philosophy.

Coffey, P., *Ontology*, Longmans Green, 1918, "General Introduction," pp. 1–31 should be read entire with the diagram presented on p. 11.

Maritain, Jacques (tr. E. I. Watkins), *An Introduction to Philosophy*, Longmans Green, 1931 for "Classification of Philosophy" see Part II. pp. 147–270 and a different diagram, p. 271.

Treatises, presenting the various departments of philosophy from the Aris-thomistic point of view are easily available, e.g.,

Aesthetics: Adler, Mortimer, *Art and Prudence*, Longmans Green, 1937, the Aris-thomistic philosophy of the beautiful applied to the cinema.

——: Maritain, Jacques, *Art and Scholasticism*, Scribner's, 1937, the nearest approach to a text presenting the Aris-thomistic point of view.

Cosmology: McWilliams, J. A., *Cosmology*, Macmillan, 1928, revised, 1935.

Epistemology: Walker, Leslie J., *Theories of Knowledge*, Longmans Green, 1910.

Ethics: Miltner, Charles A., *The Elements of Ethics*, Macmillan, 1925, revised 1939.

Logic: Crumley, Thomas, *Logic, Deductive and Inductive*, Macmillan, 1929.

Ontology: Coffey, P., *Ontology*, Longmans Green, 1918.

——: Rickaby, John, *General Metaphysics*, Longmans Green, 1905.

Philosophy of Mind: Maher, Michael, *Psychology Empirical and Rational*, Longmans Green, 1909, Book II entire, pp. 425–578.

Theodicy: Boedder, Bernard, *Natural Theology*, Longmans Green, 1915.

3. WHAT IS THE PHILOSOPHY OF EDUCATION?

Counts, G. S., "Criteria for Judging a Philosophy of Education," *School and Society*, Vol. 30, July 27, 1929, pp. 103–107.

Courtis, S. A., "Significant Criteria for the Appraisal of the Validity of Contemporary Educational Philosophy," *Educational Method*, Vol. 9, Nov. 1929, pp. 66–72.

DeHovre, Franz (tr. Jordan,) *Philosophy and Education*, Benziger, 1931, the "Introduction" carries these five titles, I. "Education and Philosophy," II. "Educational Philosophy," III. "Philosophy a Theory of Life; Pedagogy a Theory of Education," IV. "Present Day Interest in the Philosophy of Education," V. "Catholic Tradition and the Philosophy of Education," pp. XXVII–XLII.

Dewey, John, *Democracy and Education*, Macmillan, 1916, the most influential book in forming the American philosophy of education.

Finney, Ross L., *A Sociological Philosophy of Education*, Macmillan, 1928, much more conservative; racy reading.

Hamilton, William, *Lectures on Metaphysics*, Sheldon, 1860, the first eight lectures concerned with education are excellent.

Shields, Thomas E., *Philosophy of Education*, Catholic Education Press, 1917, the first formulation in English of Supernaturalism; the emphasis in the psychological part is biological.

LIFE'S THREE LEVELS

If Shakespeare, whom Jonson called the "soul of the age," was after all a typical thinking Elizabethan with the Elizabethan taste for moral philosophy, we may be sure that he meditated on nature like an Elizabethan humanist. The essence of Elizabethan as of other humanisms is the understanding of man and the definition of the sphere of properly human activity. The philosophical mind of Shakespeare's age began the work of reflection by cleaving the universe along three levels. On the lowest level is the natural world, which is the plane of instinct, appetite, animality, lust, the animal passions or affections; on this level the regulation is by necessary or natural law. On the middle level is the human world, which is regulated and, in a sense, created by the will and knowledge of man; working upon the natural world; but governed by reason, the special human faculty; and illuminated more or less from the level above. On the third level is the supernatural world, which is the plane of spiritual beings, and the home of eternal ideas.

Stuart Pratt Sherman, *On Contemporary Literature*,
Henry Holt, 1917, p. 294.

CHAPTER II

THE FOUR PHILOSOPHIES OF EDUCATION

If we take the answers that are given to the question, "What is man?" as our basis for distinguishing different philosophies of education, there are only two such philosophies. One limits man to the capacities, powers, or abilities following from his nature. For this theory the appropriate name is "naturalism." The other theory assigns to man a power above nature, a free gift from God, enabling him to live a life divine here on earth and thus earn it for life eternal. This philosophy holding out to man a supernatural destiny hereafter and endowing him here and now with supernatural means to achieve that destiny is "supernaturalism."

But naturalism is of several varieties only one of which commonly carries the name "Naturalism." There is first of all the variety that denies reality to matter. In this view man, like the universe of which he is a part, is mind or spirit. This is Idealism. The contrary view denies reality to mind or spirit. Man and the universe are nothing but matter in motion. Hence the name, Materialism. In most of the literature of today, however, this latter view carries the label "Naturalism." Opposed to both of these views is Humanism which takes the position that man is both matter and spirit and finds in his duality the struggle which puts meaning into the life of man, the struggle in which mind must dominate over

25

matter, the spirit over the flesh, if man is to live a life truly human. Thus far it agrees with Supernaturalism but as long as it remains on the natural plane it assigns to man no supernatural destiny nor does it endow him with any power above the spiritual powers, intelligence and will. These four philosophies fall into two groups. One group, monistic, explains man and the universe by a single principle, either spirit or matter. The other, dualistic, explains the struggle in the life of man as the battle between these two opposing principles each striving for mastery.

DIAGRAM 2.—THE FOUR PHILOSOPHIES OF EDUCATION

$$\left\{ \begin{array}{l} \text{Monistic} \left\{ \begin{array}{ll} \text{1. Idealism} & \text{—Spirit only} \\ \text{2. Materialism} & \text{—Matter only} \\ \quad(\text{``Naturalism''}) & \end{array} \right\} \text{naturalistic} \\ \text{Dualistic} \left\{ \begin{array}{ll} \text{3. Humanism} & \text{—Matter and spirit} \\ \text{4. Supernaturalism} & \text{—Man and God working together} \end{array} \right. \end{array} \right.$$

We will now discuss briefly each of these four philosophies in relation to education making an effort to disentangle the threads of thought which have been woven together by man ever since he began to make serious inquiry into the purpose of man's life on earth (ends) and the means available for the achievement of those purposes.

1. IDEALISM

Both Idealism and Materialism as monistic theories of the universe have this in common: they merge nature, man, and God all in one. Not merely matter and spirit, the two constituents in the nature of man, are identified, but God, the third kind of being distinguished in "natural theology" or "theodicy," (the rational basis for Supernaturalism) is identified with both nature and man. In Idealism this monistic theory works into some form of pantheism, (Germany today). Materialism finds its fulfillment in atheism, (Russia). Thus they destroy all possibility of man having a clear concept of his problem in life, the supremacy of the spiritual in his nature over the material. In this way they lull man into a false sense of security and hand him over to his lower appetites.

In this country today philosophers writing on education who call themselves "Idealists" are seldom encountered. Those that do so classify themselves thus, though poles apart from out-and-out materialists, cannot be called humanists since they deny the dualism of man's nature.[1] Reading their writings one receives the impression that they are a variety of what Babbitt calls "humanitarians." They emphasize striving to advance the good of all, but the foundation for this emphasis is feeling and sentiment, not rational thought confronting the facts of everyday experience. Dawson in his *Enquiries into Religion and Culture* says: "During the last four hundred years Spiritualism has been a steadily declining force, and the materialistic view of man has become the great rival of Catholicism." In the same place he adds in regard to the former view: "today it has its adherents among Christian Scientists and Theosophists." [2] This was written in 1933. But on January 30, 1933 something happened that radically changed this situation. On that date Adolph Hitler became Chancellor of the Third Reich and the Nazi regime came into power in Germany.

(A) IDEALISM IN GERMANY

The development of Idealism among German philosophers had its beginnings in Kant but it found its application to education in the stirring addresses to the German Nation of Fichte, calling the nation to a rebirth of power following the

[1] H. H. Horne, *Idealism in Education*, Macmillan, 1910, pp. 147–148.
[2] Christopher Dawson, *Enquiries into Religion and Culture*, Sheed & Ward, 1933, p. 311.

defeat by Napoleon at Jena in 1806. It was Hegel, however, who developed the philosophy of the state that has been taken over by the present Nazis. For him the state is the highest manifestation in the world of the great spirit whose development through time is the supreme ideal. "The State is the Divine Idea as it exists on earth." (*Philosophy of History*, Introduction) Whether Hitler or his followers have any understanding of Hegel's attempt to reconcile his doctrine of the State with the concept of freedom, we have it on the authority of Joseph H. Leighton who spent some time in presentday Germany that:

> Nazi "philosophers" are fond of appealing to Hegel as the first great formulator of the philosophy of the Totalitarian State . . . God is a pantheistic Life Force, Germany its highest incarnation and Hitler its chief prophet. It is Teutonic Islamism with a vengeance; only its Allah is not the Merciful and Compassionate, but Wotan, God of Battles.[1]

(B) IDEALISM IN ITALY

The development in Italy followed the same lines but the outcome does not present so dark a picture. For Bertrando Spaventa (1817–83) "Hegelianism was the most mature fruit of European conscience, the highest conscience to which the modern world had attained, . . . intimately rooted in Italian thought, which found in it its confirmation and a clearer and more systematic consciousness of itself. . . . Spaventa prepared the way to the Idealism of Croce and Gentile." [2] Giovanni Gentile, "the philosopher of Fascism" was appointed Minister of Instruction by Mussolini at the end of 1922. As late as 1919, according to his own statement in *The Political*

[1] Joseph H. Leighton, *Social Philosophies in Conflict*, Appleton-Century, 1937, pp. 44–47.
[2] I. L. Kandel, (editor) *Educational Year Book*, Bureau of Publications, Teachers College, Columbia University 1929, "Italy," by E. Cadignola, pp. 368–369.

and Social Doctrine of Fascism, Mussolini had no special doctrinal attitude except that of action. But six years later he not only had a doctrine but a philosophical system which put his ideas in order and Gentile was its source. Not content with merely formulating a philosophy for Fascism, Gentile's greatest contribution to the movement was the reform of Italian education carried out within the first year he was in office, 1923. It affected education on every level from the elementary school to the university as well as the technical institutions and institutions for the training of teachers. In brief the reform was a turning away from positivism which had dominated the school during the first decades of the century with its "secular and scientific proselytism," to an education aiming at the spiritual development of the pupil. Thus in the elementary schools religious teaching was made the core of the curriculum instead of artificial and abstract object teaching in the name of science; and formal grammatical analysis was replaced by an aesthetic education with the aim of disciplining the pupil's expression through drawing, molding, singing, and play as forms of language. Any great religion would have suited Gentile's purpose of emphasizing the spiritual, but through an accident of history the Catholic religion was the Italian tradition, so the crucifix was restored to the classroom.[1]

(C) MEANS IN IDEALISM

But we must not be misled by such changes in school procedure into thinking that the educational aim of Fascism is any different from that of Nazism. Germany had its Hegel but Italy had its Machiavelli. One determined the end, the state; the other the means to be used for the achievement of that end. For Machiavelli the first duty of the state was to be

[1] Giovanni Gentile, *The Reform of Education*, (tr. by Dino Bigongiari) Harcourt Brace, 1922, pp. 242–243 and passim.

strong. In the fulfillment of that duty it must use any means necessary. Thus Hegel and Machiavelli together give us the complete philosophy of the totalitarian state. How completely that philosophy has been accepted in Italy is evident from the statement by Alfredo Rocco in *The Political Doctrine of Fascism:*

> For Fascism, society is the end, the individual the means and its whole life consists in using individuals for its social ends. Individual rights are recognized only in as far as they are implied in the rights of the State . . . Our concept of liberty is this that the individual be allowed to develop his personality in behalf of the state.[1]

In the light of this doctrine we can understand the forms of social control in operation in Germany today. From it arise espionage, concentration camps and torture; the purges through firing squads and assassination when leaders get out of step with the avowed purposes of the "party"; the cloture on the press, the radio, and preaching in the churches and even private conversation, since with an efficient secret police even the walls have ears. The youth movement is the means to train neophytes for the party, but the school as the formal agency of education reaching every child in the community is the ground where the seeds are first sown. With what efficiency combined with brutality the school is now being used in Germany to spread the political doctrine of the Nazis is described with utter frankness by Erika Mann in her *School For Barbarians*, (1938). The Christian concept that each individual person is an end in himself and, without violating his rights, can never be used as a means by another, even though that other is the state, has been completely repudiated. The only immortality held out to man is the continued life of the group and each individual must find fulfillment by sacrificing even

[1] Quoted by Joseph Leighton, *Social Philosophies in Conflict*, p. 15.

life itself in advancing the life of the state. (See Figure 1, p. 32 for a diagrammatic analysis of Idealism in contrast with the other three philosophies treated in this chapter.)

2. MATERIALISM

At the other extreme from Idealism, the theory denying any-thing spiritual in the nature of man, is Materialism. It goes back to the very beginnings in the history of philosophy. When applied to the field of education, however, a new name was given to this point of view under the rallying cry of Rousseau, "Back to nature." "Naturalism" is the euphemistic label commonly used in United States today. The implication of this label is that man is one with nature, merely an animal, though the most highly developed animal the evolutionary process has yet brought forth. Belief in the indefinite perfect-ibility of man places the superman in the near future, and the business of education is to speed up the evolutionary process towards the achievement of that goal.

We can hardly overemphasize the influence exerted by the erratic genius, Rousseau. In three fields he has left his mark: in autobiographical literature with his *Confessions*, in the field of political science with his *Social Contract*, and in the field of education with his *Émile*. As Irving Babbitt has expressed it in *Democracy and Leadership:*

> Among the men of the eighteenth century who paved the way for the world in which we are now living I have, here as elsewhere in my writing, given a preëminent place to Rousseau. It is hard for anyone who has investigated the facts to deny him this preëm-inence, even though one should not go so far as to say with Lord Acton that "Rousseau produced more effect with his pen than Aristotle, or Cicero, or Saint Augustine, or Saint Thomas Aquinas, or any other man who ever lived." The great distinc-tion of Rousseau in the history of thought, if my own analysis be correct, is that he gave the wrong answers to the right questions.

FIGURE 1.—THE FOUR PHILOSOPHIES OF EDUCATION

	I IDEALISM	II MATERIALISM ("naturalism")	III HUMANISM	IV SUPER-NATURALISM
Nature of Man	A spirit	An animal	A rational animal	A religious animal
Man lives	spiritually	naturally	humanly	supernaturally
Factors Forming Human Personality	1. Heredity (racism) 2. Environment	1. Environment (e.g., Watson) 2. Heredity	the Self (intellect and will)	Grace (Divine Providence)
Foundations in Philosophies	Biological and sociological	Sociological and biological	Psychological with I and II	Theological with I, II and III
Ends in Ed.				
1. Individual ends	Man, no end in himself	Satisfaction of human wants	Self-perfection	Christian perfection
2. Social ends	Totalitarian state	Collectivist society	The "ordered life"	a. Mystical Body b. Eternal Salvation
Means in Ed.				
1. Content	Religion and art (Italy)	Science (applied)	The cultural tradition	The "spiritual inheritance"
2. Method	Social control	"Conditioning"	Mental discipline	Asceticism a. Physical b. Mental c. Moral
3. Control	State, the source of all man's rights		Natural rights of man	Supernatural right of the Church

NOTE: This figure should be read from left to right carrying over from each theory on the left whatever elements of truth are contained therein. Thus on the level "Nature of Man," Supernaturalism, column IV, recognizes that man's nature is spiritual, animal, and rational but also, that he is religious by nature.

It is no small distinction even to have asked the right questions (p. 2).

A striking illustration of Rousseau's wrong answers is the statement he makes in the opening sentences of his *Émile* in answer to the question, "What is the nature of Man?"

> Coming from the hand of the Author of all things, everything is good; in the hands of man everything degenerates . . . he desires that nothing should be as nature made it, not even man himself . . . in the present conditions of things, a man left to himself among others from his birth would be the most deformed among them all. Prejudices, authority, necessities, example, all the social institutions in which we are submerged, would stifle nature in him, and would put nothing in its place.[1]

According to Rousseau, evil enters into the life of man by his contact with social institutions. Man is corrupted by life in society. From this follows a "laissez-faire" theory of education. The child should grow up according to nature, free from all contact with society. All discipline imposed by adults is therefore taboo. The natural consequences of a child's acts will serve to inhibit some and cause the repetition of others. This doctrine of "natural goodness" was taken over bodily by the "naturalists" during the nineteenth century as a rebound against the doctrine of "total depravity" introduced by the Protestant reformers.

It was, however, the development of the biological sciences during the latter half of the century, together with the uncritical acceptance of Darwinian evolution, which gave the great impetus to the development of Materialism in education. We see this particularly in the case of Spencer. Not every "naturalist" in education would state its aim as boldly as he has done in his famous essay, *Education:* "The first requisite

[1] Jean Jacques Rousseau, *Émile*, (tr. by Worthington) Heath & Co., 1902, pp. 11–12.

to success in life is 'to be a good animal'; and to be a nation of good animals is the first condition to national prosperity." [1] His definition of education as "preparation for complete living" and his analysis of complete living set the stage for the movement which has since developed as the determination of social objectives in education. According to Spencer's analysis, complete living consists in (1) physical well-being, (2) vocational capacity, (3) parenthood, (4) citizenship, and (5) capacity to enjoy the finer things of life; and his essay is a defense of the position that for all of these, knowledge of the sciences is the knowledge of greatest worth. Not content with emphasizing the content value of science, he makes extravagant claims for its disciplinary values in training the memory and judgment, in moral training, and even religious culture.

The thing to keep in mind in regard to Spencer's fivefold analysis of the aims of education is that for him they are ultimate aims. In his philosophy, this life is all, and the goods which it holds out for the individual, as well as for society as a whole, are definitely the goods of this life: health, economic security, civic security, etc. We have a modern statement of this point of view in *The Cardinal Principles of Secondary Education*, a report of the Commission on the Reorganization of Secondary Education appointed by the National Educational Association:

This commission, therefore, regards the following as the main objectives of education:

1. Health,
2. Command of fundamental processes,
3. Worthy home membership,
4. Vocation,
5. Citizenship,

[1] Herbert Spencer, *Education, Intellectual, Moral and Physical*, Section IV, "Physical Education."

6. Worthy use of leisure,
7. Ethical character.

We hold that they should constitute the principal aims of education.[1]

The seventh objective, "ethical character," is the only one that approximates what we would commonly speak of as "religious values." But this is a statement written by public school people for public school people, and even those that believe in religious values, are not in a position to set them up for the school which, with the present temper of the American mind, must be so definitely nonsectarian in character.

The use of the word "values" in this connection introduces us to the point of view of those naturalistic philosophers who are not "educationists." "Values" is the word used by philosophers for what in educational literature is spoken of under the term "educational objectives." Thus we find in Sellars', *The Principles and Problems of Philosophy*, the following analysis under the paragraph title "A General Survey of Values":

1. Bodily values,
2. Values of primary association,
3. Economic values,
4. Political values,
5. Aesthetic values,
6. Religious values,
7. Moral values,
8. Intellectual values.[2]

Here religious values have a definite place; and in addition, moral values, which logically should be a subhead under religious values. But the question is, what does religion mean for a philosopher who is a Materialist? Sellars leaves us no

[1] *The Cardinal Principles of Secondary Education*, Bulletin No. 35, Office of Education, Washington, D. C., p. 5.
[2] Roy Wood Sellars, *The Principles and Problems of Philosophy*, Macmillan, 1926, p. 457.

doubt about his attitude in regard to this question. On page 479 he speaks of religion as a "magnificent hypothesis," and later we read:

> But I cannot forego pointing out that even strict naturalism has a place for religion if we mean by religion the concern for values. Religion can be weaned from the supernatural and stand for social and personal loyalty to the tested values of life.[1]

This is a new view of religion. Traditionally, religion has meant belief in a power above man, recognition of an obligation to live a life meriting the approval of the Being possessing this higher power, and the strivings that man puts forth to achieve this ideal. But for the naturalist, religion is a "concern for values," and these values are definitely of this life, bodily values, association values, economic values, etc. The strivings which man puts forth to achieve these values constitute the religion of Naturalism.[2]

The scientific theory behind this view today carries the name "emergent evolution." Here is a statement of the theory from the author just quoted:

> The general plan of nature which presented itself to us with this perspective we likened to a pyramid of tierlike construction. A process of creative organization led at each stage to the advent of gradients or levels above. Each new level depended upon the energies and conditions of the lower level and was adjusted to its widespreading foundation. Matter, itself, was evolved. Then came the earth with its waters, its salts and fertile earth, giving it radiant energy, the sun. Then little by little came life reaching upward to more complex forms. . . . Slowly life lifted to mind, the human mind being the latest and highest to appear. Pre-

[1] *Ibid.*, pp. 483–484.

[2] The tragedy of this situation is that the book from which these quotations are taken has been written as a text for an introductory course in philosophy (see Preface) at one of our great state universities. What pabulum for beginning students in philosophy served out with all the prestige of a great educational institution supported by the taxes of citizens who have a real belief in the true meaning of religion!

history gave way to human history, and society with its fruit, civilization, began to dominate the surface of the earth.[1]

We might call this the "saltatory" theory of evolution since it proceeds by "leaps." There is first of all the leap from a void to the physical universe. Next there is the leap from matter (the physical universe) to living things; and then the leap from living things (organic life) to man (rational life), with no adequate explanation of a cause accounting for the leaps which are all ascribed to "Nature" written with a capital letter. The statement quoted above brings out, however, the central doctrine in the theory of "Naturalism," namely, that man, as the end product of the evolutionary process, is the highest being yet evolved, but he does not differ in kind from beings of the lower orders. Rather, the only difference is one of degree of complexity. Traditionally, nature, man, and God have been recognized as three distinct orders of being; but in this theory of emergent evolution these three are all merged into one, and that one is Nature.

(A) PRAGMATIC MATERIALISM

The variety of "Naturalism" that captured the American mind during the first quarter of this century with its criterion of practical results as the test of truth was pragmatism and John Dewey has been its apostle. The extreme difficulty of following his thought has been surpassed only by the extent of his publications in the field of philosophy as well as education. Harvey Wickam quotes a famous professor as saying in a private conversation, "I have been making an intensive study of John Dewey for the last six months trying to find out what he means. I give up." [2] We would make a reservation in regard to this universal indictment. There is a sharp contrast

[1] *Ibid.*, p. 363.
[2] Harvey Wickam, *The Unrealists*, Longmans, Green, 1930, p. 196.

between Dewey's writings in psychology and those which present his social theory. As would be expected from a pragmatist, Dewey is supreme in the field of method. His insistence that all thinking is "problem solving" is sound psychology and his critique of the Herbartian steps from this point of view is very well done.[1]

Nowhere, however, is he more obstinate in his refusal to clarify his meaning than when discussing the aims of education, one place where in line with other naturalists it was to be expected that he would be clear and definite. But no, in his *Democracy and Education* (one of the most widely used texts in courses in the Philosophy of Education) in the chapter entitled "Education as Growth" he returns again and again to the idea "(1) that the educational process has no end beyond itself; it is its own end; and that (2) the educational process is one of continual reorganizing, reconstructing, transforming." And again, "There is nothing to which growth is relative save more growth, there is nothing to which education is subordinate save more education." And finally "education is all one with growing; it has no end beyond itself." [2]   We submit that if such ideas have any meaning they must be translated into terms by which we can hold them in our minds and reflect upon them. In Section 4, of this chapter we advance this same idea of education as continuous growth but growth towards an ideal described in the terms *Christian Perfection*. This concept is no "fixed goal," the idea which Dewey attacks in the same chapter. Rather, it is an everprogressing goal challenging the best efforts of the saints as we explain in detail in Chapters VII, "The Fourth Factor in Manmaking," and in our concluding Chapter XVII, "The Catholic Philosophy of Education."

From this indefiniteness in aims, many of the "Naturalists"

[1] John Dewey, *How We Think*, Heath & Co., 1910, pp. 202–213.
[2] John Dewey, *Democracy and Education*, Macmillan, 1916, pp. 59–62.

under the leadership of Dewey have turned to the Russian experiment as putting their principles into practice. In their official organ, *The Social Frontier*,[1] they avoid communism by using the term "collectivism" as descriptive of their social purposes. But Dewey and others have spent time in Russia guiding the experiment toward the realization of the millennium when all human wants will be satisfied for all men. That they accept the materialistic interpretation of history of Marx is not clear from their writings but one of the principal tenets of the school is the elimination of the profit motive from our industrial system. They seem to accept the thesis that the totalitarianism of the present Russian regime will disappear when the revolution has been effected in line with the principle of Marx that "the state will wither away." When this has been achieved, what Thorndike calls "the ultimate aim of education for man" will be realized in a classless collectivist commonwealth "the fullest satisfaction of human wants."[2]

(B) MEANS IN MATERIALISM

Dominated as it is by science the means Materialism offers for the realization of its aim are drawn from the sciences, particularly the sciences of biology and psychology. Materialistic in theory, its psychology is deterministic in both theory and practice. Heredity and environment are the only factors in the making of man. Heredity is almost a negligible factor if adherents of this view follow Watson, the extremist among the behaviorists. "Give me a dozen healthy infants, well formed, and my own specified world to bring them up in, and I'll guarantee to take any one at random and train him to

---

[1] Now discontinued but taken over by the Progressive Education Association, New York, and with the October issue, 1939, appearing under the new title *Frontiers of Democracy*.

[2] Edward L. Thorndike and Arthur I. Gates, *Elementary Principles of Education*, Macmillan, 1929, p. 18.

become any type of specialist I might select—doctor, lawyer, artist, merchant, chief and, yes, even beggar-man and thief—regardless of his talents, penchants, tendencies, abilities, vocations, and race of ancestors." [1]   In this view, environment is all-powerful.   "Conditioning" is the name for the process in the new terminology by which the behavior of the individual is to be determined.   More familiar to students of educational psychology is the S-R bond theory of Thorndike.   Determine the stimulus, S, the response, R, is inevitable.   Conditioning is the play of forces from outside the individual.   Intelligent planning, deliberation, conscious choice, free will—all these are delusions.   Training the child is precisely the same process as training an animal since he is merely an animal, but it is somewhat more difficult since the child has more abilities than the animal of highest endowment.

What is to be said concerning the outcome of such a theory applied to man?   William McDougall, the leader of the Hormic school of psychologists, answers this question for us in an essay entitled "The Psychology They Teach in New York":

I contend that the crude materialistic theory of human nature, the theory that man is a machine and nothing more, taught dogmatically every year to hundreds of thousands of innocent schoolteachers and college students, cannot fail in the long run to contribute very considerably to the decay of morals and the increase of crime.   For it is a theory utterly incompatible with any view of man as a responsible moral being and utterly incompatible with any religion that the plain man could recognize as such; a theory which represents man as incapable of choosing between good and evil, as the purely passive sport of circumstances over which he has no control; a theory which, if it is accepted, must make all talk of self-control, of self-improvement, of purpose and ideals seem sheer nonsense, survivals from an age of naive ignorance. [2]

[1] J. B. Watson, *Behaviorism*, Norton, 1930, p. 82.
[2] William P. King (editor), *Behaviorism a Battle Line*, Cokesbury Press, 1930, pp. 33–34.

Louis J. Mercier calls attention to the logical implications of this theory:

> Repudiate the supernatural, the antecedently real, the Law above man which man must discover in order that his own laws may be true and just, and you are committed to a mere pragmatic and hence everchanging social morality through man-made laws, with no appeal against the sovereign state which is to enforce them to secure the social control of the individual. Soviet Russia's conception of the state, recognizing no law above itself and no guarantee for individual rights, ever ready to make war against every institution, philosophy, or religion which asserts such a law above man and the individual responsibility of man to God, is but the political ideal which follows inevitably from naturalism.[1]

Most naturalists seem perfectly unaware of the implications of their theory which does away with the responsibility of the individual for his conduct. But the communists see these implications with a clarity that is admirable. Thus Mercier quotes Calverton writing in *The New Masses:* "It will not be long, with this new development, before the intellectuals will have to be either consistent individualists or consistent collectivists—which will ultimately mean consistent communists."[2]

There may be some comfort in the fact that schoolmen who subscribe to the mechanistic psychology and communistic sociology of Materialism do not carry out the implications of these theories in their educational practice, but in the long run the outcome must be disastrous. Thus McDougall, in the essay quoted above, referring to the former of these theories, says:

> Fortunately, human nature has a vast capacity for illogicality, for accepting a theory and acting as though it were utterly false. Hence, no doubt, most of the multitude who innocently imbibe this doctrine continue to strive conscientiously to do their duty,

[1] Louis J. Mercier, *The Challenge of Humanism*, Oxford Univ. Press, 1933, p. 266.

[2] *Ibid.*, p. 266.

continue to pursue some ideal of efficiency, honesty, and public service, and to treat their children and their pupils as moral beings. But in the long run, as the years pass and successive generations of students absorb this dogma, it is inevitable that their attitude toward life and its problems shall be affected and that the tone and manners of society shall become increasingly such as the theory requires or points to.[1]

(See Figure 1, p. 32 for a diagrammatic analysis of Materialism in contrast with the other three philosophies.)

IDEALISM AND MATERIALISM AS ONE

From this brief review of the philosophies of Idealism and Materialism it is clear when followed out to their logical conclusions, they have the same outcome as far as the nature of man is concerned. It makes little difference whether man is conceived as merely an emanation of the world Spirit (Hegel) or a product of the world's material forces in evolution (Marx). In either view he becomes a pawn for the totalitarian state to be used for its own purposes. This means the denial of the concept which is the very foundation of American government, the "inalienable rights" of man as an individual human person. The truth of this analysis is now confirmed by the pact which Germany with its Hegelian ideology, and Russia with its Marxian ideology, have entered into. Walter Lippmann predicted this a year ago when he wrote: "Marx and Hegel, Nietzsche and Alfred Rosenberg, Lenin, Stalin, Mussolini and Hitler, reached agreement on common ground. They agreed that the conscience of free men is incompatible with their purposes. The Fascists declared that liberalism corrupts the national spirit; the communists that it corrupts class consciousness." [2] American "collectivists" will probably claim they

---

[1] *Op. cit.*, p. 34.

[2] Walter Lippmann, *The Good Society*, Little, Brown, 1938, pp. 381–382.

espouse the cause of man's "inalienable rights," but since their philosophy is materialistic they deny that man is a spiritual being, that is a rational being, and only a rational being is capable of exercising rights. We will now present briefly the philosophy that makes this doctrine that man is a rational being the foundation of its whole system, the philosophy called Humanism.

3. HUMANISM

The term "Humanism" has commonly been applied to the intellectual revolution which began in Italy during the fourteenth century and spread north in Europe during the fifteenth and sixteenth centuries. Irving Babbitt interprets this movement as a revolt against the domination of theology over the life of man during the Middle Ages. In applying the term "Humanism" to the movement of which he was the leader in this country until his death, he said it is a revolt against the domination of science over the life of man, a domination characteristic of this century. Certainly this is one of the chief characteristics of what Norman Foerster calls the "rational humanism" of Hutchins and Adler.[1] These writers, following the Greeks, would restore philosophy as the Queen of the Sciences. Here is an application of this point of view to education by Adler:

The basic problems of education are normative. This means, positively, that they are problems in moral and political philosophy; and, negatively, that they cannot, they have not and never will be, solved by the methods of empirical science, by what is called educational research. The reason for the unalterable inadequacy of science is not far to seek. Science can measure and observe, can collect facts of all sorts and generalize from such collections, but neither the facts nor the generalizations can by

[1] Norman Foerster, *The Future of the Liberal College*, Appleton-Century, 1938, p. 74.

themselves answer questions about what *should* be done in education. Such questions require us to consider what is good and bad, to define the ideals or norms of human life and human philosophers.[1]

Science in its applied aspect (and for Americans its values lie in its applications) aims to make this world of ours a better place in which to live. Humanism aims to make our living in it better, that is, more human. For the Materialists dominated by the scientific point of view, man is merely an animal. He is the most complex animal yet evolved, and civilization is the evidence of this complexity, but still he is merely an animal even though he is a social animal. For the humanist, man is a *rational* animal and it is his reason that makes him human. For the supernaturalist, as de Quatrefages expresses it, "Man is a religious animal." [2] In both of these theories man is different from the lower orders of the animal kingdom not merely in degree; he is different in kind. He is partly material (body) but he is also spiritual (mind), and the conflict in the life of man arises from the duality of his nature, the struggle for supremacy between the lower, the animal part of his nature, and the higher, the spiritual part. Man is truly human only insofar as the spiritual within him gains and holds supremacy over the material, a conflict which lasts as long as life. This meaning of the term is stated by Mercier as follows:

On the basis of our analyses, it would seem therefore that, etymologically as well as historically, the term "humanist" belongs to those who recognize that man is thus distinct from other animals through the presence in him of an autonomous spiritual element which enables him to discover the universal through the particular, hence to get in touch with abiding law, and which further points to a possible coöperation of God's will with man's will in

[1] Mortimer J. Adler, "Liberalism and Liberal Education," *The Educational Record*, July 1939, p. 422.
[2] Jean Louis Armand de Quatrefages, *L'Unité de l'Espèce Humaine*, p. 38.

carrying it out; for, if man has a spiritual element in him, this element must have a spiritual Being as its origin, and ultimate human values must be in terms of that supreme Being. Thus humanism stands clearly opposed to naturalism, which would merge man with nature, either by considering him wholly material or a mere manifestation of the All-One.[1]

Humanism thus defined has been held as a theory of man in the Occident. It goes back to the great religious leaders of the fifth century, B. C., Confucius and Buddha. It received its finest philosophical expression among the Greeks particularly in Aristotle. It was held by the great schoolmen of the Middle Ages, notably St. Thomas Aquinas, as well as by Renaissance scholars like Erasmus; and its revival today among a group of American thinkers is the one encouraging sign in our civilization so overwhelmingly materialistic.

The Humanism of Babbitt, More, T. S. Eliot and their followers arose in the field of literary criticism. They attacked the equalitarian theory of democracy promising to universalize higher education with the elective system as the means to this end, but they had no following among the practical "educators" who were conducting the schools. The presentday group of humanists, Foerster, Hutchins, and Adler, etc., have gained an audience and will undoubtedly continue to win followers among practical school people. This is strikingly illustrated in the attention which President Hutchins has won for the problem of general education.[2] A decade ago the educational periodical literature was filled with articles dealing with vocational education. Today there is a very pronounced shift to discussion of the problem of general education, the education which in Newman's words, *"makes the man; it does not make*

[1] Louis J. Mercier, *The Challenge of Humanism*, Oxford Univ. Press, 1933, pp. 261–263.

[2] Robert Maynard Hutchins, *The Higher Learning in America*, Yale Univ. Press, 1936, Chapter III, "General Education," pp. 58–89.

physicians, or surgeons, or engineers, or soldiers, or bankers, or merchants, but it makes men." This is the education which is the humanist's primary concern.

(A) ENDS IN HUMANISM

This emphasis on the development of the individual stands in sharp contrast with the totalitarianism of the Idealistic philosophies and the collectivism of the Materialists, both of which make man a tool of the state. For the Humanists man is an end in himself and the advancement of his "uniquely human destiny of self-perfection" is the supreme end of education.[1] With regard to social ends they hold with Newman that "that training of the intellect which is best for the individual, best enables him to discharge his duties to society." [2] In Mercier's words in the final chapter of *The Challenge of Humanism* entitled "Naturalism or Humanism": "Whereas naturalism leaves man helpless in the flux of relativity, humanism would make him master of that flux by leading him to discover the abiding principles within and without that flux and to build on this basis an ordered life and civilization." [3] This "ordered life" is possible for man because he is endowed with reason. What means are to be used to bring about the development of man's reason so that an ordered civilization may be realized?

(B) MEANS IN HUMANISM

The primary emphasis of Humanism is that the individual is the determiner of his own acts. Heredity and environment are factors in the making of man but there is a third factor

---

[1] Mortimer J. Adler, "The Crisis in Contemporary Education," *The Social Frontier*, February, 1939, p. 141.

[2] John Henry Newman, *Idea of a University*, VII, "Knowledge Viewed in Relation to Professional Skill."

[3] *Op. cit.*, p. 259.

which in the last analysis is superior to either in determining whether an individual achieves a human personality and lives an ordered life, and this third factor is man himself. Environment can, within limits, be made over to man's liking. Man is superior to his environment, and this superiority arises from the fact that he is a rational animal. He has intelligence and free will, and these capacities are what mark him off from the rest of the animal kingdom.

But if man is to bring about his development as a personality truly human, he must take himself in hand through these two capacities. Through the exercise of intelligence he must lay out a plan of life and through the exercise of will he must submit himself to a regimen of self-discipline aimed at the realization of his life ideal. Naturalism rejects the doctrine of self-discipline, and Rousseau, with all his perversions and inconsistencies is a striking illustration of the outcomes of such an attitude. But for Humanism, the necessity of self-discipline is the central doctrine in its theory of the good life. This idea, self-discipline, runs all through the writings of Babbitt with his "will to refrain," "the inner check" and the *frein vital* over against the *élan vital*. Sherlock Bronson Gass contributes an essay to *Humanism and America* entitled "The Well of Discipline" in which he calls attention to "the contrast between the fruitfulness of the scientific world, its vitality, its harmony, its world-wide coöperation, and our frankly acknowledged moral bankruptcy;—vigor and fecundity in the area to which discipline has been shifted, futility and chaos in the area from which discipline has been withdrawn." (p. 283) For Humanism this power of self-restraint performs for man the same function that instinct performs for the brute creation, namely, control. Applied to education this means in Adler's words:

If man is a rational animal, constant in nature throughout history, then there must be certain constant features in every sound

educational program, regardless of culture or epoch. The basic
education of a rational animal is the *discipline of his rational
powers* and the cultivation of his intellect. This discipline is
achieved by the liberal arts, the arts of reading and listening, of
writing and speaking, and, perforce, of thinking, since man is a
social animal as well as a rational one, and his intellectual life is
lived in a community which can exist only through the communication of men. . . .

But one cannot learn to read and write without subject matter.
The reason is trained in its proper operations by these arts, but
the intellect is not cultivated by them. That can be accomplished
only through furnishing it with knowledge and wisdom, by ac-
quainting it with truth, by giving it a mastery of ideas. At this
point, the other basic feature of liberal education appears, namely,
the great books, the master productions in all fields, philosophy,
science, history, and belles lettres. They are not only the material which must be used to teach students how to read and
write, but they constitute the *cultural tradition* by which the
intellects of each generation must first be cultivated.[1]

HUMANISM AND RELIGION

This reference to the "cultural tradition" leads us to inquire,
"What is the attitude of humanists towards religion?" That
they are greatly interested in religion there can be no doubt.
Babbitt himself, in his contribution to the series of essays
edited by Norman Foerster under the title *Humanism and
America*, says quite positively: "For my own part, I range
myself unhesitatingly on the side of the supernaturalists.
Though I see no evidence that humanism is necessarily ineffec-
tive apart from dogmatic and revealed religion, there is, as it
seems to me, evidence that it gains immensely in effectiveness
when it has a background of religious insight." [2]   T. S. Eliot
has contributed to the same book an essay entitled "Religion

[1] *Op. cit.*, pp. 143–144.
[2] Norman Foerster (editor), *Humanism and America*, Farrar and Rinehart,
1930, p. 39.

Without Humanism," the opening sentences of which read: "I must reply, in these few pages, upon a brief summary of the limitations within which I believe humanism must work, which I published in the *Hound and Horn*, June, 1929. In that paper I stated my belief that humanism is in the end futile without religion." [1]   The logic of his belief is shown by the fact that he is an adherent of the Anglican Church.   Chesterton, in *The Thing*, has a sympathetic chapter entitled "Is Humanism a Religion?" and he has given what we would hold to be even a more logical demonstration of belief and practice in this idea by entering the Catholic Church.   (See Figure 1, p. 32 for a diagrammatic analysis of Humanism in contrast with the other three philosophies.)

4. SUPERNATURALISM

Since this book is an attempt to state the philosophy of Supernaturalism applied to education, this section will give merely a brief statement of this philosophy from the point of view of ends and means in education, leaving to succeeding chapters the details of this exposition.   Supernaturalism as a theory of man, and hence as a Philosophy of Education distinct from Idealism, Materialism, and Humanism, has for its basis belief in a personal God, the author of man's nature and creator of the universe, with the doctrine that God having created man and placed him on this earth, did not desert him; but through His Providence watches over his struggles to achieve his end and offers him assistance in that endeavor.   Evidence of that interest in man and offer of assistance on the part of God is revelation.   Within this revelation two facts stand out with definite clearness which mark this theory off from all natural-istic theories.   They are first, that man's nature is a fallen nature and second, that this fallen nature is lifted up through

[1] *Ibid.*, p. 105.

7977

the merits of Jesus Christ, the Son of God, whom He sent to restore man to his high estate. This is what we mean by redemption.

This fact of man's fallen nature is a stumbling block for all materialists. Nevertheless, it is within the experience of reasoning man apart from revelation. Pascal says that without it, "we are incomprehensible to ourselves." (See p. 564 for the complete quotation.) This is the explanation of the stories found in so many ancient mythologies of which Pandora's box in Greek mythology is a striking example. The same thought is expressed by Newman as follows:

> Starting then with the being of a God, I look out of myself into the world of men, and there I see a sight which fills me with unspeakable distress . . . the greatness and littleness of man, his far-reaching aims, his short duration, the curtain hung over his futurity, the disappointments of life, the defeat of good, the success of evil, physical pain, mental anguish, the prevalence and intensity of sin, the prevailing idolatries, the corruptions, the dreary hopeless irreligion, that condition of the whole race, so fearfully yet exactly described in the Apostle's words, "having no hope and without God in the world,"—all this is a vision to dizzy and appall; and inflicts upon the mind the sense of a profound mystery, which is absolutely beyond human solution. . . . The human race is implicated in some terrible aboriginal calamity. It is out of joint with the purposes of its Creator. This is a fact, a fact as true as the fact of its existence; and thus the doctrine of what is theologically called original sin becomes to me almost as certain as that the world exists, and as the existence of God.[1]

But the doctrine of man's fallen nature is not the doctrine of "total depravity" introduced in the sixteenth century by Protestant theology. In this theory, man is capable of no act morally good. Hence he is to be saved not by works but through being predestined (Calvin) or by faith alone (Luther).

[1] Quoted by Robert Shafer, *Christianity and Nationalism*, Yale Univ. Press, 1926, pp. 86–87.

In this theory, man is morally dead; for the Materialists (Rousseau), man is morally well; in the Catholic theory, man is morally sick. He needs a physician but he must use his own natural powers to call that physician and he must coöperate with Him to insure complete recovery. The physician is Christ, and his ministrations to man calling upon him are what is meant by the doctrine of Grace, help from God to live the Christian life. Christ opened the gates of heaven; man must walk in.

The ultimate ends of Christian education in the theory of Supernaturalism therefore, are twofold: one concerning the life of man hereafter, the other his life here below. The final goal of man on earth is to get back to God from Whom he came. He needs help to achieve this objective, but help is at hand. His ultimate end here below is the perfection of his own personality as a human being (Humanism), but more than that, this natural life must be supernaturalized. For this the model, Christ, is ever before him, and help is at hand to aid him if he will make use of it. We may, therefore, state the ultimate ends of Supernaturalism: (1) Christian perfection here below and (2) life with God hereafter.

(A) MEANS IN SUPERNATURALISM

Supernaturalism holds with Humanism the theory of the dual nature of man, matter and spirit, animality and rationality. Out of this duality arises what Emerson calls "law for man" and "law for thing." St. Paul's terminology is similar:

> I find then a law, that when I have a will to do good, evil is present with me. For I am delighted with the law of God, according to the inward man; But I see another law in my members, fighting against the law of my mind, and captivating me in the law of sin, that is in my members. Unhappy man that I am, who shall

deliver me from the body of this death? The grace of God, by Jesus Christ, our Lord.[1]

Here is the fourth factor in the making of man. God's grace as a help to lead the good life is offered to all men, but man must ask for that help and he must coöperate with it when it is presented to him. What is the form of coöperation commonly called for? St. Paul answers this question for us: "I chastise my body and bring it into subjection; lest perhaps when I have preached to others, I myself should become a castaway."[2] Again we are confronted with the necessity of self-discipline. It is refreshing to have a scientist, Arthur H. Compton, emphasizing this necessity: "Since the days of Pythagoras it has been recognized that a world of law implies a life of self-discipline if that life is to reach its highest development. Thus in an era when many old conventions become outworn, the clear teaching of science is of special value: If man will learn the truth and abide by it, that truth will make him free."[3] In the mind of this eminent physicist, no longer can the naturalists claim science supports them in their rejection of the doctrine of discipline. It is the universal law of life: *self-development through self-discipline.* In the field of morals we call it asceticism (from the Greek word meaning exercise), that is, "spiritual exercises in pursuit of virtue"; in the field of athletics and physical education we call it training, or "physical exercises in pursuit of strength, and skill"; in the field of mind we call it mental discipline, or "mental exercises in pursuit of mental power."

Discipline alone is no guarantee of victory for man in his struggle to master the appetites of his animal nature. But discipline that is self-imposed with a worthy motive is a sure guarantee that help will be forthcoming. St. Augustine states

[1] Romans vii, 21–25.
[2] 1 Corinthians, ix, 27.
[3] Arthur H. Compton, *The Freedom of Man,* Yale Univ. Press, 1935, p. 111.

this beautifully: *Facienti quod in se est, Deus non denegat gratiam.* ("To him who does what lies within him, God does not deny grace.") "My grace is sufficient for thee," was Our Lord's promise to St. Paul, and He makes this same promise to every man of good will. But grace does not destroy nature; rather, it perfects it. As the late Holy Father expressed it:

> The supernatural order . . . not only does not in the least destroy the natural order . . . but elevates the natural and perfects it, each affording mutual aid to the other, completing it in a manner proportioned to its respective nature and dignity. The reason is because both come from God, Who cannot contradict Himself.[1]

St. Thomas's phrase *gratia supponit naturam* may be freely rendered, "grace builds on nature." With nature and grace working together, victory is assured. (See Figure 1, p. 32 for a diagrammatic analysis of Supernaturalism in contrast with the other three philosophies.)

CONCLUSION

We have now stated in brief the aims (ends) of the four philosophies of education, Idealism, Materialism, Humanism, and Supernaturalism, and the means which they offer whereby these aims are to be achieved. Our special concern, however, is with the philosophy of Supernaturalism and the remaining chapters in this presentation will be devoted to a detailed analysis of this philosophy of education, keeping in mind the fundamental principle stated above, *grace builds on nature.*

Our first inquiry is, therefore, into the nature of the pupil, to which is devoted the whole of Part I, "Foundations," the biological, psychological, sociological, and theological foundations of education. This is concluded in Chapter VIII, "The

[1] Pope Pius XI, *The Christian Education of Youth,* 1933.

Hierarchy of Educational Objectives," in which all three groups of objectives, the psychological, social, and philosophical, are integrated in one general scheme, giving us our answer to the first of the pivotal problems of education, (1) the *pupil*, his nature and needs. In Part II, "Applications" we pass on to the other three pivotal problems, concerned as they are with the means of education, (2) the *curriculum* (materials to be taught), (3) the *teacher* (method), and (4) the *institution* (administration).

Section A of Part I is entitled "Biological and Psychological Foundations." Our problem here is to discover how learning takes place, what are its outcomes, and how it may be facilitated. In the following Chapter, III, "The Nature of Man," we seek to deepen our insight into the dual nature of man as a somatopsychic, that is, a body-mind organism, since the recognition of this fact is basic to any understanding of learning.

SUGGESTED READINGS

Brubacher, John S., *Modern Philosophies of Education*, McGraw-Hill, 1939, Chap. XIV, "Systematic Philosophies of Education" presents the philosophies of pragmatism, naturalism, essentialism, idealism and "scholastic realism," the latter, p. 345.

Demiashkevitch, Michael, *An Introduction to the Philosophy of Education*, American Book, 1935, Chap. II. "Philosophy of Education and Philosophy" discusses Monism, Materialism, Idealism, Skepticism, Dualism and Pragmatism.

Fitzpatrick, Edward, *Readings in the Philosophy of Education*, Appleton-Century, 1936, selections by a Supernaturalist.

Kilpatrick, W. H., *Source Book in the Philosophy of Education*, Macmillan, 1923, rev. 1934, selections by a Materialist.

Kuehner, Quincy, *A Philosophy of Education*, Prentice-Hall, 1935, selections from various sources, Chaps. III, IV and V, deal with Naturalism, Pragmatism and Idealism respectively.

Lodge, Rupert C., *Philosophy of Education*, Harper, 1937, the three chapters following Chapter I. "The Three Types of Philosophy" discuss the nature of education as interpreted by Realism, Idealism and Pragmatism, pp. 1–69.

Skinner, Langfitt and others, *An Introduction to Modern Education*, Heath, 1937, Chap. XVII "The Philosophy of Education" by H. H. Horne discusses four philosophies, Naturalism, Pragmatism, Idealism and Realism, pp. 442–463.

Thomas, Frank W. and Albert R. Lang, *Principles of Modern Education*, Houghton Mifflin, 1937, Chap. II. "Philosophies of Education" discusses Idealism, Naturalism and Pragmatism, pp. 38–62.

I. IDEALISM

De Hovre, Franz E. (tr. by E. B. Jordan), *Philosophy and Education*, Benziger, 1931, Part III, "Nationalism as a Philosophy of Life and Education" contains a short chapter on Fichte pp. 293–301; for Hegel see index.

Gentile, Giovanni (tr. by Dino Bigongiari), *The Reform of Education*, Harcourt, Brace, 1922, Idealism in Italy, passim.

Horne, H. H., *Idealism in Education*, Macmillan, 1910, Chaps. II, III and IV, treat heredity, environment and will from the point of view of an idealist.

——, *The Democratic Philosophy of Education*, Macmillan, 1933, a critique of Dewey's *Democracy and Education* by one who calls himself a "Christian idealist."

Leighton, Joseph A., *Social Philosophies in Conflict*, Appleton Century, 1937, a critique of totalitarianism.

Lodge, Rupert C., *Philosophy of Education*, Harper, 1937, idealistic.

Rauschnigg, Herman, *The Revolution of Nihilism*, Alliance Book Corporation, 1939, world domination, the aim of Hitlerism by the one time president of the Senate of Danzig.

Rusk, Robert R., *The Philosophical Bases of Education*, Houghton Mifflin, 1928, idealistic.

Whitehead, Alfred N., *The Aims of Education*, Macmillan, 1929, idealistic.

2. MATERIALISM

Breed, Frederick S., *Education and the New Realism*, Macmillan, 1939, an excellent critique of pragmatism and the "progressives" from the point of view of the new realism.

Childs, John L., *Education and the Philosophy of Experimentalism*, Century, 1931, the scientism of Materialism.

Curoe, Philip R., *History of Education*, Globe, 1921, Chap. XVI, "The Naturalistic Movement in Education" is a brief presentation of Rousseau and his influence in education, pp. 139–147.

De Hovre, Franz E. (tr. by E. B. Jordan), *Catholicism and Education*, Benziger, 1931, Part I is entitled "The Philosophy and Pedagogy of Naturalism" p. 1–82; for a critique of Dewey as a "Radical-social" educator see pp. 101–116.

Dewey, John, *Democracy and Education*, Macmillan, 1916, pragmatic naturalism.

Kandel, Isaac L., "The Philosophy Underlying the System of Education in the United States," *Educational Year Book*, Bureau of Publications, Teachers College, Columbia Univ., 1930.

Kilpatrick, W. H., *The Educational Frontier*, Century, 1933, chapters by prominent "Naturalists."

O'Connell, Geoffrey, *Naturalism in American Education*, Benziger, 1938, a critique of the naturalism of Dewey, Kilpatrick, Rugg and Thorndike from the point of view of Supernaturalism.

Shafer, Robert, *Christianity and Naturalism*, Yale Univ. Press, 1926, a critique by a Humanist.

Woefel, Norman, *Molders of the American Mind*, Columbia Univ. Press, 1933 presents the views of a group of American naturalists.

3. HUMANISM

Adler, Mortimer J., "Liberalism and Liberal Education," *Educational Record*, July, 1939, an excellent critique of totalitarianism and liberalism from the point of view of a rational humanist.

——, "The Crisis in Contemporary Education," *The Social Frontier*, Feb. 1939 a critique of "progressive" education contrasting science and philosophy.

Babbitt, Irving, *Rousseau and Romanticism*, Houghton Mifflin, 1919, one of the best statements by a Humanist.

Foerster, Norman, *Humanism and America*, Farrar and Rinehart, 1930, a comprehensive statement with chapters by prominent Humanists.

——, *The American State University*, N. Car. Univ. Press, 1937, contrasts Naturalism, Humanism and Supernaturalism p. 120; see also chapt. 7, "The Idea of a Liberal Education."

——, *The Future of the Liberal College*, Appleton-Century, 1938, Chap. V. "Education Leads the Way," a critique of *The Educational Frontier* edited by Kilpatrick.

Hutchins, Robert, *The Higher Learning in America*, Yale Univ. Press, 1936, a severe critique of the present situation in American education.

Mercier, Louis J., *The Challenge of Humanism*, Oxford Univ. Press, 1933, compares the Humanism of Babbitt with Supernaturalism.

The references for Humanism are largely in periodicals notably the *Bookman* and its successor *The American Review*, e.g., Elliott, "The Religions of Babbitt and More," Summer, 1937.

4. SUPERNATURALISM

De Hovre, Franz E. (tr. by E. B. Jordan), *Catholicism in Education*, Benziger, 1934, presents the theory of Supernaturalism as interpreted by five great Catholic educators.

Fitzpatrick, Edward, *I Believe in Education*, Sheed & Ward, 1938, the educational creed of a Supernaturalist.

Maritain, Jacques, *True Humanism*, Scribner, 1938. This is a statement of Christian Humanism, hence Supernaturalism.

McGucken, William J., *The Catholic Way in Education*, Bruce, 1934, contains an excellent chapter entitled "The Supernatural and Education" pp. 27–36.

Newman, John Henry, *Idea of a University*, any edition.

——, *Discussions and Arguments*, "The Tamworth Reading Room."

——, *Sermons on Various Occasions*, Sermon I. "Intellect, the Instrument of Religious Training."

Pius XI, *The Christian Education of Youth*, 1931, the Authoritative statement of Supernaturalism.

Shields, Thomas E., *Philosophy of Education*, Catholic Ed. Press, 1917, an early statement of Supernaturalism.

Vann, Gerald, *On Being Human*, Sheed & Ward, 1934, presents the general thesis that the Supernaturalism of St. Thomas is the perfection of Humanism on the principle: *gratia perficit naturam*, p. 18.

THE NATURE OF MAN

On earth, there is nothing great but man; in man, there is nothing great but mind.

Phavorinus.

THE NATURE OF MIND

TRIPARTITE DIVISION.—Hamilton adopts the threefold distribution of the facts of consciousness into phenomena of *Knowledge*, of *Feeling*, and of *Conation*. This classification, first propounded last century by Tetens, a German philosopher, . . . probably enjoys most general favour among psychologists of the present day. It bases its claims on the assumption of three ultimate radically distinct modes of conscious activity to one or other of which all forms of mental life are reducible, while none of these, it is asserted, can be identified with, or resolved into, either of the other two. Consciousness assures me, it is urged that I am capable of Knowledge, of seeing, hearing, imagining, reasoning, and the rest. It also testifies to the fact that I may be drawn towards or repelled from objects, in other words, that I am endowed with the faculty of Desire. Finally, it reveals to me that I experience pleasure and pain, and that I am subject to various emotions, such as curiosity, pride, anger, and admiration, which are not acts of cognition, nor yet of desire. Accordingly there must be postulated as the basis of this last class of states a third capability in the mind, the Faculty of Feeling.

Michael Maher, S.J., *Psychology*, Longmans Green, 1909, pp. 34–35; for continuation of this quotation and critique see p. 75.

CHAPTER III

THE NATURE OF MAN

The mystery in the make-up of man is the same mystery that runs all through philosophy, the mystery of the one and the many. Man is one. He is a unitary organism. Yet man is two. He is mind and matter, soul and body, spiritual substance and material substance. How can this be? Through the history of philosophy three different answers have been given to this question. Two of the answers deny one of the terms of this combination. Materialists say man is all matter—no mind! Idealists say man is all mind—no matter! Both of these schools of thought are current in the modern world though, with the presentday worship of science, the materialists far outnumber the idealists. The third answer retains both terms in the make-up of man, and various are the ways in which that combination is presented to preserve its unity. No answer gives complete satisfaction to the mind endeavoring to understand the relationship between matter and spirit in their union to form man. Hence, the mystery. But there are many mysteries in the world of nature (what is gravitation, electricity, etc.,?), why should we be surprised that there is a mystery in the nature of man? Our purpose in the Philosophy of Education is to delve as deeply as possible into that mystery, clear up all we can concerning it and, as we grow in knowledge, apply this knowledge to the advancement of human living.

The answer to this problem which we briefly present here is an answer that has come down to us from the greatest minds of antiquity, from perhaps the greatest mind of all time, in Dante's fine phrase, "the master of those who know," the Greek philosopher, Aristotle. This answer was taken over by the Christian thinkers, notably by St. Thomas Aquinas in the thirteenth century, and with the added light of divine revelation was built into what we are calling the Aris-thomistic system of philosophy. The key to understanding the nature of man as interpreted in this system is understanding the distinctions between substance and accident and between matter and form in the philosophical meaning of these terms. Substance is that which exists *per se*, which does not need another in which to exist, which, if we may repeat the word in explaining it, subsists by itself. An accident on the contrary is that which does need another in which to exist. Thus, color, size, shape, etc., are accidents of material substance. Man is a substance; his acts are accidents. They come and go but man the substance remains through all these changes. Now in every created substance there are two constitutive elements, namely, matter and form. Matter is the undetermined element, form the determining element. Thus in man, body is the material element and spirit is the formal element which makes man man. We speak of material substance and spiritual substance, but relative to man they are incomplete substances, i.e., they have a natural affinity to unite to form the complete substance, man. Hence the union of these two, the material and the spiritual in man is a substantial union, that is, they together constitute one substance, man. To help us understand this problem we use the analogy of the combination of two elements, hydrogen and oxygen, the union of which in right proportions, brings into being a third substance, water, with its own characteristics clearly differentiating it from either of the two that go to make it up.

So with man. We say that he is a somatopsychic organism. This word "somatopsychic" is made up of the two Greek words, "soma," meaning body, and "psyche," meaning soul or mind. To say, then, that man is a somatopsychic organism is the same as saying that he is a body-mind organism. The advantage of putting these two words into one is that it emphasizes the essential unity in the nature of man. He is not a body merely; this without the mind or soul would be a corpse; nor is he a soul (mind) only; this would be a purely spiritual being like an angel. Rather, he is a living organism; a spirit (soul, mind) animating, *i.e.*, giving life to, a body. Once these two are separated even in thought, we are not thinking of man. Rather are we thinking of a pure spirit, *i.e.*, an angel, or of a dead body, *i.e.*, a corpse.

The science of psychology is the science of this somatopsychic organism, man. Though we do not separate the two constituent elements of his nature, body and mind, we do make a distinction between them and we do study these two distinct elements of his nature under separate headings, "body facts" and "mind facts." But the student should realize that this is done merely for purposes of study. This is the way our minds work. *"Divide et impera!"* is as true in the kingdom of mind as it was true in the Roman Empire. If we wish to deepen our understanding of the nature of the human being, we must divide and classify the great mass of facts bearing on this problem and give our attention to particular groups of these facts one after another until we have covered all the groups and have thus assimilated a body of knowledge all of which bears upon the problem of psychology, the nature of the human being.

The primary division of this body of knowledge, called the "science of psychology," is threefold: first, body facts, studied through observation and the experimental method in general; second, mind facts (conscious experience) studied through inner observation, *i.e.*, introspection, observation of self, the inner experience of each individual and his reflections thereon; and third, behavior facts, the "soma" and the "psyche" in action. This third group of facts is studied through the use of both methods, observation of the behavior of others and introspection or, self-observation of our own behavior. This latter method, introspection, is a much more difficult method of arriving at knowledge than the first, but it is fallacious to say, as the extreme Behaviorists do, that it does not result in scientific knowledge. Knowledge derived through this method is limited, of course, as is knowledge derived through any other method, but it is real knowledge nevertheless and serves the twofold purpose of knowledge in the same way as does knowledge derived through the objective method, *i.e.*, observation of others.

KNOWLEDGE AS APPRECIATION AND KNOWLEDGE FOR USE

What are the two purposes which knowledge serves? To put it another way, why do we study psychology? We study psychology for the same reasons we study any science—first, for the satisfaction that comes from knowing (knowledge for its own sake, *i.e.*, knowledge as appreciation); and second, for the use we can make of knowledge for the advancement of human living. From the point of view of intellectual satisfactions no knowledge is superior to a knowledge of ourselves and our fellows with whom we live. In the second place no knowledge is more practical or utilitarian. Knowledge means power to predict what will happen. In the natural sciences with their exact measurements, this power of prediction makes possible the control of the forces of physical nature and their application to the needs of man. Similarly, though not with the same degree of exactness, since the personal factor enters here in a way that is unknown in the field of exact sciences, knowledge gained through the study of psychology makes possible within limits prediction of how human beings will act under such and such circumstances. From this power of prediction follows the power of control (again within limits) since, if we can determine the circumstances in which a human individual is placed, we can thereby regulate to a great degree his behavior. The whole process of education rests upon this belief. We determine the environment of the child in school by freeing him from certain influences which we believe would be harmful and we bring to him experiences which we believe will be beneficial insofar as they advance understandings, generate certain life ideals, and have as their outcomes desirable habits. On the basis of such experiences we feel we have set up *controls of conduct* which will function all through life. Unlike the control exerted from the outside on physical forces, such as electricity, the controls of conduct in human beings must be self-administered. Knowledge within limits does, however, establish control of human behavior, a control made possible only through our power of prediction, which is the outcome of knowledge.

This leads to one of the most significant aspects of the study of psychology for every individual college student, namely, its utilitarian value (knowledge for use). Through our power to predict the behavior of others we will, within limits, be able to control their behavior. But the behavior control that should be the chief interest of every individual human being is the control of his own behavior. That this can be advanced through the study of psychology there is no doubt. An understanding of the motives that move men and women and hence influence their behavior, comes partly through observation of their behavior, but it comes in the first instance and much more deeply through a thorough acquaintance with the motives which move ourselves (self-observation) provided we are normal personalities. And this knowledge of self, altogether apart from its value in dealing with other normal human beings like ourselves, has its chief value in the aid it offers in regulating our own behavior. Here again we emphasize the difference between the control of the forces of physical nature for our own purposes, an extraneous control, and control of the forces of human nature which must be self-administered if human personality is to achieve its full development. The study of psychology should be an aid in both fields, *i.e.*, in the field of self-control and in the field of influencing others, the latter field being the essential work of the teacher. We now take up the first group of facts which constitute the subject matter of psychology.

1. THE MECHANISM OF BEHAVIOR
(BODY FACTS)

We remind the student that the word "mechanism" is used in two senses, first referring to a machine and its parts or as the dictionary says, "something comparable to a machine" (*Webster's Secondary School Dictionary*), and second to the operations or actions of a machine. In this section we are using the word in both senses applied to the human body. Structurally, it is only certain parts of the body, certain organs, which serve as the mechanism of behavior, the remainder carrying on the other vital processes, *e.g.*, digestion, circulation, etc. The former, taken together as a unit, constitute what is called the "integrating mechanism," *i.e.*, the mechanism through which the organism functions *as a whole*. This mechanism is divided into three groups of organs, each group with a particular function. There is first of all group I, called *receptors*, the sense organs, eye, ear, skin, etc., whose function is to receive messages from the outside world or from within the body, these messages being registered in conscious experience as sensations. At the other end of this integrating mechanism is group III, called *effectors*, the muscles and glands through which a particular

type of behavior-act is effected, *i.e.*, carried out.   These organs
determine whether in any particular situation we run away or
stand our ground, whether we weep in sorrow or cry with joy.
In between these two parts of the mechanism is group II, the
connectors.   These are the nervous systems.   We use the plural
advisedly, for there are two nervous systems intimately connected one with the other, the cerebro-spinal and the autonomic.   It is through the functioning of this central part of the
mechanism that the particular behavior-act at any given moment is adapted to the situation presented by the receptor
organs.   The whole mechanism analyzed into its three parts
together with the organs in each part are presented in Diagram
3 (p. 66).

So much for the structure of this mechanism.   But each one
of these three parts of the mechanism has a particular function.
The function of the receptors is stimulation, that is, the arousing of sensations; that of the effectors is response; and that of
the connectors is adaptation.   This word is well chosen.[1]   Literally, from the Latin *ad* (to) and *aptare* (fit), adaptation means
a *fitting* of the response *to* the stimulation.   In human behavior,
since the response is generally to a total situation rather than
to an isolated stimulus, we may well say that the function of the
receptors is to present the situation and the response is the behavior which the organism carries out.   (See Figure 2, page 67.)

The most effective way of bringing out clearly the meaning of
this diagram is to take a simple behavior-act and analyze it into
the elements thus: We come down to breakfast in the morning
in the normal state of health, deeply engrossed in endeavoring

[1] Howard C. Warren, *Human Psychology*, Houghton Mifflin, 1919, Chapter V
is entitled "Stimulation, Adjustment and Response."   From the point of view of
terminology this is unfortunate.   The term "adjustment" is now used almost
universally by psychologists for the various forms of behavior which are effected
through Sector 5 of the circuit.   The selection or, in the case of habit the determination of these behavior forms, the function of Sector 3, is what we mean
by "adaptation."

DIAGRAM 3.—THE HUMAN INTEGRATING MECHANISM

(Anatomical, i.e., structural analysis)

I. Receptors (terminals) Receiving mechanisms
- 1. End organs
  - a. Eye
  - b. Ear (semicircular canals)
  - c. Skin
  - d. Nasal cavity
  - e. Taste buds (mouth)
  - f. g., etc.
- 2. Free nerve endings, in muscles, visceral organs, etc.

II. Connectors (nervous systems) Adapting mechanisms
- 1. Cerebro-spinal
  - a. Central
    - 1. Brain
    - 2. Spinal cord
  - b. Peripheral
    - 1. Cranial nerves (12 pairs)
    - 2. Spinal nerves (31 pairs)
- 2. Autonomic
  - a. Cranial
    - 1. Mid-brain
    - 2. Upper spine
  - b. Sympathetic
    - 1. Spine
    - 2. Body cavity
  - c. Sacral —Lower spine

III. Effectors (terminals) Reacting mechanisms
- 1. Muscles
  - a. Voluntary (striped-skeletal)
  - b. Non-voluntary (smooth-systemic)
- 2. Glands
  - a. With ducts
  - b. Ductless

to think through some problem we are confronted with that day. Our behavior through habit runs along quite smoothly, leaving us free to continue our search for the solution of our problem. Let us analyze the overt bodily activity we are carrying on meanwhile, *i.e.*, our behavior. Light rays from the fruit

FIGURE 2.—THE INTEGRATING MECHANISM AND THE NEURO-TERMINAL CIRCUIT

THE MECHANISM (structural analysis)		THE CIRCUIT (functional analysis)	
Parts	*Organs*	*Sectors*	*Functions*
Receptors (terminals)	Sense organs: eye, ear, skin, etc.	1. Receiving	Stimulation
Connectors (nervous arc)	Sensory neurones	2. Afferent	Sensory conduction
	Brain, spinal cord, other centers	3. Conversion	Adaptation
	Motor neurones	4. Efferent	Motor conduction
Effectors (terminals)	Muscles and glands	5. Reacting	Response

at our place on the table impinge on the retina of the eyes, and after taking our seat, unfolding our napkin, we reach for a spoon as usual each morning, take hold of an orange and using the spoon, eat the edible part, a feat requiring some skill. While these muscular coördinations are going on, the glands have been pouring saliva into the mouth (our mouth waters) and down along the digestive tract, the organs (stomach, etc.) have been preparing themselves for the reception of food and the carrying out of their part in the digestive process. So through the whole of the breakfast period, muscular contractions and relaxations and glandular secretions go on, regulated by the reflex mechanism and habit. The tension of hunger dominant in our body situation when we entered the room has been relieved and lighting a cigarette we give ourselves to some piece of news which has caught our eye in the headlines of the morning paper. In this simple piece of everyday behavior we have numerous illustrations of stimulation of sense organs, adaptations to the situations presented, and responses which carry over those adaptations into behavior. This type of behavior we call habit. It undoubtedly makes up the vast majority of our actions during the day.

THE NEURAL THEORY

The explanation of a behavior-act such as any of the above, is based on what is called the neural theory. Due to the great advance in anatomy, physiology, and particularly neurology, we now know much more about what is happening within the body in any simple behavior-act than James did in 1890 when he brought out his *Principles of Psychology*. Today, instead of speaking of gross areas of neural structure, we speak of the neurone as the structural unit of the neural mechanism. Similarly, the reflex arc (Figures 2 and 3, sectors 2, 3, and 4.)

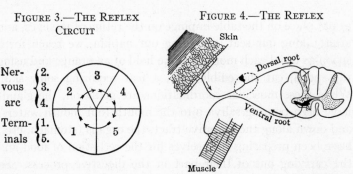

FIGURE 3.—THE REFLEX CIRCUIT

FIGURE 4.—THE REFLEX

A sensory impulse travels from a skin receptor to the spinal cord, entering by the dorsal root. Connecting neurones convey the impulse to the motor neurone, which, leaving by the ventral root, goes to the muscle, producing a contraction. (Figure 4 from Charles J. Herrick, *Introduction to Neurology*, W. B. Saunders, 1931.)

is the functional unit of the neural mechanism. The neural mechanism made up of neurones is the central part of the integrating mechanism, with terminals on either end, the sense organs on one end and the muscles and glands on the other. The functioning of the whole gives us the reflex circuit. The reflex act is the unit of behavior made possible through this mechanism, though, as we will see later, this statement will have to be modified. The central concept in the neural theory presented by Waldeyer, is according to Murphy in his *Historical Introduction to Modern Psychology:*

the anatomical independence of nerve cells and their physiological interconnection at junction points or "synapses." (page 204)

Evidently on this basis from a functional point of view the most important sector of the circuit is No. 3, the Conversion Sector, in which the incoming sensory impulses are converted into the outgoing motor impulses, giving rise to behavior.

Since an insight into this concept of the reflex circuit is absolutely necessary for understanding the approach which has been made to the study of learning during the first quarter of this century we analyze in detail the operations which take place in each of the sectors of the circuit.

DIAGRAM 4.—THE REFLEX CIRCUIT

Sectors of the circuit

1. Receiving: sector — physical energy, orange light rays, odor, etc., arouses physiological energy, *i.e.*, sensory impulses (stimulation)

2. Afferent: sector — sensory impulses travel over sensory paths (sensory conduction)

3. Conversion: sector — sensory impulses, image, color, odor of orange, etc., are summated as a unit—orange (integration) and motor impulses are distributed to appropriate motor neurones (coördination), the two together, (adaptation)

4. Efferent: sector — motor impulses travel over motor paths (motor conduction) and

5. Reacting: sector — physiological energy, the moror impulses, liberate
   a. physical energy: grasping orange, spoon, etc., and
   b. chemical energy: salivary, gastric secretions (response).

Such an act of behavior as eating an orange at table carries with it the idea of completion, and therefore a full stop at its terminus, but in many ordinary actions of the day like walking, the responses made furnish further stimulation and "the music goes 'round and 'round." Hence the significance of the term "circuit." In the instance just described each functioning of this circuit is called a reflex. We said above that the reflex is the unit of behavior, but this is true only of nonvoluntary behavior. There is another type of behavior that is of supreme importance in the life of man, which brings in an element not present in the reflex at all. Occasions arise every day in the life of the ordinary person in which habit cannot determine the adaptation to be selected. Thus in the illustration of the breakfast table let us suppose that on sitting down to breakfast this morning, as we pick up our spoon to eat the orange, we recall that following breakfast yesterday we did not feel very well. This remembrance brings to mind a peculiar taste of the orange. Possibly it was spoiled? All this takes place in a very short time, but after a moment of hesitation we push the orange aside and ask for a glass of tomato juice.

Here is a new type of adaptation to a situation different from that of yesterday. The dominant characteristic of the adaptations yesterday was that they all went on unconsciously. That is, we were *not aware* of what we were doing. Today the situation is totally different. Awareness is the distinctive feature, and this awareness presents a problem. Adaptation means solving this problem. It is solved only following the recall of yesterday's indisposition (memory), recall of the peculiar tonal quality of that indisposition (feeling), search for its cause (intellection), and final decision resulting in choice (volition). All these are conscious activities. They and many others are what we mean by mind. In the case of habit we speak of the control of our behavior as turned over to the nervous mechanism through repetition. This, of course, is a manner of speaking. Philosophically, the soul is as much the principle of unconscious habitual acts, or systemic activities of the organism, digestion, circulation, respiration, etc., as it is of mental activities. Further in the neural theory, all mental activities have a basis in neural process. "No psychosis without neurosis," it is phrased. But we cannot convert this proposition, "No neurosis without psychosis." In dreamless sleep we have a great deal of neurosis without psychosis. And in this sense we say these activities, *i.e.*, automatic systemic activities and habits, are controlled by the neural mechanism. The other group of activities, where mind enters in, we call conscious experience. The very function of mind in this concept is to control behavior, that is, that part of our behavior for which we have no established neural mechanisms, either inherited or acquired, and which are fixed in their functioning. In the next section we analyze the activities of conscious experience.

2. CONSCIOUS CONTROLS OF BEHAVIOR
(MIND FACTS)

Adaptation, that is, the fitting of the response to the situation resulting in human behavior, is of two kinds, that which takes place unconsciously (reflexes and habits), and that which is effected through consciousness, that is, the mental functions. What are the various mental activities which play a part in determining the behavior an individual carries on? Again, this is a problem of classification. Always remembering that the mind is a unit, that as a spiritual entity it has no parts, that the divisions which we set up in our attempts to classify its activities are logical divisions made for purposes of study although they have a basis in fact, we proceed to this task.

DISTINCTIONS IN MENTAL ACTIVITIES

Let us represent all mental activities as included within a circle. Divide these mental activities into two great classes, namely, those man carries on in common with the other members of the animal kingdom, sensation, perception, etc., and those which are peculiar to man as a *rational* animal, intellection, volition, etc. We divide the circle horizontally to indicate this division of mental operations and speak of the lower part of the circle as the sensuous level, and the upper part as the rational level. This is *the horizontal distinction* in mental activities. (Figure 5, p. 73.)

But traditionally there is another distinction in mental operations which runs through both of these levels of sense and reason. This we will call *the vertical distinction* in mental activities. It is one thing to experience a sensation of hunger; it is another to do something about it that this hunger may be relieved. Similarly, on the rational level, reflective thinking, deliberation, and planning a course of action in the presence of some baffling problem is a peculiarly human attribute, but carrying out that plan with purpose and determination is just as truly a human characteristic. Let us divide the circle vertically to represent this distinction in mental operations, shading the left portion with vertical lines and the right with horizontal. Then in the left lower sector we locate the sensory powers leading to knowledge, and in the left upper sector the intellectual powers leading to knowledge with the two words, "sensation" and "intellection." In the right lower sector we write the word "impulse" to cover all those tendencies to action which man has in common with other animals, and in the right upper sector the word "volition" to represent those decisions, choices, etc., peculiar to man which follow deliberation in his attempts to meet the problems of life. Here is the vertical dis-

FIGURE 5.—DISTINCTIONS IN MENTAL FUNCTIONS

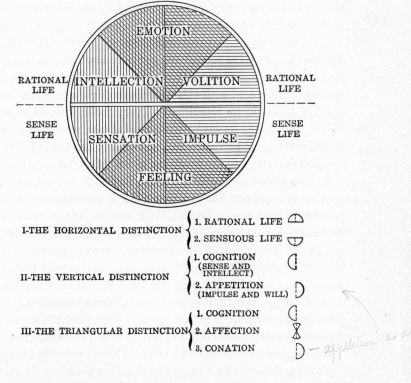

I-THE HORIZONTAL DISTINCTION
  1. RATIONAL LIFE
  2. SENSUOUS LIFE

II-THE VERTICAL DISTINCTION
  1. COGNITION (SENSE AND INTELLECT)
  2. APPETITION (IMPULSE AND WILL)

III-THE TRIANGULAR DISTINCTION
  1. COGNITION
  2. AFFECTION
  3. CONATION

tinction in mental activities between cognition and conation, activities which in man have been traditionally labeled by the two words, intellect and will (Figure 5 above).

THE TRIANGULAR DISTINCTION

But there is another distinction in our mental operations which is all-important for education. Let us illustrate by a simple example. We are walking along the sidewalk, and leaves on the branch of a tree protruding in our direction lightly touch our cheek as we pass by. We are aware of the leaves, that is, we have a conscious experience called the sensation of touch, but there is nothing particularly agreeable or disagreeable about the experience. On another day, however, let the wind be blowing and let this branch swaying in the wind strike our cheek with some force. We not only have a sensation but this sensation has a peculiar tonal quality which we call the feeling of pain, and with this experience of pain we draw back quickly to avoid its repetition. Every feeling begins in sensation, but it has its own peculiar tonal quality which marks it off from a mere sensation and this quality has a great deal to do with determining the reactions which follow the experience, reactions aimed at avoidance if the feeling is painful, at preserving or repeating the experience if it is pleasurable. So too on the rational level. Ordinarily, a mature person would not become angry if slapped in the face by a branch of a tree swaying in the wind, even if the experience proved painful. But let him be slapped by a fellow man, causing less pain than the impact of a branch of a tree, and the emotion of anger arises immediately. Why? Because a new element is present in the emotional complex. This new element is an *intellectual insight.* That is, we are insulted if slapped by a fellow being; not so, when slapped by a branch of a tree. We read *meaning* into the situation. Moore emphasizes the situation thus:

> This emotional state is dependent upon an insight into the situation and knowledge of an external individual and his relationships to the one who experiences the emotion. Such an insight transcends completely the qualities of sense. It is an intellectual something and not sensory. So, also, with all our emotions. They are insights and memories of a very complex nature which lie at the root of the emotion and which rise and fall in consciousness during the emotional outbreak, giving rise to renewed intensity by their repeated occurrence.[1]

[1] Thomas Verner Moore, *Dynamic Psychology*, Lippincott, 1924, p. 109.

Here, then, is *the triangular distinction* in mental functions:
(1) cognition (knowing), (2) affection (feeling) and (3) conation
(doing). (Figure 5, p. 43.) It is of great importance for education. We realize that in philosophy traditionally the mental
functions have been divided into cognitive and appetitive, and
the affective and conative functions classified as subdivisions
of the appetitive thus:

Mental Functions [1] { Cognitive
{ Appetitive { Affective
{ Conative

We will point out later why for our purpose in education it is
better to drop the word "appetitive" and put the three terms,
cognitive, affective, and conative together on the same plane.

Of more importance to philosophy, however, is the distinction between sensuous life and rational life. One of the quotations introducing this chapter (p. 58) giving the origin of the
triangular distinction we are recommending here, is from
Maher's *Psychology*. This passage continues: "Our objection
to this is that it sins both by excess and defect. On the one
hand it ignores the fundamental distinction between the lower
and higher grades of mental life and on the other it asserts
without sufficient grounds the existence of a separate third
faculty." [2] We realize the importance of this distinction in
philosophy. The main argument for the spirituality of the
soul is based upon it; the difference in nature of the activities of
the sensuous life, sensation, perception, etc., which man shares
in common with animals, and those of the rational life, abstraction, conception, reasoning, etc., peculiar to man. But the
parallel horizontal lines in Figure 5 dividing the circle into

[1] *Ibid.*, See "Mental Products" in the bracket diagram entitled "Elements of
Mind," p. 50.
[2] *Op. cit.*, p. 35.

lower and upper halves indicate this distinction in an emphatic way and give it its name the "horizontal distinction." But the triangular distinction is present on both levels in these terms: sensuous level, sensation, feeling, impulse; rational level, intellection, emotion, volition.

In regard to Maher's second objection that the triangular distinction is "without sufficient grounds" we answer in the words of Moore, the foremost Catholic psychologist today:

> I. The effective mental states must be distinguished clearly from our representative processes, for they have characteristics of their own which cannot be confounded with our sensations, mental images, and concepts.
>
> II. In the affective mental states themselves we may distinguish two groups: The first group consists of simple feelings, such as pleasure and pain. The number of these simple feelings is as yet an unsettled problem. . . . The other group consists of more complex states which are usually termed emotions.[1]

Moore is here emphasing the necessity of distinguishing feelings and emotions as "affective mental states" from states which are "cognitive" in character, namely, sensations, images and concepts, etc. In addition to this distinction we wish to point out that they are also to be distinguished from states which are distinctly "conative" in character, i.e., those that are concerned with reactions of the organism. Even though slapped in the face by a person whom the world lists as our enemy, we need not necessarily reply in kind and strike back, although the impulse so do so is very strong. The exercise of free will is a distinctive human prerogative which calls forth all the more praise when provocation is the stronger. "The will to refrain," the "inner check" of Babbitt,[2] is a reality in

[1] *Op. cit.* Chap. III, "Summary of the Theory of the Affective Mental States" p. 132.

[2] Chap. II, Section 2, page 147.

the life of man, as real as the finest discriminations of sense made by the scientist in the laboratory or the highest intellections of the philosopher in his periods of reflection. The latter are cognitive operations, the outcome of which is knowledge. The former are conative operations, the outcome of which is action, skill, ability to do something, or to refrain from doing something. Mediating between the two are the affective operations, the outcome of which is attitudes, called in the field of the arts, appreciations; in the field of conduct, ideals. In Figure 5 (p. 73) "affection," the third of the mental functions is represented by the hatched portion of the circle both above and below the horizontal line. Following Moore we carry the distinction one step further than is ordinarily done by Aris-thomistic philosophers and base feelings on sensations and emotions on intellectual insights. In this interpretation animals are not capable of emotions properly so called since they are not capable of intellectual insights. We may phrase it thus: emotion has its foundation in the intellect, its fruition in the will.

It is of some interest that in spite of his objections, the organization of subject matter in Maher's *Psychology* suggests the triangular distinction insofar as Part I, "Sensuous Life," has Chapter XI, "Feelings of Pleasure and Pain," pp. 221–228 and Part II, "Rational Life," has Chapter XX, "The Emotions" pp. 425–454, thus on both levels treating the affective phase of mental life separately from the cognitive and conative phases. But in a book of 610 pages only 38 pages are devoted to this subject. If, as Moore defines it, "psychology is the science of human personality," does feeling and emotion play such a minor role in the development of personality? The fact is the world is still waiting for a psychology of the feelings and emotions. Up to the present the psychoanalysts have made the greatest contribution in revealing what an important

factor feelings and emotions are in determining human behavior, the subject for study in the following Chapter IV,
"The Motivation of Human Behavior." The least we can do
is to keep the affective phase of our mental life as a subject of
study on a parity with the cognitive and conative phases,
without destroying the unity of the organism. This is the
point of view presented by a presentday psychologist in the
following statement:

> In *Chapter one* we pointed out a very old classification of human
> activities. We saw that, according to this way of thinking, the
> individual is one who *does* things, who *enjoys* things, and who
> *knows* things. Here we have a start toward classification. We
> are quite sure that the organism functions in these ways. More-
> over, it appears that these large classes include within their broad
> limits all of the activities of the organism. It should be clearly
> recognized that any attempt to divide up the activities of such
> a highly unified organism as the human must be quite arbitrary.
> The organism does not function in a single way at any given
> moment any more than an animal may truthfully be said to di-
> gest during eight hours per day, to respire for a second eight
> hours, and to reproduce and carry on such functions as circula-
> tion and excretion for another like period. The animal may, and
> probably does, do all of these during the course of a short time.
> In most cases, they are undoubtedly concomitant rather than
> sequent. The same statement holds for the psychological activ-
> ities of a human being. He may be behaving in two or more un-
> like ways at the same time. He may be enjoying what he is doing;
> or he may "work" and think at the same time. One psycholog-
> ical function does not come to an abrupt end to be followed by
> other functions. Operations go on; they are events. One form
> may cease while another continues. It is obviously true that
> during one's waking life one continuously functions psycholog-
> ically. As a rule, each function is very intimately related to all
> others.
> CLASSES OF PSYCHOLOGICAL FUNCTIONS. Of the various kinds
> of psychological activities, or functions, which stand as sub-

heads under the gross divisions of *doing*, *feeling*, and *knowing*, the first to appear in the life of the individual is perception.[1]

THE TRIANGULAR DISTINCTION AND CATHOLIC EDUCATION

That this threefold analysis of mental life is within the Catholic tradition appears clearly when we recall the answer in the first chapter of the Catechism to the question "Why did God make you?" For centuries this has been memorized by generation after generation of children: "(1) to know Him, (2) to love Him, (3) to serve Him in this world, and to be happy with Him forever in the next." Similarly, great Catholic educators have emphasized this threefold phase of man's mental life. Thus, in Bishop Spalding's writings, we find:

> The whole purpose of Education is to favor acquirement of habits; habits of feeling, thinking and doing.[2]

And in DeHovre-Jordan's *Catholicism in Education* we find, in Chapter IX, entitled "Newman as an Exponent of the Catholic Ideals of Character Formation," the following:

> If Christianity is "the Completion of Natural Virtue," it is the only spiritual environment in which man's character can attain to full perfection. The importance of such information is obvious when we reflect that man's powers of *knowing*, *feeling* and *willing* (or acting), which together constitute the sum total of his specifically human activities, not only differ as to their nature and object, but are often in conflict with one another. This lack of harmony is one of the consequences of original sin. To restore that harmony by incorporating man in Christianity, which is "the completion of natural virtue;" this is the task of Catholic Character Education.

Now, it will be asked, how is this harmony to be achieved?

[1] Glenn De Vere Higginson, *Fields of Psychology*, Holt, 1931, pp. 67–68.
[2] John Lancaster Spalding, *Aphorisms and Reflections*, McClurg, 1901, p. 215.

The first step is to recognize clearly the fact that *knowing, feeling,* and *willing* are three distinct powers of the soul. While related one to the other they must never be confused. Each enjoys a certain autonomy, so to speak. Thinking is not willing, and feeling is not thinking. Catholic education never loses sight of this distinction. The next step is to guide and direct each of these powers aright. Beginning with the intellect, which is so often confused as it wanders about in a labyrinth of fragmentary truths, Catholic philosophy points out the way that leads to ultimate Truth in which all partial truths find their explanation. Thus unity and harmony are established in the intellectual life of man. The procedure is the same in the case of the will and of the effective life. Left to itself the will may attain to one or other virtue but seems incapable of orienting itself properly in a world where, as Chesterton says, "the virtues have gone mad because they have been isolated from each other and are wandering alone." [1] Catholic moral training will enable the individual to bring these virtues together into a harmonious whole and to lead a truly virtuous life. So, too, with the emotional life. How Catholic education harmonizes the discordant elements here may be seen from the fact that the genuine Christian finds no difficulty in reconciling the fear of God with the love of God.

The complete formation of man, or complete character education, according to Catholic ideals means that each of these faculties is directed to the attainment of its proper object and that all work together harmoniously for the attainment of his eternal destiny. [2]

EDUCATION AND THE OUTCOMES OF LEARNING

That the most practical classification of mental functions for education is this threefold one of cognition, affection, and conation, is evident the moment we take up the problem of the outcomes of learning. This is the most important inquiry in educational psychology. Only insofar as the learning outcomes are identified can procedures be planned intelligently for

[1] G. K. Chesterton, *Orthodoxy*, Dodd Mead, 1936, p. 53.

[2] Franz de Hovre (tr. by Edward B. Jordan), *Catholicism in Education*, Benziger, 1934, pp. 358–359.

realizing these outcomes. Now there is a growing unanimity among educational psychologists and writers on methods and technique of teaching that the primary classification of these learning outcomes is threefold. Many words are used to label these outcomes, but they all fall naturally into one of these three groups: (1) *cognition*, *e.g.*, knowledge, facts, meanings, concepts, understandings, laws, principles, etc.; (2) *affection*, *e.g.*, attitudes, ideals, appreciations, tastes, interests, dispositions, etc.; and (3) *conation*, *e.g.*, abilities, skills, habits, techniques, procedures, etc. (Figure 6, p. 82.)

Following this same line of thought we see now the full significance of our analysis in Chapter I of the educative process into three kinds of changes, namely: (1) the change from ignorance to knowledge (cognition); (2) the change from domination by impulses to motivation by ideals (affection); and (3) the change from undeveloped capacities to developed abilities (conation).

It is the aim of education to bring about these three kinds of changes and by so doing set up controls for behavior. Without such controls man may live an animal existence, but he has no place in civilized society. We now turn to an analysis of the types of behavior within which these learning outcomes are to function as controls.

3. TYPES OF BEHAVIOR
(BEHAVIOR FACTS)

Following this analysis of the integrating mechanism (body functions) and the controls of behavior (mental functions) the student must continually bear in mind that the distinctions involved have been made for purposes of study. After all, there is only one organism, man. Man is a somatopsychic organism, that is, a body-mind organism, but this organism functions as a whole in any behavior act. We are in sympathy

FIGURE 6.—THE OUTCOMES OF LEARNING, THAT IS, TEACHER OBJECTIVES
(controls of behavior)

AUTHORS, TITLES, DATES AND LABELS	PRIMARY DISTINCTIONS IN MENTAL FUNCTIONS		
	Cognition (knowing)	Affection (feeling)	Conation (doing)
Cunningham, *The Pivotal Problems of Education*, 1940, "outcomes of learning or teacher objectives"	I. Knowledge (facts and meanings) III. p. 81	2. Attitudes (ideals and appreciations) III. p. 81	3. Abilities (habits and skills) III. p. 81
1. Bagley, *Educational Values*, 1911, "controls of conduct"	Intellectual controls (B) Ideas, meanings, concepts, facts, principles p. 26	Emotionalized controls (C) Ideals—p. 54 (D) Tastes (E) Attitudes p. 64	Automatic controls (A) Specific habits p. 14
2. Bossing, *Teaching in Secondary Schools*, 1935, "functions of secondary education"	1. Knowledge p. 28	3. Conditioned response p. 31	2. Skills and techniques p. 30
3. Douglass, *Modern Methods in High School Teaching*, 1926, "outcomes of teaching"	1. Information— p. 3 2. Retention of information— p. 18	4. Ideals and attitudes p. 24	3. Habits and skills p. 21
4. Garrison, *Technique and Administration of Teaching*, 1933, "learning outcomes"	1. The knowledge outcomes p. 90	3. Attitudes and appreciations as outcomes p. 92	2. Skills and habits as outcomes p. 90
5. Melvin, *Technique of Progressive Teaching*, 1932, "learning products"	2. Knowledge 3. Understanding p. 125	4. Appreciation of worth or value p. 125	1. Ability to do, make or achieve p. 125

(The number and letters in the last three columns indicate the order in which these "outcomes" are listed by the various authors.)

FIGURE 6.—(*Continued*)

Authors, Titles, Dates and Labels	Primary Distinctions in Mental Functions		
	Cognition (*knowing*)	Affection (*feeling*)	Conation (*doing*)
6. Monroe, *Directing Learning in the High School*, 1929, "immediate objectives of teaching"	II. Adaptive controls of conduct (knowledge) p. 61	III. General patterns of conduct (generalized controls) p. 61	I. Fixed controls of conduct (specific habits) p. 61
7. Morrison, *Practice of Teaching in the Secondary School*, revised 1931, "objectives of teaching"	1. Attitudes of understanding p. 19	2. Attitudes of appreciation p. 19	3. Abilities (skills) p. 19
8. Thomas, *Principles and Technique of Teaching*, 1927, "products of learning"	(3) Knowledge or information p. 46	(2) Attitudes and appreciations p. 40	(1) Habits and skills p. 37
9. Waples, *Procedures in High School Teaching*, 1926, "pupil responses"	Thought response p. 188	Appreciation response p. 188	Habit response p. 188
10. *Core Curriculum of Virginia Secondary Schools*, 1934, "aims of education"	Generalizations, understanding of, p. 7	Emotionalized attitudes, appreciation of, p. 3	Special abilities, ability to, p. 13

with this statement by Thorndike: "In presentday psychology, little effort is made to divide a man's mind up into intellectual, emotional, and volitional functions. There are all sorts of combinations." [1] The crux of the matter, however,

[1] E. L. Thorndike, *The Psychology of Wants, Interests and Attitudes*, Appleton-Century, 1935, p. 3.

is the meaning given to the word "divide." Distinction without separation is the very heart of reflective thinking. As the French put it, *distinguer pour unir*; we distinguish in order to unify. So here the distinctions in this primary analysis of mental functions unify our view of the organism as a whole and serve as the basis for our definition of education presented in Chapter I (p. 9). They will serve also as the basis for our analysis of the "values" of a school activity, (Chapter X) as well as for that of the teaching techniques (Chapter XIII). But this does not invalidate our contention that man is a unitary organism and that in all activities he functions as a whole.

Similarly we have analyzed the body functions (Figure 2, p. 67) separately from the mental functions (Figure 5, p. 73). But again this is for purposes of study. If this results in separation, rather than clarification in thought, the student becomes a dualist in the Cartesian sense. Descartes said extension was the essence of matter and thought the essence of mind, and, with this separation of the two, the relationship between man's mind and his body was no closer than that between man and a machine. We explained at the beginning of this chapter that in the Aris-thomistic theory the union of the two is the closest possible, namely, a *substantial* union, the two together forming the one substance, man. We may not have available any satisfactory explanation of the union. Here is one of the central mysteries in the makeup of the universe: how can the material and the spiritual, so different by nature, enter into union at all? But everyday experience compels us to recognize the fact of this union, even though presentday theory offers no adequate explanation of the "how." We are reminded here of Samuel Johnson's statement about freewill. "All argument is against it; all experience, for it." And again of Dean Swift's reply to Bishop Berkeley who

stopped him on the street one day and began to press upon
him the arguments in favor of the idealist's position. After
a period of forebearance, Swift kicked a stone down the street,
turned around and walked off. If a man does not accept the
evidence presented to him by his senses, there is no use arguing
with him. Similarly in our problem, the union of body and
mind constituting man; the facts of everyday experience
outweigh all theoretical arguments which may be brought
against it.

The "soma" and the "psyche" of the organism in action,
give us human behavior. We have attempted an integration
of the two by bringing together Figure 3, "The Reflex Circuit,"
and Figure 5, "Mental Functions," in Figure 7, "The Somatopsychic Organism" (p. 86), and now we make an analysis of the
organism in operation, that is, an analysis of behavior. The
word itself causes difficulty. Some psychologists consider
thoughts, feelings, volitions, etc., types of behavior. In our
terminology mental functions are rather controls of behavior,
and behavior takes place through the functioning of the soma
(body) and the psyche (mind) as the constituents of the living
organism, man. This may appear like a concession to the
"behaviorists," the materialistic school of psychologists who
deny the reality of mind and the validity of introspection as a
method in scientific psychology. But, as a matter of fact,
this is the ordinary meaning of the term as given in the dictionary and as used in everyday speech referring to overt
bodily activity observable by others. Mental activity, *i.e.*,
"conscious experience," is observable only by the self through
introspection, and although it acts as a determiner of behavior,
i.e., it controls behavior, it is not behavior itself.

In analyzing behavior into its various types, our first problem is to decide on a basis of classification. A basis was
suggested in the functional analysis of the neuroterminal

circuit. This functional analysis gave us stimulation, adaptation, and response as the elemental functions in every behavior act. But we saw that there are two different types of adaptation, and with this analysis as our basis we distinguish two different types of behavior. The adaptation which fits the response to the stimulation may be conscious or wholly un-

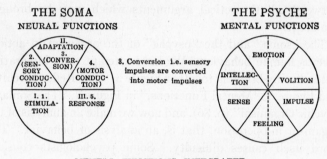

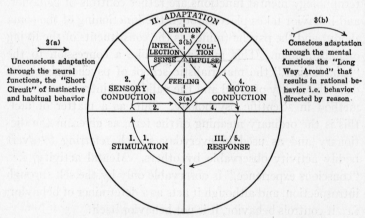

* The fact that the arc 3(b) passes through the center of the circle "Mental Functions" means that all six mental functions may be involved in II. ADAPTATION leading to behavior

FIGURE 7.—THE SOMATOPSYCHIC ORGANISM

conscious. Unconscious adaptation may be inherited or it may have been acquired by experience. If unconscious adaptation is inherited, its outcome is instinctive behavior. If it has been learned, we call the outcome habit. If the adaptation is conscious, that is, if the behavior resulting is under conscious control we call it rational behavior, *i.e.*, subject to reason. Since habits in the forming were subject to reason, (*i.e.*, were learned) they are to be grouped with rational behavior under the general term, intelligent behavior. The relationship of the types of adaptations to the types of behavior are presented in the following diagram.

DIAGRAM 5.—ADAPTATIONS AND BEHAVIOR

ADAPTATIONS		TYPES OF BEHAVIOR
I. Unconscious	1. Inherited (neural functions)	1. Instinctive
	2. Acquired	2. Habitual
II. Conscious	3. (mental functions)	3. Rational

(intelligent)

Interpreting this diagramatic analysis in terms of Figure 7, "The Somatopsychic Organism" (p. 86), we see that unconscious activities are the result of the functioning of sectors 1, 2, 3a, 4, and 5; whereas conscious activities come about through the functioning of 1, 2, 3b, 4 and 5. The line 3b passes through the center of the circle "Mental Functions" to indicate that in the case of rational behavior any or all of the mental functions may be involved. The greatest difficulty is encountered in attempting to explain by Figure 7 what happens in the case of instincts. The difficulty arises because of the two meanings of the word "instinct," its popular meaning, and its scientific meaning. As used by "objective" psychologists today instincts are types of behavior *unmodified by learning*. They eliminate mind as a determiner of behavior.

For McDougal, on the other hand, instincts with their impulses "are the mental forces that maintain and shape all the life of individuals and societies." [1] So viewed, even instinctive behavior follows the line 3b and not 3a leaving to 3a only purely unconscious activities such as circulation and respiration and motor habits. In the case of habits too, we must distinguish between those which are totally unconscious (such motor habits as walking, writing, etc., with adaptations determined by the neural mechanism, 3a) and those other which are mental in character, intellectual, emotional and volitional habits. When the word "habit" is used in such phrases as "habits of thinking," it refers to a facility that has been developed through practice in dealing with certain ideational content. Thought is the very *content of consciousness* along with feelings of pleasure or displeasure and the resulting urge to action. Hence in mental habits it is the *mode of operation* of which we are unconscious.

Even though this classification of behavior as instinctive, habitual, and rational does not completely satisfy us, we will find it useful as we continue our study. Our objective is to render all human behavior, intelligent behavior. This is the very business of education. In the following chapter, Chapter IV, "The Motivation of Human Behavior," we will study what the psychologists call instinctive tendencies and modified instincts and indicate how in the philosophy of Supernaturalism they are to be converted into intelligent behavior with the outcome, Christian conduct.

SUGGESTED READINGS

This chapter deals mainly with psychology as a natural or perhaps better, a humanistic science. The Aris-thomistic philosophical theory is stated briefly in the introduction. These books are recommended for further study of this philosophical approach:

[1] See quotation introducing the following chapter, p. 92.

Brennan, Robert Edward, *General Psychology*, Macmillan, 1937, is divided into "Book One: Organic Life; Book Two: Sensory Life; Book Three: Intellectual Life." Each of these three books is subdivided into "Section 1. The Science of" and "Section 2. The Philosophy of." The word "General" in the title signifies that both the scientific and philosophical approaches are made in all three parts.

Fearon, Arthur D., *The Two Sciences of Psychology*, Prentice-Hall, 1937, "a correlation of experimental (physical) and philosophical (metaphysical) psychology," Preface.

Maher, Michael, *Psychology Empirical and Rational*, Longmans Green, 1909, the standard text for the philosophical approach, "Book II, Rational Psychology" pp. 459–578.

McDougall, William, *Body and Mind*, Methuen & Co., Ltd., 1911, subtitle, "A History and Defense of Animism"; a scientific psychologist who says in the Preface: "I am aware that to many minds it must appear nothing short of a scandal that anyone occupying a position in an academy of learning other than a Roman Catholic seminary, should in this twentieth century defend the old world notion of the soul of man." p. XI.

I. THE MECHANISM OF BEHAVIOR

Gates, Arthur I., *Elementary Psychology*, Macmillan, 1929, Chapters II, III and IV carry the titles: "The Receiving Mechanisms," "The Connecting Mechanisms," "The Reacting Mechanisms."

——, *Psychology for Students of Education*, Macmillan 1924, Chapters II, III and IV carry the same titles given above.

Herrick, Charles J., *Introduction to Neurology*, W. B. Saunders, 1931, the anatomy and physiology of the neural theory by a neurologist.

Murphy, Gardner, *An Historical Introduction to Modern Psychology*, Harcourt Brace, 1929, the neural theory as formulated by Waldeyer in 1891, pp. 203–204.

Warren, Howard C., *Human Psychology*, Houghton Mifflin, 1919, Chapters III, "The Neuro-Terminal Mechanism" and V, "Stimulation, Adjustment and Response."

Wheeler and Perkins, *Principles of Mental Development*, Thomas Y. Crowell, 1932, Chapter IV, "Functions of the Adult Nervous System."

Woodworth, Robert S., *Psychology*, Henry Holt, (fourth ed. revised) 1939, Chapter VIII, "The Nervous System" a simplified presentation to make it significant to the student.

2. CONSCIOUS CONTROLS OF BEHAVIOR

Barrett, James Francis, *Elements of Psychology*, Bruce, 1931, the first thirteen chapters are a brief summary of "General Psychology" by a Supernaturalist; Chapters XIV–XVII inclusive are a brief summary of "Philosophy of Mind."

Higginson, Glenn Devere, *Fields of Psychology*, Henry Holt, 1931, the section entitled "Psychology of the Psycho-physical Organism," pp. 61–71 stresses the unity of the organism with analyses of the body's contribution to function and that of the mind, the latter in the three-fold classification, cognition, affection and conation, as most serviceable in applying psychology to education; see also pp. 1–6 for the same classification as "fundamental attitudes."

Maher, Michael, *Psychology*, Longmans Green, 1909, rejects the "Tripartite Division" of mental faculties pp. 34–35; the triangular distinction in mental functions on both the sensuous and rational levels is implied in Maher in that the concluding chapter of "Part 1. Sensuous Life" is entitled XI "Feelings of Pleasure and Pain," pp. 211–218, and that of "Part 2. Rational Life," XX "The Emotions," pp. 425–458.

Moore, Thomas Verner, *Dynamic Psychology*, Lippincott, 1924, as indicated by the title, deals with the affective and conative life, not the cognitive; Part III, "Human Emotional Life," pp. 101–136, is the best treatment available from the point of view of Supernaturalism.

——, *Cognitive Psychology*, Lippincott, 1939, with the foregoing completes what is commonly called "General Psychology" but both books give some treatment to the philosophical implications.

Reymert, Martin L., (editor) *Feelings and Emotions the Wittenberg Symposium*, Clark Univ. Press, 1928, 34 papers by prominent European and American psychologists treating different aspects of this problem.

Thorndike, Edward L., *The Psychology of Wants, Interests and At-*

titudes, Appleton Century, 1935, is a treatment of one group of mental functions by an objective psychologist.

Outcomes of Learning: page references to the classifications of learning outcomes by ten authors are given in Figure 6, pp. 82–83.

3. TYPES OF BEHAVIOR

Moore, Thomas Verner, *Dynamic Psychology*, Lippincott, 1924, we have adopted here the distinction between instinct and impulse presented in Part IV, Chapter I, "Instinct and Impulse" pp. 137–147.

Shaffer, Laurence Frederic, *The Psychology of Adjustment*, Houghton Mifflin, 1936, Chapter II, "The Origins of Behavior," III, "The Modification of Behavior" by an objective psychologist.

Warren, Howard C., *Human Psychology*, Houghton Mifflin, 1919, Chaps. VI and VII both entitled "Behavior," 1. "Reflex Behavior," 2. "Instinctive Behavior" and 3. "Intelligent Behavior" pp. 92–132.

Wheeler and Perkins, *Principles of Mental Development*, Thos. Y. Crowell, 1932, Chap. IX, "The Source of Intelligent Behavior."

THE NATURE OF INSTINCTS

Habits are formed only in the service of the instincts . . .

Directly or indirectly the instincts are the prime movers of all human activity; by the conative or impulsive force of some instinct (or of some habit derived from an instinct), every train of thought, however cold and passionless it may seem, is borne along towards its end, and every bodily activity is initiated and sustained. The instinctive impulses determine the ends of all activities and supply the driving power by which all mental activities are sustained; and all the complex intellectual apparatus of the most highly developed mind is but a means towards these ends, is but the instrument by which these impulses seek their satisfaction, while pleasure and pain do but serve to guide them in their choice of the means.

Take away these instinctive dispositions with their powerful impulses, and the organism would become incapable of activity of any kind; it would lie inert and motionless like a wonderful clockwork whose mainspring has been removed or a steam-engine whose fires had been drawn. These impulses are the mental forces that maintain and shape all the life of individuals and societies, and in them we are confronted with the central mystery of life and mind and will.

William McDougall, *Social Psychology*,
15th Edition, J. W. Luce, 1933; pp. 44,
46.

CHAPTER IV

THE MOTIVATION OF HUMAN BEHAVIOR

As students of education our primary interest is in human behavior. We wish to help students do better the things they will do anyway, to set up controls that they may avoid doing things harmful to themselves and to the society in which they live, and to stimulate them to certain forms of behavior which, apart from genius, would be impossible without education, or at least very unlikely to take place at all. Since this is the aim of the educator, it behooves him to have as deep an understanding of human behavior as can be developed through observation and study.

In the last chapter we began this study with a structural and functional analysis of the mechanism of behavior, that is, those organs through which behavior is carried on. In the second place, we gave attention to the control of behavior most significant for human living, namely, conscious control, that is, the control exerted by mind studied in our analysis under the concept of mental functions. Following this we gave brief attention to the two predominant types of behavior, namely, that which goes on without the intervention of consciousness, instinct and habit, and that due to consciousness itself, that is, under the direction of reason, hence called rational behavior. In this chapter and the one that follows, our purpose will be to carry this analysis further in order that we may deepen our understanding of human behavior and prepare ourselves as educators for directing and guiding it in students.

1. HEREDITY AND BEHAVIOR

We may well begin this inquiry with the question, Why should behavior take place at all? At first sight this may seem a baffling inquiry and yet a little consideration reveals that the answer is at hand. It lies in the statement, "to be alive is to be active." To state it negatively, for any living organism, when activity ceases, life itself ceases. The activities of the human organism *acting as a whole* are called human behavior. Our problem is, what forms of behavior does the human organism begin life with, how are these modified through living, and what new forms come forth as growth and development progresses. The first question, what forms of behavior does the organism begin life with, brings up for consideration the problem of heredity.

It is interesting to note the change which has come about in the thinking and writing of psychologists on this question of inherited forms of behavior during the past half-century. The older point of view was popularized by James in his *Principles of Psychology* in 1890. At the end of Chapter XXIV, entitled "Instinct," he states:

> These are the most prominent of the tendencies which are worthy of being called instinctive in the human species. It will be observed that *no other mammal, not even the monkey, shows so large an array.*[1]

At the other extreme we have this statement by Shaffer:

[1] William James, *Principles of Psychology*, Henry Holt, 1890, Vol. II, pp. 440–441.

The theory of instinct has ceased to be significant and useful in psychology, but demands recognition because of its great influence on popular thought.[1]

If an instinct is defined as "an inherited mode of behavior" and if we ask ourselves what does man do, what activities does he carry on which have *not been modified in some way by learning*, we see immediately why the scientific psychologist is so severe on the concept "instinct." The adult human being does nothing which has not been modified by learning. From this point of view, then, there are no human instincts in the sense in which the word is used in reference to animal life (particularly the insects), that is, fixed, unlearned, and unchanging modes of behavior. But surely we are not going to discard heredity as one of the factors in the making of man. After all, children do look like their parents, and they act like them. Scientific psychologists may explain their acting like their parents by the concept "social heredity," that is, the influence of environment or learning. Through the impulse of imitation they learn to act like their parents just as they learn the language of their parents and not some other language which they never hear. But the question goes deeper: why should they *imitate* their parents? Have we here arrived at a native tendency which meets the criteria of heredity, namely, (1) it arises without opportunity for learning and (2) it is universal in the species? Let us look at the newly born infant from the point of view of these criteria. In the first place, the bodily structure which makes behavior possible is inherited. We have made both a structural and functional analysis of the organs of the human body, making up this structure under the term "the integrating mechanism," that is, those organs through which the organism acts as a whole. But the term

[1] Laurence F. Shaffer, *Psychology of Adjustment*, Houghton Mifflin, 1936, p. 23.

"mechanism" refers not only to the parts of a machine, it is also used in reference to the operations of the machine. Are mechanisms in the functional sense of the word inherited? Most certainly some are. We described in the previous chapter the reflex as the functional unit of behavior. The human infant comes into the world possessed of many reflexes (for example, the pupilary reflex of the eye) and many combinations of reflexes. If this were not so survival would be impossible. Warren gives a list of some sixty-six reflexes in a fivefold classification.[1] Some of the reflexes listed by Warren commonly occur in combination and give us the elementary forms of behavior necessary for survival, for example, the grasping, sucking, swallowing activities of the infant. Another form of behavior that is certainly inherited is what is called "mass reactions."

> . . . the infant displays a considerable amount of diffused and nonspecific activity in which the body reacts as a whole. To any kind of stimulation, he kicks his legs, waves his arms, wiggles, squirms, and vocalizes. This behavior occurs under the ordinary stimulation of light, skin contacts, and internal states as well as in response to more clearly defined stimuli and is sometimes described as spontaneous or random. This characterization is unfortunate, for no movement occurs without a cause or stimulus, and the child is never without some stimulation, either external or internal. Violent stimulation such as loud noises will intensify this diffused type of activity, as will intense inner states such as those of hunger and pain. In general, there is a proportional relationship between the intensity and scope of the stimulation and the strength and diffusion of the response. The explanation of the mass reaction lies in the unorganized condition of the infant's nervous system. Any stimulus tends to spread its effect over many pathways, causing, the activity of a wide variety of effectors.[2]

[1] Howard C. Warren, *Human Psychology*, Houghton Mifflin, 1919, p. 100.
[2] Laurence F. Shaffer, *op. cit.*, pp. 30–31.

THE QUESTION OF INSTINCT

The significance of the above analysis is that it just about exhausts the varieties of behavior a human being is capable of apart from learning. All psychologists are now agreed on this. Nevertheless, the term "instinct" does persist. Thus Warren says:

There are two modes of behavior in man which take the place of pure instinct: *modified instincts and instinctive tendencies.*[1]

and then he gives a list of twenty-six of these "modified instincts" in a fivefold classification:

1. Nutritive
2. Reproductive
3. Defensive
4. Aggressive
5. Social Organization

He defines an instinctive tendency as

a mode of behavior comprising many distinct sorts of actions, all of which are individually learned, but which resemble one another in general type: the type itself is not learned but belongs to the constitution of the species . . . The most fundamental types are *imitativeness, playfulness, and curiosity.*[2]

These three terms are old acquaintances to anyone familiar with the educational literature of the first quarter of this century. It is of some interest to point out that these tendencies have a definite relationship with the three changes which we emphasized in our definition of education in Chapter I, thus: (1) imitation, the change from capacities to abilities; (2) play, the change from domination by impulses to motivation by ideals; (3) curiosity, the change from ignorance to

[1] *Op. cit.*, p. 104.
[2] *Ibid.*, p. 107.

knowledge. The importance of these original tendencies in the field of education, whether called "modified instincts" or "instinctive tendencies" is emphasized by Chapman and Counts:

> Only as initially we can use the drive attaching to these original tendencies, and later as we can use the drive attached to acquired tendencies which have evolved from the original ones, can we train and educate the individual.
>
> Though the instinctive basis of his conduct becomes increasingly less and less obvious as habit formation and intelligence modify and direct its original modes of expression, human life is permeated through and through with instinctive action. This instinctive equipment, regarded by certain stern moralists as essentially bad, viewed by certain irresponsible lovers of liberty as essentially good, furnishes the only groundwork for the process of training and education. To eradicate these innate tendencies is no more possible than to allow them an uncharted liberty. Any system of education or morals is certain to fail unless it recognizes these inextinguishable forces . . . To spend time evaluating the equipment is futile; whether we like it or not, this equipment is *the raw material of the educative process.*[1]

THE URGES AND DRIVES

As is evident from the above quotation, with the loss of caste by the word "instinct" among psychologists, other words are coming into use to label these native tendencies, chief among which are "urge" and "drive." Thus Gates, in his *Elementary Psychology* has a chapter entitled, "The Dominant Human Urges." His first classification is "Urges Aroused Primarily by Organic Conditions," listed as eleven, characteristic among which are "(1) the urge to secure food" and "(9) the urge to mate." (p. 223). The second classification, entitled, "Other Dominant Urges," he introduces with this statement:

[1] J. Crosby Chapman and George S. Counts, *Principles of Education*, Houghton Mifflin, 1924, p. 67.

Each "urge" moreover is not to be thought of as single and in-divisible but rather as a name applied to a group of particular impulses which are more or less similar.

(1) The urge to collect and hoard.

(2) The urge to excel and succeed—the "mastery impulse," etc.[1]

This reference to an "urge" as "a group of particular impulses" suggests a way out of the difficulty. We find it stated definitely by Moore in these words

We may, therefore, define an impulse as a *tendency that we experience, in the presence of an actual opportunity, to make use of any of our human abilities.*

Impulses are the real psychological elements in instincts. Much of the discussion about the number and nature of instincts is rendered superfluous by this concept. There are just as many impulses as there are human abilities. Instincts are merely groups of impulses or desires to which popular parlance has given names. In danger the "instinct of preservation" is called into play. This means nothing more than that every human ability that can help to extricate one from the danger is called into action. The parental instinct makes parents employ all their abilities in protecting their children, caring for them and furthering their welfare, etc.

Valuable as would be the study of those groups of impulses in detail to which popular psychology has given names, we must refer this study to social psychology to which it more properly belongs.[2]

It is as social psychologists, therefore, that we now take up this problem of classifying "instincts" *i.e.*, these urges or drives which are groups of impulses aimed at some particular end in social living. Before doing this, however, we must present the

[1] Arthur I. Gates, *Elementary Psychology*, Macmillan, (revised) 1928, Chapter VIII, "The Dominant Human Urges," pp. 216–244.

[2] Thomas Verner Moore, *Dynamic Psychology*, Lippincott, 1924, pp. 140–141.

definition of instinct which has exerted the most influence among students of social psychology. We introduce it by a quotation which links it with the threefold analysis we have made of mental functions in the previous chapter:

> There is every reason to believe that even the most purely instinctive action is the outcome of a distinctly mental process, one which is incapable of being described in purely mechanical terms, because it is a psycho-physical process, involving psychical as well as physical changes, and one which, like every other mental process, has, and can only be fully described in terms of, the three aspects of all mental process—the cognitive, the affective, and the conative aspects; that is to say, every instance of instinctive behaviour involves a knowing of some thing or object, a feeling in regard to it, and a striving towards or away from that object. . . .
>
> We may, then, define an instinct as an inherited or innate psycho-physical disposition which determines its possessor to perceive, and *to pay attention* to, objects of a certain class, *to experience an emotional excitement* of a particular quality upon perceiving such an object, and *to act in regard to it* in a particular manner, or, at least, to experience an impulse to such action.[1]

McDougall listed seven "major instincts" in 1911, but by 1923 the number had expanded to fourteen.

2. THE DOMINANT HUMAN DRIVES

Shaffer, referring to attempts to classify instincts, makes this statement: "These categories are only the attempt of the philosopher to gain a unitary view of animal behavior."[2] We accept this position and now proceed as advocates of the Christian philosophy of life to find a basis for a unitary view of human behavior in terms of the fundamental drives which

[1] William McDougall, *Social Psychology*, J. W. Luce, 1921, pp. 27, 30.
[2] *Op. cit.*, p. 24.

account for man's activities.   There is one such classification found among the poets as well as among philosophers and the founders of religion.   Dante, in the first canto of *The Inferno*, tells of meeting three beasts which hindered him in his attempt to ascend the hill of life, the leopard of luxury, the lion of ambition, and the wolf of avarice.   Buddha under the Bo-tree saw in a vision the root of evil in man's life, desire, "the lust of gold, and fame, and pleasure." [1]   Spinoza in the Introduction to his *Ethics* made an analysis identical with that of Buddha. (See Figure 8, Section B, p. 102.)

But it is the Christian concept of life which is our particular interest.   What are the obstacles in the path of man which would hinder him from achieving his full development?   We see them portrayed for us in the three temptations which Our Lord underwent in the desert before beginning His public ministry.   These are *the three temptations of humanity*.   "Command that these stones be made bread"—the temptation to sense pleasure, the body appetite for food at the same time a symbol of that other dominant body appetite, sex.   Then the devil took Him up into the holy city and set Him on the highest pinnacle of the temple and told Him to cast Himself down, the angels would bear Him up, and the people seeing Him supported by the angels would fall down in worship of Him.   This was the temptation to power.   Finally, the devil took Him up on a high mountain and showed Him all the kingdoms of the world.   "All these will I give thee, if falling down thou wilt adore me." [2]   This was the temptation to amass possessions. Here, then are the three desires, the three drives, the failure to control which, in the Christian philosophy of life, causes the failure of life.   St. John labels them "concupiscences," from the

[1] Edmund Davidson Soper, *The Religions of Mankind*, Abingdon Press, 1921, p. 185.
[2] Matthew, IV, 1–11.

Latin word for desire. "For all that is in the world, is the concupiscence of the flesh, and the concupiscence of the eyes, and
the pride of life." [1] (See Figure 8, Section A, below.)

In the organized asceticism of the Church the controls which
are set up for these three drives are the three vows, poverty
(possessions), chastity (pleasure), and obedience (power). Life
under the vows means the life-long effort to establish and maintain strict control over these impulses in order that life itself

FIGURE 8.—THE DOMINANT HUMAN DRIVES

A. *The Drives in Scripture*

THE THREE DOMINANT DRIVES:	THE TEMPTA-TIONS OF HUMANITY:	THE THREEFOLD CONCUPISCENCE OF ST. JOHN:	ST. PAUL: "WE SHOULD LIVE	JEREMIAS' AND DANTE'S THREE BEASTS:
I Possessions	"All these will I give thee."	"of the eyes" (the world)	justly	The Wolf of Avarice
II Pleasure	"Command that these stones be made bread"	"of the flesh" (the flesh)	soberly	The Leopard of Luxury
III Power	"Cast thyself down."	"the pride of life" (the devil)	and godly in this world."	The Lion of Ambition

B. *Life in Religion and the Drives*

CONTROLS, THE THREE VOWS:	REPRESSION: DETACHMENT FROM	EXPRESSION: THROUGH	ONE OF THE WORLD RELI-GIONS, BUDDHA:	THE FOUR CARDINAL VIRTUES:
I Poverty	Things	Work	Gold	Justice (prudence)
II Chastity	Persons	Communal life	Pleasure	Temperance (prudence)
III Obedience	Self	Prayer	Fame	Fortitude (prudence)

[1] 1 John II, 16.

FIGURE 8.—(*Continued*)

C. *Life in the World and the Drives*

TANSLEY'S THREE GREAT COMPLEXES:	CONTROLS, THE TEN COMMANDMENTS:	UNCONTROLLED, THE CAPITAL VICES:	CONTROLLED, THE CAPITAL VIRTUES:	OUTLETS IN THE WORLD:
I Ego	III, VII, X	1. Covetousness 2. Sloth	1. Liberality 2. Industry	Vocational calling
II Sex	IV, VI, IX	3. Lust 4. Gluttony	3. Purity 4. Temperance	Family life
III Herd	I, II, V, VIII	5. Pride 6. Envy 7. Anger	5. Humility 6. Brotherly love 7. Meekness	Hierarchy of life ideals

D. *The Drives in Other Authors*

PSYCHOLOGICAL THEORISTS:	ST. THOMAS, THE END OF MAN NOT	ARISTOTLE'S THREE LIVES:	MILTON'S PARADISE REGAINED:	SHAKESPEARE'S LIFE TRAGEDIES:
I Economic determinists	Wealth	The life of moneymaking (wealth)	Riches (Book II)	Merchant of Venice (Shylock)
II Freud (sex)	Pleasures of the body	The life of enjoyment (pleasure)	Food (Book I)	Anthony and Cleopatra
III Adler (power)	Honor, glory, power	The life of action (honor)	Glory (Book III)	Henry VIII (Woolsey) Macbeth

may be devoted to serving God in a life of prayer and of service to fellowman, depending on whichever of the spiritual or corporal works of mercy the person vowed to religion is engaged in.   The controls for people living in the world are, of course, the commandments, and no more wholesome activity can be offered to students of psychology (as well as of religion) for deepening their understanding of the fundamental problem in life—the control of the animal part of our nature by the spiritual—than the allocation of the commandments to the particular drives over which their keeping means control. The same should be done with the seven capital sins and the seven capital virtues thus setting up definite goals for the conduct of life. (See Figure 8, Section C, p. 103.)

It may seem strange to some that concepts so definitely religious in origin are presented here as part of the psychological foundations of education. There are two things to be said in reply to this objection. In the first place, our approach to the problem of education is that of the Christian philosopher. Hence we cannot ignore what is now, and has been for centuries, the classification of the human urges most helpful in setting up controls for the conduct of life. In the second place, the work of the psychologists who have devoted themselves to this field suggests this classification. Thus among the psychoanalysts, Freud would explain all human striving in terms of the sex urge (sense pleasure), although of course he gives a wider extension to that term than is ordinarily done. Adler would explain all human activity in terms of the urge to power. And while we cannot say that Jung explains it in terms of the urge to amass possessions, nevertheless, it is true that possessions, worldly wealth and man's effort to amass the same, do play a real part in his concept of the "libido" as the general life urge from which springs all activity, since possessions are the ordinary means to the satisfaction of both the urge to pleasure and the urge to power. It is another group of theorists, however, who have brought into prominence the part that the urge to amass possessions plays in human living, namely, those who in their theorizing advance what is called the "economic determination of history." In this theory as in the theory of

Freud and Adler, all human striving is explained in terms of one dominating drive but in this case the motivation is economic. (See Figure 8, Section D, p. 103.)

Following the tradition of Christianity, however, we believe it more satisfactory to see man's life driven by these three dominating drives. As life becomes more and more complex with the increasing complexity of civilization, opportunity for the satisfaction of the urges are more numerous, but hindrances and preventions of these satisfactions are also more numerous. The drive on the one hand, and failure to find an outlet for the drive, create the situation called conflict. Following conflict, many various types of adjustment arise, some of which are rational, others irrational. The educator, if he is to be of help to the student in working out a plan for the management of his life, must understand these situations which are characterized by conflict and adjustment. We now turn to their consideration.

3. CONFLICT AND ADJUSTMENT

The impulses, then, are the real psychological elements in human drives. As inherited tendencies to exercise abilities they group themselves around those centers of interests which have the greatest attraction for man. We have adopted the traditional Christian classification of these "centers of interest" under these names, the drives towards possessions, pleasure, and power. Every impulse in the makeup of man tends to express itself as some form of activity which makes it possible for the individual to dominate over his environment (power); or will bring the experience of sense pleasure for the most part in terms of the two body appetites, food and sex; or to amass worldly wealth, not perhaps for its own sake like the miser, but because wealth is the ordinary means for the satisfaction of the other two drives, pleasure and power. When satisfaction of these drives is not possible there arises the experience called desire. Desire means an unsatisfied impulse, and as this becomes intensified, there is experienced a craving to seek or to produce a situation in which the impulse may be satisfied. Our desires, however, are so many that early in the life of the child a situation arises in which some of them cannot be gratified, *e.g.*, the infant crying for the moon. Here we are in the presence of conflict. Conflicts arise when either nature or man hinders the satisfaction of desire. This is a lesson the child must learn early in life. He cannot satisfy all his desires.

If he can secure anything he wishes by crying, he soon becomes a tyrant over those who should be regulating his behavior. This is anything but adequate preparation for life in society where many desires cannot be satisfied. But conflict in the child arises from within also. The child who is restrained from certain impulsive actions by the admonition "Mother does not want you to do that," has already begun building a life ideal. The great conflicts in life arise precisely here, *i.e.*, in the struggle between satisfying desires on the one hand and living up to a life ideal on the other. Dark and devious are the ways in which all normal people work out adjustments in their attempts to resolve these conflicts without sacrificing either alternative.

We follow Moore in this analysis of the various types of mental adjustments which people make in presence of life's problems.[1] The positive tendency to enjoy pleasant situations he calls "the persistent drive." It is the negative tendency to avoid the unpleasant which produces the great variety in human behavior. Here we distinguish two types of adjustment. The first offers no solution to the problem. It is

[1] *Op. cit.*, Part IV, "The Driving Sources of Human Nature and Their Adjustment," pp. 137–249.

characterized by depression and anxiety, the natural tendency
to be depressed and to worry and fret over unpleasant situations.   The second class of adjustments offer some kind of
solution, however inadequate:

There are three possibilities here.   The unhappy eventuality
may in some manner be avoided.   Tendencies which merely aim
at avoiding unpleasant situations have been aptly termed *defense*
reactions.   Here we have a large group of reactions.   One may
put the unpleasant situation out of mind if it is a mental affair.
One *may shut out* the world from contact with his mind, if surroundings are harsh and unpleasant, and become surly, cynical,
sour, silent, secretive, negativistic.   One may *become incapacitated*
by general weakness or special disability, if his duties become very
unpleasant, and there is any way of throwing the burden of self-
support or family sustenance on relatives, friends, or the associated charities.   One may *avoid* the *realization* of *personal blame*
by an exalted sense of his own righteousness, and transfer it to
others by suspicions and accusations.   One may *keep others from
realizing* his own real desires by a solemn face, or a violent, old-
maid shock-reaction at the recountal of the sins of others.   All
these examples are instances of native human tendencies which
appear spontaneously in anyone, given the proper circumstances,
but not all appear with equal facility in all types of individuals.
Besides getting out of an unpleasant situation, one may seek
to make up for its unpleasantness by some new form of enjoyment.   If this is attempted along more or less the same level of
satisfaction as the lost pleasure which creates the unpleasant situation, then the reaction is termed *compensation*.   Thus, one may
imagine the fulfillment of unsatisfied desire.   One may compensate for an unhappy life by becoming a wit.   One may go to a
vaudeville show to drown his discontent.   One may *transfer his
affections* from one person to another.   One may *appeal for sympathy*—sometimes by making himself appear sicker than he is—
by convulsive seizures, etc.   Some throw themselves against their
enemy hoping for unjust severity that others may see how badly
they are treated.
If, however, satisfaction is sought in pleasures of a higher na-

ture, we speak of the reaction as *sublimation*. Thus, a woman disappointed in love may become a social worker, or give of her millions to build an orphan asylum, or become devoted to music, art, literature, etc. Music offers to certain natures channels of outlet when the ordinary interests and affections of life are denied them. So, also, literature, art, and science. Religion is the natural *sublimation* of human desires, always possible and always effective, no matter how great the calamities that confront us." [1]

The types of adjustments just described in the terminology of the psychoanalytic school have been called "unconscious." The terminology seems unfortunate since the person who compensates for an unhappy life by becoming a wit is not unconscious in his witticisms. But there is one element in the complex of which he is unconscious, namely, the causal connection between the impulses denied expression and the behavior which furnishes compensation. In this sense these adjustments are unconscious, or perhaps better, irrational, *i.e.*, not subject to reason.

The rational way to adjust oneself to an unpleasant situation is to face the facts, hiding nothing from oneself, admitting that not all desires can be satisfied. Those desires which can properly be satisfied should be selected and an orderly plan for a normal, healthy life laid out. The plan should then be carried out through determined and persevering effort. Sublimation in religion should be such a plan.

Without doubt, the evils of repression of natural desires have been grossly exaggerated. Repression of native tendencies must characterize all life in society today. There is no road to peace and contentment which is not characterized by self-discipline. Nevertheless, a proper understanding of the organized asceticism of the Church under the three vows sees clearly that this life is not mere repression. On the contrary, life in religion makes definite provision for the expression of

[1] *Op. cit.*, pp. 185–186.

these fundamental human drives. Through the vow of chastity (detachment from persons) the religious gives up the pleasures of family life in the world but he substitutes therefor *communal life* in the monastery. The life of the anchorite did too much violence to human nature to endure as a permanent institution in the Church. Through the vow of poverty (detachment from things) the religious gives up amassing worldly wealth for himself—but through his *work* he plays his part in advancing the economic interests of the community. Through the vow of obedience (detachment from self) he gives up the ambitions and opportunities which the world holds out to all individuals in varying degrees for their own advancement, but there is one field in which he need put no limit to his vaulting ambition, namely, the spiritual life through *prayer*. When there is added to such an interpretation of the religious life a strong supernatural motive, no one can deny that it offers peace and contentment to normal men and women voluntarily choosing to live it. (See Figure 8, Section B, p. 102.)

The Christian teacher should seize every opportunity to bring home to students that the same principles govern life in the world. Repression of the impulses in terms of self-discipline is absolutely necessary for any well-ordered life aiming at any worth-while goal. Suppression is impossible if life is to go on. This was the answer of Buddha with his Nirvana, but it is not the Christian answer. Young people should be led to understand that the two body appetites as part of our nature are good in themselves. Food and drink are necessary for the preservation of the individual, sex for the preservation of the race. Evil enters only when they get out of control. In the first the outcome is the sin of gluttony; in the second, the sin of lust. Control must be established and the controls are the virtues, temperance instead of gluttony, purity instead of lust. For the ordinary individual the situation most conducive to establishing these controls is the expression of these impulses in family life. For the drive for sense pleasure, we have the full meaning of the phrase, "bed and board." Similarly with the other two dominant drives. Any worthy ambition, with the exercise of authority over the children as an auxiliary, is the outlet for the drive toward domination. A person's vocation (the wife as home-builder as well as husband as home-provider) is the avenue along which this drive to amass possessions should find its expression. In every instance control of the impulses means taking the middle ground as illustrated in this last example, not becoming a miser on the one hand or an improvident spender on the other.

In all the above we have been speaking of the impulse as the true psychological unit operative in the drives leading to behavior. For the most part the impulses are inherited, not acquired, though Woodworth stresses the fact that every acquired mode of behavior, every habit, carries its own drive. He who has learned to swim has the impulse to swim, given the occasion where swimming promises satisfaction. Whether or not this is true in every case, the outstanding fact about adult human behavior is that it is acquired, *i.e.*, learned. Man has no instincts in the sense that the animals have, but he has a much greater power of learning. In fact, this ability to learn is what marks him off from the rest of the animal kingdom. How does learning take place on the animal level and on the level that is distinctly human? This is our inquiry in the chapter that follows.

SUGGESTED READINGS

Warren, Howard C., *Dictionary of Psychology*, Houghton Mifflin, 1934, definitions of behavior, impulse and instinct, etc.

I. HEREDITY AND BEHAVIOR

Bernard, L. L., *Instinct: A Study in Social Psychology*, Holt, 1924, the scientific approach to instincts as social factors.

Caldwell, V. W., C. E. Skinner, and J. W. Tilty, *Biological Foundations of Education*, Ginn, 1931.

James, William, *Principles of Psychology*, Holt, 1890, the older point of view on instincts Vol. II.   Chapter XXIV "Instinct," pp. 383–441.

Jennings, H. S., *The Biological Basis of Human Nature*, Norton, 1930, the best presentation of heredity and environment as complementary factors in the determination of traits, particularly pp. 133–134.

McDougall, William, *Social Psychology*, J. W. Luce, 1921, 15th ed. 1933, the most extensive use of instincts in explaining man's social life.

Moore, Thomas Vernon, *Dynamic Psychology*, Lippincott, 1931, distinction between instinct and impulse and the two uses of the word "instinct," its popular and scientific use, pp. 137–148.

Warren, Howard C., *Human Psychology*, Houghton Mifflin, 1919, Chap. VI "Behavior" for human reflexes, human instincts and "instinctive tendencies," pp. 92–111.

Woodworth, Robert S., *Psychology*, Henry Holt (fourth rev. ed.), 1939, Chap. VII, "Heredity and Environment."

2.   THE DOMINANT HUMAN DRIVES

Most of the references that follow give the sources for the classifications in Figure 8, pp. 102–3.

Aquinas, St. Thomas, *Contra Gentiles*, Book Three, Chaps. XXV–XXXVI, rejects the ends listed in Figure 8, concluding with Chap. XXXVII, "That the Final Happiness of Man Consists in the Contemplation of God," tr. by English Dominican Fathers, Vol. III, Part 1.

Aristotle, *Ethics I*, the "three lives" rejected as leading to the highest good in favor of the "Life of Contemplation"; the English translation used here is that of H. Rockham in the Loeb Classical Library, pp. 11–17.

Bible, Old Testament, the Commandments, Exodus XX.   1–17, Deuteronomy V, 6–21; Jeremias, "the three beasts" V, 6.   New Testament, the Temptations, Matthew IV, 1–11; Mark I, 12–13, Luke, 1–13; the threefold concupiscence, 1 St. John II, 16; St. Paul, "The grace of God instructing us that we should live, etc., Titus II, 11–12; Apocalypse, the "three unclean spirits," XVI, 13.

Boethius, *The Consolations of Philosophy*, Book III, Section II, discusses the "divers desires" of man as (1) riches, (2) pleasure and (3) honour, power, and glory.

Buddha: Edmund Davidson Soper, *The Religions of Mankind*, Abingdon Press, 1921, the three desires, p. 185; also, article in *Encyclopedia Americana*.

Cram, Ralph Adams, *Gold, Frankincense and Myrrh*, Marshall Jones, 1919, the positive aspect of monasticism, pp. 6–7.

Cunningham, W. F., "The New Psychology and Ancient Asceticism," *Homiletic Monthly*, May and June, 1935.

Dante, *Inferno*, Canto I, "the three beasts."

Dawson, Christopher, *Enquiries into Religion and Culture*, Sheed & Ward, 1933, III, "The Nature and Destiny of Man" discusses the dominant role of the three "instincts" in Naturalism, pp. 320–323.

Gates, Arthur I., *Elementary Psychology*, Macmillan, 1929, Chap. VIII is entitled "The Dominant Human Urges" and IX "Motivation and Adjustment."

Milton, John, *Paradise Regained*, the temptations, Books I to IV.

Pythagoras (Jamblicus, *Vit. Pytha.* 58.), reference in Aristotle's *Ethics*, "The Loeb Classical Library," comparing the three kinds of men to the three classes of strangers who went to the Games, "competitors, spectators and traders," note p. 14.

Shakespeare's life tragedies, as listed and the famous speech of Cardinal Wolsey "Cromwell, I charge thee fling away ambition" in *Henry VIII*, Act III, Scene 2; *Antony and Cleopatra*, the lust of the flesh, Act III, Scene 6.

Spinoza, *Ethics*, the three desires, "Introduction, the Improvement of the Understanding"; also article in *Americana*.

Tanquery, Adolphe, *The Spiritual Life*, Descleé & Co., Tournai (Belgium) 1932, is an excellent introduction to ascetical theology; the "capital vices" pp. 392–426; the "moral virtues" pp. 472–548.

Tansley, A. G., *The New Psychology*, Dodd Mead, 1922, "the great complexes," Part VI entire.

· 3. CONFLICT AND ADJUSTMENT

Adler, Mortimer, *What Man Has Made of Man*, Longmans Green, 1937, notes on lectures delivered before the Institute of Psychoanalysis, with notes on the notes, very difficult reading; names psychoanalysis as one of the two "exceptions to the inductive sterility of psychological research" pp. 90–91; states that "William McDougall declared Freud to have done more for psychology than anyone since Aristotle." p. 202.

Allers, Rudolph, *The New Psychologies*, Sheed & Ward, 1933, Chap. III is entitled "The New Psychologies and the Old Faith."

Chapman, J. Crosby and George S. Counts, *Principles of Education*, Houghton Mifflin, 1924, discusses conflict and the "complexes," pp. 143–153.

Dollard, John and others, *Frustration and Aggression*, Yale Univ. Press, 1939, takes as its basic postulate, "aggression is always a consequence of frustration." p. 1.

Maturin, B. W., *Selfknowledge and Selfdiscipline*, Longmans, Green, 1915, should be read by all students confronted with personal problems demanding adjustment.

Morgan, John, *The Psychology of the Unadjusted School Child*, Macmillan, 1926, Chapter XII, "Distorting Reality—Rationalization."

Moore, Thomas Verner, *Dynamic Psychology*, Lippincott, 1924, Part IV is entitled "The Driving Forces of Human Nature," pp. 137–249, critiques of Freud, Jung and Adler.

Shaffer, Laurence Frederic, *The Psychology of Adjustment*, Houghton Mifflin, 1936, the approach of the "objective psychologist"; Chap. IX "Adjustment by Ailments" treats psychoneuroses, hysteria, stammering, etc., pp. 227–249; Chap. X "Persistent Nonadjustive Reactions" treats anxiety, worry, so-called "nervous" conditions and "nervous breakdown," pp. 269–277.

Woodworth, Robert S., *Psychology*, Henry Holt (fourth rev. ed.), 1939, Chap. XVIII, "Personal Applications" the main problem of life, adjustment, and mastery; the three drives as "security, pleasure, and achievement."

A NEW THEORY OF LEARNING

At the present time . . . Americans find themselves in a serious dilemma. They have come to realize that they are living in the most dynamic civilization of history and that the world about them is undergoing constant transformation. Obviously the doctrine of specific training, the doctrine of psychological mechanism, the doctrine that all learning is essentially the formation within the nervous system of bonds between particular situations and particular responses, the doctrine which was welcomed half a generation ago as the sure road to educational salvation, makes no provision for adjustment to a changing civilization. As a consequence, educators find themselves constrained to prepare the coming generation for the rapidly shifting scenes of industrialism with a psychology which implies that this is impossible. They are therefore turning to the reëxamination of theories once discarded and the formulation of a new theory of learning.

George S. Counts, *The American Road to Culture*, John Day Co., 1930, p. 168.

CHAPTER V

THEORIES OF LEARNING

In the two preceding chapters we have been dealing with topics which play a major part in the course commonly called "General Psychology." We now turn to the topic which is the central theme of "Educational Psychology," namely, learning. How does learning take place? What is the nature of the learning process? These are the questions which confront us in this chapter. Their difficulty is equalled only by their importance. If teachers are to help pupils learn rapidly and effectively without loss of time and effort, they must have some knowledge of how learning takes place so that they may plan teaching procedures in terms of the learning process and be a help, not a hindrance, to pupils to whom they minister.

The human organism is the most complicated organism life offers us for study. It is small wonder then, that when we consider even a part of its activities, the learning activities, we find many conflicting theories. Woodworth makes this statement:

The present situation regarding the learning process is certainly interesting. We have what is really a three-cornered debate going on. We have a variety of facts, all of which need to be accounted for by an adequate theory; and we have a choice of theories, none of which has attempted to take care of all of the facts. We have the fact of trial-and-error learning, with the law of effect put forward in interpretation. We have the fact of the conditioned reflex, with the theory of conditioning as interpretation. And we have the fact of learning by insight, with the theory of tensions bridging the gap as interpretation.[1]

The experimental work on which these theories of learning have been based, was done on animals. The student of education with some philosophical background may react unfavorably to this. "Why," he may ask, "since our interest is in human learning, have not the theories advanced to explain human learning been based on studies of human beings in their attempts at learning?" Many studies, of course, have been based on the learning activities of human subjects, but there are two particular reasons why most of the experimental work in this field has been confined to the study of animals. The first reason is that, dealing with animals, it is possible to set up *controlled conditions*, a necessary feature of any experiment that merits the name "scientific." Ordinarily we do not let children become hungry and then place them in a cage with a trick door to discover how they learn to open the door to get food placed outside the cage. In the second place, and this is more significant, we have every reason to believe that learning in animals is a *much simpler process* than it is in children. If we could get some real insight into how animals learn we would have a start towards understanding at least some phases of human learning. After all, man is an animal. The fact which we are continually stressing in this presentation that he is a *rational* animal, does not deny that much of his activity is on the sensuous level, similar to that of animals not endowed with reason. If, through the study of animals, we can deepen our understanding of the sense life of man, this may serve as a key

[1] Robert S. Woodworth, *Contemporary Schools of Psychology*, Ronald Press, 1931, pp. 123–124.

for deepening our understanding of learning that is truly human, that is, ideational learning. Certainly we would deepen our understanding of human nature if we understood better those activities which man carries on in common with animals of the lower orders, one of the most significant of which activities is learning.

In the quotation from Woodworth above, the word "law" is used in reference to learning. The student should understand clearly the meaning of the word when used in this connection. Science is systematized or organized knowledge. Factual knowledge is the first objective of science, but it is not content to stop there. Factual description aims to pass on to explanation. In the process of working out explanations of observed phenomena the first step is hypothesis, which often is little more than a guess attempting to explain the phenomena. If the explanation seems to serve, it becomes a theory; and a theory receiving acceptance by a group of scientists working in a field, becomes a law. In this use of the word, there is no implication of obligation, which is the meaning of the word in the field of ethics, the science of human conduct, *e.g.*, the moral law. Rather, a law in science is simply a statement of uniformity. In the dictionary definition, as used in science, law means "a statement of invariable order or relation of phenomena under given conditions." [1] It is in this sense that the word is used in the phrase "laws of learning." Such "laws" are set forth merely as descriptive statements of how learning takes place. Pure science is concerned with description and explanation, but applied science strives to pass on to prediction and control. Little as we know about the ultimate nature of electricity as one of the forces of nature, what knowledge we have of its operations is stated in laws and on the basis of these laws we can predict what will happen

[1] Webster, *Secondary School Dictionary.*

under such and such circumstances. This power of prediction leads to control. We produce a current and send it along a wire, all regulated by law. Then according to our needs we can flood a room with light merely by pressing a button.

Such is the outcome of our power of prediction and control in the physical sciences, which are called the "exact sciences." No such precision is attainable in those sciences dealing with man—biology, psychology, and the social sciences. As Thompson says in his *Outline of Science*, even the biologist doesn't know which way the cat will jump. Little wonder the problem is more complicated in the case of children, and particularly when we study the adult human being. Education is striving to become one of the applied social sciences. Like all applied sciences, its aim is prediction and control, only in this case the objective is the control of the forces of human nature, not the control of the forces of physical nature. We realize, of course, how much more difficult this problem is. In human behavior the element of freedom, characteristic of any humanistic or supernaturalistic philosophy, puts complete control of human behavior beyond the realm of possibility. Nevertheless, we know that human behavior is subject to control far in excess of what the ordinary man on the street realizes. In James' phrase, we are all "walking bundles of habits." Every habit is set off by a stimulus. Hence if we can determine the stimulus we can secure the desired response. Everyone is doing this every day in his efforts to control the behavior of others. The child who says "please" is setting the stimulus for the parent that he may secure the desired candy. So, too, is the industrial manager who offers a bonus to workmen for certain unusual services. The trouble with this type of control is that it is not based on organized knowledge. That is, it is not scientific.

Psychology, as the science of human nature, seeks to ac-

cumulate accurate information about man and his behavior
Education, as an applied social science, seeks to systematize
this knowledge so that it may proceed to formulate hypotheses,
theories, and finally, "laws," regulating human behavior. One
type of human behavior is of particular interest to the teacher,
namely, learning. Hence our desire to formulate statements
descriptive of how learning takes place so that, as teachers,
we may help it take place more effectively than it would without our ministrations. When universal applicability in a
certain area of learning is ascribed to these descriptive statements, they are called "laws." With new knowledge coming in
as study and research on the learning process continues, these
so-called "laws" will be modified and restated from time to
time. They are always tentative, subject to refinement, and
will undergo changes as knowledge of the learning process
progresses. But this is true of the laws of the exact sciences.
Exactness is a relative term; and although it will never be
achieved in our knowledge of human nature to the same degree
it has already been achieved in our knowledge of physical
nature, it will always be the scientific ideal.

With this introductory statement on the significance of the
term "law," we now take up for consideration the so-called
"laws of learning." Since in our philosophy there is a radical
difference between the mental life of animals and of man, we
will treat this topic under the two headings, "Laws of Animal
Learning" and "Principles of Human Learning."

1. LAWS OF ANIMAL LEARNING

The laws of learning, as commonly presented in educational
psychologies today, have been worked out on the basis of
elaborate experiments with animals in psychological laboratories under controlled conditions. They are applications of

the neural theory explained in Chapter III, "The Nature of Man." Insofar as stimulus, adaptation, and response is a statement of the life cycle, a formula summarizing the process through which life goes on, it must be significant for learning, which is one phase of the living process. The heart of the neural theory is "the anatomical independence of nerve cells and their physiological interconnection at junction points or 'synapses'." [1] Out of this concept of the physiological, i.e., functional interconnection of neurons at junction points called "synapses," has come the "bond" theory of Thorndike. Here is his statement of one of the experiments on which it is based:

We take a box twenty by fifteen by twelve inches, replace its cover and front side by bars an inch apart, and make in this front side a door arranged so as to fall open when a wooden button inside is turned from a vertical to a horizontal position. . . . A kitten three to six months old, if put into this box when hungry, a bit of fish being left outside, reacts as follows: it tries to squeeze through between the bars, and bites and claws at its confining walls. Some one of all these promiscuous clawings, squeezings, and bitings turns round the wooden button, and the kitten gains freedom and food. By repeating the experience again and again, the animal comes gradually to omit all the useless clawings and squirming, jumping actions, and to manifest only the particular impulse (e.g., to claw hard at the top of the button with the paw, or to push against one side of it with the nose) which has resulted successfully. It turns the button around without delay whenever it is put in the box. It has formed an association between the situation, *confinement in a box of a certain appearance*, and the response of *clawing at a certain part of that box in a certain definite way*. Popularly speaking, it has learned to open a door by turning a button. [2]

[1] Gardner Murphy, *Historical Introduction to Modern Psychology*, Harcourt Brace, 1929, p. 204.
[2] E. L. Thorndike, *Educational Psychology*, Bureau of Publications, Teachers College, Columbia Univ., 1931, Vol. II, p. 9.

(A) THE LAW OF EXERCISE

This description of animal learning calls attention to the fact which everyone knows, that repetition is a factor in learning. But what is the explanation? What happens within the organism that brings it about that the act of opening the door of the cage, at first beyond the ability of the kitten, later through learning is performed with facility and without delay? The Law of Exercise is an attempt to answer this question. As stated by Gates, a disciple of Thorndike, this law says:

Whenever a modifiable connection between a situation and a response is exercised, other things being equal, the strength of that connection is increased.[1]

The connection, the strength of which has been increased, becomes a "bond" between the stimulus and the response, hence the formula, S-R bonds. According to the description we have given in Chapter III of the functional operations of the neural mechanism, an A should be placed between the S and the R, giving us the formula S-A-R, in which A stands for adaptation, either automatic (*e.g.*, the simple reflexes), handled by the neural mechanism alone, or conscious adaptation, when the mind (*i.e.*, deliberation, feeling, and choice) enters into the determining of the response.

(B) THE LAW OF EFFECT

But repetition alone does not explain all learning. Gates reports a famous experiment performed by G. W. and E. G. Peckham which illustrates this well:

These observers found that a spider dropped hurriedly from its web at the sound of a tuning fork. When it had climbed back, a repetition of the stimulus produced the same dropping reaction;

[1] Arthur I. Gates, *Psychology for Students of Education*, Macmillan, 1924, p. 208.

but after eight or nine trials the stimulus suddenly lost its power; the spider failed to react by dropping from the web. Next day, however, the stimulus was effective for a time but failed after six or seven repetitions, and after about ten days the dropping reaction ceased entirely—at least for a time.[1]

If repetition were the whole of learning the spider should have learned to drop with greater facility the more often the experience was repeated. Just the contrary happened. It learned *not to drop at all* in the presense of the stimulus. The interpretation given to this fact is the *attitude* of the learner. Dropping was annoying to the spider, whereas remaining in his web was satisfying. Here is a definite limitation on the Law of Exercise. Gates states this interpretation as the Law of Effect in these terms:

> The individual tends to repeat and learn quickly those reactions which are accompanied or followed by a satisfying state of affairs. The individual tends not to repeat or learn quickly those reactions which are accompanied or followed by an annoying state of affairs.[2]

Every teacher applies this law every day in the classroom when he praises or blames his pupils for desirable or undesirable responses.

(c) THE LAW OF READINESS

But if the Law of Effect were to take precedence over the Law of Exercise and be the final arbiter in determining the learning activities to be carried on in school, we can readily see how "soft pedagogy" would be the result. Satisfaction after activity is certainly a factor in learning, but the real task is to initiate those activities, the carrying on of which will result in learnings demanded by pupils' present needs and those

[1] *Ibid.*, pp. 224–225.
[2] *Ibid.*, p. 230.

which will inevitably arise in later life. Here our attack must
be on the impulses. In Chapter IV, "The Motivation of
Behavior," we have followed Moore and defined an impulse as
a tendency to exercise an ability. We have as many impulses
as we have abilities. These impulses go into operation whenever there is a felt need which the exercise of the ability gives
promise of satisfying. If there is no felt need, there is no
tendency to action. The cat in the cage in the experiment
described above was hungry, and the fish outside was an effective stimulus under that circumstance to initiate activity.
But if the cat had just been satiated with fish before being
placed in the cage, the fact that there was more fish outside
would not arouse any activity. The cat probably would have
been quite content to roll up in the corner and sleep, digesting
the fish it had just eaten. Activity may be the key to learning,
but there must be a certain readiness upon the part of the
learner if activity is to be initiated. Fatigue is a common
hindrance to learning. When we are learning to play tennis,
the exercise at first is enjoyable (gives satisfaction), but if,
under compulsion, it is carried on beyond the point of fatigue,
instead of continued improvement in the execution of a stroke
(learning), bungling will be the outcome. This limitation on
the Laws of Exercise and Effect is called the Law of Readiness.
Reeder quoting Thorndike gives the following statement in
neurological terms in which the "conduction unit" is the
combination of sensory and motor neurons united by a bond.

> When a conduction unit is ready to conduct, conduction by it is
> satisfying. For a conduction unit ready to conduct not to con-
> duct is annoying. When a conduction unit unready for conduc-
> tion is forced to conduct, conduction by it is annoying. [1]

Possibly the neurological metaphysics of the technical jargon
in this statement may be made somewhat intelligible through

[1] Edwin H. Reeder, *Simplifying Teaching*, Laidlaw Bros., 1920, p. 30.

the analysis presented in the following figure adapted from Reeder:

FIGURE 9.—THE LAWS OF LEARNING [1]

STATE OF NEURONS	ACTIVITY	RESULTS
Law of Readiness	Law of Exercise	Law of Effect
Readiness to act	Acting	Satisfaction
Readiness to act	Not acting	Annoyance
Unreadiness to act	Acting	Annoyance
Unreadiness to act	Not acting	Satisfaction

This analysis suggests a time sequence in which the laws of learning operate. Readiness is a condition which should be present *before* activity is initiated if learning is to take place effectively; satisfaction is a condition following *after* or concomitant with the exercise of the activity. The real value of the figure, however, lies in the fact that it emphasizes that all three laws are operative in any learning act. The laws do not operate successively, one beginning to function when another ceases. Rather, all are operative all the time, although at any point in the learning process one may be primary. We make this analysis so that the student may deepen his insight into the learning process. But learning is a unitary function and, though different phases may be distinguished, it should be thought of as a whole.

"CONDITIONING" AS A THEORY OF LEARNING

One series of experiments in the physiological laboratory that had great influence in modifying the interpretations of learning based on the neural theory, was that carried forward by Pavlov in Russia in the early part of this century. He was

[1] *Ibid.*, p. 30.

studying digestion in dogs. An apparatus was set up so that when meat was fed to a hungry dog, the secreted saliva was drained off through a tube and carefully measured. In the course of the experiment Pavlov noticed that saliva began to flow before the meat was placed in the dog's mouth. After some trials, not merely the sight of the meat but even the sound of the footsteps of the attendant bringing it, was sufficient to stimulate the saliva flow. This gave Pavlov an idea. Each time when food was brought to the dog he had a bell rung. After repeated trials the bell was rung without the bringing of food and the saliva began to flow just as it did when food was brought. What had happened was that a purely artificial stimulus, the ringing of a bell, had become a substitute for the natural stimulus, food in the mouth. Pavlov saw that the ability to acquire such signals must be an important factor in an animal's ability to adapt itself to its environment. Here he believed was a lead for the study of the higher brain centers and accordingly he turned the activities of his laboratory in that direction. He coined the phrase "conditioned reflex" to label the reflex in which the response had become attached to a new stimulus acting as a substitute for the natural stimulus. Pavlov as a physiologist had little sympathy with psychologists and thought of his own work as brain physiology. But Woodworth says that when he heard of Thorndike's experiments with animal learning, he deemed them pertinent to his own investigations.[1]

This concept of the "conditioned reflex" was adopted with enthusiasm by the materialist school of psychologists, the Behaviorists. The experimentation fitted in perfectly with their definition of what was scientific, since it was purely objective and "conditioning" for them became the universal explanation of all learning. The word was soon taken over by

[1] *Op. cit.*, p. 62.

the social scientists and has now passed into language as a part of every-day speech. Definition "number 8., Psychol." in Webster's *New International Dictionary* (2nd edition, 1937, p. 557) is stated in terms of Pavlov's famous experiment.

Conditioning as the substitution of a new artificial stimulus for the old natural one is certainly within the experience of everyone. If an individual who has been relying on appetite for the determination of his meal times, enters an institution where all are called to meals by the ringing of a bell, and if for any length of time he responds promptly to the bell stimulus, he will soon be conditioned as effectively as Pavlov's dog, even to the flow of saliva. Traditionally we have called behavior of this type, habit. Now that we have more accurate knowledge of the physiological functioning of the organism in such behavior, it is not evident what progress has been made by calling the process "conditioning" instead of "habituation."

THE GESTALT THEORY OF LEARNING

A different approach to the problem is made by the Gestalt school of psychologists. They are in protest against what they call the "constancy hypothesis" implied in Thorndike's statement of his findings, that is, a 1-to-1 relationship between a specific isolated stimulus (sensory impulse) and a specific motor reaction. The Gestaltists attack the problem from the point of view of perception. The "gestalt" or "configuration" (the word used to translate the German *gestalt*) must be perceived as a whole, if there is to be any insight into the problem. They criticize Thorndike's experiments on the ground that the animals could not perceive the nature of the problem (rats in a maze) or it was too difficult to be grasped as a whole (the cat in the cage). In Koffka's experiments with apes, a banana was hung out of reach in the cage with a box at hand which made it possible to reach the fruit when the box was placed beneath it. In another case a banana was placed outside the cage and a couple of sticks within the cage, both of which were too short to reach the banana. But when these sticks were fitted together, the banana could be reached. The most intelligent of the apes solved this problem. Now the significant feature of this learning is that once the problem was solved there was a sudden drop in the learning curve, not a gradual one with progressive elimination of useless movements by trial and error. Once the problem was solved it was learned, and repetition was not a significant factor. This sudden drop in the learning curve was explained as *insight* into the nature of the problem and its solution. Another experiment on animal learning in support of the Gestalt theory and against the "constancy hypothesis" is related by Woodworth.

Let an animal first be trained to find his food in that one of two boxes which is marked by a patch of a certain shade of gray. Suppose two boxes are always placed before him, A and B, of which A is marked with a light gray, and B with a medium gray. After the animal has learned to go always to B, box A is removed and box C, marked with a gray still darker than B, is substituted. Will the animal preserve his supposed fixed association, his positive response to B? As a matter of fact he goes now to C. He still goes to the darker of the two boxes. What he has learned, then, is not a response to a certain particular gray; he has learned to respond to the lighter-darker pattern by going to the darker side. Whether we can generalize from the behavior toward shades of gray, and conclude that the animal always responds to patterns or configurations, rather than to separate stimuli, is a question that has not been sufficiently studied. But on the basis of this experiment, it has been argued that all of the older theory of learning must be given up. In particular Thorndike's laws of learning are held to be now overthrown.[1]

[1] Robert S. Woodworth, *Contemporary Schools of Psychology*, Ronald Press, 1931, p. 121.

An American Gestaltist, M. Howell Lewis, reports experiments in absolute and relative choices among lights of varying intensities in confirmation of the configurational view.

> The 'laws' of Thorndike under consideration in this study grow out of a number of assumptions, among them, first, the assumption that a given isolated stimulus will always and inevitably produce the same response and secondly, the assumption that the 'laws' of learning deal with hypothetical units of behavior designated by the formula S-R. Behavior thus atomized logically leads us to look for elements in a given situation, and to regard these elements, if found or assumed, as the primary components which we must add together in order to produce and to explain learning.[1]

If the reader will refer to Thorndike's statement of the experiment with the cat in the cage (p. 120), he will see that Thorndike does not describe the cat as reacting to an isolated stimulus. Rather, he speaks of the "situation, confinement in a box of a certain appearance." So, too, in Gates' statement of the Law of Exercise (p. 121), the connection spoken of is between "a situation and a response." S in the S-R formula may more properly be said to stand for situation rather than stimulus, since even on the animal level it is to situations that reactions occur. Certainly except in the case of simple reflexes like the pupillary reflex of the eye, to think of any behavior response as following an isolated stimulus is an extreme oversimplification. All teachers know definitely how pupils react to the total situation in the classroom; not merely to the question asked but to the sound of the teacher's voice, his facial expression, the attitude of other pupils, the temperature of the room, the nature of the subject matter being taught, etc.

It was Lashley's experiment with excision of parts of the

[1] M. Howell Lewis, "Elemental Versus Configural Response in the Chick," *Journal of Experimental Psychology*, Feb. 1930, p. 61.

central nervous system of animals, however, that gave the *coup de grace* to any interpretation of learning based on isolated neural elements. He found that after the removal of parts of the central nervous system necessarily including the assumed "synaptic connections," animals were still able to perform the learned acts. From this he concluded, the nervous system works in terms of "mass action" instead of isolated elements.[1]

Bode, in his *Conflicting Psychologies of Education*, following a presentation of the theory of learning according to the Gestalt school makes this statement with reference to the laws:

> Thorndike's laws of learning—the law of use, the law of disuse (exercise), and the law of effect—are laws of habit-formation and nothing more. If we give a place to "insight" in the learning process, these laws become of subordinate importance. The core of the learning process is not habit, but intelligence.[2]

We fail to see how the statement that Thorndike's laws "are laws of habit-formation and nothing more" places much of a restriction upon them, unless the term "habit" is limited to motor habits only. Of more significance for man are mental habits. All knowledge is a habit. The child who *knows* his tables has learned a series of useful habits which, as occasion demands, will go into action in solving problems in ordinary living. On the rational level we speak of habits which are intellectual, emotional, and volitional. These habits have traditionally been spoken of as the virtues, the intellectual virtues and the moral virtues. Volitional habits in conflict with the moral law are vices. The virtues like all habits are developed through the repeated performance of separate acts. The last

[1] K. S. Lashley, "Nervous Mechanisms in Learning," Murchison, (editor), *Handbook of General Experimental Psychology*, Clark University Press, 1929, pp. 524–566.

[2] Boyd H. Bode, *Conflicting Psychologies of Learning*, Heath, 1929, p. 231.

eight pages of James' chapter "Habit" in his *Principles of Psychology* (1890) is said to be the finest lay sermon ever written. It emphasizes the importance of early establishment of both intellectual and moral habits in the life of the pupil. "Habit is the fly-wheel of society," "Make your nervous system your ally instead of your enemy," "Keep the faculty of effort alive in you by a little gratuitous exercise every day," "The man who has daily inured himself to habits of concentrated attention, energetic volition, and self-denial in unnecessary things . . . will stand like a tower when everything rocks around him and his softer fellow-mortals are winnowed like chaff in the blast"; these are the finest preachments of natural asceticism. The chapter concludes with this stirring peroration:

The hell to be endured hereafter, of which theology tells, is no worse than the hell we make for ourselves in this world by habitually fashioning our characters in the wrong way. Could the young but realize how soon they will become mere *walking bundles of habits*, they would give more heed to their conduct while in the plastic state. We are spinning our own fates, good or evil, and never to be undone. Every smallest stroke of virtue or of vice leaves its ever so little scar. The drunken Rip Van Winkle, in Jefferson's play, excuses himself for every fresh dereliction by saying, I won't count this time! Well! he may not count it, and a kind Heaven may not count it; but it is being counted none the less. Down among his nerve cells and fibres the molecules are counting it, registering and storing it up to be used against him when the next temptation comes. Nothing we ever do is, in strict scientific literalness, wiped out. Of course, this has its good side as well as its bad one. As we become permanent drunkards by so many separate drinks, so we become saints in the moral, and authorities and experts in the practical and scientific spheres, by so many acts and hours of work. Let no youth have any anxiety about the upshot of his education, whatever the line of it may be. If he keep faithfully busy each hour of the working day, he may safely leave the final result to itself. He can with perfect certainty count on waking up some fine morning, to find himself one of the competent ones of his generation, in whatever pursuit he may have singled out. Silently, between all the details of his business, the *power of judging* in all that class of matter will have built itself up within him as a possession that will never pass away.[1]

This is James, the philosopher, speaking, not James the scientist. The fact of habit is perhaps the most fundamental in the whole problem of learning. Nevertheless it is a question how far the great amount of experimental work based on the neutral theory has brought us in understanding how learning takes place. At one extreme we have the claim of Reeder in *Simplifying Teaching*, who after stating Thorndike's laws, says, "All learning may be explained psychologically by the operation of three laws." [2] At the other extreme we have this statement by Lashley in the paper referred to above, "Nervous Mechanisms in Learning":

> The conclusions from this review of the problem of learning must be largely negative. In spite of the vast experimental literature which has grown up since the studies of Ebbinghaus and the advancement which has been made in the study of nervous structure, it is doubtful that we know anything more about the mechanism of learning than did Descartes when he described the opening of the pores in the nerves by the passage of animal spirits. His statement sounds remarkably like the reduction of synaptic resistance by the passage of the nerve-impulse.[3]

A still severer indictment of the neurological approach to the problem of learning is made by Adler:

> The inductive sterility of experimental research in psychology is plain to anyone who has examined vast amounts of data and found no significant generalizations yielded by them. What are the "laws" of learning, of reaction time, of memory, of perception,

---

[1] William James, *Psychology*, Henry Holt, 1890, Vol. I, p. 127.
[2] *Op. cit.*, p. 30.
[3] *Op. cit.*, p. 561.

of attention, of association?   These are all fields in which the pile of raw data is tremendous.   At best the generalizations with which experimental reports conclude are matters of common sense knowledge, given an air of precision and elegance by a pseudo-technical language and a parade of metrical determinations.   I do not mean to say that we have not learned a great many details about the functioning of sense-organs, muscular fatigue, drug-effects, the role of the glands in emotional disturbances, and so forth.   But this is all physiology.[1]

But the approach through the technics of the exact sciences is not the only approach to the study of learning.   There has been a distillation of man's knowledge concerning this important problem through the centuries as man has observed human behavior and reflected upon his observations.   This is the philosophical approach.   It finds its formulations in "principles" rather than "laws" since these principles, though true and verifiable, do not claim the exactitude of the laws of the physical sciences.   These principles can be made meaningful to the student teacher.   They are verified by his own experience first as a student, and then as a teacher.   When through observation and reflective thinking he has effected these verifications, they should function as helpful guides in planning his own teaching procedures.   Before stating the more important of these principles it will be worth while to explain their source in contrast with scientific laws.

2. PRINCIPLES OF HUMAN LEARNING

The dictionary defines science as organized or systematized knowledge.   This is the widest use of the term and includes all fields of knowledge in which organization has been achieved, the natural, the social, and the philosophical sciences.   In its narrower significance science means knowledge derived through

[1] Mortimer J. Adler, *What Man Has Made of Man*, Longmans Green, 1937, p. 201.

experimental procedures. The characteristic feature of science in this meaning of the term is *measurement*. All the sciences so interpreted have become or are in the process of becoming mathematical. The great advances in the physical sciences in both their pure and applied aspects have been made possible through perfecting instruments of precision with the result that we speak of them as the "exact sciences." The success achieved by these sciences dealing with the operable things of the physical world is the envy of the humanistic sciences dealing with man, more commonly called the "social sciences." Psychology belongs to this group. Psychometrics has made great advance in mental measurements. Educational psychology as an applied social science endeavors to carry over from the field of pure psychology, and carry forward in their applications to the problems of education, those findings which have significance for the learning and teaching process. The I. Q. concept and its application to school procedures is the outstanding achievement in the psychometric field to date.

When we turn now to philosophy to determine how far its findings are applicable to the educative process, we see a sharp contrast with the natural sciences in regard to the kind of subject matter dealt with. All knowledge comes from experience. The scientist and the philosopher both attempt to use all the mental powers possessed by man in their search for meanings in experience. Both carry on observation and reflection, using the powers of sense and the powers of intellect. Analysis and synthesis, induction and deduction are characteristic of both. The outstanding difference is in the kind of experience they deal with. For the scientist it is a very special kind of experience with which he works. In a sense, it is artificial experience. It goes on under controlled conditions in the laboratory, the clinic, or the research field. He tries to eliminate all possible variables but one, and this one is the object of his investigations.   The philosopher, on the other hand, deals with general experience rather than with special. The object of his study is the experience common to all mankind.   It is not under controlled conditions in a laboratory, although in thought he will segregate part of it for special consideration.   This is the way all rational thinking goes on. But the laboratory for the philosopher is life itself.   Figure 10 contrasts the two kinds of experience with which science and philosophy deal.

FIGURE 10.—THE SCIENTIFIC AND PHILOSOPHICAL APPROACHES

APPROACHES	KINDS OF EXPERIENCES		OUTCOMES
Science	Special experience	under controlled conditions (laboratory, clinic, etc.)	Laws
Philosophy	General experience	common to all mankind	Principles

This distinction between science and philosophy on the basis of the kind of experience they deal with is indicated by the use of the word "data."   We never speak of the data of philosophy for the simple reason that the experience the philosopher reflects upon and from which he draws principles for the guidance of life, is the experience shared by everyone leading a normal life. It does not have to be sought out in the laboratory. But for the scientist the facts of ordinary everyday experience are insufficient.   He must supplement them by investigation. He creates an artificial situation not encountered in life and he applies mathematics to details which in life never stand by themselves.   Thus in anatomy through dissection he counts the number of cranial or spinal nerves.

Jaime Castiello, trained in the psychological laboratories of this country and Europe, calls attention to the "halo of infallibility" which in this country seems to invest anyone putting on a white apron in a psychological laboratory. If "experiment" as such is a contact with reality, so too is "experience." He reminds us

> that outside psychological laboratories, very great minds indeed, have thought out the fundamental problems of psychology applied to education and that such minds came to certain very definite conclusions; that the history of ideas is very old and that there is any amount of solid psychological wisdom embedded in the writings of all great thinkers. As Hegel so pithily puts it, living custom and tradition is, after all, nothing but crystallized reason and worth taking into consideration. . . . I propose to control modern psychological research with tradition and at the same time I want to control tradition with experiment.[1]

What are some of these "definite conclusions" which the history of ideas reveals as "solid psychological wisdom"? We will state three and at the same time indicate where in the history of thought they have received definite formulation.

(A) THE PRINCIPLE OF SELF-ACTIVITY

In attempting to formulate principles which apply with special significance to human learning, we begin with one which is universal in its application and is subscribed to by all educational psychologists, no matter of what school. We will call this "The Principle of Self-Activity," and it may be stated thus: *a student learns through his own activities*. Learning as a part of living, like living, is an eminently personal process. Each student must develop his own habits. These are the central factor in learning. A teacher can no more hand over his own habits ready-made to the pupil than he can hand over his own toothache. True enough, he can display those habits

[1] Jaime Castiello, S.J., "Real Psychology in Education," *Proceedings of the Catholic Educational Association*, 1936, pp. 213–215.

before the pupil (*e.g.*, logical reasoning, clear and forceful expression, or motor skills like handwriting, etc.) and in this way set a pattern for the pupil to imitate; but the imitative activities are the pupil's own, and it is these activities, not those of the teacher, which result in pupil learnings. Once a teacher has grasped this central fact in all learning, he is prepared to analyze the teaching function into its elements. He sees that what a teacher must do is (1) *provide and explain a pattern* for the pupil to imitate (instruction), (2) *arouse the pupil to activity* (motivation), and (3) *demand achievement* in that activity giving him guidance through helpful criticism and appropriate praise and censure (discipline). This is the teacher's task and this analysis holds, no matter which of the learning outcomes is aimed at in any teaching act, whether it be new knowledge, a new attitude, a new ability, or improvement in an old one. These three phases of teaching are much more in evidence in teaching the motor skills but they are present in all teaching. And activity on the part of the pupil is the aim of all three.

This principle as stated is so simple and so universal in application it would be strange, indeed, if elaborate experiments in psychological laboratories had to be performed and verified before it could be formulated. Nor has this been the case. Aristotle expresses the same idea in these words: "The intellect is perfected not by knowledge but by activity." [1] St. Thomas, in his tract on the teacher, phrases it in this way:

> Sicut ergo medicus dicitur causare sanitatem in infirmo natura operante, ita, etiam, homo dicitur causare scientiam in alio *operatione rationis naturalis illius;* et hoc est docere. (*De Veritate,* Quaestio XI., De Magistro, Articulus Primus.)

translated by Mary Ellen Mayer as follows:

> As, then, a doctor is said to cause health in a sick person through the operation of nature, so man is said to cause knowledge in an-

[1] Aristotle, *Ethics Nic.*, 1. 3.

other *through the operation of the learner's natural reason*—and this is to teach.[1]

Possibly the first formal statement in English of this principle is that by Hamilton, in the appendix to his *Lectures on Metaphysics*, dated 1836, over a hundred years ago.

> By the application of that primary principle of education, which wherever employed, has been employed with success I mean,— *the determination of the pupil to self-activity,*—doing nothing for him which he is able to do for himself. This principle which has always been inculcated by theorists on education, has however, by few been carried fully into effect.[2]

In his first lecture in the paragraph entitled "Application of the foregoing principles to the conduct of a class in philosophy," he says:

> Holding that the paramount end of liberal study is the development of the student's mind, and that knowledge is principally useful as a means of determining the faculties to that exercise, through which this development is accomplished,—it follows, that I must regard the main duty of a Professor to consist not simply in communicating information, but in doing this in such a manner, and with such an accompaniment of subsidiary means, that the information he conveys may be the occasion of awakening his pupils to a vigorous and varied exertion of their faculties. Self-activity is the indispensable condition of improvement; and education is only education,—that is, accomplishes its purpose, only by affording objects and supplying incitements to this spontaneous exertion. *Strictly speaking, every one must educate himself.*[3]

Newman frequently stresses this same idea that all education is self-education (*cf.* DeHovre-Jordan, *Catholicism in Education*, p. 328). We do not believe the restrictions which Hamilton

[1] Mary Ellen Mayer, *The Philosophy of Teaching of St. Thomas Aquinas*, Bruce, 1929, Part II, St. Thomas Aquinas' De Magistro, p. 53.
[2] *Op. cit.*, p. 638.
[3] *Ibid.*, p. 10.

placed on the teaching of his day are merited by teachers in any typical modern school. Certainly in the training of these teachers in courses in education no principle has been more forcibly and more continuously dinned into their ears than this: a pupil learns only insofar as he is active. The writer once heard a University president with a flair for striking statements, phrase it in these words: "a student learns through his own activities, *not by being sprayed with ideas.*" The last part of the statement was, no doubt, a stricture on the lecture system. This is justified when the method is used in dealing with children and early adolescent pupils since they do not have the ability to listen to a formal lecture with profit. But in the case of later adolescent pupils and particularly for college and university students whose minds are mature or approaching maturity, the lecture may be one of the most effective methods of teaching, if students listen with comprehension. Listening is being active, mentally active; and we must not think of the principle of self-activity as regulative of motor learning only.

The Boy Scout program may well adopt the slogan "We learn by doing," and the program is the series of activities planned by this free-time agency (corresponding to the curriculum of the school) for the leisure-time education of boys twelve years of age and older. But if the "doing" engaged in by Scouts consists for the most part in going out into somebody's woods and chopping down trees to build a bridge over which no one will ever have need to walk, it will hardly win the respect of the community. Nor need it. The program is without doubt the best ever planned for this age boy and the principle for its conduction "learning by doing" is absolutely sound. Peters says: "Scouting embodies perhaps the best pedagogical principles exemplified in any educational institution now existing. The basis of the work is chiefly "projects," units of achievement."[1] But the leadership must direct the activities if worthwhile learnings are to be the outcome, in the same way that teachers must plan and direct intelligently the activities within the school. "Busy work" may develop merely "busybodies."

No one questions the importance of repetition in the development of the motor skills. Here the outcome of intelligent practice is so evident in terms of improved skill it is accepted by everyone. The only way to learn to swim is to practice swimming. But when it is a question of what we may call the mental skills, universal acceptance is not the rule. But the law is just as valid in the world of mind as it is in the world of body. The only way to learn to think is to practice thinking. Thinking is hard work. Too difficult, Nicholas Murray Butler says, for most men and practically all women! Hence we need not expect that anyone will engage long in this activity who is not willing to submit himself to a regimen of self-discipline. But the individual who does submit himself to such a regimen, given ordinary native talent, will realize in himself the principle we are stressing all through this treatise, namely, *self-development through self-discipline*, the road to which is *self-activity*.

That repetition of an activity has long been recognized as an important factor in learning is evident from the fact of this Latin adage coming down to us through the centuries: *Repetitio est mater studiorum*. Repetition may be the mother of learning, but it is not the whole family of factors which condition learning. If repetition were the whole of the matter, we never could learn anything new at all. The learner at tennis repeats the stroke but his aim at the beginning at least is not to give a perfect repetition; rather, it is to change it slightly in the direction of improved skill. The spider's learning in the experiment

---

[1] Charles C. Peters, *Foundations of Educational Sociology*, Macmillan, 1924, p. 219.

recounted on page 121 was not to repeat the fall; although, of course, we could state it differently and say he was repeating remaining in the web in spite of the sounding of the tuning fork. But why should he do either? Here, obviously, is another factor in learning.

(B) THE PRINCIPLE OF MOTIVATION

The name of Thorndike's second law, "Satisfaction," is well-chosen when we speak of it as one of the laws of animal learning. It suggests immediately satisfaction of the two body appetites, food and sex. But surely in the life of man, the satisfactions most significant for the development of worthy personalities are on a higher level than this. Man is a rational animal. If he is going to live up to this rationality, the satisfactions which are most meaningful for him are intellectual. Intellectual satisfactions are the higher type of interests, and we know it is man's interests which determine the activities he carries on, particularly his mental activities. Here, then, is the second principle of human learning: *an activity is learned the more easily, to the extent that it is motivated by interest.* Interest has long been stressed by writers on education as the key to learning. Herbart, "the first of educational psychologists," made it one of the cardinal points in his psychology of learning. Reeder seems to relegate "satisfaction" to something that takes place after the activity. This surely is a misreading of the Law of Effect as stated by Gates: "The individual tends to repeat and learn quickly those reactions which *are accompanied* or followed by a satisfying state of affairs." The accompanying is often, though not always, in terms of deferred satisfactions. Listening to music is certainly satisfying to many people, but in the case of the student working over a difficult problem, the satisfaction is of the future if he can only solve the problem. We say he is driven on by his interest in the problem, though his inability to solve it may be a great source of annoyance.

Man's interests are, of course, manifold, and this is what marks him off from the animal which lives in terms of the body appetites. The modern emphasis in educational literature on arousing interests is in terms of setting up problems. Dewey never made a truer statement than when he said: "Thinking begins in what may fairly enough be called a forked road situation, a situation which is ambiguous, which presents a dilemma, which proposes alternatives. . . . When there is no question of a problem to be solved or a difficulty to be surmounted, the course of suggestions flows on at random." [1] Habit takes care of the vast majority of our actions during the day, and thinking in the sense of reflective thought arises only when we are confronted with a problem. We are driving a car, performing all the motor reactions necessary for this activity through habit perfected by repetition, but let the engine stop running, reflective thinking begins immediately. We look to our supply of gas. If this is satisfactory we check the feed pipe; and if this is operating we suspect some fault in the electrical connections. With these checked to our satisfaction, we are at a loss and finally call up a garage to get an expert to think for us. When he arrives, he detaches a cup from the carburetor, spills the contents on the ground and watches it evaporate slowly. "See," he says, "Water!" Driving back to the station where we just purchased the gas, he calls our attention to the water bubbles in the glass container overhead. We receive our money back, go to another garage, and wait for the draining and refilling of the tank and then proceed on our way rejoicing. We have learned a lesson about the quality of gas which may be purchased on occasions, a lesson that calls for no repetition to be remembered, and is a striking illustration

[1] John Dewey, *How We Think*, Heath, 1910, p. 11.

of the law of interest or if you will, of insight, since once this experience occurs it is never forgotten. The teacher in the classroom can seldom set up problems as real as the one just described, but that is the purpose of "projects" and all problem teaching. With little interest there will be little learning, no matter how much repetition may be demanded.

(c) THE PRINCIPLE OF APPERCEPTION

In the experience just described, what were the conditions present which made it possible for the new knowledge to enter the mind as a permanent possession without any repetition? Interest certainly was one of them, since being stalled in a little country town one hundred miles from home was not a very pleasant prospect. But that was not the only factor. We all knew something about gas engines, and when our instructor, the garage mechanic, presented the new knowledge about the quality of gasoline sometimes purchased and ways of testing for it, this new knowledge was easily assimilated. Here is the third principle of human learning. It means "readiness," surely, but we will not ascribe this readiness to the neurons in a "conduction unit." This only clouds the issue. The readiness in this case is a mental something. The mind is ready to assimilate new ideas. This process of assimilation, since the time of Herbart, has been called apperception. Hence we will call this principle the Principle of Apperception. It reads thus: *Every new idea is learned to the degree that it is assimilated to other ideas already in the mind.*

We can make the meaning of the principle clear by the following example. Perception is commonly defined by psychologists as the interpretation of the data furnished by sensation. In the instance we used in Chapter III, coming to the breakfast table in the morning, we have sensations of a certain color shading away from lemon, certain olfactory sensations, of touch, the skin of the fruit, kinesthetic sensations, its weight, and finally, gustatory sensations. Interpreting, that is, reading meaning into some or all of these, we *perceive* an orange. What does it mean to apperceive? This illustration will help make this clear. Three men come down a road passing a stately oak tree. The first says, "Think of the number of feet of lumber you could get out of that tree!" The second says, "I'll bet there's a squirrel's nest up in that tree!" The third: "My, see the beautiful symmetry of that tree. How those branches balance one another!" They all perceive the same tree. But they apperceive it in terms of their past experience. The first was a lumberman, the second a hunter, the third an artist. Here we have a good illustration of how *thinking is linking*. But the linking in this case is not a mere mechanical association. Rather, it is a vital something, the perceptions of meanings in terms of past experience. Here is the difficulty very young children experience in learning. They have had so little experience, there isn't much in their minds to link a new experience to. We don't teach calculus to kindergarteners. It is difficult enough to teach the simple arithmetic processes to the immature mind of the child.

The principle of apperception is often violated in school in either of two ways, teaching over the heads of pupils or under their feet. If the subject matter we are offering is so far above pupils that there is no possibility of vital association with the present content of their minds, no learning results. On the other hand, if the subject offered is "old stuff" for some in a class, no learning results in their case for the simple reason that they already know the matter being offered.

Thus far in Section A, "Biological and Psychological Foundations of Education" (Chapters III, IV and V), we have been considering characteristics common to all human kind. The illustrations just given of how the Principle of Apperception may be violated in two ways in teaching, brings us face to face with the fact that individuals are not alike in the possession of traits that are of significance to the school. The trait of most significance for the school is, of course, the ability to learn. The principles of learning assume common likenesses in all pupils in the process through which learning takes place; but the fact of individual differences in pupils' ability to learn is even more striking than the likenesses. We turn now to consider briefly this problem.

3. INDIVIDUAL AND GROUP DIFFERENCES

Nature never repeats herself, is a common saying. No two grains of sand on the shore, no two blades of grass in the field, no two leaves on the tree are exactly alike. The differences may be very slight, requiring microscopic analysis for detection, but they are real. If this is true of grains of sand, blades of grass, leaves of the tree, how much more must it be true of human kind, the most complex organism in the created universe. That human beings differ definitely one from another is the basis for the detection of criminals through fingerprints. No two prints are ever alike. If this is true of the anatomical features of man's body, how much more must we expect it to be true of the psychological features of man's mind, chief among which is the ability to learn.

This, of course, is no new discovery for the school. Plato, in his Republic, in which he describes the educational system of the ideal state as he visioned it, divided the citizens into three classes: the philosophers, whose function was to rule the state; the soldiers, who were to protect and defend it; and the workers, whose function was to obey and support the other two classes. The task for education was to discover and develop the qualifications of each individual and then train him for the function for which he was best fitted, though the system of education presented in the Republic is concerned for the most part with that of the philosophers only. Monroe's comment, on Plato's solution of the educational problem is worth quoting:

> While it must be admitted that this solution is but a formal one, yet any practical solution is determined largely by a previous formal solution. The value of a formal solution which will give an ideal to work toward is clearly indicated by the chaotic condition of our educational practice of today, which possesses neither formal ideal nor unified practice.[1]

American education may be in a chaotic condition today, as Monroe says, but if so, part of that chaos is caused by our attempt to educate all the children of all the people in a single system with little or no segregation of pupils into different type schools, a segregation commonly found in Europe. Our system is democratic, equal opportunity for all; but can it be effective in the achievement of its purposes when all pupils receive substantially the same training? A major problem in this country is the extent and magnitude of differences among pupils when dealing with an unselected group in our cosmopolitan schools.

THE NORMAL DISTRIBUTION CURVE

Every one knows that if we measure a physical trait like height in any large unselected group, say a thousand entering college freshmen, there will be a few very short individuals at one extreme and a few very tall at the other extreme, with the majority grouping themselves in the middle, close to the average. The distribution for the whole group will fall into, what is called in the language of the statistician, the curve of normal distribution, or the normal probability curve, or the normal

[1] Paul Monroe, *Textbook in the History of Education*, Macmillan, 1925, p. 139.

frequency curve.   This probability curve is symmetrical and bell-shaped.   Now the theory is that mental traits distribute themselves in the same way, and thousands of measurements of pupils in school have confirmed this prediction.   In the

FIGURE 11.—THE NORMAL DISTRIBUTION CURVE

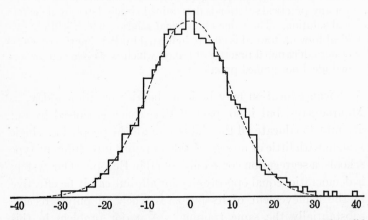

The Normal Curve of Distribution is indicated by the dotted line.   The solid lines show the actual distribution of the scores in mental tests of 1656 pupils in Grade IX.   Note how closely the curve based on actual scores approximates the theoretical curve.   (Thorndike and Gates, *Elementary Principles of Education*, Macmillan, p. 218.   From E. L. Thorndike, *Journal of Educational Research*, November, 1924.)

illustration (Figure 11, above) the base line shows the variations from the least to the greatest amount of the trait being measured and the height of the curve above the base line, the frequency of the trait.   The first thing evident from an inspection of the curve is that variations from the average are continuous.   This means that human beings are not divided into "types."   There is only one type, the human type, indicated by the mythical average in the middle, and variations from this type are shown by small intervals tapering off in both directions.   In measuring a combination of traits, the old theory of compensation held that if a child was weak in one trait, in all probability he would be strong in another trait, thus restoring the balance and making all individuals approach the average. Just the contrary is the case. If a child has a high intelligence rating he is more than likely to be superior in other traits, to children of low intelligence. This fact emphasizes individual differences rather than reducing them through compensation. The significance of individual differences is one of the outstanding contributions of educational psychology to the science of education. The phrase, "provision for individual differences," from the point of view of the school, is however, pretentious. It has become a catch word, and some school people, capitalizing its popularity, have advertized their schools as furnishing "an individual curriculum for the individual pupil." If they do anything besides tutoring, such a claim renders them suspect. The school is one of the social agencies brought forth by society to do a very special work, the education of youth; but to claim that all instruction in a school of any size is individual is preposterous. Nor should it be. There are real values in group instruction which are not attainable at all in highly individualized teaching procedures. When the school divides up its large unselected group into classes, the slow, the average, and the fast, for example, it is setting up divisions that do not exist in nature; they are artificial and mere matters of definition since all variations are continuous. Nevertheless, that is the way the school must work. From the fact of individual differences, any large school must proceed to group differences and do everything it can to meet the needs of these variant groups in classes as homogeneous as possible. This presents a serious problem for the American cosmopolitan high school, that is, a school which all the children of all the people attend. Sectioning on the basis of ability is now making headway in high school, but with the great increase in the number of college students following the war the same problem is there. Ability grouping is most common in freshman English. Here there are specific skills which can be tested for, and when found wanting, can be provided for by special sections emphasizing drill in the fundamentals, leaving the other students free to travel at a pace commensurate with their abilities.

In the Catholic college the most serious situation in this regard is in the teaching of religion. It should be our special concern, but it has been the most neglected from the point of view of student ability and student needs. In the large college and university entering students come from Catholic high schools in all stages of preparation for college work in religion, and from public high schools with no preparation at all. As a result, too often instruction is geared to the pace of the average student, with the result that it is too slow for the fast and too fast for the slow. But religion placement tests are now available for college freshmen (Bruce Publishing Company, Milwaukee), and there is some prospect that the situation will be materially improved. Students scoring high on these tests and high in a general psychological examination should be placed in special sections which both in name and in content are real courses in theology. At the other extreme, students scoring low in a religion placement test should be given special coaching classes stressing the fundamentals and daily prayers. We return to this situation confronting the school with an unselected student body and the significance of group differences in Chapter XI, "The Dilemma of Democratic Education."

In bringing to a conclusion this treatment of theories of learning, we link up the laws of learning with the outcomes of learning. In the diagram which follows, the laws of learning are allocated to the three primary mental functions. This allocation is, however, merely a matter of emphasis. As a spiritual substance, the mind is a unit and it functions as a unit; but there are different ways in which it functions. The classification of functions of most significance for education is the one we are following here. But it would be a fatal blunder for the student to think of the different functions as three logic-tight compartments. Rather, they go on concomitantly, not serially or one after the other. We know and feel at the

FIGURE 12.—PRINCIPLES OF HUMAN LEARNING

MENTAL FUNCTIONS	ANIMAL LEARNING	HUMAN LEARNING	OUTCOMES OF HUMAN LEARNING	DURANT'S GOALS
Cognition (knowing)	Law of Readiness	Principle of Apperception	Knowledge (facts and meanings)	the understanding of life
Affection (feeling)	Law of Effect	Principle of Motivation	Attitudes (ideals and appreciations)	the enjoyment of life
Conation (doing)	Law of Exercise	Principle of Self-activity	Abilities (habits and skills)	the control of life

same moment and also act or, at least, experience a tendency to action. Similarly, the laws of learning are operative in all mental functioning though they have special reference to one. These are logical distinctions made for purposes of study. Growth in knowledge, for example, is conditioned by motivation and self-activity, but it has special reference to apperception. And so with the other outcomes of learning. If the principles of learning are applied in teaching, there is every prospect that the outcomes of learning will be realized. If they are not applied, learning will be definitely hindered; in fact it may fail to take place at all. With the principles of learning adhered to, and the outcomes of learning, knowledges, attitudes, and abilities, realized, the pupil is on his way to the achievement of what Durant calls the goals of education: "First, the control of life . . . second, the enjoyment of life . . . third, the understanding of life." [1] (Figure 12, p. 149.)

Which are the knowledges, attitudes, and abilities the school must develop within the pupil in order that he may understand, enjoy, and control life? The answer to this question requires an excursion into the field of educational sociology, the study of man's social life and its meaning for the school. Knowledges, attitudes, and abilities must be developed in all fields of social living. This is the problem we discuss in the next chapter treating the universal human needs.

SUGGESTED READINGS

I. LAWS OF ANIMAL LEARNING

Dashiel, J. F., "A Survey and Synthesis of Learning Theories," *Psychological Bulletin*, XXXII, 1935, pp. 261–275.

Heibreder, Edna, *Seven Psychologies*, Century, 1933, for learning and the conditioned reflex see pp. 245–248; the stimulus-response concept as psychology's "most useful tool," p. 302.

Koffka, Kurt, *The Growth of the Mind*, Harcourt Brace, 1924, a Gestaltist.

Kohler, Wolfgang, *Gestalt Psychology*, Paul, French, Trubner, London, 1932.

Pavlov, I. P., (tr. by Amrep.) *Conditioned Reflexes*, Oxford Univ., London, 1927.

Pressy, S. L., *Psychology and the New Education*, Harper, 1933, "Part II: Learning in School" the second half of the book, pp. 305–586.

Thorndike, Edward L., *Educational Psychology, Vol. II. The Psychology of Learning*, Bureau of Publications, Teachers College, Columbia Univ., 1913.

——, *Educational Psychology; Briefer Course*, Bureau of Publications, Teachers College, Columbia Univ., 1914.

——, and others, *Adult Learning*, Macmillan, 1928.

[1] Will Durant, "What Education Is of Most Worth," *Saturday Evening Post*, April 11, 1936.

——, *Human Learning*, Century, 1931, replies to the many criticisms of his theory of learning, particularly, pp. 122–131.

2. PRINCIPLES OF HUMAN LEARNING

Castiello, Jaime, *Humane Psychology*, Sheed & Ward, 1936, psychology as a science backed by the philosophy of supernaturalism.

Commins, W. D., *Principles of Educational Psychology*, Ronald Press, 1937, a presentation of the organismic point of view, Chaps. 10, "Heredity and Mentality;" 11, "Learning" and 12, "Habits and Skills" particularly worthwhile.

Kelly, William A., *Educational Psychology*, Bruce, 1935, Chap. XV, "The Learning Process," background Supernaturalism.

Skinner, Charles E., (editor) *Educational Psychology*, Prentice-Hall, 1936, eclectic viewpoint by various authors, keynote, that learning is a process of continuous growth; the child, a growing and functioning organism. Part III "Learning."

Woodworth, Robert S., *Psychology*, Henry Holt, (fourth revised ed.) 1939, Chapter IX, "Learning," how man surpasses animals in learning ability; the conditioned reflex in human subjects.

3. INDIVIDUAL AND GROUP DIFFERENCES

Chapman, J. C., and George S. Counts, *Principles of Education*, Houghton Mifflin, 1924, Problem 11, "How Is Education Conditioned by Individual Differences," pp. 174–194, an excellent summary up to the date 1924.

Ellis, R. S., *The Psychology of Individual Differences*, Appleton, 1928, a good summary with bibliography.

Mort, Paul R., *The Individual Pupil in the Management of Class and School*, American Book Co., 1928.

Wentworth, Mary M., *Individual Differences in Intelligence of School Children*, Harvard Studies in Education No. 7, Harvard Univ., 1927, case studies and group characteristics.

Woodworth, Robert S., *Psychology*, Henry Holt, (fourth revised ed.) 1939, Chapter III, "Individual Differences in Ability," uses new tests for verbal, numerical and spatial abilities illustrating statistical methods.

What are the functions which these non-vocational educations can serve in the lives of adult Americans from twenty-five to seventy years of age into which our highly advantaged liberal-college students mature? These can best be brought into relief by analyzing what figuratively may be designated the several "careers" of most normal adults under the complex conditions produced by what Spengler rather happily calls our "megalopolitan" civilization. These careers can for the present be differentiated conveniently into seven classes; namely,

(1) The Vocational,
(2) The Family-rearing,
(3) The Civistic,
(4) The Religious,
(5) The Health-conserving,
(6) The Personal-culture-enhancing,
(7) The Pleasure-seeking.

Space is not available here to describe either the "core contents" of these careers as realized by our more wholesome and socially effective citizens, or the numerous more or less pathological cases in which painful disharmonies are often allowed to develop among them.

It must be insisted, however, that realistic sociological analysis of the lives of large proportions of the mature men and women with which the readers of these pages are familiar will provide much evidence to support these contentions: First, that under present conditions of civilized living, and especially of urban living, adequate pursuit of the seven careers listed tends largely to differentiate and even to specialize the allocations of time, effort, income, and even personal associations which each person must make; second, that under the pressure of intense preoccupation with one of several of these careers, pursuit of the others may be neglected for long periods, but almost invariably with pathological consequences to personality and to society; and third, that effective preparations for entry upon life-long pursuit of these careers not only give us really functional foundations for all pre-college school educations, but should and can give us the foundations of values and objectives for liberal-college non-vocational educations as well.

David Snedden, "Toward Free and Efficient Liberal Colleges," *Journal of Higher Education*, June, 1935, pp. 311–312.

CHAPTER VI

THE UNIVERSAL HUMAN NEEDS

In the preceding Part, Section A., "Biological and Psychological Foundations," we studied the nature of man as an individual and hence of the pupil, the individual learner in the school. We considered man from the two points of view indicated when we say he is a somatopsychic organism, *i.e.*, a body-mind organism. Biology is the science concerned primarily with body, psychology primarily with mind, although we saw that neither of these two aspects can be completely separated from the other. We make this logical separation for purposes of study only, in order that we may develop a deeper understanding of the fact that while man is a unitary organism, he is, at the same time a rational animal.

But no man lives alone. Man is a social animal. He lives in society. He is immersed in an environment both physical and social which plays a great part in determining the kind of personality that emerges as the process of living and learning goes on. In the process of living he experiences certain needs which must be met if life is to continue at all, *e.g.*, the need for food and drink; and other needs which must be met if life is to be at all satisfying, *e.g.*, the desire for human companionship; and still others which must be provided for if what the Great Teacher called the "abundant life" is to be achieved. In the light of this fact it is only to be expected that if man experiences any fundamental need he will use his intelligence to bring into being a means adapted to the satisfaction of that need. When such a need is universal, *i.e.*, when it is experienced by all men, men will work together to bring that means into being. This is what we mean by society, and this is the origin of what we call the social institutions.

Each social institution or social agency has been brought into being by society to meet some universal need of man living in society. This is its specific, its essential function. It may help another agency achieve its specific function, *e.g.*, the school helps the church achieve its function, the eternal salvation of its members, but this is a supplementary, an instrumental function. In the same way the church as the patron of the arts and sciences through the centuries helps the school achieve its function, namely, advancing the intellectual life of man, but this is not the specific function of the church. In the same way the intelligently conducted school will not be neglectful of the health of its pupils by requiring of them a regimen injurious to health. On the contrary, any school under intelligent administration not only avoids such excesses but makes a positive contribution to the health of its pupils by developing health knowledge and proper attitudes relative to health, while at the same time, through its daily regimen, training them in health habits. But this is a supplementary not the specific function of the school. This distinction is important because out of it arises a principle which is applicable to all the social agencies, namely this: no social agency should so concern itself with supplementary functions, *i.e.*, help other agencies achieve their functions, that it must neglect or fail to give proper time and consideration to the carrying out of its own specific function.

What are the fundamental needs of man, needs which

through their universality have brought into being the primary social agencies?   Obviously these needs were fewer in primitive society than they are today in the complex social organization in which we are now living.   How many such universal needs are there in the life of man today in our complex social organization, and what are the agencies which society has brought into being to meet these needs?

Approaching the problem historically as these needs arise in the life of the individual, we distinguish seven universal needs as follows: The first is (1) *health*, that general well-being of the organism which at birth makes survival possible and through life makes living enjoyable.   The new-born babe, however, unlike the young of animals of the lower species, cannot survive without help from his fellows, in this case his parents or those who take the place of parents.   This need, through which in the first instance, the physical necessities of life are supplied continues all through life as a mental something which we call (2) *human companionship*.   In the first instance it is met through the family, the primary social agency, the foundation of society.   But if the child is to continue in health and enjoy the associations of family life he must be supplied with food, shelter and clothing, and material goods, all of which are forms of material wealth.   The need for these essentials of life we will call (3) *economic security*, and the social agency which society has created to meet this need is the economic order. But if the individual is to remain secure in the possession of the material goods he has accumulated—yes, even the possession of his own life as well as family life—he needs protection against anyone who would rob him of these goods.   We will call this need (4) *civic security*, and the state (government) is the agency society has created to insure it.   But the individual citizen living in the state, if he is to live the extremely complex life of a modern civilized human being, must come into the

FIGURE 13.— THE UNIVERSAL HUMAN NEEDS

Human Needs—Careers—Values—Social Objectives of Education

CUNNINGHAM'S "NEEDS" 1936	SNEDDEN'S "CAREERS" 1935	SELLARS' "VALUES" 1926	CHAPMAN & COUNTS' "INTERESTS" 1924	"CARDINAL PRINCIPLES" 1918	SPENCER 1860
1. Education (mental life)	6. Personal-culture-enhancing career	8. Intellectual values		2. Fundamental processes	
2. Health (organic life)	5. Health-conserving career	1. Bodily values	1. Health	1. Health	1. Health
3. Human companionship (family life)	2. Family rearing career	2. Values of Primary association	2. Family life	3. Worthy home membership	3. Parenthood
4. Economic security (economic life)	1. Vocational career	3. Economic values	3. Economic life	4. Vocation	2. Vocation
5. Leisure (leisure life)	7. Pleasure-seeking career	5. Aesthetic values	5. Recreational life	6. Worthy leisure	5. Leisure
6. Civic security (civic life)	3. Civistic career	4. Political values	4. Civic life	5. Citizenship	4. Citizenship
7. Divine security (religious life)	4. Religious career	6. Religious values 7. Moral values	6. Religious life	7. Ethical character	

possession of the achievements of that society, at the same
time developing his own abilities so that he may become both
a cooperating and a contributing member of that society. This
need we call (5) *education*, and the school is the agency society
has created to provide it. But man does not live by bread
alone. There are aspirations arising within him for a higher
life than that of the animal, aspirations of the spirit in which
he seeks to penetrate into the meaning of his life, his origin,
nature, and destiny. In this quest the universal answer of
mankind says that his origin is God, his nature is freedom, and
his destiny is life with God hereafter if he uses that freedom in
conformity with God's will. If he does not so use it, his spirit
is restless and ill at ease, his "conscience troubles him"; he is
failing to satisfy a fundamental need which we will call (6)
divine security, the conviction that all is right between him and
his Creator, God. Finally, even when man performs all the
duties arising out of these six situations in life, there are certain
marginal interests he seeks to satisfy for the pure pleasure of
the satisfactions which arise in following these interests.
The more heavily his obligations press upon him, whether they
arise from the necessity of caring for his health, from the family,
from his work, from membership in the state, the church, or the
school, the more desperately he feels the need for a surcease
from these pressures to have some time for himself in which he
can follow his own sweet will apart from the call of duty. This
need we call (7) *leisure*. "Six days shalt thou labor. . . . But
on the seventh day . . . thou shalt do no work." was the Divine Command on Mount Sinai.[1]

Many other analyses of the fundamental human needs have
been made by different individuals or groups of individuals at
different times. Spencer was the first to apply this type of
analysis to the aims of the school. He named only five social

[1] Exodus XX, 9–10.

aims, omitting education and religion from his list, although, of
course, the former was implied since he was writing about education.   As for religion, the third part of his essay is entitled
"Moral Education," which is one of three elements in religious
education, *faith, worship,* and *works.*   In Figure 13 on page 156
we have indicated how this analysis has been carried forward,
leading to the one we are presenting in this chapter.   The Cardinal Principles are seven, but certainly command of the Fundamental Processes is not synonymous with Education, and
Ethical Character refers only to the conduct phase of religion,
a phase which is essentially the same as Spencer's Moral Education, not the Dogmatic and Liturgical phases.   Thus, in a
Catholic school the Dogmatic aspect determines the conduct
objective as *Christian Character*—not merely Ethical Character, which may be the ethics of paganism.   Sellars' Values
similarly confuse Religious and Moral Values.   The writer of
this presentation was greatly pleased to discover Snedden's
analysis of "careers" as identical with the one he is offering here
but in strikingly different terminology. [1]   (See quotation introducing this chapter, p. 152.)

These needs are universal for all men in all climes.   Since our
chief concern is Education, we will treat that first with the aim
of determining the specific, *i.e.,* the essential, function of the
school, and in the light of this decision, as we treat the other
needs, conclude each discussion by attempting to determine the
supplementary or instrumental function of the school relative
to the six other needs.

1. EDUCATION—THE SCHOOL

Time was when there was no school.   In primitive society the
family took the place of what we now call the school.   Parents

[1] David Snedden, "Toward Free and Efficient Liberal Colleges," *Journal of
Higher Education,* June, 1935.

were the first teachers then, just as today parents, particularly the mother, continue to be the first teachers of the child in its early years. But as the social inheritance grew in size and in extent, and particularly when man brought forth a written language and the language and number arts had developed, then came forth the school. For centuries this was all the education the great masses of people were to receive, training in the three R's, the reading, writing, and reckoning of the elementary schools. Even this was not won without a struggle. Governor Berkeley of Virginia in his reply to the authorities of England in 1761 reported: "Learning has brought disobedience, and heresy, and sects into the world, and printing has divulged them, and libels against the best governments. God keep us from both!" He said he hoped there would be no free schools and printing presses in that province for a hundred years. Governor Berkeley to the contrary, however, printing presses were established and, to make use of their products, schools arose to prepare the youth of the land in the art of reading. Here we have indicated the two phases of the educative process, social transmission on the one hand and individual development on the other. But it is the latter of the two which is the primary function of the school. Transmission of the social inheritance to each oncoming generation is the *means* through which the development of the individual is brought about. This, therefore, is the primary function of the school. The ability to think is the supreme human ability. Man is a rational, that is, a reasoning animal. But if this reasoning power is to be developed at all adequately he must come into contact with the reasonings of those who have gone before him. Here is the second distinctive human ability, the ability to express thought in language, and through language, written and oral, come to know the thoughts of his fellow man as well as to communicate his own. Hence the importance of the language arts. But literacy spread throughout a people is no guarantee of a stable society. Language may be used to deceive as well as to communicate knowledge. Back of literacy there must be a mind, an intellect with power of insight and critical judgment, an emotional life inspiring man to strive after the higher good and a will enabling him to realize that good in his life with fellow man. The prime function of the school, therefore, is the making of minds. Knowledge is an adornment of the mind, but for education the *pursuit* of knowledge is what brings about mental growth and development. Here the process is more important than the product, though, of course, if the process is wisely directed, the product will be an inevitable outcome. The emphasis today in American education is upon knowledge. Education is conceived more as a pouring-in process than a bringing forth of the best possibilities each mind is capable of. This pouring-in process has received euphemistic names to cover up the fallacy that is inherent in its very nature. Thus we hear much of the "enriched curriculum," but seldom of the crowded curriculum. Through this enriched curriculum all important knowledge and training not provided for by other social agencies must be provided for by the school. In this theory the school is a *residual* agency and only incidentally an intellectual agency. Thus Peters says:

> As pointed out in earlier chapters the school should do only what the other agencies leave undone. Its function is distinctly a residual one.[1]

Conceived in this way the school is to handle the residue. It has no specific essential function of its own as have all the other social agencies. During the past two decades, a vast literature concerning educational objectives and therefore the function

[1] Charles C. Peters, *Foundations of Educational Sociology*, Macmillan, 1924, p. 364.

of the school, has been pouring from the printing presses. Amid this plethora of opinion only one voice has been heard protesting against this mistaken theory of the purpose of the school and rebuking it for its failure to see its own specific function, the perfection of human personality through perfecting the human mind. This means planning and carrying out a program that gives some promise of the achievement of that purpose. The voice crying in the wilderness of American educational theory has been that of Henry Smith Pritchett, formerly President of The Carnegie Foundation for the Advancement of Teaching, in his annual reports, from one of which the following quotation is typical.

The school is primarily an intellectual agency. It will serve society best if it keeps always in mind this primary obligation. The school system that dissipates its energy in the endeavor to compass all manner of social activities will in time forget or neglect the primary intellectual purpose for which it exists. . . .

The curriculum of the old-time common school was meagre, the classical program of studies in the colleges of fifty years ago was narrow, but they both stood for the conception that a liberal education lay in training the habits and powers of the mind. In the enormous expansion of the course of study, in making the high school a vestibule to the college, in adding ever new activities that now overshadow the intellectual purposes of high school and college, Americans have come to look upon a liberal education as the acquiring of knowledge. To learn to observe, to marshal the facts of observation, and to think out the correct answers to be drawn from these facts, constitute the foundation of a liberal education.

The school exists in order to train the minds of children and youth for this process. The acquiring of knowledge is altogether a secondary matter. It has become the main thing. Our high schools and colleges seek to give their pupils something from every field of thought. Following the advice of Herbert Spencer, they labor to present these packages of knowledge in the most agreeable forms. The textbooks offer every variety of predigested knowledge. Our youth are spoon-fed as are those of no other nation. Breadth of knowledge is obtained at the expense of independent individual training in finding the facts, sifting them, and drawing accurate conclusions. The method makes for intellectual dependence. "The boy who has become accustomed to depend on the teacher for his knowledge in school tends to take his knowledge second hand in after life. The boy who can study only what he likes in school is governed in after life by his likes and dislikes rather than by his reason." (Hadley, *Economic Problems of Democracy*, p. 154.)

This is the far-reaching change that has come to be characteristic of our educational system of to-day. It is exactly the reverse of that intellectual training which the study of science ought to bring. To get the facts, to put them in logical order, to deduce the reasonable conclusions therefrom, constitute the essential part of the scientific method. In our teaching we have obscured the method of science in the process of filling the minds of children and youth with information put up in pleasing packages.

To recognize once more that a liberal education does not consist in imparting knowledge but in training the habits and powers of the mind must be the beginning of any freshening of our school system.[1]

That this theory of the school as primarily an intellectual agency is the Catholic theory, we have no less an authority than Newman who wrote the great educational classic of the English language, *The Idea of a University*. In reading this work of Newman we must remember he was describing the English university made up of many colleges, not the German university, with its emphasis on research and professional training, which has been followed in this country. Newman's theme is liberal education and his university is what we call in this country the Liberal College. What is its function?

It is, I believe, as a matter of history, the business of a University to make this intellectual culture its direct scope, or to employ itself in the education of the intellect—just as the work of a Hospi-

[1] Henry Smith Pritchett, *Nineteenth Annual Report*, The Carnegie Foundation for the Advancement of Teaching, 1924, Condensed edition, pp. 36–37.

tal lies in healing the sick or wounded, or of a Riding or Fencing School, or of a Gymnasium, in exercising the limbs, or an Alms-house, in aiding and solacing the old, or an Orphanage, in pro-tecting innocence, of a Penitentiary, in restoring the guilty. I say, a University, taken in its bare idea, and before we view it as an instrument of the Church, has this object and this mission; it con-templates neither moral impression nor mechanical production; it professes to exercise the mind neither in art nor in duty; its function is intellectual culture; here it may leave its scholars, and it has done its work when it has done as much as this. It educates the intellect to reason well in all matters, to reach out towards truth, and to grasp it.[1]

The position we are presenting here is that the school on all levels of general education is primarily an intellectual agency. We call attention to the fact, however, that Newman in this statement makes a distinction between what we will call the *essential* function of the school, that is, "taken in its bare idea, and before we view it as an instrument of the Church," and this latter function which, using Newman's word, we will call its *instrumental* function. Our position is that the school like all the great social agencies has its own specific essential function, the making of minds. It has in addition other supplementary instrumental functions in which it aids the other social agencies achieve their specific functions. We now turn to study the other fundamental needs of man and the agencies whose specific function it is to make provision for them, in each case concluding our study with an answer to the question: What is the supplementary, *i.e.*, the instrumen-tal, function of the school in regard to each need.

2. HEALTH—THE HEALTH-CONSERVING AGENCIES

The educator's attitude toward health will be determined fundamentally by his philosophy of life. The naturalist will

[1] John Henry Newman, *Idea of a University*, Discourse VI, "Knowledge Viewed in Relation to Learning."

have a comparatively simple problem. If he is a materialist, health education will resolve itself into the cultivation of a sound animal. If he is an idealist, he will adopt the Christian Science technique. The humanist's objective will involve greater complexity since he will consider not only physical well-being, but also mental health. For the supernaturalist, the humanist's view of health must necessarily be enlarged by the fact of man's supernatural destiny. His concept of health will include that physical, mental, and emotional well-being which will enable the individual to live a normal, happy life here, leading to life hereafter.

The first place in the scale of human needs is accorded to health not only because it is the first to arise in the life of the individual, but also because of its fundamental character in relation to the other needs. The universal recognition of the importance of health can be judged from the fact that an inquiry concerning it is the customary greeting of friends; and drinking to the health of another is an ancient custom that has lasted through the centuries. Health is not, however, to be regarded as the ultimate end of education, or as the primary objective of the school. Wood, in *Health and Education*, states:

> Health is not the end of life or education but it is an essential condition for the realization of worthy ends, more immediate or ultimate, in the career of the individual. (p. 57)

The relation of physical and mental health to the other universal human needs is obvious. The explanation in Chapters III, IV, and V of the nature of man, and the learning process as it goes on in the somatopsychic organism is proof enough of the dependence of education upon health. Observation of the life about us needs no theoretical confirmation to assist in impressing us with the dependence of domestic, economic, and civic security upon physical and mental health. The cases of family dissension, of poverty, and crime, the root of which lies in unhealthfulness, are legion.

Moreover, health is intimately related to divine security—to man's ultimate end, Christian perfection, which we commonly call holiness. "Holiness," "wholeness," and "health" are all derived from the same Anglo-Saxon root, "hāl" meaning "whole." Doctor James J. Walsh epitomizes this relationship as it exists in man:

> Wholeness of body and soul—that is, health and holiness—work together for good in that mysterious compound we know as man.

In *Health and Holiness*, Francis Thompson goes so far as to say:

> Health, I have well-nigh said is Holiness. What if Holiness be Health? Two sides of one truth. In their coordination and embrace resides the rounded answer.[1]

The fact that the supernaturalist takes this comprehensive view of man's nature, and recognizes the importance of health as a factor in the attainment of his end, enriches his concept of the ends and means of health education far beyond that of the others. With them he appreciates the importance of health habits which will develop and maintain a vigorous physique. Chapman and Counts [2] in accounting for the fact that health practice lags behind health knowledge hints strongly in such expressions as "morbid interest in other-worldliness," and "pathological unconcern about health," that religion has militated against effective health education, a charge which the numerous quotations cited by Lockington in *Bodily Health and Spiritual Vigor* adequately refute, putting the blame for

[1] Francis Thompson, *Health and Holiness*, Herder, 1905, p. 80.
[2] J. Crosby Chapman and George S. Counts, *Principles of Education*, Houghton Mifflin, 1924, p. 203.

our modern conception of the saints' attitude toward care of the body upon the misunderstanding and shortsightedness of their biographers.[1]

The supernaturalist recognizes man to be a unitary organism and consequently he emphasizes the importance of mental hygiene not only as a supplement to physical hygiene, but also as its necessary concomitant. Doctor James J. Walsh says:

> While we talk of the influence of the mind on the body, and the body on the mind, we must not forget that these two constitute one being; and there is quite literally no idea which does not make itself felt in the body.

The mental phase of health is the basis for rational adjustment to the condition of impaired physical health. Though the individual suffer severe loss of some physical power, he realizes that all is not lost; that, on the contrary, such handicaps can be converted into assets. History furnishes many examples of men and women with seriously impaired health who have achieved success in the affairs of this life and in those of salvation. These are, of course, the exceptions that prove the rule of the dependence of success upon health, yet they are possibilities that serve for exemplification and motivation. Thomas A. Edison regarded his partial deafness as a great aid to concentration, and we have all seen individuals (like the college professor of whom his friends said that contracting diabetes made a man of him) who have developed strong characters as a result of subjecting themselves to a regimen of therapy demanding a high degree of self-mastery.

But the highest contribution of supernaturalism to the problem of health is in this twofold concept: First, health is a gift of God; the right to live bestowed by the Creator connotes

[1] William Lockington, *Bodily Health and Spiritual Vigor*, Longmans Green, 1914, pp. 13–21.

essentially the duty to respect life and to preserve health in order to achieve the purposes of life. This further impresses us with the relation of health and personal holiness, and health and Catholic Action. Saint Ignatius said: "An ounce of sanctity with exceptionally good health does more for the saving of souls than striking sanctity with an ounce of health," and Pius X wrote to the seminarians of Venice: "It is my wish to watch the progress of my young men, both in piety and learning, but I do not attach less importance to their health on which depends in great measure the exercise of their ministry later on." The second fundamental attitude is this: Although this high correlation between health and success does exist, man's essential worth is measured in terms of eternal values because of his supernatural end; consequently, loss of health does not mean that life is no longer worth living. The logical naturalist will recognize suicide as the only reasonable end of a life impaired by incurable disease. Facts testify that there have been many such practical naturalists. But to the supernaturalist, belief in life hereafter and the recognition of the temporality of this life make loss of health not an irreparable catastrophe, but a problem to be coped with in the light of his supernatural destiny.

THE SCHOOL'S PART

Granted the importance of health to the individual and to society, the question is: What part has the school to play in health education. Payne and Schroeder state that health education is the business of the school for two reasons:

First, because the progress of the child in school is directly dependent upon his physical condition. . . . Secondly, because it depends on the observance of specific and well-known practices related to nutrition, exercise, sleep, rest, cleanliness, and the like, and these in turn are dependent on specific habits, adequate knowledge, and appropriate attitudes of healthful living. The development of habits, knowledge, and attitudes that will control the behavior of the child is the purpose of the school and the function of education.[1]

It devolves upon the school, then, to provide for the pupil experiences which will influence habits, knowledge, and attitudes so as to promote individual, racial, and community health.

The first duty of the school to the pupil's health is one of administration, and demands that hygienic conditions in building, equipment, and personnel be provided so that the physical well-being of the pupil is safeguarded while he is in school.

The formation of health habits stands first in the educative process in the order of time. Even in the earliest years, it will have in most cases a twofold aspect: correction of bad habits already formed, and the formation of new good habits proper to the growing child. Certain problems of healthful living, such as good posture, care of the eyesight, and food selection in the school cafeteria, are directly connected with school life. The extent to which problems of personal hygiene will enter into the school's work will depend largely upon the age of the pupils, and the extent to which these matters are neglected in the home.

As the pupil advances, the element of health knowledge will assume increasing importance. Physiology, understanding of the causes of health and disease, knowledge of the principles of mental hygiene, and an acquaintance with the growing body of scientific knowledge regarding the promotion of health and the cure and prevention of disease will be necessary to enable the pupil critically to evaluate his own somatopsychic make-up, and reasonably to direct his own health habits. It is impor-

---

[1] E. G. Payne and L. C. Schroeder, *Health and Safety in the New Curriculum*, American Viewpoint Society, 1927, p. 13.

tant that this health knowledge be imparted under conditions favorable for the maximum transfer of knowledge into habits and attitudes of healthful living.

Most important of all is the development of health attitudes that will result in a wholesome health-consciousness, and a consequent optimum adjustment of the individual to himself and his environment. It is in this matter of developing health attitudes that health education in the Catholic school will be unique. In forming health habits and imparting health knowledge, materialist, humanist, and supernaturalist will proceed in much the same way, but it is obvious that a system that regards man, body and soul, as the temple of the Holy Ghost, the object of future glorification in heaven, will inculcate in the pupil widely different attitudes toward his health than will a system that regards him as a good animal only, and esteems temporal efficiency as his highest achievement. What Chapman and Counts term "health conscience" will embrace for the supernaturalist a wider scope than it denotes to these authors.[1] It will embrace not only the individual's responsibility to self and to the community, but will include responsibility to the Creator and belief in the divine sanction. Health education in the Catholic school will include the development in the pupil of the recognition and acceptance of the health ideals consequent upon the philosophy of supernaturalism.

The school's responsibility for health education will find expression in all the "pivotal problems of education." In the curriculum and the co-curricular activities the school has its own peculiar opportunity for health education. The program of physical education where bodily activities are motivated and mental attitudes conducive to healthy bodily functioning are attained; the development of the cultural, vocational, and recreational aspects of life so necessary for the attainment of

[1] *Op. cit.*, pp. 208–209.

mental health; as well as the direct approaches to the pupil's health problems; all are within the proper scope of the school's program.   The teacher, too, sets up in his own personality patterns of physical and mental health that will be powerful in their effects upon pupils.   The problem of the institution can be solved adequately only by due consideration of its duty to provide means for healthful living, and to coöperate with the health-promoting agencies.

The latter function of the school is today becoming more and more important.   Because of its social nature, the school offers opportunities to public health agencies to reach the child, and often through the child, the home.   The school seems to be the best place for the application of the prophylactic phase of medical science.   In coördination with almost every school from the nursery school to the university level, we find some kind of student health service.   In many of our city systems, children in the parochial schools as well as those in the public schools are receiving at school the services of physicians and nurses supplied by the city department of health.   The worth of such service has already expressed itself in terms of disease prevention, increased positive health of pupils, and consequent improvement in school work.   It is the obvious duty of the school to coöperate with these agencies in the interest of the physical well-being of the individual pupil and of the social group.

3. HUMAN COMPANIONSHIP—THE HOME

"What are the most precious gifts for which an old man, looking back on his life, ought to thank God?" is the question which Dean Inge proposes in his book, *Vale*.   In his answer he considers health, and recognition, but his conclusion is:

I have not the slightest doubt that domestic happiness is the greatest of all good gifts, next to that of "wisdom," for which Solomon prayed, and which, I suppose, may be defined as a right judgment of the relative value of things. The blessings which God has given me in my wife and children are in a different class from all other sources of happiness and pleasure that have come to me. At a time when many persons are not ashamed to assert that marriage is generally a failure, it is permissible to give this personal testimony.

This statement raises the two contrasting issues that concern us in our study of human companionship as a universal human need. (1) What does it offer that affords man such satisfying happiness? and, (2) Why are many persons asserting that marriage is generally a failure? The first question we have already answered briefly in Chapter IV. Here we shall consider more fully how worthy home membership provides the normal outlet for man's three dominant urges: to enjoy pleasures, to amass possessions, and to exercise power.

Pleasure may be thought of on two distinct levels, on the level of sense, which we share with other members of the animal kingdom, and on the rational level, which is peculiarly human. On the sense level the two impulses which offer the greatest satisfaction are, in the Providence of God, coupled with the maintenance and perpetuation of the human race. The first is the impulse to partake of food and drink, and the second is the sex impulse. In any social organization, worthy of the name society, these two impulses find their expression through family life. Human companionship is an important function of the home because it satisfies the urge for pleasure on the rational level. Man is a social animal and craves the society of his fellows. The intensity of this desire is suggested by recalling that the severest punishment which the penitentiary inflicts is solitary confinement. Family life alone makes adequate provision for this universal need of companionship. Without the ministration of his parents, or someone to take their place, the new-born babe could not survive the long period of dependence which the human infant experiences. In a good home the first lessons in human relations are learned under the guidance of sympathetic but wise teachers. The sense of security provided by its protection offers the first stabilizing influence. As intelligence and appreciation develop there is an increase in the charm of shared cultural enjoyment. Nothing yet has been discovered which surpasses a wholesome family circle for teaching people how to get along with one another. Here every variety of companionship exists: youth with age, boy with boy, girl with girl, boy with girl, and man with woman. Those who are denied the opportunity of membership in a happy home are robbed of one of the most priceless possessions of human kind.

From the natural point of view the craving to beget children and thus to reproduce one's own idealized personality in the personality of another offers the most enduring satisfaction in life. When it is achieved, and children come to complete the home, the urge to amass worldly possessions becomes very real indeed. Man, through his work in the world, labors to provide not only the necessities of food, shelter, and clothing, but also the comforts and luxuries which will maintain his family in a desirable social position. Woman, in addition to being the mother of the children, plays an important part in the economic administration of the family goods. The third primary drive, the drive to power, also finds its fullest expression in the home. The father may be a low subordinate in his industrial position, but here he is master. Household tasks are not drudgery to a mother who directs her own domestic world. In the authority that parents exert over their family, they have not merely the opportunity but the definite duty to see that their children will be governed by discipline. In the first instance this discipline will be superimposed, but as the full development of the natural powers approaches it must be taken over by youth and become self-imposed. It is in this process that the American home is failing to meet one of its prime obligations today, and the result in adult life will be immaturity.

We emphasize throughout this discussion that worthy family life is the highest *natural* ambition. The religious, the priest, the brother, or the nun, bound to the religious life by the vows of the organized asceticism of the Church, sublimates this natural ambition in a supernatural one, and strives to reproduce in his own personality the personality of Jesus Christ. Of course all members of a Christian home have the obligation to form themselves after the model of Christ, but in St. Paul's phrase, parents are "divided." The husband is interested in how he may please his wife; the wife in how she may please her husband. The religious who labors for the sanctification of the human race, gives up his right to a family of the flesh for the family of the spirit, and endeavors to increase the number of God's children who find their way to heaven. He sacrifices home life to communal life so that all his energies may be better consecrated, first, to reproducing in himself the personality of Jesus Christ, and then to the spreading of His kingdom. (See Figure 14, "Rights and Duties in Three Societies," p. 176.)

THE SCHOOL'S PART

What can the school do to promote successful home life? The point of view we are offering in this presentation is that the school is primarily an intellectual agency. Its specific function is the making of minds by teaching students how to think and how to express their thoughts. Its aim is to enable the individual to develop his complete personality so that he may lead a life of Christian perfection here and attain eternal happiness hereafter. Consequently, the immediate objective of the school is to cultivate the student's mind in such a way as to enable him to think through and to meet the problems of adult life.   There he will need to assume the responsibilities of the three societies of which he is a member, the family, the state, and the Church.   Pius XI points out this in *The Christian Education of Youth:*

> Education, which is concerned with man as a whole, individually and socially, in the order of nature and the order of grace, necessarily belongs to all these three societies, in due proportion, corresponding, according to the disposition of Divine Providence, to the coördination of their respective ends.

Without infringing, then, on the school's prime purpose of mind-making, education must perform, in so far as it can, its instrumental function of preparing the student for enriched family living.   This can be brought about by both a direct and an indirect process.

THE HOME IN TRANSITION

This responsibility of the school has become more grave with the passing of years and the threatened disintegration of the American home.   A brief sketch of the major transitions through which family life has passed will suffice to remind the educator of the nature of the problem that has been deposited at his door step.   It will also explain the gloomy note that concluded Dean Inge's remark quoted above (pp. 170–171).

In the Middle Ages the permanency of family life was insured by its industrial function, and during that period the home reached the highest point it has ever attained as a stabilized social institution.   The cultivation of the fields and the home-production of commodities kept all hands busy.   From the youngest to the eldest, all worked for the common good.   Then there came a series of revolutions which set to work powerful disintegrating forces that have almost imperceptibly undermined the prime social group, the home. In the wake of the Renaissance came the Religious Revolution with its accent on individualism. Self-expression, self-gratification, self-interest, began to replace interdependence with independence in the home. The Scientific Revolution, which occurred a century later, placed its emphasis on reason, and the "rationalization" of conduct soon led to contempt for authority and disregard of self-control in the moral order. The consequence was a let-down of integrity in family bonds.

The nineteenth century brought the labor-saving devices of the Industrial Revolution, which completed the destruction of integrated economic life in the family circle. More and more leisure time, combined with the new cry for freedom from all restraint, introduced a faulty romanticism and a pleasure philosophy of life. Through the vigilance of the Church, these forces among Catholics were kept in comparative check until the devastating era of the World War. Then a distinct break in home traditions occurred. One whole generation was left at the mercy of the dogs of War, and modern warfare knows no mercy. The moral disintegration, the shattering of ideals, the frantic pursuit of such pleasure as may be found, far surpassed in havoc the casualties of the battle-field. Rev. Edgar Schmiedler, O.S.B., points out the resulting situation in the modern home.

> Frequently the father is shorn of his power, the mother is no longer queen of the domestic world, the child is in revolt. There is parental irresponsibility and youthful precocity. With an ever-mounting divorce rate, and with desertion on the increase there are broken homes, unhappy homes, unsuccessful homes. With a decreasing birthrate there are fewer children in the homes. There are homeless children and childless homes. In many instances the purpose of the family goes unfulfilled.[1]

[1] Edgar Schmiedler O.S.B., *An Introductory Study of the Family*, Century, 1930, p. 78.

We like to feel that this sorry picture finds no place in Catholic home life, but the "leakage from the Barque of Peter" is sufficient to warn us that we cannot live in a fool's paradise. Catholic homes are the small minority, and the number of Catholic children in public schools is shockingly large.   Young

FIGURE 14.—RIGHTS AND DUTIES IN THREE SOCIETIES

Chapter VI. "Universal Human Needs" {
Section 3.   Domestic Security
Section 4.   Economic Security
Section 6.   Civic Security
}

THE THREE SOCIETIES	ENDS, WHAT ARE THESE SOCIETIES FOR?	RIGHT, A "MORAL POWER" TO	DUTY, A "MORAL OBLIGATION" TO
I. Domestic society (the family)	(End in general: to propagate the race through consecrated communal life)		
	1.* (A.) procreation of children 2.* (Rat. A.) Education of children 3.* (Soc. A.) Human companionship 4.* (Rel. A.) Consecration of the union by the sacrament	1. marry and have children 2. educate their children as conscience dictates 3. enjoy domestic security	1. be loyal to each other 2. educate their children as Christian parents 3. respect the security of other families
II. Economic society (the economic order)	(End in general: to provide a decent livelihood for all)		
	1. (A.) Subsistence 2. (Rat. A.) Education 3. (Soc. A.) Security in one's station in life 4. (Rel. A.) Religious needs	1. Employees: receive a family living wage 2. Employers: receive an honest day's work for wages paid	1. Employees: do an honest day's work for wages received 2. Employers: pay a family living wage

* Explanation of abbreviations:
1.* A. Animal; 2.* Rat. Rational; 3.* Soc. Social; 4.* Rel. Religious.

FIGURE 14.—(*Continued*)

THE THREE SOCIETIES	ENDS, WHAT ARE THESE SOCIETIES FOR?	RIGHT, A "MORAL POWER" TO	DUTY, A "MORAL OBLIGATION" TO
III. Civil society (the state)	(End in general: to promote the welfare of the governed by safeguarding: 1. (A.) Economic needs 2. (Rat. A.) Intellectual needs (education) 3. (Soc. A.) Peace and order 4. (Rel. A.) Religious liberty	1. Citizens (a) "life (b) liberty and (c) pursuit of happiness." 2. Government (a) obedience to the laws (b) levy taxes (c) intelligent voting and honest office holding (d) wage a just war	1. Citizens (a) obey the laws (b) pay taxes (c) vote intelligently; hold office honestly (d) support war with possessions and life itself 2. Government protect the rights of all to (a) "life (b) liberty and (c) pursuit of happiness."

people cannot escape the conscious and unconscious indoctrination that comes from atheistic teachers, from bad movies, and worse magazines. Unless some daily agency is at work offsetting these malicious influences, we are presumptuous to feel that our children will be unaffected. Even parents with the highest ideals and best intentions are turning helplessly to any agency that promises to guide them in the precarious task of bringing a young family safely through a chaotic era. If the Catholic school does not offer this help, parents will seek it elsewhere, and probably follow will-o-the-wisps of modern superficial theories. That the school has a definite responsibility to meet in this problem has already been asserted by many authorities. The Holy Father stresses the need of education for family welfare in the encyclical on *The Christian Education of Youth:*

> We wish to call attention in a special manner to the present day lamentable decline in family education. The offices and professions of a transitory and earthly life, which are certainly of far less importance, are prepared for by long and careful study: whereas for the fundamental duty and obligation of educating their children, many parents have little or no preparation, immersed as they are in temporal affairs.

But it is one thing to be convinced that a problem exists, and quite another thing to know what to do about it. Certainly the school has some share in safe-guarding the rights and encouraging the duties of family life.

A CATHOLIC FAMILY WELFARE PROGRAM

In sifting through the situation to determine how much of the responsibility the school should assume, two cautions must be observed. The school cannot interfere with its own prime function as an intellectual agency, nor can it interfere with the rights and obligations of the home. It becomes evident, however, that the Catholic school with its emphasis on a supernatural philosophy of life has the ideal program ready at its disposal for meeting the situation. No radical revision of curricular subject matter is required. No attempt to join forces with the fantastic remedies offered by secular colleges and universities is encouraged. These institutions, trying to meet the rising tide of demand all over the country for help in making marriage and home life more successful, are resorting to such specialized courses as "Choosing a Mate." They are merely treating the symptoms, not the disease. The emphasis must be placed, from the elementary school through the Liberal

Arts college, upon cultivating a philosophy of values in family life, upon discovering the roots of social disintegration and controlling them at their source.   In this process there is a definite goal in the growth of knowledge, attitudes, and abilities which the Catholic school should seek.

The Elementary School will do its best by indirection, provided the teacher is able to create sympathetic attitudes. Under proper supervision the growing popularity of the pre-school movement may be used to advantage.   Psychologists and educators have demonstrated that the ideals and habits which the child develops before he is seven are the ones that are going to dominate his life.   Experiences in fair play in group projects which he meets here will provide social adjustments that amplify his home training.   In striving to imitate the Boy Christ and His Immaculate Mother, the growing child will give to his tendency towards hero worship an ennobling outlet. In general, the art of getting along happily with himself and others, of establishing correct behavior patterns, and of being a satisfactory member of his own home circle are the major concerns of this problem in the primary years, and are of vital importance in determining the kind of a home the child will one day build.   As the youth reaches the upper grades and his intelligence begins to unfold, he will make rapid strides in the ability to think.   Since "thinking is linking" and vitalizing education means associating it with life, here the teacher has a fertile field to work indeed.   The home is still the center of the child's life, and the teacher who is alert can link almost any study, but particularly literature and history, with the ideals of family relationship on the youth's own level.   Social habits and skills in work and play can be developed which eliminate timidity and self-consciousness as the budding adolescent faces new social situations.

The Secondary School offers more opportunity for direct

teaching. Twenty years ago secular educators began to realize the need of educating for family welfare and made the mistake of placing their emphasis on sex-instruction and household skills. The attitudes of the present generation are the unfortunate result. The question of sex-instruction for the Catholic school has been decided in no uncertain terms in the Holy Father's Encyclical on Education. This decision is in line with the best judgment of mankind from the purely natural point of view. In a matter so intimate and delicate as sex, all instruction must be of a personal nature, by one who is older to one who is younger. The first obligation, of course, rests with the parents, ordinarily the father with the boys and the mother with the girls. But so often is this obligation neglected that teachers will long have to assume a great part of the burden. In doing this, however, they will be acting as personal counselors to youth, not as instructors of a group in class. One principle can be laid down which should be operative whenever teachers are dealing with this delicate problem. It is this: questions of children and youths on this matter should be answered with clarity and ample fullness to satisfy their curiosity *at the time the question is asked*. Here there should be no holding back. If these questions are not answered to their satisfaction when asked, they will seek information elsewhere and in all probability receive answers which will give them a perverted view on the whole matter. But if their questions are explained adequately, and if, with the answer is associated the religious significance of the part sex plays in the life of man, we have good reason to believe that a wholesome attitude will be developed. But we stress again that little good can be accomplished unless we treat this matter on the basis of a personal relationship, the parent in the home, the teacher in private conference, the priest in the confessional; these are the life situations which offer the greatest opportunity for helping youth to work out an adjustment to this difficult problem.

Household arts have a legitimate place in secondary education in America's cosmopolitan-comprehensive high school. Here all the children of all the people are receiving their final preparation for adult living, and the curriculum has to be adjusted to permit everyone to derive suitable profit. The non-academic-minded group, and those who for economic reasons must enter the industrial world at once, have a right to such vocational education as they desire and are fitted for. For many girls, courses in the principles of foods study, clothing construction, marketing, and interior decorating; and for many boys, training in the elements of the manual arts, will be the most valuable type of instruction that high school can offer them. But the question that arises is, should the academic group, those capable and desirous of preparing for higher education, be permitted to spend their time "studying" household arts? The answer must be in the negative if they wish a thorough foundation on which to build their Liberal Arts career. Those skills will undoubtedly be an asset to any boy or girl, but they are merely the mechanics of home-making, and time has shown that they do not insure domestic happiness any more than they afford mental discipline. If they are substituted for academic requirements the college student faces his new work with a distinct handicap. Provision is made, however, in many secondary schools by clubs and noncredit "hobby courses," for anyone who is interested to take advantage of this training without interfering with the academic program. This would seem to be the best solution to a much mooted question.

During these adolescent years the formation of ideals on worthy home life reaches its culmination and too much care cannot be taken in wise guidance. Renewed emphasis may be placed on social and moral values by their immediate association with various studies. Readings in both poetry and prose will present pictures of all types of homes, thus affording the teacher an excellent opportunity to inculcate idealism in family relationships. In interpreting the social background of history the significance of family solidarity in the rise and fall of nations can stimulate useful thinking. The sciences, particularly biology, offer a place where life principles may be studied without embarrassing anyone. But it is in the religion classes that the Catholic school can establish its most secure foundations.

The past generation made its mistake in Family Welfare education by emphasizing sex and household mechanics. The present group are pinning all their hope in social adjustment. Unless this concentration on human relations rests squarely on a firm basis of divine relations it is going to be a house built on sand. In treating the sixth and ninth commandments, the religion teacher must present the sex instinct in its proper light, not as an evil in itself. He must make clear that evil enters only when it gets out of control and that parents, in bringing children into the world are coöperating with the creative power of God. Under the sacrament of Matrimony the Catholic youth learns that as a social institution "the primary end of marriage is the procreation and education of children." (Canon Law.) With these eternal truths as his balance wheel he is ready to weigh new theories and to shape his own philosophy according to their worth. The danger that state schools are running in emphasizing social values to the neglect of moral standards may offer some element of warning to us. For that reason, towards the end of the secondary school division one orientation course on family welfare, similar to the one to be recommended for the Liberal Arts college but graded to high school level, should be required of all boys and girls. This could easily be incorporated in the last year of religion and would do much to prepare young people for the responsibilities of parenthood.

The Liberal College marks the time when character is pretty well set. The student has already acquired the views and habits which are going to equip him for family life. Nevertheless, his increased intellectual capacity will make it possible for him to understand the "whys" behind many of his problems. In psychology classes there is ample opportunity to learn "how to win friends and influence people" and so to get along with his family. Here also the elements of child development, essential for successful parenthood may be introduced. Economics will teach him the value and method of family budgeting. History and literature will increase in their cultural and social significance. Philosophy will unify all of his knowledge and give life a purpose, and so on through the various departments. But all of this will occur on one condition only. That is, that the individual teacher of each subject be the stimulating influence in cultivating the right attitudes; that by his own idealism he will arouse the student to transfer his theoretical knowledge into actual practice in the family circle of which he is a member, and to project it to the one he hopes to form. This is for the student, after all, but a phase of completing the learning cycle, and as such, a contribution to his mental acumen. All that may be gained from direct teaching in promoting successful family relations in the liberal arts college can easily be included in a single course. In the Catholic college this course may find a place in the department of religion, for domestic happiness has its strongest roots in the supernaturalization of the union. Unless mutual loyalty and respect for one's own domestic security as well as that of his neighbor, is grounded here, the home is apt to be a mushroom growth.

Such a course should cover the rights and duties of the marriage contract, based on a study of the *Encyclicals* on Marriage and Education. It should set up a philosophy of life which gives proper place in a scale of values, to the moral home virtues, to genuine and sacrificial love versus false romanticism, to the importance of intellectual, cultural, and social equality in marriage partners; to the inculcation of the hardy Christian virtues of self-control and self-discipline versus the soft creed of individualism; and to nonmaterial values in a standard of living. Finally, it should include some reference to the psychology of child development and to the relationship of parents to each other and to their children. The unifying force of religion will integrate these basic problems which make for success or failure in building a home. Flexner ridicules Yale for upsetting the whole university to establish an "Institute of Human Relations," and Vassar for its "Institute of Euthenics" made up of an "artificially pieced together of bits" from all departments to promote "the science of efficient living." [1] They are but two instances of the countless major attempts being made to check the tide of family disintegration. What the Catholic college needs primarily is an awakened sensitivity to the simple but genuinely effective program it can put in operation at will, with no interference in its scholastic standards.

The place of Home Economics on the college level is a more debatable issue. Such sequences as the dietetics or the art of costume design, if arranged in such a way as to insure their being taught as a science, or as an art, may find a legitimate place. But again, if they are debased to mere manual skills, their proper place is in the vocational school, not the liberal college. Experience has demonstrated that one who possesses a disciplined and cultured mind can acquire these mechanics in a short time without the necessity of repetitiously "learning" them over for a series of years on elementary, secondary, and higher levels of education.

Shields, in *The Philosophy of Education* discussing the ques-

[1] Abraham Flexner, *Universities, American English German*, Oxford Uni. Press, 1930, pp. 72, 112–117.

tion of preparation for family life, would make adequate provision for motherhood, but overlooks the responsibilities which fatherhood entails.[1] Unless both parents are aware of the difficulties they are facing, and are agreed on their methods of meeting them, the father can tear down in his hour around home what the mother has spent the day building up. Home tasks today are practically eliminated and careful study and planning are required to devise means for training the young in responsibility. All the rosy dreams of domestic security through the social sciences are due for a sad awakening unless the home of the future can reëstablish itself on bonds of religious, cultural, affectionate, and authoritative integrity. This is a far cry from the old industrial and economic ties of dependence, and a problem in which the school undoubtedly must share.

COEDUCATION

It is the theory of many educators that if young people are thrown together daily in school life, any training necessary for social adjustment will automatically take care of itself. This method, particularly in the adolescent age, is equivalent to bringing high explosives closely together and expecting them to fuse. The encyclical, *Christian Education of Youth*, sums up the Catholic view on coeducation in an authoritative statement. While economic considerations have permitted it to exist in this country, traditionally Catholic education has always been conducted on a basis of segregation, except for the elementary years and the graduate and professional schools. That men and women are fundamentally different is clearly stated by Jennings in his *Biological Basis of Human Nature*. In discussing the chromosomes as the carriers of all hereditary traits he says: "In the male, therefore, every cell of the body

[1] Thomas E. Shields, *Philosophy of Education*, Cath. Education Press, 1917, p. 283.

differs in chromosomes from every cell of the female body." [1]
With this as a basis, it is only reasonable to expect that
obvious anatomical and physiological differences will be reflected in psychological differences.   Just as boys do not
play like girls, work like girls, nor act like girls, so neither
do they feel and think like girls.   Adequate provision should
be made for this fact during their formative years with caution
exercised while their new-found emotions are in a volatile
and uncontrolled condition.   Rudolf Allers, an outstanding
Catholic psychologist, in his *Psychology of Character* emphatically supports this position:

> The careful investigations of K. Buhler show that the time-factor
> in the development of the two sexes is so different that coedu-
> cation is impracticable except in the period before school and the
> early school years.   Even if considerations of possible moral risk
> be ignored, the idea of complete coeducation throughout the whole
> period of youth is shown to be completely mistaken; but this by
> no means justifies the segregation of sexes.   A part of the prep-
> aration for the realities of life is social intercourse and collabora-
> tion between the two sexes.   People who to a large extent grow up
> isolated from persons of the opposite sex often learn only with
> difficulty to enter into relations with them when the occasion
> demands it.   Many marital and even occupational difficulties are
> attributable to this.[2]

In line with Allers' suggestion in the last part of this quotation, we believe that practically all of the advantages of coeducation in high school and college may be achieved by a well-
planned and well-conducted program of co-recreation free from
the distractions and the dangers of coeducation.   But this is
part of the school's leisure time problem.   We will discuss
co-recreation in a later section of this chapter, in Section 5,
"Leisure," p. 204.

[1] H. S. Jennings, *Biological Basis of Human Nature*, Norton, 1930, p. 40.
[2] Rudolf Allers, *Psychology of Character*, Sheed & Ward, 1931, p. 275.

4. ECONOMIC SECURITY

When a youth is confronted with the problem of leaving the home of his childhood to establish the home of his choice, he is face to face with another need which up to this time may not have been very real to him, the economic need. "Social infancy," the period of dependence on parents, is now over. Social maturity, the period of self-dependence, is at hand. One aspect of this maturity is the ability to provide for his own maintenance and, when he enters the family relation, for the maintenance of those dependent upon him. Before the industrial revolution this situation was simple compared with the constantly increasing complexity of modern life. The rapid strides made during the past fifty years in perfecting the agencies productive of material wealth (the factory system of manufacture in contrast with the old domestic system) have not been paralleled by a proportionate development in our system of distribution so that this wealth may be shared equitably by all willing to play their part in its production. Statistics released to the press by Hildegard Kneeland, in charge of a study made by the National Resources Committee, 1938, give a distribution of consumers' incomes upon which Table I is based: [1]

TABLE I.—CONSUMER INCOME CATEGORIES

LEVELS	DESCRIPTION OF FAMILIES	NUMBER OF FAMILIES
1. Top level	Families "living not only luxuriously but piling up fortunes."	800,000
2. Second level	Families "habitually able to afford luxuries."	1,585,000
3. Middle level	Families of the "comfortable middle class."	8,000,000
4. Fourth level	Families "fighting poverty."	11,000,000
5. Bottom level	Families "facing starvation."	8,000,000
	Total	29,385,000

[1] *Consumer Incomes in the United States*, National Resources Committee, United States Government Printing Office, Washington, 1938.

This report states further that 283,000 families (1 per cent of the population) have a gross income equal to the total annual earnings of the poorest 11,000,000 families (40 per cent of the population) and that 75 families at the top get more money than 1,200,000 families at the bottom. Such a condition of unequal distribution of wealth is certainly not conducive to peace and order. This is not what we mean by a "commonwealth." Rather, here is a "commonpoverty" shared in by 19,000,000 families out of a total of 29,000,000, or more than 65 per cent. If these statistics have any foundation in fact the situation is indeed serious.

Here is another part of the picture. During the fall of 1937 the writer, while residing in Portland, Oregon, returned every day from his teaching assignment by a route that took him past the gate leading to a large lumber mill. Stationed at this gate during several months was a squad of forty or fifty policemen. Every morning these policemen brought to work the men employed in the mill; they remained there all day and in the late afternoon escorted the workers back to their homes, while across the street in front of the gate, particularly when the men were leaving, was a motley crowd of men, women, and children, jeering at the workers and threatening violence. Here was a state of industrial war not industrial peace, and the war was not between capital and labor but between two rival unions fighting out a jurisdictional dispute.

When we ask the question "What is the economic order for?" there can be only one answer. Any economic order whether capitalism, communism, or any other, when rationally interpreted has only one primary purpose and that purpose is *to provide a decent livelihood for all*. Communism, the economic order in Russia, claims that it will provide a decent livelihood for everyone better than capitalism has ever done in any country. To what extent it will make good this claim, history alone will tell, but there is no doubt that capitalism as the economic system of the United States has been a miserable failure when measured in terms of this purpose. If 19,000,000 families are "fighting poverty" or "facing starvation" government relief is not a charity; it is a necessity. Men will steal before they will starve, and if economic security cannot be brought to the great mass through the economic order as it functions in any country, then there will be no security either of person or property, for those responsible for this failure.

Statistical studies of the social situation give us a vivid picture of this failure in the United States during the decade now closed. But no study limited to investigating the state of society will disclose the remedies that must be applied if the economy order within which we are living is to be reconstructed so that a decent livelihood for all willing to carry their share of the burden involved, will be secure. Rather, we must study the nature of man. We must face the fact of the driving forces within man and we must build an economic order in which these forces will find an outlet, expressing themselves along lines that will make for human comfort and human happiness.

In Chapter IV, "The Motivation of Human Behavior," Section 2, "The Dominant Human Drives," discarding the elaborate classifications of "instincts" proposed by some psychologists, we adopted as our analysis the threefold classification of these driving forces that has always characterized the Christian interpretation of life, the drives for (1) possessions, (2) pleasure, (3) power. Here are the three centers around which man's life revolves in his efforts to achieve for himself and his dependants the satisfactions which make life worth living. If they are universal in life, they must be important in man's economic life also. A brief analysis of this situation will reveal that two of them are of paramount importance.

We may reject the theory of the economic determinists "that

in every historical epoch the prevailing mode of economic production and exchange, and the social organization necessarily following from it, form the basis upon which is built up, and from which alone can be explained, the political and intellectual history of that epoch." [1] Human living is too complicated to be explained in all its ramifications by any such simple formula. Motivation of human behavior arising from love, loyalty, patriotism, and intellectual interests of a thousand varieties, often to the sacrifice of economic interests, is a very real fact in the life of man. Man is not merely an animal. He is a rational animal and this means a *spiritual* animal. A crude materialistic theory can never explain his behavior in striving for the finer things of life. These are spiritual and it is these which build a cultural civilization based on the search for truth, the love of beauty, and lives of virtue. "Not in bread alone doth man live." [2] Nevertheless, we must face the fact that man cannot live without bread. In this connection "bread" means not merely food but clothing and shelter also, the necessities for bare subsistence. These the economic order must furnish to all if it is to have any stability. But more than this, in the financial organization of society today the fulfillment of the drive for possessing worldly wealth determines to a great extent the degree to which any individual can satisfy the basic drives for pleasure and power. This is so potent a fact that it explains why economic determinists have universalized the economic motive in their explanation of human behavior. The drive for pleasure finds its expression for the most part in satisfying three of the universal human needs, health, family life, and leisure. The drive for power finds expression in these three needs: (1) education as preparation for a life of

[1] Max Eastman (editor), *The Communistic Manifesto and Other Writings*, The Modern Library, New York, 1932, Preface to the Communist Manifesto by Friederick Engels in "Capital," p. 318.

[2] Mat. IV, 4.

power; (2) civic life, the ordinary field for its expression; and (3) religious life, man's search for God, who, for the believer, is the source of all power. But it is through the economic life itself that power passes into the hands of those who control the material wealth in any community. "Who pays the piper, calls the tune," is more true today than it was in the simple civilization in which it found expression in this proverb.

When we apply this analysis to the economic order one fact stands out with startling clearness and it is this: no economic order has the slightest chance of stability and permanence unless it offers to the great generality of men opportunity for satisfying these two drives, (1) the drive for possessions and (2) the drive for power. This latter means an opportunity to play a part in controlling the circumstances which condition the production and distribution of wealth. There is no other basis which gives any hope of industrial peace. Capitalists have been slow to recognize this fact but it seems to be dawning upon the more intelligent leaders of industry today. This analysis takes us far beyond the right to a living wage. That battle in the realm of theory seems to be won. Now the next advance is to recognize that if industrial peace is to be ours, these two principles must be its basis: first, employees must *share in the ownership* of the means of production and second, they must *participate in the management*. This is not revolutionary economics. Rather, it is sound psychology and good common sense. But it is more than that. It is social justice and Christian charity. It is the doctrine of Pius XI in his encyclical *Reconstructing the Social Order (Quadragesimo Anno)*. In this letter to the world he says:

We deem it advisable that the wage-contract should, when possible, be modified somewhat by a contract of partnership, as is already being tried in various ways to the no small gain both of the wage-earners and of the employers. In this way wage-earners are made sharers in some sort in the *ownership*, or the *management*, or the profits.

As philosophers analyzing the economic problem for the purpose of determining what the school can do as an aid towards its solution, it is not our part to invent or to evaluate the various devices now being tried out to give employees a share in the ownership and participation in the management of business enterprises. That is the part of experts in the field of practical business procedure. They should give guidance to both employers and employees in order that this problem may be worked out to the satisfaction of all concerned including the consumer. It is encouraging, however, to see the many procedures now in operation which have as their purpose the achievement of one or both of these aims. Here are some devices for sharing ownership and profits: stock-ownership, sharing the profits with or without a sharing of the losses; bonuses in times of increased profits, labor-shares and wage dividends based on employee's annual wage, etc. According to Joseph F. Thorning writing in the *Commonweal*, the Jantzen Knitting Mills of Portland, Oregon, will give workers "a dividend or share in the profits in proportion to the amount of their annual wage. In many instances this will add $500 each year to the laborer's income." [1] The same article reports that the Eastman Kodak Company of Rochester, New York, on November 11, 1936 declared "a wage dividend of $2,200,000 over and above an extra stock dividend for the stockholders aggregating $1,688,000. The wage dividend is $1,000,000 larger than that paid out in 1936 and was payable on March 1, 1937 to each employee who had completed five years of service in the company. The share for each worker was to be com-

---

[1] Joseph F. Thorning, "Share the Profits," *Commonweal*, July 16, 1937, p. 301.

puted on the basis of his average wage per week during the five year period." In the matter of participation in the management there are many devices and "plans:" union-management cooperation, shop-committees, works-councils, employee representation, etc. Carroll Daugherty lists five types of employee representative plans: (1) The Colorado Plan, (2) The Mitten Plan, (3) The Proctor and Gamble Plan, (4) The Filene Plan and (5) The Goodyear Plan.[1] Organized labor has not favored the extension of these, since they tend to take on the nature of company unions. In so far as they do this, it is claimed, they cease to be democratic and labor enjoys only the show of participating in the management with the substance denied by the domination of the owners over labor's "representatives."

COLLECTIVE BARGAINING AND THE DRIVES

In all the struggles which have been going on between labor and capital during the past several decades, the big bone of contention has been the right of labor to collective bargaining. With the growth of unionism and a change to a sympathetic and intelligent attitude on the part of the public we may say that labor has won this battle. The Wagner Labor Relations Act is concrete evidence of this gain for labor. Labor is now in danger of losing the ground already won through self-centered and unintelligent leadership which precipitates factional disputes alienating the sympathy and good will of the general public. A striking example of what can be accomplished by strong and intelligent leadership is the case of the International Ladies Garment Workers Union. As reported in *Life*, August 1, 1938, this union of 250,000 men and women, now free from graft, racketeering, and communist control, has made the following advances:

[1] Carroll Daugherty, *Labor Problems in American Industry*, Houghton Mifflin, 1933, pp. 787–791.

1. It has brought about a reduction in hours per week from a working day of 16 hours, 90 hours a week, to a working week of 35 hours.
2. It has increased pay from salaries ranging from $2 to $8 a week to $15 to $35 a week.
3. It conducts an educational program on the history and present problems of labor.
4. It conducts a social program, including a $1,000,000 Unity House two hours from New York where members may spend their vacations at low cost.
5. It functions through an Arbitration Board impartially chosen by the union and employers which settles all disputes.

And these benefits are shared by all members of the union at a cost of $0.35 a week for a worker receiving a weekly wage of $17.00. Others pay dues proportionately. This gives the union an annual budget of $5,000,000. When we analyse these gains of collective bargaining as effected by this union in terms of the three "drives," we see that all three receive recognition. Even the drive for pleasure is included. The social program of the union has made provision for a healthy and wholesome use of leisure time. In this case there is no provision as yet for sharing the ownership of the producing agency. There has, however, been affected a sharing of the profits through greatly increased wages. In the case of the third drive, the drive for power, this union through the Arbitration Board now plays a real part in the management of the industry. Abuses are corrected; recommendations for the betterment of working conditions are made and acted upon; and the rank and file of workers have real reason to believe that they have a voice in determining policies.

As the industrial revolution carried us further and further away from the guild system of the Middle Ages, where the master workman ruled over his own shop and the more capable among the workmen themselves, as apprentices or journeymen, looked forward to the day when they too would be "masters," the new economic order which came into being denied to the great mass of workers any opportunity for the expression of the basic urges which are part of the nature of every human being. Today a new approach to this problem is being made through the organization of Coöperatives.

THE COÖPERATIVE MOVEMENT

The coöperative movement is a striking illustration of the practical application of these two basic principles in working towards industrial democracy. It embraces three types of coöperative enterprises: (1) consumers' coöperatives (2) producers' coöperatives, and (3) credit coöperatives, but it is the first which has undergone the greatest development, particularly in England, the original home of the idea.

Its first great advocate was the utopian Robert Owen, and the first group to apply his principles with favorable results were the now famous flannel weavers of Rochdale. In 1844, financially broken after a lost strike, they subscribed small sums toward the co-operative purchase of foot necessities and gradually saved enough capital to open a regular store. Other capital was made available through other wage-earning consumers who bought one or more shares of stock at the low par value of five dollars. As the sales expanded, profits were made because of the margin of retail sales prices over wholesale purchase prices. A fixed rate of five per cent was always paid on stock before any further distribution of profits. If there was a surplus, it was divided among purchasers rather than among stockholders according to the total value of their purchases in any given quarter year. All sales were strictly cash and the prices were those of the market; that is, no credit accounts were permitted and no effort was made to sell at cut prices. The managers were elected by the stockholder members from among their own number. Democratic control was secured by the provision that, unlike the practice in corporations, every stockholder had only one vote, no matter how many shares he owned. In other words, it was one vote per man instead of one vote for every share. New members were always encouraged to join by wide publicity and propaganda. Their participation was made easy by allowing stock purchase to begin with an initial payment of twenty-five cents "down" and the balance taken out of shares of profits.

The details of the Rochdale plan are important here because they show the *basic principles which must be followed* if any venture wishes to succeed on a truly co-operative basis. There can be no doubt of the Rochdale success. Within two decades there were co-operatives all over Great Britian and Ireland.[1]

In the United States most of the consumer coöperatives are in the Middle West with Minnesota in the lead. As reported in the Bureau of Labor Statistics, the membership of the movement is given as about 500,000, capital investment as about $20,000,000, and total volume of business as about $200,000,000.[2] A national agency has been formed, the Coöperative League of America, annual conferences are held and information is disseminated.

In producer coöperatives the workers themselves own and operate the plant. But this type of coöperative has received little development because of the inherent difficulties of the problems they create. For efficient production more capital is required than workers themselves can ordinarily supply, and managerial competence is not always available among the members of a unit. The development in the United States of the third type of coöperatives, credit coöperatives, has been almost spectacular. These societies are organized for making small loans to members. The funds of the association are provided from low membership fees, and, after adequate reserves are made, dividends are paid on shares of stock. The

[1] *Ibid.*, pp. 661–662.
[2] *Consumers' Credit and Productive Cooperative Societies*, Bureau of Labor Statistics, Bulletin No. 351, Washington, 1931.

Rochdale principle of one vote per member is almost always preserved. At the end of 1929, 974 Credit Unions had been established in the United States, there were almost 300,000 members and the total volume of loans was almost $60,000,000.[1] The extension of coöperatives throughout the United States will probably be a slow process. The American temperament nourished throughout our history on the doctrine of individualism is opposed to its basic principle that the individual finds the fullest expression of his personality in loyalty to a group enterprise. But it is of significance that coöperatives conducted on the Rochdale principle are truly democratic and that they provide for expression of the dominant drives, possession and power, for all members, through *sharing the ownership* and *participating in the management*. Not until our "captains of industry" recognize the necessity of doing this and work out a practical plan for putting this principle into practice, can there be any basis for an economic order that holds promise of peace and stability. (For an analysis of "Rights and Duties" in Economic Society see Figure 14, p. 176.)

THE SCHOOL'S PART

When we inquire what the school concerned with general and not vocational education, can do to help promote economic security, we see that its first obligation is instruction in this phase of the social problem. The curriculum of schools on all levels, elementary, secondary, and collegiate, is giving a greater place to the social studies. Some high-school administrators are making social studies the one constant that all pupils must take in all four years of high school. The Minnesota State Department of Education has recently issued a syllabus to meet this situation. We doubt that the multiplication of new courses under high-sounding names will do much

[1] *Ibid.*, pp. 6 and 55.

to deepen pupils' understanding of the difficulties of the social problem. There is one thing, however, that should be done and it lies in the field of history. Too long has history been taught with a military emphasis, stressing wars and glorifying military heroes. History should be the story of man's social life in all its phases, domestic, economic, civic, and cultural. The problems with which we are confronted today are the same problems which have always confronted man, but a discussion of the modern version of these problems will vitalize the life story of peoples who have been confronted by them in times past. Thus, government relief through made work is certainly an improvement over the "bread and circus" of the decaying Roman empire.

Some schools are conducting programs aimed at developing habits of thrift. Bank days are set up and each pupil is expected to make a deposit, no matter how small, so that he may have the experience of saving for a purpose. Budgeting is taught as a primary principle of household economy with the thought that this practice will be carried back and introduced into the parental home of the child as well as carried forward to the day when he will establish his own home.

But it is in the matter of developing attitudes that the school, at least the Catholic school, can do its best work. The great encyclicals of the present Holy Father and Leo XIII are available as teaching materials. Here the principles of social justice and Christian charity are exposed with a force and clarity seldom met with in the writings of the scientific economists. Yet these principles, such as the right to a living wage and the duty of giving an honest day's work for wages received, are basic to any science of economics that gives any hope of reconstructing the social order in such a way as to bring economic security to all. Some years ago the writer was teaching in a college which planned to have its economics department accredited by a state university as giving adequate preparation for graduate work in economics. An instructor from the state university in the course of his visit to the college spent some time in a class called "Distributive Justice" in which Fr. John A. Ryan's book by that title was used as text. Afterwards the visitor expressed admiration for the teaching he saw in the class but with regard to the content he said: "That is good ethics but it is not economics." For the Catholic institution all the social sciences are ethical sciences since their basic principles come from the latter field. Here is no "dismal science" but one which carries hope for the betterment of man's life on earth.

Undoubtedly the outstanding illustrations of how the school can contribute to the betterment of the economic life of a people is the case of St. Francis Xavier University in Antigonish, Nova Scotia, Canada. Here at the instigation of Father James J. Tompkins and under the leadership of Father Moses Coady, the Rector, the university branched out into the field of adult education. Hundreds of local study groups were formed among the farmers, miners and fishermen under the directions of the University Extension Department. The subject studied was coöperatives. As a result today there are 142 flourishing credit unions laying the foundations of a true coöperative banking structure, 42 coöperative stores, and more than 50 coöperative lobster- and fish-processing plants and sawmills. But more was accomplished than this. Coöperation was preached and put into practice not as a mere economic movement but as an application of Christianity to presentday problems. The result has been a spiritual and cultural regeneration. Church attendance increased in proportion as the coöperative organizations multiplied. As Bertram F. Fowler puts it writing in the *Commonweal:* "They have learned what few in the world have learned today, namely, to unify the whole process of living, applying to the whole seven days of the week—to the business of obtaining

bread and shelter, to the handling of their fish and farm products, to the making of homes and happiness—but one rule of
life, that men should live like brothers and help each other mu-
tually instead of destroying each other." [1] Here is true Christianity in action. As a result of this regeneration, the Communist party which had been making gains in Cape Breton "has
today shrunk into insignificant proportions." [2]

But man cannot work all of his waking hours. Today we
recognize that leisure is not a luxury. It is a universal need and
therefore one of the rights of man. We will now consider this
need and the school's part in meeting it.

5. LEISURE—THE LEISURE TIME AGENCIES

Leisure, as we intimated in the foregoing section, has possibilities of becoming a Frankenstein, possibilities which grow
more threatening every day. The problem of how to obtain
leisure has been nearly five thousand years in the solving.
Among the Greeks and Romans the vast majority of the people
were slaves. During the Middle Ages they were serfs. Today
all men are free, not only in the sense of enjoying political freedom, but in that larger sense, free to order as they will, much of
their own time. The great social changes which affected the
home so vitally have also brought about a new distribution of
the classes. Throughout the older civilizations and until the
modern period was well begun, society was made up of a
leisure class and a labor class. This inequality was one of the
causes of the political revolutions of the Eighteenth Century which, theoretically at least, ended that situation. No
longer was the leisure class to be supported by the drudgery of
the workers. In the democratic ideal every man has the obli-

---

[1] Bertram F. Fowler, "Cooperation as a Technique," *Commonweal*, August 19,
1938, p. 423.
[2] *Ibid.*, p. 423.

gation to work, to be a self-supporting member of the society to which he belongs.   But he has also the right to leisure, through the judicious management of his own time.

This hard-won prize would have proved futile had not another great social change taken place.   The scientific discoveries which brought on the industrial revolution have given man an opportunity to use his right with constantly increasing degrees of satisfaction.   At first, however, the new inventions set up new barriers which had to be destroyed.   Pure science was teaching man, largely by the use of steam and electricity, how to control the forces of nature.   Applied science, making use of this new-found control, was giving him labor-saving machinery which brought on the factory system.   This meant long hours of monotonous labor not only for men, but for women and children as well.   In the beginning the laborer did not know how to fight this new tyrant, and there were years when miners never saw the sunlight and children never learned to play.   Gradually leaders began to demand social legislation, shorter hours, and better working conditions.   Sixteen-hour days were not unheard of, and it is not so many years ago that a group of laborers in Boston were striking for a twelve hour day.   With the perfection of machinery however, production has been speeded up beyond maximum consumption until now the six-hour day and the five-day week are realities and there is reasonable assurance of further reduction of working hours in the immediate future.   The addition of the great masses of unemployed to the leisure situation increases the importance of this problem.

It is not only the industrial world but also the home which has been revolutionized by scientific improvements.   Electric lights, refrigerators, ranges, vacuum cleaners, washing machines, mangles, irons, oil and gas heaters have reduced housework to a minimum.   Canned goods and delicatessen shops provide better meals than many a housewife can prepare.   Department stores, telephones, and motor transportation eliminate still more tasks, until many homes, too, have achieved a maximum six-hour working day. We have already noted the disastrous effect on children. In the pioneer home "chores" were a real part of the education of youth, developing a sense of responsibility and cultivating a familiarity with home management. Only a generation ago, in the writer's own boyhood as a city-dweller, there were many after-school tasks to be performed. In the fall, there was wood to be chopped and stored for the winter. In the winter there was the wood box to be kept filled. And in the spring there was the garden to be spaded, planted, and hoed. With the urbanization of our population and the increase of labor-saving devices in the home this source of real training has almost totally disappeared and artificial devices must be set up to occupy the extensive leisure of youth in a worthy manner. And so it is that the big problem had become, not how to get leisure, but what to do with it.

The fact that the industrial revolution was not an unmixed blessing becomes evident when one observes how man is spending his abundant free time. The recent flood of publications on the market bearing such titles as, "The Threat of Leisure," "The Curse of Leisure"; the organization and activity of the National Recreation Association; the movement for organized play-centers all attest that society is aware of the grave new danger menacing it, and is trying to do something about it. Viscount Grey has said that America is a pleasure-seeking but not a pleasure-finding nation. The fact is accounted for by Nash in this statement:

> This machine age has already supplied as unexampled wealth of leisure and what happens? The average man who has time on his hands turns out to be a spectator, a watcher of somebody else, merely because that is the easiest thing. He becomes a victim of spectatoritis—a blanket description to cover all kinds of passive

amusement. . . . He is willing to sit back and have his leisure time pursuits slapped onto him like mustard plasters,—external, temporary, and in the end, "dust in the mouth."[1]

Man has almost lost the art of entertaining himself, and commercialized recreation is more of a drain on the nervous system than a relaxation. Moving pictures, radios, theatres, stadiums, and automobiles, which supply the bulk of American amusement, dissipate energy, overtax incomes, and offer little, if any, adequate compensation. The result justifies Nash's remark, "The mechanical age has handed leisure to us upon a silver platter. Now we are wondering if we dare accept it."[2] That the school has a major responsibility with reference to this problem is evident.

THE SCHOOL'S PART

In facing the problem of the enrichment of leisure time, the school meets the same difficulty it encounters in adjusting the curriculum. There must be provision for individual differences. Boys and girls have as varied capacities for enjoyment as they have for intellectual achievement. The one guiding principle of *active participation* rather than passive observation must be kept in mind in all recommendations. In the field of sports and athletics, which will take care of one large group, there must be less concentration on interscholastic competition and more on intramural activities, especially such sports as will carry over into adult life. Physicians and psychiatrists are urging every individual to find a hobby for leisure moments which will offer some outlet to pent-up creative impulses. An interesting hobby gives to the tired mind what rest and sleep give to the tired body. The various school clubs and co-curricular organizations have splendid opportunity to engage

[1] Jay B. Nash, *Spectatoritis*, Sears Publishing Co., 1932, p. 5.
[2] *Ibid.*, p. 9.

youthful interests in this field and to provide the necessary guidance, particularly on the high school level.

These activities, while part of school life, might be taken care of in recreation centers and elsewhere, but there is one distinct and valuable obligation to the leisure problem which the school must fulfill. That is to stimulate an interest in reading and the fine arts. If the social inheritance of mankind is going to be adequately assimilated and transmitted, there must be wider reading than will be done in the mere fulfillment of assigned lessons. An introduction to the five fields of knowledge (Chapter IX, Section 3, p. 298) which compose the curriculum is about all the school can guarantee. But it can open up avenues of interest over which the real student will travel with understanding and delight for the rest of his life. Little leisure-time reading will be done, however, unless there has been an attractive presentation to awaken interest in the backgrounds of society. The fine arts, even on the level of appreciation, have been woefully neglected, but there is indication now that they are rapidly rising to their place of merit on all levels of education. Here too, participation, rather than observation, will be the clue to real interest.

CO-RECREATION

In rejecting the claims of coeducation for promoting wholesome intercourse between the sexes and thus advancing the probability of subsequent successful family life, we advocated in its place co-recreation. We present here the considerations which lead us to conclude that shared leisure-time activities will achieve most of the benefits that coeducation hopes for, and discourage most of its evils. The principle argument advanced for coeducation is that since men and women are going to live together in adult life, they must learn to know each other by living together during the school day. But it is just that claim that we wish to investigate. Which part of adult life do men and women spend together? Is it their work time or their play time?

The benefits of co-recreation arise out of what we may call the social function of men and women. So long as men continue to beget children and women continue to bear them, just so long must we recognize that with respect to the basic social institution, the family, their functions are complementary, not identical. The industrial order of the presentday society has only helped to accentuate this fact. Today the builder of the home, the mother, remains within it to do her work, whereas the provider therefor, the father, leaves the home to go to his work whether it be in a factory or on the farm, in the business or in the professional world. And what part of their time is it these two, husband and wife, mother and father spend together? It is *their leisure time, i.e.,* their play time. The common table, the evening together with the children, excursions in the great outdoors together in summer and winter, reading the same books, enjoying the same entertainments at the theatre and the concert, a common taste in all these things, next to an enduring mutual love and a common religion, is without doubt the surest foundation upon which to build a wholesome and happy home life for themselves and for their children.

The school that is awake to its opportunities as well as to its obligations must take its cue from this life situation. Complete segregation of adolescents during the later high school and college years, when these young people are drawn so powerfully to share each other's company, is an artificial barrier bound to have harmful effects even if it could be strictly maintained. By all means keep them apart during their work time so that they will not be a distraction to each other, but during their leisure time co-recreation offers the opportunity whereby they may learn to live with each other by the only method that anyone can learn any activity, namely, by practising that activity. Co-recreation offers opportunity for this practice through common participation in all those activities that are not strictly curricular.   These activities include, of course dances and other social parties initiated by the various student organizations of institutions sponsoring programs of co-recreation.   But it means more than this.   Dramatics offer a great opportunity for putting into operation a program of co-recreation that not only realizes distinct educational values but also provides wholesome entertainment for those participating, whether they be in the audience or in the cast on the stage.   Some schools have extended this type of activity to include debating.   Not that girls and boys compete against each other.   Rather, teams are made up of students from both schools and debates are presented at the convocations before the two student bodies.

At first sight athletics offers meager opportunities for extending this program.   But even in athletics many opportunities present themselves.   The students of girls' high schools and women's colleges become ardent supporters of the boys' high schools and men's colleges at athletic contests, admitted on student tickets and sitting in the student section of the bleachers. Since the institutions for girls and women in general do not engage in intercollegiate competition in athletics, the students of boys and men's institutions cannot reciprocate in this matter. But certain of the minor sports offer opportunity for common participation by students from both institutions, notably tennis in mixed doubles, and golf in mixed foursomes.   Winter sports offer the greatest variety of occasions for common participation in outdoor sports.   Skating, skiing, and tobogganing are activities the pleasure of which is greatly heightened by participation in mixed groups.   Hiking is another activity of this type with the additional advantage that it is a delightful sport for all three seasons of the school year, fall, winter, and spring.

No one questions that all work and no play makes Jack a dull boy. The same may be said for Jill. Jack and Jill did not make much of a job of it when they set out to fetch that pail of water, but if it had been a game of tennis they had embarked on we have reason to believe a more pleasant outcome would have resulted. Herein is the principle of co-recreation. Man's work in the world is different from the work of woman. Let the school take its cue from this. School time is the work time of youth. In school let young women prepare themselves for their work in the world in an environment adapted to their nature and needs, *i.e.*, a school conducted by women. Let young men prepare themselves for their work in the world in the same type of environment, a school conducted by men. But in school, as in the world when building a home together, let them share their leisure time together under sympathetic guidance, of course, for they are still youths and maidens, not mature men and women. Such a policy whole-heartedly entered into and extended throughout the whole group of co-curricular activities is what we mean by a program of co-recreation. As an offset to the only too common practice of mixed marriages, it is perhaps the most efficacious means the school can use in playing its part in the upbuilding of Catholic family life.

6. CIVIC SECURITY—THE STATE

One circumstance that conditions the satisfaction of the universal human needs already treated, education, health, and home, leisure and the possession of material wealth ordinarily derived from labor, is freedom and protection in the use of those things which make the satisfaction of these needs possible. If we add religious freedom (to be treated in the following section, 7. "Divine Security") to these five needs we have an analysis of the "inalienable rights" named in the Declaration of Independence as "life, liberty, and the pursuit of happiness." The same paragraph of this famous document continues, "to secure these rights, governments are instituted among men." Here is a seventh need, security as a citizen in the exercise of these rights; hence our label for this need, "Civic Security."

For Aristotle there were only three types of government, monarchy, the rule of one, oligarchy, the rule of a few, and democracy, the rule of the people, that is, the many. History presents us with the tragic failures of all three forms. Today in Europe democracy has degenerated into dictatorship under the name "National Socialism." This label is used in Germany alone by Nazism, but it is equally apt for Communism in Russia and Fascism in Italy, since all three make the state supreme over the individual. For a century and a half in this country democracy has achieved notable results in securing man's inalienable rights for all law-abiding citizens. Can it continue to function as effectively in the new era we are now entering?

THE AMERICAN THEORY OF GOVERNMENT

What are the dominant ideas in the American theory of government that account for its outstanding success and hold promise of continued success if these ideas continue to function in governmental procedures? They are two, and both are definitely stated in the second paragraph of the Declaration of Independence:

> We hold these truths to be self-evident, that all men are created equal, that they are endowed by their Creator with certain inalienable Rights, that among these are Life, Liberty, and the pursuit of Happiness. That to secure these rights, Governments are instituted among Men, deriving their just powers from the consent of the governed.

These ten words "All men are endowed by their Creator with inalienable rights" are the charter of American liberty. The concept of "inalienable rights" was not new in political theory. It had been stated definitely by Bellarmine and Suarez as arising out of the concept "natural law" and has always been a part of the ethical principles of Scholastic philosophy. How did it come to be included in the Declaration of Independence? The two treatises on government which were popular in the colonies were Algernon Sidney's *Discourses Concerning Government* 1698, and John Locke's *Two Treatises on Government,* 1690. Both were written to refute a book by Robert Filmer, the private theologian of James I, called *Patriarcha* which was a defense of the Divine Right of Kings. This book was written for the expressed purpose of refuting Cardinal Bellarmine's political theories on popular sovereignty. As quoted in John C. Rager's *Democracy and Bellarmine,* pp. 134–135, the opening sentence of the book reads:

> Since the time that School-Divinity began to flourish there hath been a common opinion maintained, as well by Divines, as by divers other Learned Men, which affirms:
> 'Mankind is naturally endowed and born with Freedom from all Subjection, and at liberty to choose what Form of Government it please: And that the Power which any one man hath over others, was at first bestowed according to the discretion of the Multitude.'
> *This tenet was first hatched in the schools and hath been fostered by all succeeding papists for good divinity.*

On the fourth page of *Patriarcha* we read:

> To make evident the Grounds of this Question, about the Natural Liberty of Mankind, I will lay down some passages of Cardinal Bellarmine, that may best unfold the State of this controversie. Secular or Civil Power (saith he) is instituted by men; It is in the people, unless they bestow it on a Prince. This Power is immediately in the whole Multitude, as in the subject of it; for this Power is in Divine Law, but the Divine Law hath given this power to no particular man. If the Positive Law be taken away, there is left

no Reason why amongst a Multitude (who are Equal) one rather than another should bear Rule over the Rest. Power is given by the multitude to one man, or to more, by the same Law of Nature; for the Commonwealth cannot exercise this Power, therefore it is bound to bestow it upon some One man or some Few. It depends upon the Consent of the multitude to ordain over themselves a King, Counsel, or other Magistrates; and if there be a lawful cause the multitude may change the Kingdom into an Aristocracy or Democracy. Thus far Bellarmine; in which passages are comprised the strength of all that I have read or heard produced for the Natural Liberty of the Subject.

Sylvester J. McNamara in *American Democracy and Catholic Doctrine* says:

> Jefferson's own copy of Filmer's *Patriarcha* still exists in the Library of Congress. Jefferson, therefore, must have read this epitome of Bellarmine as given by Filmer. The word *"must"* has been used, we think, justifiably, because it was undoubtedly the attacks made on Filmer by Locke and Sidney, Jefferson's two favorite authors, that caused Jefferson to get and read a copy of Filmer's controversy with Bellarmine. . . .
> It is generally admitted by Jefferson's biographers that he read everything he heard of and could find written on political philosophy (pp. 117–119).

This concept of "inalienable rights" written by Jefferson into the Declaration of Independence is the fundamental idea in American government. Following the Revolution the Constitution was written as an instrument of government to safeguard the citizens of the new republic in the exercise of these rights, and they were specified in detail in the first ten amendments to the constitution commonly called the "Bill of Rights."

The second idea which forms the basis of the American theory of democratic government is the concept of civic duty. True enough the word "duty" does not occur in the ten words we have quoted above as the charter of American liberties. But the idea is there by implication. With these rights endowed upon man *"by his Creator"* an entirely new aspect is given to the picture. If man is a creature of God his nature comes from God. Everything he is or possesses has its origin in God. Man is God's property. He gave man life and, in constituting his nature, gave him the means to live that life in a way that would lead to his own happiness. So to live is an obligation that no man can escape. It is the very meaning of the natural law. In this concept "duty" enters in as a basic fact in the life of man. The Declaration of Independence makes it a basic fact in the theory and practice of government.

Any proper interpretation of these two concepts "right" and "duty" reveals at once that they are correlative terms. This means one cannot be understood without the other. Simply defined, a right is a *moral power to do or to refrain from doing something*, a power which others must respect. A duty is a *moral obligation to do or to refrain from doing something* in favor of others. If a citizen has the right to "life, liberty, and the pursuit of happiness," all other members of society have the duty to do nothing that would prevent the individual from exercising this right. Here then are the two ideas upon which the American theory of government is founded—individual rights and social duties. We hear much today of individual rights. What is needed is to develop an understanding of social duty and have it accepted in a way that will make it operative in the lives of citizens in their dealings with one another. This alone is what will make it possible for the democratic theory to function effectively in practical politics.

So conceived, democracy in this country is an attempt to institutionalize the Christian concept of man. In China possibly one day a Chinese Republic may institutionalize the political implications of Confucianism. But it is Christianity that brought to a pagan world the inherent dignity of man as a rational being with consequent inalienable rights, the right to all things necessary as means to obtain his end as a rational animal. But man by nature is also a social animal "And the Lord said: It is not good for man to be alone." [1] To the concept "respect for the individual" therefore, must be added "regard for the group." On these two foundation stones the American theory says that democracy must be built.

When it came to formulating an instrument of government that would put these two principles into operation in a practical way, the outcome was the Constitution, with the separation of the three governmental functions, legislative, judicial, and executive in three distinct departments, Congress, the Courts, and the President. This may be but a series of compromises between the advocates of a highly centralized government on the one hand, and those fearing such centralization on the other. Yet Gladstone pronounced the Constitution "the greatest work ever struck off by the hand and brain of man." And it has worked for a century and a half. What made this possible?

MAJORITY RULE AND MINORITY RIGHTS

Democracy worked through the employment of one simple device of practical politics, majority rule. But notice we speak of this procedure of practical politics as a "device." It is not a principle from which power flows. All power is from God. The people in a democracy determine through this device who is to exercise power and within what limitations. Here is precisely the error of the dictatorships which are now annihilating the concept of true democracy. This error stems from Rousseau's theory of social contract. John Herman Randall says:

Rousseau's deification of the majority in practice has led to the abandonment of any conception of natural rights for the individ-

[1] Genesis II, 18.

ual which cannot be infringed; it is the very antithesis of the theory of Locke, admirably expressed in John Adams, that the majority is as much to be feared as any monarch. It gives supreme power to a popular government to do what it wishes, where the English theory had tried to prevent government from doing much. . . . Where Locke's natural rights justified constitutional restrictions on government, Rousseau's popular sovereignty supported an actual revolution that would establish the rule of the majority.[1]

The principle of majority rule received philosophical justification in the writings of Hegel. The Divine Right of Kings had been discarded with the development of democracy but Hegel brought forth a new "divine right" when he identified the state with God. "The state incarnates the divine idea upon earth." are his words and all forms of National Socialism rest upon this theory. The state is God. As quoted by Joseph Leighton, Mussolini in his book *The Doctrine of Fascism* (Firenze, 1935) expounds this theory in these words: "For Fascism the State is absolute, individuals and groups relative." [2] He has expressly declared: "The state creates rights." [3] The state speaks through the majority; therefore, the majority creates rights. In this theory natural rights of the individual human being disappear. A device of practical politics, majority rule, becomes a political doctrine. If civic security is to be a reality the only defense against this interpretation of democracy is the principle, majority rule *with minority rights*. With this principle in operation there is some basis for the hope that democracy will rest on its two foundation stones which alone can make it function as a stable government, (1) respect for individual rights on the one hand, and (2) regard for social duties on the other. (For an

[1] John Herman Randall, *The Making of the Modern Mind*, Houghton Mifflin, 1926, pp. 354–355.

[2] Joseph A. Leighton, *Social Philosophies in Conflict*, Appleton-Century, 1937, p. 16.

[3] *American Mercury*, November, 1936.

analysis of "Rights and Duties" in Civil Society see Figure 14, p. 177.)

THE SCHOOL'S PART

What is the contribution that the school can make towards rendering civic security, so interpreted, a reality? Henry Suzzallo speaking of the state says:

> It seems not to be able to develop a training system within its own domain through which the beginners in politics will gradually become better, more wholesome, and serviceable leaders.[1]

The totalitarian states of Europe today are cognizant of this fact. Therefore their first endeavor is to control the schools so that the new generation will issue from them imbued with their ideology. So too in this country if the American dream of a democratic state guaranteeing to all citizens their God-given rights is to be realized, we must give attention to the schools. The first obligation of the schools is instruction. The concepts, natural rights and social duties, can be communicated to pupils by direct instruction. How necessary it is that this be done is made clear by McNamara in his book already quoted. He quotes a passage from a textbook, which, he says: "is used in one of the largest public school systems in the United States." At the outset the passage is an attack on property but it extends the same argument to "personal liberty." Thus, it is an attack on the doctrine of natural rights as stated in the Declaration of Independence. Here is the passage in full:

> The right of private property is so fundamental in our modern civilization that we hardly think of it as resting on the will or consent of society, maintained only by the constant vigilance on the part of society, and subject even now to slow and gradual modification. Still less, perhaps, has it ever appeared to most of us as

[1] Henry Suzzallo, *Our Faith in Education*, Lippincott, 1924, pp. 40–41.

a right that is open to question. The reason for this attitude of mind is that people are ruled in great measure by custom rather than by the light of history and of reason. When any customary right has spread very widely and become deeply rooted in society, men fall into the error of calling it a 'natural right,' There is, to be sure, a sense in which the property right may be called natural, namely, that the right has been rather the result of a natural evolution than of any conscious convention. But, as usually employed, the term natural right implies that the right is 'established by nature' and hence is not to be called in question. In reality there are no such rights. A man in isolation could obviously have no 'rights' whatever. The word rights necessarily implies society, and points to the origin of rights not in any abstract nature, but in the grouping of men.

The Basis of Human Rights.—What then, is the basis of human rights? The preceding discussion should have made it clear that rights do not come from nature in the sense that they thus gain a standing and authority independent of the will or consent of society. Neither are such rights absolute or inherent, though those words have often been mistakenly used in describing them. Private property, contract, personal liberty, and all the other 'rights of men' must justify themselves by proving that they promote the highest welfare of mankind. As the Latin phrase has it, *"Sal publica suprema lex."* Some of us may believe that it is in the "very nature of things" that personal liberty, for example, will best serve human welfare, but we cannot ask or expect others to take this for granted on our unsupported assertion. And when we admit we must prove the social beneficence of private property or personal liberty, we have already practically abandoned the 'natural rights' argument, in the dogmatic form already described. Practically speaking, therefore, we may all agree that the *basis of human rights is social expediency—the proved power to promote the well-being of man in society.* [1]

This is the doctrine of Utilitarianism as developed by Jeremy Bentham, "The greatest good for the greatest number," the

---

[1] Sylvester J. McNamara, *American Democracy and Catholic Doctrine*, International Truth Society, Brooklyn, pp. 126–127.

basis for all law.   Bentham in his *Anarchical Fallacies*, Article II, as quoted by Randall states categorically: "There are no such things as natural rights—no such things as rights anterior to the establishment of government." [1]   Commenting on the passage from an American school textbook quoted above, McNamara says:

> Had the author of the above passages been ruled, to use his own words, "by the light of history and of reason," he would have written something like the following: historically, the individual existed before the family, therefore his rights are prior to the family's; the family existed before the State, therefore its rights are prior to, and independent of the State's, which possesses no rights other than those delegated by the families constituting it.   Or writing philosophically he should have argued: since man by his natural form is capable of living, he has a natural right to life. But if he has a natural right to life he must have a natural right to that which sustains life, namely the fruits of the earth.   And if he has a natural right to the fruits of the earth he has a natural right to that which produces the fruits, which is property.   His abstract right to property, then, is independent of the State, exists before society is established, and would be possessed and exercised by him even though he were in a state of "isolation." [2]

McNamara continues on the following page: "To preserve the equilibrium of one's political thought in this age of intellectual anarchy, it is necessary to keep constantly in mind that the State is the servant, not the master, of those who compose it." The Catholic school is particularly fortunate in this situation since it has available the encyclicals of the recent Popes, which are acknowledged by all to be the best statements in print dealing with these problems.   *"The Constitution of the Christian State"* by Leo XIII and *"Atheistic Communism"* (Divini Redemptoris) by the late Holy Father, Pius XI, should be required readings in every Catholic high school and college.

[1] *Op. cit.*, p. 362.
[2] *Op cit.*, pp. 127–128.

From a purely naturalistic point of view, here is a summary of what the school can do through its instructional activities towards meeting this problem:

> Schools can lead their older pupils to examine critically the social situations about them. Supporting this right to examine the contemporary scene, there is quite a body of tradition which only the more arrogant pressure groups dare to deny. In an honest examination of contemporary life, numerous *social problems are indicated* clearly. These may be safely *described and explored* as problems which our country is facing, without indoctrinating young people to belief in the particular solutions put forward by one or another pressure group. To get perspective on these problems, young people can be led to *trace the factors which gave rise to them*, and this usually shows each problem to be the latest condition following a long series of social changes: the culmination of many different influences. Through such a study, pupils almost inevitably come to *expect further change* and get an opinion about *the direction of the expected* change. This is about as far as schools can go in dealing directly with the controversial issues of the present, but it is as far as they need to go. By this procedure, young people will be *habituated in the use of a scientific methodology in thinking about social problems*. Also, they should have *discovered* for themselves, the *social values* for which succeeding generations of mankind have struggled.
>
> If these italicized objectives can be realized in any considerable proportion of the secondary school and college populations, the educational system will have done its share to maintain our democracy.[1]

But we would not limit the influence of the school in developing the qualities of good citizenship to its instructional activities. "Use of a scientific methodology in thinking about social problems" should be aimed at, but knowledge alone is no guarantee of virtuous living. The second of the learning outcomes,

---

[1] Daniel A. Prescott, *Emotion and the Educative Process*, American Council on Education, Washington, 1938, pp. 156–157.

"attitudes," is of paramount importance here.   The public school can do something towards developing the natural virtues of coöperation and mutual helpfulness but when seeking to develop a sense of obligation it is limited to social sanctions.   Not so the Catholic school.   Religion is the firm foundation for the concept, social duties.   The fatherhood of God and the brotherhood of man was the gift of Christianity to a pagan world. When a doctor of the law asked: "Master which is the greatest commandment in the law?   Jesus said to him: Thou shalt love the Lord thy God with thy whole heart . . . and soul . . . and mind.   This is the greatest and the first commandment.   And the second is like to this: Thou shalt love thy neighbor as thyself.   On these two commandments defendeth the whole law." [1] Here is the spirit that must dominate the school that would be truly Christian.   In a school where teachers and taught are animated by this spirit, social duties will be recognized as having their origin in God and their fulfillment in service to one's fellows as brothers in Christ.

In the third place the school must give to youth an opportunity to practice the social virtues.   The whole life of the school offers such an opportunity, but the administration must realize that the discipline imposed upon younger pupils must be transformed into a self-imposed discipline as these pupils mature. Participation in student government offers an opportunity. This does not mean turning over completely the administration or even the recreational activities of the school to pupils.   But it does mean giving them a part to play in maintaining peace and order in the school community and in this way preparing them to play their part in maintaining peace and order in the larger community of which they will soon be a part.   Our guide here is the principle of progressive freedom.   This means that pupils as citizens of the school community should share the re-

[1] Matt. XXII, 36–40.

sponsibilities of maintaining order within that community *insofar as they are capable of doing so*. As they grow older they become more capable and therefore should exercise more power. Perhaps the outstanding illustration of this procedure in a Catholic institution is that of St. Joseph's College for Women in Brooklyn, N. Y. The story of this experiment in student government is told by the Dean, the Right Rev. Msgr. William T. Dillon, J.D., in a paper read before the N.C.E.A., College Department, from which these excerpts are taken:

> The constitution gave the students complete control of all activities that were not purely academic or clearly within the disciplinary purview of the dean. . . .
> The students control examinations under an honor system which is *sui-generis* . . . They are in immediate charge of attendance and are empowered to pass upon the legitimacy of excuses for absence . . . Moreover, no Faculty member is allowed to remain in a room where an examination is being administered.
> The students control their own finances, offering a budget to a committee that reviews, but cannot coerce. Coaches in dramatics, athletics, and in all the various fields of interest are hired and "fired" by the governing boards of the individual societies.
> Believe it or not, the students of the Senior Class have the right to vote upon the matter of academic honors as might be expected in such a system as ours. . . .
> We have no problems of discipline as they are known in most colleges, but that is only the negative aspect. Positively, and this is so much more important, we find undergraduates assuming responsibilities that we had carried not too effectively. They have absolute right as well as supreme responsibility and they are not officious. They are impressed with their burden and it makes them humble. When crises occur, as they did in the inception, they have asked for grace of time to remedy them and they have remedied them always.[1]

[1] William T. Dillon, "Student Organization in a Catholic College," *Proceedings, The National Catholic Educational Association*. Vol. XXXIII, 1937, pp. 203–209.

Here is training for citizenship. If we believe that Catholic education lifted above the natural by the supernatural influence of Divine Grace prepares youth to lead a life that is self-controlled, students in our high schools and colleges should have more opportunity than they now have to practice self-control since self-control by the large majority in any democratic community is the only guarantee of civic security.

7. DIVINE SECURITY—THE CHURCH

If we could imagine an individual in whose life all the fundamental needs thus far treated have been met; for whom education, health, a happy home, economic and civic security along with time for leisure are a reality, there is still one fundamental need which must be met if he is to live at peace in the universe which surrounds him. What is the meaning of life? What is it all about? Are we here for a day to be gone tomorrow? Or has life some purpose; and if so, am I achieving that purpose in the life I am living? These are questions which, in moments of reflection, confront every individual, no matter how busy, how preoccupied his life may be from day to day. Moreover they are questions which demand an answer from every intelligent being who would avoid the pitfall of despair, for peace and contentment are banished from the life of that individual who has found no answer to them. Since this is true, it is to be expected that man through the ages has sought and found an answer to these questions. That answer is what we mean by religion.

The origin of the word "religion" is in dispute, but we follow those authorities who derive it from the Latin word "religare," to bind. But if there is a binding, two things are involved, one of which is bound to the other. In this case man is bound to God, and religion is the sum total of the relations between man and God. It includes the whole of his being, body and mind, and the whole of his mental life, intellect, emotions, and will.

This comprehensiveness is well stated in this definition: "Religion is the sum total of beliefs, sentiments, and practices, individual and social, which have for their object a power which man recognizes as supreme, on which he depends, and with which he can enter (or has entered) into relation." [1]

This supreme power is God, and man has need of God to give meaning to his life. With God recognized as the author of his being, life means the opportunity for growth and development of man's personality, and death means returning to God from whom we came, provided we have lived our lives in conformity with the Divine Will. This is the only satisfying answer to the riddle of the universe. And it is the answer which accounts for the universality of religion among all people at all times.

We can make a more definite approach to explain this universality through psychology. In Chapter IV, "The Motivation of Human Behavior," we analyzed the primary drives accounting for man's behavior as three, the drives we called possession, pleasure, and power. In the case of pleasure we saw how this is made up of two fundamental impulses, one concerned with the welfare of the individual, the impulse for food and drink, the other the welfare of the race, the sex impulse. In the same way further analysis reveals that the impulse to power is balanced by an impulse of submission. Both these impulses reveal themselves in the life of every individual. We not only crave to exercise power over others but we crave a higher power over ourselves. This is the psychological basis for the social phenomena of the universality of religion. Man craves for a power superior to himself to whom he can pay homage and under the shelter of whose authority he finds security. Some psychologists carrying the analysis further make the observation that the impulse to submission is stronger in women than it is in men, and account thereby for the fact that

[1] L. de Grandmaison, *The History of Religion*, Herder, 1914, Vol. I, p. 3.

religion plays a larger part in the life of woman than it does in the life of man. Whether or not this is the explanation for this universally recognized fact that women contribute more than their share to filling the churches, nevertheless we must admit that universally in mankind there is a universal craving to seek approval from a superior being and out of this universal craving arises the social phenomenon of religion.

Besides this sense of security for the individual found in religion, there is another reason why religion must be fostered by the social group. Let a visitor from a foreign country tell graphically what that instrumental function of religion is:

Standing in the midst of a great American city, and watching the throngs of eager figures streaming hither and thither, marking the sharp contrasts of poverty and wealth, an increasing mass of wretchedness and an increasing display of luxury, knowing that before long a hundred millions of men will be living between ocean and ocean under this one government—a government which their own hands have made, and which they feel to be the work of their own hands—one is startled by the thought of what might befall this huge yet delicate fabric of laws and commerce and social institutions were the foundations it has rested on to crumble away. Suppose that all these men ceased to believe that there was any power above them, any future before them, anything in heaven or earth but what their senses told them of; suppose that their consciousness of individual force and responsibility, already dwarfed by the overwhelming power of the multitude, and the fatalistic submission it engenders, were further weakened by the feeling that their swiftly fleeting life was rounded by a perpetual sleep— . . . Would the moral code stand unshaken, and with it the reverence for law, the sense of duty towards the community, and even towards the generations yet to come? Would men say "Let us eat and drink, for tomorrow we die." Or would custom, and sympathy, and a perception of the advantages which stable government offers to the citizens as a whole, and which orderly self-restraint offers to each one, replace supernatural sanctions, and hold in check the violence of masses and the self-indulgent im-

pulses of the individual? History, if she cannot give a complete
answer to this question, tells us that hitherto civilized society has
rested on religion, and that free government has prospered best
among religious peoples.[1]

Today the press is filled with reports that the situation which
Bryce says never has existed in history, "a civilized nation without religion," is being realized in Soviet Russia. To what extent the Russian experiment will rob the Russian people of their
religion and realize a "free government" among a nonreligious
people history alone can tell. But whatever comes of it, what
we already know about Russia today reveals clearly that freedom will not be one of the prominent characteristics of a system
of government created by communism. Here is Christopher
Dawson's statement of the situation there:

> The Communist rejection of religion and Christian morality has
> not led to the abandonment of social control and the unrestricted
> freedom of opinion in matters of belief. On the contrary, it has
> involved an intensification of social control over the beliefs and
> the spiritual life of the individual citizen. In fact, what the
> Communists have done is not to get rid of religion, but merely to
> substitute a new and stricter Communist religion for the old
> official orthodoxy. The Communist Party is a religious sect
> which exists to spread the true faith. It has its inquisition for
> the detection and punishment of heresy. It employs the weapon
> of excommunication against disloyal or unorthodox members.
> It possesses in the writings of Marx its infallible scriptures, and
> it reveres in Lenin, if not a God, at least a saviour and a prophet.[2]

THE SCHOOL'S PART

If, then, religion has two distinct values, its essential value,
divine security, giving meaning to the life of the individual, and
its instrumental value, social security, functioning as the most

[1] James Bryce, *The American Commonwealth*, 1888, Vol. II, pp. 582–583.
[2] Christopher Dawson, *The Modern Dilemma*, Sheed & Ward, 1933, pp. 94–95.

powerful control of human conduct in group life, it would seem to be apparent that it deserves a prominent place in the school program. Such it had in the early days in this country. In the beginning all education in the colonies was dominated by a religious purpose. But about the middle of the last century the war of the religious sects clamoring for their share of the public funds to support their schools finally drove the states to withdraw all funds from any schools conducted under religious auspices and the tax-supported school was on its way to complete secularization. This was a stupid and most un-American solution of the problem. Why we could not have worked out some other solution as has been done in Quebec and Holland, for example, whereby religion might have remained an integral part of the educational program, at least in those schools where a considerable group wanted it so, is not our inquiry here. How we must work towards some such solution today will be subject matter for discussion in Chapter XVI. "Rights and Duties in Education." The effect of the compromise, if we may call it such, was disastrous in the extreme. Harper, one-time President of Chicago University, discussing this subject some years ago, said: "It is difficult to foretell the outcome of another fifty years of our educational system, which trains the mind only, and leaves the moral side untouched. The Roman Catholics meet this difficulty while our Protestant Churches utterly ignore it." For public school people to claim that leaving religion out of the school program is being neutral is a naive assumption. By completely ignoring it they have already taken sides and they are on the side of the antireligious forces. In the mind of the child and youth the school is teaching them all the important lessons of life. Religion is not one of those lessons,—therefore! Public school people today are becoming conscious of this serious defect in their program. "Character education" is now a frequent topic for discussion within the profession, and many public schools are making provision for character training within their curriculum. We are sympathetic with these efforts and realize that something can be accomplished in developing the natural virtues such as honesty, truthfulness, etc. But since religion is the only adequate basis of morality, to attempt to teach morality without religion cannot but be fraught with failure. We can teach the evil consequences of immoral living but knowledge is no guarantee of virtue. It may be true what Bryce says, that "many highly civilized individual men live without religion." We think of the pagan philosophers of Greece as possible examples, since for some of them the pagan worship of the gods had lost all significance. For them the "good life" had such attraction they needed no supernatural sanction to lead them to live it. Virtue was its own reward. But when we think of the great mass of common men subject as they are to the driving forces of animal impulses, we cannot believe that they have no need of sanctions other than those of the virtuous life itself. Newman knew the human heart, and here is what he says about the power of education and knowledge to regulate the life of man:

> Knowledge is one thing, virtue is another; good sense is not conscience, refinement is not humility, nor is largeness and justness of view faith. Philosophy, however enlightened, however profound, gives no command over the passions, no influential motives, no vivifying principles. . . . Quarry the granite rock with razors, or moor the vessel with a thread of silk; then may you hope with such keen and delicate instruments as human knowledge and human reason to contend against those giants, the passion and the pride of man.[1]

A great Catholic educator discussing this problem before a group of public school people some years ago made this state-

[1] John Henry Newman, *Idea of a University*, Discource V, "Knowledge Its Own End."

ment: "If we cannot put religion in the curriculum of the public school, let us put it in the teachers." The same point of view is expressed by Chapman and Counts:

> Of decisive importance is the attitude and equipment of the teachers. To a large degree they form the traditions of the school and create its atmosphere. If they are religious men and women, the boys and girls who come under their influence will partake of their character. But if they pass lightly over, ignore, or, as is sometimes the case, mock at the deeper meanings of life, or if they are embarrassed when faced with a religious problem, no amount of theoretical religious instruction can set at naught the perpetual operation of the silent forces of example. Those in charge of our schools, therefore, must themselves frankly wrestle with those great problems of life which are styled religious. Until this defect is remedied, until our teachers are given a thorough religious training, the school cannot foster the religious life.[1]

In this discussion we have made no mention of the Church. We have been discussing this question of religious education from the point of view of "natural religion." The philosophy of supernaturalism has definite answers to these questions expressed in the teachings of the Catholic Church. Since it is our purpose to present these teachings in some detail we will devote the next chapter to this important matter.

We have now treated all the universal human needs which man experiences living in society. This analysis is, we believe, exhaustive. With (1) health and (2) human companionship; (3) economic security and (4) leisure; (5) civic security and (6) divine security provided for and all having their place in the (7) educational program of the school, any other need that arises in the life of man will fall logically under one of these seven rubrics. For Naturalism "divine security" has no refer-

[1] *Op. cit.*, p. 362.

ence to future life, the interpretation which we give to it. In the *Cardinal Principles of Education* it is listed as "Ethical Character" and described as "a spirit of service" to fellow man with no reference to God.[1] In a Bulletin of the Office of Education, 1926, entitled *Character Education*, the bold statement is made: "The aim of life is life itself." [2] It is evident from this that for naturalism these social aims of education are the ultimate aims. For Supernaturalism they are mediate aims, that is, through the mediation of them the ultimate aims of Christian education, Christian perfection here and now and life with God hereafter, are to be achieved.

In our treatment of divine security above, we stated that we had not completed our consideration of this subject. The religion we spoke of was what we call "natural religion." We referred to the natural impulse in man to seek for, and having found, to worship and conform his will to, the will of the superior Being, God. Through the knowledge, love and service of God, in faith, worship, and good works, man finds meaning in life and attains the measure of divine security he is entitled to on the basis of the perfection or lack of perfection with which he practices these virtues. But with a natural impulse implanted in man to seek God, the author of his being, it would be strange, indeed, if God, having created man and placed him here on earth, should then ignore him and leave him to work out his own purposes and his own devices for the achievement of those purposes without a word of enlightenment, of encouragement, and if necessary, of discipline, when those purposes are beneath the dignity of the spiritual nature of man. Looked at in this light, the fact of revelation is reasonable indeed. Revelation means light from on High to clarify in

---

[1] *Op. cit.*, p. 9.
[2] Bulletin No. 7, *Character Education*, 1926, Office of Education, Government Printing Office, p. 12.

man's mind the meaning of life here on earth and the means at his disposal for the achievement of the supreme purpose of living, returning to God from Whom he came. Revelation, then, is a supernatural gift not an absolute necessity of man's nature in its pure state, but one that has come to man out of the goodness of God's mercy because of His love for man, the creature of His hand.

We are not concerned here with proving the fact of revelation and its implications for the life of man on earth. That is the business of the Theological Sciences, the sciences which deal with God and man's relations to Him. Rather, we accept that fact and inquire into the nature of the supernatural life promised to man in revelation and then ask what the school can do in the performance of one of its instrumental functions, religious education, in deepening that supernatural life in the lives of its pupils. This is what we mean by the Theological Foundations of Education. Does God give man any light beyond reason, and does He offer him help in working towards his own perfection? The succeeding chapter is devoted to this problem under the title, "The Fourth Factor in Man-Making."

SUGGESTED READINGS

Chapman, J. Crosby and George S. Counts, *Principles of Education*, Houghton Mifflin, 1924, gives an excellent treatment from the point of view of a naturalist of what are called the "Six Life Interests" (Part III. "Sociological Foundations," Problems 12 to 17 inclusive). Problem 4. "Why has Society Established the School to Promote Education?" treats what in our analysis is the first human need, education.

Commission on Reorganization of Secondary Education, *Cardinal Principles of Education*, Office of Education, Bulletin No. 35 1918, 27 pages, should be read by every student of American secondary education.

Douglas, Aubrey A., *Secondary Education*, Houghton Mifflin, 1927, discusses the seven human needs in seven chapters, XIV to XX inclusive.

Sanders, William J., "Fallacies Underlying Curriculum Theory," *Educational Administration and Supervision*, March, 1939, a severe critique of the concept "security" as a basis for curriculum construction, notably, "physical security," health, p. 177.

Sellars, Roy Wood, *Principles and Problems of Philosophy*, Macmillan, 1926, presents an analysis characteristic of the philosophy of materialism, pp. 457–462.

Shields, Thomas E., *Philosophy of Education*, Cath. Ed. Press, 1917, beginning with Part II. "Educational Aims," has one or more chapters treating all the human needs except leisure. This treatment is from the point of view of Supernaturalism.

Snedden, David, "Toward Free and Efficient Liberal Colleges," *Journal of Higher Education*, June, 1935, analyzes seven "careers" which correspond to our seven "needs."

Spencer, Herbert, *Essay on Education*, Fitzgerald, 1885, the English educational classic, which inaugurated the analyses of the social aims of education, should be read by every student of education; for the fallacies it contains see Inglis, *Principles of Secondary Education*, Houghton Mifflin, 1918, "I. Direct Values," pp. 388–394.

I. EDUCATION

Chapman, J. Crosby and George S. Counts, *Principles of Education*, Houghton Mifflin, 1924, Problem 4, "Why Has Society Established the School to Promote Education?" pp. 37–54.

Douglas, Aubrey A., *Secondary Education*, Houghton Mifflin, 1927, Chap. XIV "The Fundamental Processes" pp. 373–410, a good analysis of the contribution of the tool subjects to the first universal need, education.

Newman, John Henry, *Idea of a University*, should be read entire by anyone interested in the school as an intellectual agency.

Peters, Charles C., *Foundations of Educational Sociology*, Macmillan, 1924, for "residual theory" see p. 364.

Shields, Thomas E., *Philosophy of Education*, Cath. Ed. Press, 1917, Chap. XIX, "The School," pp. 321–347.

230   THE PIVOTAL PROBLEMS OF EDUCATION

2. HEALTH

Kirsch, Felix M., *The Catholic Teacher's Companion*, Benziger, 1924, the quotations from Dr. Walsh are taken from this volume.

Lockington, William, *Bodily Health and Spiritual Vigour*, Longmans Green, 1914, carries the subtitle "A Book for Preachers and Teachers"; it advocates asceticism for both health and holiness.

McCarthy, Ralph H., *Safeguarding Mental Health*, Bruce, 1937, presents the Catholic point of view on this problem.

Payne, E. G. and L. C. Schroeder, *Health and Safety in the New Curriculum*, American Viewpoint Society, 1927.

Thompson, Francis, *Health and Holiness*, Herder, 1905, is a short essay by the famous English Catholic poet.

The Journal of Health and Physical Education carries numerous articles by educators on health education in the schools, e.g., "Some Implications of the Objective Health" by F. G. Lloyd, 3:5 pp. 9–11, May 1932.

All texts in Scholastic Ethics give the ethical principles basic to this problem e.g., Charles Miltner, *Elements of Ethics*, Macmillan, 1939, Chap. VI, "Duties Towards the Body," pp. 199–215.

3. HUMAN COMPANIONSHIP—THE HOME

Allers, Rudolph, *The Psychology of Character*, Sheed & Ward, 1931, discusses "The Characterology of the Sexes" in Chap. V., and the "mistaken idea of coeducation" p. 275.

Doms, Herbert, *The Meaning of Marriage*, Sheed & Ward, 1940, "The way in which husband and wife form each other and work towards the perfection of each other, can be considered the essential meaning of marriage" (publishers' announcement).

Flexner, Abraham, *Universities, American, English, German*, Oxford Univ. Press, 1930, exposes the abuse of vocationalism, particularly domestic science in the college and graduate schools, pp. 150–169; the recent outcropping of the various "Institutes" and their futility is discussed, pp. 72–112.

Howard, Frank E., and Frederick Patry, *Mental Health*, Harper, 1935, discusses the importance of the fundamental urges from a naturalistic viewpoint, Chapter IV.

Jennings, H. S., *Biological Basis of Human Nature*, Norton, 1930, gives the biological basis for the physiological differences in the sexes, p. 40.

McCarthy, Raphael, *Training the Adolescent*, Bruce, 1934, discusses the importance of the home and school during this important stage of life.

——, *Safeguarding Mental Health*, Bruce, 1937, offers a popular but sound interpretation of the current mental hygiene movement, particularly as it affects child development.

McGucken, William, *Catholic Way in Education*, Bruce, 1934, proposes psychological reasons for segregation in education, pp. 52–53.

Pius XI. Encyclicals, *The Christian Education of Youth*, Paulist Press, 1931.

——, *Christian Marriage*, Paulist Press, 1931, the Catholic doctrine and attitude on the nature and purpose of marriage.

Plant, James S., *Personality and the Cultural Patterns*, Oxford Univ. Press, 1937, discusses how personality is a direct result of the cultural atmosphere in which a child is reared.

Schmiedeler, Edgar, *An Introductory Study of the Family*, Century, 1930, is the best presentation from the Catholic viewpoint of the disintegration of the home and the possibilities of reconstruction.

—— and Sister M. Rosa McDonough, *Parent and Child*, Appleton-Century, 1934, offers through the whole book recommendations on child development.

Shields, Thomas E., *Philosophy of Education*, Catholic Education Press, 1917, devotes Chap. XVII "The Home," particularly to the education of girls.

Thom, Douglas A., *Every Day Problems of the Every Day Child*, Appleton, 1927, is recommended to parents for suggestions on how to rear children successfully.

All texts in Scholastic Ethics give the ethical principles basic to this problem, *e.g.*, Charles Miltner, *The Elements of Ethics*, Chap. XIV. "The Family" pp. 289–304.

4. ECONOMIC SECURITY

Adams, Arthur B., *Our Economic Revolution*, Univ. Oklahoma Press, 1934, this book has been called a "farewell to laissez faire." It favors limited governmental control of our industrial system.

Andrews, John B., *Labor Problems and Labor Legislation*, American Assoc. for Labor Legislation, 1932.

Catlin, W. G., *The Labor Problem in the United States and Great Britain*, Harper, 1935.

Cummins, Earl F., *The Labor Problem in the United States*, Van Nostrand, 1932.

Daugherty, Carroll, *Labor Problems in American Industry*, Houghton Mifflin, 1933, rev. 1937, the title of Chapter II. "Psychological Aspects of Labor Problems" is promising but the content disappointing; the "basic urges" are referred to but no application of this concept to industry is made. The cooperative movement is discussed pp. 659–669 and Chap. XXVII "Employee Representation" presents various "plans" for giving labor participation in management, pp. 787–798.

Leo, XIII, *The Condition of Labor*. (Rerum Novarum) the encyclical which forty years later (1931) gave the title to Pius XI's "Quadragesimo Anno."

Michel, Virgil G., *Christian Social Reconstruction*, Bruce, 1937, carries the subtitle "Some Fundamentals of the Quadragesimo Anno."

Moon, Parker T., *The Labor Problem and the Social Catholic Movement in France*, Macmillan, 1921.

Pius, XI, *Reconstructing the Social Order*, (Quadragesimo Anno) economics enlightened by the ethical principles of Christianity.

Ryan, John A., *A Living Wage*, Macmillan, 1906.

——, *Capital and Labor*, Paulist Pamphlets.

——, *Distributive Justice*, Macmillan, 1927.

——, *The Labor Problem*, Paulist Press, 1921, "What it is—How to solve it."

Thorning, Joseph F., "Share the Profits," *Commonweal*, July 16, 1937, cites a number of cases where corporations have given labor a "wage dividend."

Van Nell—Breuning, (tr. by Bernard W. Dempsey) *Reorganization of the Social-Economy*, Bruce, 1937, advertised as "the most enlightening commentary on the great encyclical, Quadragesimo Anno."

COÖPERATIVES

Coady, M. M., *Masters of Their Own Destiny*, Harper, 1939, the story of the Antigonish movement in the Maritime Provinces of Eastern Canada by one who has been engaged in it.

Cowling, Ellis., *A Short Introduction to Consumers' Coöperation*, Central Coöperative League, Bloomington, Ill., 1935.

Fichter, Joseph, "Workers Coöperatives," *Commonweal*, Dec. 10, 1937, presents the coöperatives as developing a "sense of ownership" and raising the worker to "the exalted status of self-employer."

Fowler, Bertram, *Consumers' Coöperation in America*, Vanguard, 1936.

Hall and Watkins, *Coöperation, the Hope of the Consumer*, Coöperative Union, Manchester, Eng. 1934.

Kress, A. J., *Capitalism, Coöperation, Communism*, Ransdell, Washington, D. C., 1932.

The People's Year Book, Cooperative Wholesale Society Ltd, Manchester Eng., Annual, 1936.

All texts in Scholastic Ethics give the ethical principles basic to this problem, e.g., Charles Miltner, *Elements of Ethics*, Chapter X "Ownership" and XI "Contracts" pp. 247–269.

5. LEISURE

Allers, Rudolf, *The Psychology of Character*, Sheed & Ward, 1938, gives the psychological basis for a program of co-recreation, p. 275.

Antonine, Sister, "Co-recreation and Social Adjustment in Catholic Colleges," *Journal of Religious Instruction*, Nov. 1933, Vol. IV. No. 3, pp. 259–267, discusses co-recreation in Catholic Colleges; the *Proceedings of the Catholic Educational Association*, Vol. XXX, 1933, pp. 124–132, also contain this article.

Baugh, A. C. and N. E. McClure, *Essays towards Living*, Ronald, 1929, a book of essays for college students, devotes Part II to the right use of leisure.

Calkins, E. E., *Care and Feeding of Hobby Horses*, Leisure League of America, 1934, gives a survey of the field of hobbies with helps for discovering your own.

Cunningham, William F., "Co-recreation," *The Catholic Educational Review*, Vol. XXXII, No. 9, Nov. 1934, pp. 531–539, theory and practice of a program of co-recreation in Catholic high schools and colleges.

Cutten, George C., *The Threat of Leisure*, Yale Univ. Press, 1926, Chap. VII, "Is Education a Solution?" gives an affirmative answer.

Jacks, Lawrence P., *Education through Recreation*, Harpers, 1932, a series of lectures delivered in the United States by this English gentleman under the auspices of the National Recreation Association.

May, H. L., and Dorothy Petgen, *Leisure and Its Use*, Barnes, 1928, discusses the way foreign countries have handled the leisure problem.

Nash, Jay B., *Spectatoritis*, Sears Pub., 1932, describes the national affliction of America.

National Recreation Association, *The New Leisure Challenges the School*, National Recreation Assoc. Press, 1933, the leisure problem tells what the school should do, how to do it, and what has been done.

Veblen, Thorstein, *The Theory of the Leisure Class*, Vanguard, 1932, criticizes the mentality of the American leisure class, Chap. XIV discusses how it has effected Higher Education.

6. CIVIC SECURITY—THE STATE

Dawson, Christopher, *Religion and the Modern State*, Sheed & Ward, 1935, Chap. VIII, "The Catholic Doctrine of the State," pp. 129–141.

Dillon, William T., "Student Organization in Catholic Colleges," *Proceedings*, National Catholic Educational Assoc. 1937, pp. 203–209, gives the origin and development of the outstanding example of student government in a Catholic college.

Francis Joseph, Sister, *Our Government and Our Civic Duties*, Benziger, 1938, a text for the 8th grade showing "how we are governed and how civil authority depends upon divine."

Lapp, John Augustus, and Robert Weaver, *The Citizen and His Government*, Silver Burdett, 1936, a good text for high school.

Leo, XIII, "The Christian Constitution of States," *The Catholic Mind*, Vol. XXXIV, Nov. 8, 1937; "Christian Democracy," Vol. XXXV, Oct. 22, 1937.

Manion, Clarence E., *Lessons in Liberty*, Univ. of Notre Dame Press, 1939, subtitle "A Study of God in Government," an excellent text for high schools.

McNamara, Sylvester J., *American Democracy and Catholic Doctrine*, International Truth Society, Brooklyn, presents in parallel columns the preambles of the constitutions of Virginia and
the United States with a summary of Bellarmine's democratic
theory suggesting that this was the source of Jefferson's idea
of natural rights.

Pius, XI, *Atheistic Communism* (Divini Redemptoris) gives the
Catholic theory of natural right and social duty set over
against the theory of communism.

Rager, John C., *Democracy and Bellarmine*, Qualityprint, Shelby-
ville, Ind., 1926, discusses the influence of Bellarmine's political theory upon the American Declaration of Independence.

Randall, John Herman, *The Making of the Modern Mind*, Houghton
Mifflin, 1926, Chap. XIV, "The Science of Government," pp.
334–364, shows the influence of Rousseau on American Political theory *after* the revolution *not before;* therefore with no
influence on the Declaration of Independence.

Ryan, John A., *The Christian Doctrine of Property*, Paulist Press,
1923.

All texts in Scholastic Ethics give the ethical principles basic to
this problem e.g., Charles Miltner, *The Elements of Ethics*, Chapters II. "Rights"; III. "Duties," pp. 161–173, and XVIII, "Civil
Society," pp. 332–351.

7. DIVINE SECURITY—THE CHURCH

All texts in Scholastic Ethics give the ethical principles basic to
this need from the point of view of Natural Religion, e.g., Charles
Miltner, *The Elements of Ethics*, Chapter IV, "Man's Duties to
God," pp. 187–194.

References for this need as interpreted by the philosophy of
Supernaturalism are given at the conclusion of the following Chapter
VII, "The Fourth Factor in Man-Making."

RELIGIOUS EDUCATION

We can be content with no less than the old summary of educational ideal which has been current at any time from the dawn of our civilization. The essence of education is that it be religious.

> A. N. Whitehead, *The Aims of Education*, Macmillan, 1929, p. 23.

Christianity, and nothing short of it, must be made the element and principle of all education.

> John Henry Newman, *Arguments and Discussions*, IV. "The Tamworth Reading Room, 3. Secular Knowledge not a Direct Means of Moral Improvement."

The mere fact that a school gives some religious instruction (often extremely stinted), does not bring it into accord with the rights of the Church and of the Christian family, or make it a fit place for Catholic students. To be this, it is necessary that all the teaching and the whole organization of the school, and its teachers, syllabi and textbooks in every branch, be regulated by *the Christian spirit*, under the direction and maternal supervision of the Church; so that religion may be in very truth the foundation and crown of the youth's entire training; and this in every grade of school, not only the elementary, but the intermediate and the higher institutions of learning as well.

> Pope Pius XI, *The Christian Education of Youth*.

236

CHAPTER VII

THE FOURTH FACTOR IN MAN-MAKING

Education is man-making. This fact so simply stated involves a process that is complicated in the extreme. Every experience an individual goes through is educative if he learns therefrom. In studying this process our endeavor is to isolate in thought the factors which play prominent roles therein, recognizing that never in life do they operate in isolation. Rather, all are at work all the time with the result that no two individuals are identical in characteristics. What are the factors which play the chief roles in the making of any individual human being?

The educational literature of the past half century, for the most part written from the materialistic point of view, recognizes only two factors in the making of man, heredity and environment. From this have arisen two schools of thought, the hereditarians and the environmentalists. With the development of the biological sciences during the latter half of the last century, the hereditarians were first in the field, but the development of the social sciences during the past thirty years has brought about the ascendancy of the environmentalists. The theory of the immutability of the I.Q. was a typical product of the school of heredity, whereas now the changeableness of the I.Q. in response to environment influences has been sufficiently demonstrated for all environmentalists.   Evidence from the biological sciences suggests the equal importance of both in the determination of any one characteristic.   Jennings in his *Biological Basis of Human Nature* gives an account of the development of giants in Drosophila, a fruit fly which multiplies rapidly and hence serves as a suitable subject for this study.   The varying factors were a modified gene in the x-chromosome and feeding.   The presence of this particular gene

> causes the animals which have no other type of x-chromosome than this to grow to nearly twice the size of ordinary Drosophilas. But this increase in size takes place only if the animals are well fed during a certain period of their larval lives.   Individuals without this gene do not become giants, no matter how well fed.   And individuals bearing this gene, if not well fed at the particular required period, do not grow larger than the usual flies.   The giant size therefore requires for its realization a particular type of environment acting on a particular type of gene.   If either condition is not fulfilled, giants are not produced. . . .
>
> What do such cases show about the nature of inheritance, and of its relation to environment? . . . Characteristics do not fall into two mutually exclusive classes, one hereditary, the other environmental.   A given characteristic may be altered by changing the genes; and this is the ground on which it is called hereditary. But the same characteristic may be altered by changing the environment; and this is the ground on which it is called environmental.[1]

Jennings is here dealing with insects.   Is man merely an insect with acquirements?   Such a view is crude materialism denying the spiritual in the make-up of man.   Horne, an Idealist, in his *Idealism in Education* entitles Chapter II, "Heredity and Education;" Chapter III, "Environment and Education"; and Chapter IV, "Will and Education." [2]   For the Humanist

[1] H. S. Jennings, *The Biological Basis of Human Nature*, Norton, 1930, pp. 133–134.

[2] H. H. Horne, *Idealism in Education*, Macmillan, 1910.

also, there is a third factor. (Cf. Chapter II, Section 3, "Humanism," pp. 43–49.) Heredity and environment are factors playing a part in man's development, but more important than either of these is that quality which makes him man, namely, rationality. To a very great extent man using the capital that comes to him through heredity is free and able to mold his environment to his won purposes or to allow himself to be overcome by it. The social institutions, the most significant aspect of man's environment, are the products of his freedom and intelligence. In this view each individual has a part to play in determining his own personality. To deny this is to deny man's greatest attribute, reason, and his most prized possession, freedom.

For the supernaturalists, however, there is a fourth factor in the make-up of man. In this view God did not merely create man; He watches over his every action (Providence) and offers him assistance above and beyond his natural powers to attain the high estate to which He has called him. This factor we call grace. It means help from on High to lead the good life and it is offered to all men of good will. Grace does not destroy nature; it builds upon it. *Gratia supponit naturam.* Grace makes it possible for man to live a life above nature, the supernatural life, our subject for study in this chapter. Here we are presenting the theological foundations of education. (1) What is the nature of this supernatural life? (2) What must man do to live it? And (3) how can the school help to lift man to this plane? These are the questions we now consider.

1. THE MEANING OF THE SUPERNATURAL

We have been emphasizing all through this presentation of educational theory that man is a rational animal. This means he is partly material and partly spiritual. The two elements in his nature are united in a substantial union to form the one substance, man. This is the dictum of philosophy based on natural reason interpreting the facts of man's life or, at least, it is the dictum of those philosophers following Aristotle who see a duality in this unitary organism we call man. But theology through revelation tells us something more about the nature of man, something of which we might have had a suspicion through the unaided light of human reason (See quotation from Newman, Chapter II, Section 4, p. 50) but which we never could have known in all its clearness had not revelation added its light to that of reason. Theology tells us that to man created in the image and likeness of God there were added gifts beyond anything due his nature, supernatural gifts, and that man in the period of probation to which he was submitted lost these gifts through his fall. Not only did he lose these supernatural gifts which brought him close to God but in addition he was wounded in his natural attributes. His intellect was darkened and his will weakened by that first transgression of the law of God, leaving him inclined to evil rather than to good. But despite this unfaithfulness, God did not forsake man. He promised him a Redeemer who in due time came in the person of Jesus Christ, and through His death on the Cross restored man to the favor of God, and, through His life and teachings on earth with man, gave an example of the good life man should live and instructions as to how to achieve it. Man's nature, therefore, though a rational nature, is a fallen nature. It was wounded in its highest attributes, intellect and will, but it was to be healed through the ministrations of Christ, Who came on earth to restore man to the high estate from which he had fallen.

This teaching of theology on man's fallen nature should not be confused with the teachings of the Protestant reformers who taught the doctrine of the "total depravity" of man. Here are Calvin's words:

Original sin, therefore, appears to be an hereditary depravity and corruption of our nature, diffused through all the parts of the soul, rendering us obnoxious to the Divine wrath, and producing in us those works which the Scripture calls "works of the flesh." . . . These two things therefore should be distinctly observed: first, that our nature being so totally vitiated and depraved, we are, on account of this very corruption, considered as convicted and justly condemned in the sight of God, to whom nothing is acceptable but righteousness, innocence, and purity. . . . The other thing to be remarked is, that this depravity never ceases in us, but is perpetually producing new fruits, those works of the flesh, which we have before described, ... My intention here is only to hint, in a brief way, that man is so totally overwhelmed, as with a deluge, that no part is free from sin; and therefore that whatever proceeds from him is accounted sin; [1]

But this is not the Catholic theory of the nature of man. As McGucken states it,[2] man's nature is *deprived*, not *depraved;* deprived of the supernatural gifts which had been bestowed upon it at creation and through this deprivation man is wounded in those high attributes, intellect and will, which mark him off from the animals of the lower kingdoms. But man was still able to do something for himself. He was not totally "depraved" to be saved by faith alone. Jesus Christ had opened for him the gates of heaven, but man must walk in; and this walking in consists in coöperating with the help God offers men, the help called grace.

There is a mystery in the operations of grace, in the same way that there is a mystery in the Incarnation, the doctrine that Jesus Christ is true God and true man. We do not attempt to explain the mystery of the Incarnation, but it is important that we understand clearly wherein the mystery

---

[1] Frederick Eby, *Early Protestant Reformers*, McGraw-Hill, 1931, pp. 236–240, from *Institutes of the Christian Religion*, tr. by John Allen, I, pp. 229–231.

[2] William J. McGucken, S. J., *The Catholic Way in Education*, Bruce, 1934, p. 31.

lies.   In the Incarnation as an article of faith we are not asked
to believe that one Divine nature is two natures, human and
divine; nor that one Divine person is two persons.   This would
be impossible since both statements are contradictions.   The
mystery of the Incarnation is that one Divine person animates
two natures, one divine and one human; that Jesus Christ is
true God and true man.   Similarly in the case of grace, there
is a mystery.   How can God lead man to win back those lost
gifts and at the same time leave man free to reject that help?
This we do not attempt to explain.   Nor need we.   Everyone
of good will has immediate experience of this help from God.
Looking back over his life, everyone sees occasions when he was
confronted with grave temptation to evil, but by a power more
than human he surmounted these temptations and lived his
life with and for God.   The naturalists may call it chance or
good luck, but for the supernaturalist it is providence and he
sees in these occasions the hand of God beckoning him to Himself.   What are the means through which man receives this help
from God to make progress towards his own perfection here
and now, and his eternal salvation hereafter?

THE CHURCH HUMAN AND DIVINE

When Christ had finished his mission on earth and ascended
into heaven He did not leave man limited to his own resources
to lead the good life which He had taught in all its fullness and
of which He had given such an inspiring example.   Rather,
before leaving He set up an organization which was to continue
the work He had begun and carry it on to the end of time.
This organization was the Church, and it is of real significance
to those engaged in the work of education that Christ's command to his apostles and disciples, when last He spoke to them,
was not to preach but to *teach:*

All power is given to me in Heaven and in earth.

Going there, *teach ye all nations;* baptizing them in the name of the Father, and of the Son, and of the Holy Ghost.

Teaching them to observe all things whatsoever I have commanded you: and behold I am with you all days, even to the consummation of the world.[1]

What was the content of this message that the apostles and disciples were to teach to men, calling them to a new life, a life to be modelled after that of Christ Himself?   Roughly we may say that this message falls into three parts, the first supplying the *motives* for leading the Christian life; the second, the *means* which make this new life possible for fallen man; and third, the *discipline* demanded by the life itself.   The first is a body of doctrine, the element of faith; the second, the sacramental system of the Church, the element of worship; and the third, the regulations whereby these means are to be put into operation, resulting in the Christian life actually lived, the element of good works.   These three, then, make up the supernatural life, faith, worship, and works.   The organization responsible for realizing all three in the life of man is the Church.   Now the Church instituted by Christ to carry on his work is not merely the exterior organization, the hierarchy of pope, bishop, priest, and people.   It is much more than that. It is a spirit animating the whole of the body in the same way as the soul animates the body of man, giving it life and making it possible for man not merely to live his own life but to reproduce that life in others.   Similarly, the Church reproduces itself in the life of all its members lifting them up when they fall and propagating itself to the end of time as promised by Christ Himself.   The Church, then, made up of human members, is both human and divine, since its head is Christ Himself.   This characteristic of the Church is what we mean by the phrase "the Mystical Body of Christ."

[1] Matthew XXVIII, 18–20.

THE MYSTICAL BODY OF CHRIST

This doctrine of the Church runs all through the Scriptures in which we find Christ identifying His life in the world with that of His followers. For three years he had prepared His disciples for this new doctrine by His miracles, the healing of the sick, the raising of the dead to life, and the forgiveness of sins, making this transition from the life of the body to the life of the soul. It was, however, in His sermon at the Last Supper that He identified the life of His followers with His own life: "I am the vine; you the branches: he that abideth in me, and I in him, the same beareth much fruit: for without me you can do nothing." [1] This theme runs all through the five chapters of St. John giving His last discourse the night before He died: "I in them, and thou in me; that they may be made perfect in one." [2] In the Acts, at the conversion of St. Paul when he was stricken on the road to Damascus, the voice which called to him from heaven said: "Saul, Saul, why persecutest thou me?" [3] Saul, or St. Paul, as he came to be known, had been "persecuting the church of God" as he tells us in his Epistle to the Galatians (I, 13), and he, "breathing out threatenings and slaughter against the disciples of the Lord, went to the high priest and asked of him letters to Damascus, . . . that if he found any men and women of this way, he might bring them bound to Jerusalem." [4] Yet the voice said to him, "Why persecutest thou *me?*" To persecute the followers of Christ was to persecute Christ Himself who still lived on earth in them. St. Paul is the first to use the analogy of the body, and after stating it in the twelfth chapter of his first Epistle to the Corinthians in these words: "For as the body is one, and hath

[1] John XV, 5.
[2] *Ibid.*, XVII, 23.
[3] Acts VIII, 4.
[4] Acts I, 1–2.

many members; and all the members of the body, whereas they are many, yet are one body, so also is Christ." [1] he adds, "Now you are the body of Christ, and members of member." [2]

Benson, in his *Christ in the Church*, develops this analogy of the Church as the Body of Christ considered as a whole, and of its members, as members of the Body of Christ considered separately, in terms of the findings of modern science dealing with the living organism:

> Every organic body—the body, let us say, of a man or a dog—may be regarded under two aspects. First, it possesses its one single and unique life, that may properly be called the life of the body, beginning before birth and ending at the moment called death. Yet, sheltering, so to speak, under this unity—in fact contributing to it—are lives whose number is beyond computation—viz.: the lives of the innumerable "cells" that compose the body. Those cells are continually coming into being, living each its life, and finally dying and passing away with the destruction of the tissues, yet in no sense interrupting by these changes the one continuous life of the body as a whole. The body of a full-grown man has no single cell, at any given moment, which it possessed at the time of his birth; yet his body, we say, has lived continuously from his birth up to that given moment. The cells are indeed individuals, but they are a great deal more, in virtue of their mystical cohesion. . . .
>
> Now this physical illustration may perhaps appear a little forced; yet surely the analogy is too remarkable to be passed over. We considered just now whether it was possible to speak of the Life of the Church as identical with the Life of Christ—of the identity, that is, of the myriad consciousnesses of Catholic Christians with that Divine consciousness of Christ; and we see that recent research supplies us with a parallel, exact, so far as we have considered it, with the entire Catholic claim on the point. We see how it is not only possible, but essential, for an organic body—that is, for the highest form of physical life with

[1] *Op. cit.*, XII, 12.
[2] *Op. cit.*, XII, 27.

which we are acquainted—that it should consist from one point of view of a myriad infinitesimal lives that lose themselves, and yet save themselves, in the unity of the whole, and that the unity of the whole, while it transcends the sum of the individual cell-lives, is at once dependent on them and apart.   If this is true of physical life, literally and actually, it is surely not unreasonable to expect that it should be true also of spiritual life; and the coincidence is the more remarkable when we remember that the science of cell-life is of very recent date.[1]

To the Protestant, the church is generally an "institution of social service" [2] and Christianity is the union of each individual with Christ without any priest or prelate, any church or sacrament to act as intermediary between him and the Savior.   The Catholic concept of the Church as the Mystical Body of Christ is much larger than this.   As developed by Benson, the meaning is that Christ living in the Church today is going through the same experience He went through when He was on earth in the flesh.   Christ was worshipped in the crib by shepherds and kings; the Church contains in her membership both the rich and the poor, the lowly and those of high estate.   Christ underwent the three temptations in the desert; the Church is undergoing these same three temptations every day in the life of each individual member.   Christ performed miracles and they were explained as the work of the devil; miracles are performed in the Church today, *e.g.*, at Lourdes, and they are explained away as some form of psychosis.   Christ had his Judas; the Church has her Judases in unfaithful ministers. Christ was crucified on the Cross; the Church is crucified in Mexico and Russia.   Christ was buried in the Sepulchre; the Church was buried when the Popes deserted Rome.   And finally, Christ rose again from the dead, just as the Church,

[1] Robert Hugh Benson, *Christ in the Church*, Herder, 1911, pp. 14–17.

[2] Norman Foerster, *The American State University*, U. of North Carolina Press, 1937, p. 41.

after it had been buried by Nero, by Arius, by Henry VIII and by Voltaire, rose again to a new life and continued to spread throughout the world.

So much for the corporate life of the Church as the Mystical Body of Christ. How does each cell of that body, each individual in the Church, participate in this supernatural life? The answer to this question is the sacramental system. A sacrament is an outward sign instituted by Christ to give grace. In Baptism, for example, the sign is washing with water; its effect is washing away original sin. The seven sacraments cover all the important areas in the life of man. Through Baptism, he is born into the Church; through Penance, sins committed after Baptism are remitted; through the reception of the Holy Eucharist, food is supplied to nourish his spiritual life; in Confirmation, he is strengthened to serve as a soldier in the army of Christ the King; those who enter Matrimony sanctify their love for each other preparatory to building a Christian home; those who enter Holy Orders receive the grace to perform their sacred duties as ministers of the Church; and finally, as death approaches, the sacrament of Extreme Unction gives health and strength to the soul in preparation for its departure from this life. The sacraments are the ordinary channels through which grace flows into the soul, but man's every good act performed with a supernatural motive increases that grace. Man in the state of sanctifying grace is united with God. He is living the supernatural life but it may be on a high or a low level. The Holy Spirit is dwelling within him and he is sharing in the gifts of the Holy Ghost. What are these gifts which are the evidence that man is living the supernatural life? They are seven and they cover the whole of man's rational life, as is evident when they are allocated to three mental functions, as follows:

FIGURE 15.—MENTAL FUNCTIONS AND THE GIFTS OF THE HOLY GHOST

COGNITION (knowing)	AFFECTION (feeling)	CONATION (doing)
1. Knowledge	4. Piety	6. Counsel
2. Understanding	5. Fear of the Lord	7. Fortitude
3. Wisdom		

The gift of (1) knowledge enables us to know the will of God in all things; (2) understanding to penetrate more deeply into the mysteries of faith; (4) piety leads us to obey God because we love Him; (5) fear of the Lord fills us with a dread of sin; (6) counsel warns us of the dangers to salvation; (7) fortitude strengthens us to do the will of God in all things; and (3) wisdom directs our whole life and all our actions to His honor and glory. This is the supernatural life analyzed in detail.

We listed above three elements in the supernatural life, faith, worship, and good works. All three are included in the gifts of the Holy Ghost as analyzed above. But there is one phase of good works that is so foreign to the spirit of the world (the natural life) and so characteristic of the life of Christ on earth (the supernatural life) that we give it more extended treatment.

2. ASCETICISM AND THE SUPERNATURAL

A life above nature, the supernatural life, is possible for man in spite of his fallen nature, because God comes to his assistance. Divine grace is help from God to share in Christ's life on earth. But grace can be refused. Further, help to lead the Christian life will not be forthcoming in abundance to anyone who does not coöperate with that grace when it is offered. In what does this coöperation consist? One form of coöperation which must characterize the Christian, that is, the follower of Christ, is the practice of self-denial. "If any man will come after me, let him deny himself and take up his cross daily, and follow me." [1] are the words of Our Lord. St. Paul as an apostle surely was showered with graces. Yet St. Paul tells us: "I chastise my body, and bring it into subjection: lest perhaps, when I have preached to others, I myself should become a castaway." [2] The Church in dealing with the faithful makes continued requests upon them to deny themselves pleasures, that they may become more like Christ. This is the meaning of Advent, of Lent, and of Friday abstinence. These periods of penance are followed by feasts of joy, Christmas and Easter, but penance must be a constant practice if the supernatural life is to be lived on a high level. There is perhaps no doctrine of the Church so hateful to the world as this, that self-denial must be practised if self-development is to be achieved. This practice of penance by those who would be true followers of Christ is called asceticism. What is asceticism?

The word comes from the Greek word meaning exercise, and a dictionary definition is "spiritual exercises in pursuit of virtue." The moral virtues like the intellectual virtues are perfected through exercise. This is the law of life. In physical education we call it training. In the education of the mind we call it mental discipline. In the education of the body and soul we call it asceticism, and ascetics are those who through rigorous self-discipline set out to put the soul in the saddle riding the beast of their animality on earth's road to heaven. The organized asceticism of the church means the religious life lived under the three vows of poverty, chastity, and obedience. In contrast with this, the energies of the world are spent in pursuit of possessions, pleasure, and power. [3] Celibacy is one

[1] Luke IX, 23.
[2] 1. Cor. IX, 27.
[3] See Figure 8 "The Dominant Human Drives" in Chapter IV, p. 102.

form of asceticism at which the world scoffs in derision. "It is unnatural," the worldling says, "and even if it were possible for men and women to lead such a life in peace and content- ment, it would only be a form of selfishness, a refusal to shoulder the burdens of family life." They miss the point entirely. Of course, celibacy is unnatural. It is meant to be. But it is *supernatural* when it is chosen voluntarily in order to live closer to God, and if so entered into, it is made possible by the grace of God. Our Lord Himself lived this life during His thirty-three years on earth, and he said to the rich young man "Come follow me." [1] That was an invitation, not a command; but those who accept that invitation were promised rest for their souls. In the Mystical Body of Christ, ascetics, within the monasteries or without, are performing a double function. Sin is rife in the world. Much of this sin is never atoned for by the perpetrators of it. But it must be atoned for if the insult to God which sin involves, is to be requited. Christian ascetics voluntarily take upon themselves the task of suffering for the sins of others. In this they are imitating Christ in his vicarious atonement on the Cross, that is, atonement in the place of another. The second function of the ascetics is to advance their own perfection. This function must be carried on by all Christians who would make any advance in living the super- natural life. And this is the lesson that must be taught to Christian youth. They must be brought to realize that their purpose in life is different from that of those animated by the spirit of the world. Their end in life is different and the means which they must take to achieve that end is different. These means are two, the help from God to live the Christian life which we call grace, and self-help in the form of self-denial. This second means, self-help through self-discipline, is the

[1] Matthew XIX, 21.

guarantee of receiving the other means in abundance. God helps those who help themselves. It is refreshing to find one outside the Church stating this difference between the spirit of the world and the spirit of Christ in terms that are of real significance for the religious education of youth:

> If the undergraduate can only get it through his head that Christian morals and natural morals are two quite different things, get it out of his head that the former is merely old-fashioned while the latter is up-to-date, get it into his head that they differ in aim and in purpose, a vast confusion may be resolved . . . Anyone with half an eye can see that natural morality differs from Christ's morality and that the difference is due to a differing definition of man and his highest good. . . .
>
> The usual man of the moment may admit that there is a soul, but only in the sense of a higher function of the body. Man may be a superbeast, but he is essentially a beast. So people think. And because they think it the impulse toward chastity and monogamy loses force. This is to be expected, for the simple reason that chastity is not an animal virtue and never was . . . If man is only a socialized beast, if his highest goods are animal goods, there is not the slightest reason why companionate marriage, so called, or some other form of thinly disguised promiscuity should not prevail. . . .
>
> What is the Christian to do about it? Nothing can be done about it as long as people believe that man is a higher animal and nothing more. We may as well abandon the attempt to make people live like Christians when they are not Christians, to preserve a Christian civilization without belief in that God-search which alone justifies a Christian civilization. One's God implies one's good. To ask people who worship Mammon to live lives of sacrifice, to expect devotees of Venus to be chaste, to hope that people whose real God is comfort at any price will suffer gladly for the truth is grotesque. . . .
>
> We live in a pagan world, as did the Hebrew prophets, as did the Christ, as did His early disciples. Christians are now—they probably always have been and always will be—a chosen people,

set apart.   What is right or wrong for others may not be right or wrong for them.   They have been bought by Christ's love, at the price of His blood. . . .

It would help the undergraduate a good deal if the Church would plainly say: "If you wish Christ's grace, if you believe that He is the Way, the Truth, the Life, the Sustainer of souls, then you must try to live according to that morality which is of Him. If you do not desire Christ, if you are satisfied with lesser aims, then conform to the standards of conduct prevalent about you. If you do, the Church will be very sorry, but she cannot then be held responsible for your eventual, or present, happiness or unhappiness." [1]

We have been stressing here that this principle of self-development through self-discipline is the law of life with special emphasis on its significance for the supernatural life. In Chapter V, p. 130, we quoted from the famous chapter on "Habit" in James' *Psychology*, Vol. II, in which he even uses the word "asceticism" and urges its practice in "little unnecessary things" upon all who would succeed in any arduous life occupation. In Chapter X, "Values and the Disciplines in School Activities," we will return to this theme when treating the disciplinary values of a school activity. Youth knows the truth of the principle in the field of athletics, but we must bring home to them its validity in all domains of life, particularly in the religious life and the intellectual life. The Church must preach it as well as administer the sacraments; the school must teach it along with its other lessons; and the home must demand it, at the same time setting an example for youth to follow. With this lesson learned, youth are well on their way towards the realization of that goal which was the ardent desire of Christ for all: "I am come that they may have life, and have it more abundantly." [2] We turn now to the question, "What can the school do to help pupils learn to live the supernatural life?"

3. EDUCATION AND THE SUPERNATURAL

In the preceding chapter, "The Universal Human Needs," we developed the thesis that each of the great social agencies has its own specific function in making provision for one of these needs but that, in addition to this, each agency may have many instrumental functions insofar as it aids other agencies in meeting the need which is specific to them. The specific function of the school is the making of minds. It is, first of all, an intellectual agency. But the school by its very nature, since it is the agency of formal education and since education should pervade the whole of life, has an instrumental function relative to each of the other fundamental human needs. Chief among these for the Christian Supernaturalist (since he sets Christian perfection in this life and life with God in the next as the ultimate objective of all living and therefore of education) is its instrumental function to assist the Church in achieving its end, that is, the eternal salvation of its members. The school does this in three ways, which are the three modes in which man lives his life. "Why did God make you?" is a question in the first chapter of the Catechism. And the answer says: "to know Him, to love Him, and to serve Him in this world, and to be happy with Him forever in the next." This answer presents the life of religion in its traditional organization of faith, worship, and works. And the Catholic school helps the Church in all three phases, whether it be elementary school, high school, college, or university. The three agencies which carry the primary responsibility for the upbringing of youth are the home, the church, and the school. On the lower levels of the educational ladder, and sometimes on the higher, these three agencies work separately, though, of course, they should coöperate with one another since all have the common interest of making it possible for childhood and youth to attain their optimum development as Christian men and women. But on the college and university level it not infrequently happens that home, church, and school are all combined in one institution, in that the priest is not only minister of the church in administering the sacraments and in the pulpit, but he is at the same time teacher in the classroom and laboratory, and father in the home (the dormitory) as well as companion in hours of leisure. This presents an ideal situation for the religious education of later adolescents. For this reason and because the writer's experience has been in the Catholic college and university where the students for the most part are housed on the campus, he will limit his description of the School's religious education program to this situation, leaving to others the description of the ideal religious education program of the elementary and high school.

(A) INSTRUCTIONAL PHASE—KNOW GOD!

That students may know God with the deepest understanding possible, religion has its place in the curriculum as a requirement during the first two years of college, when the student's time is distributed over the great fields of knowledge. The aim of formal instruction in Theology, as for the other religious activities of the college, is to implant in the heart of youth the Christian Life Ideal. Someone has defined ideals as master ideas. The master idea in this case, is the personality of Jesus Christ. Hence, the practice is growing in favor in the Catholic college of building the syllabus for the freshman course in theology around the personality of the God-man, with the Bible as text. Introduced to theology, the science of God, by reading the three discourses in Newman's *Idea of a University* on this subject, the student follows the story of the God-man as told in the Liturgical year with its feasts and seasons. He begins with the fall of man and the promise of the Redeemer, and studies God's patience with man in the history of the Jewish people. The historical books of the Old Testament are studied with emphasis on the Commandments and are followed by the Moral books, leading to the Prophetical through Advent to Christmas. Now, the New Testament is the text. The obedience of the boy-Christ is followed by the Temptations of Humanity as undergone by Christ in the desert. Then comes Christ's public life and, through Lent, His passion and death—to Easter; after Easter—the founding of the Church—its missionary enterprises, through The Acts of the Apostles, with the remaining time devoted to the Epistles and the Apocalypse. The second year's work consists of apologetics, emphasizing the Church as the Mystical Body of Christ, living the same life He lived with saints and sinners throughout its nineteen hundred years of history.

The work of these two required years is brought to completion by a comprehensive examination, satisfactory performance on which is a requirement for graduation. Following this, theology courses are offered in the upper biennium, so that students may follow these courses in the same way that they follow any elective course in which an intellectual interest has been aroused. Further, colleges are now offering a major sequence in theology, sometimes combined with philosophy, so that students may major in theology just as they major in any field of knowledge—not with the intention of training seminarians, but simply so that the intellectual discipline of mastering a subject may be available here as in the other fields of knowledge. Through distribution of the student's time over the great bodies of knowledge during the lower biennium, and concentration in one field during the upper biennium, the aim is to produce the college graduate with an informed, cultured, disciplined mind.   Religious knowledge, surely, has a part to play in this process.

(B)   DEVOTIONAL PHASE—LOVE GOD!

We turn now to the devotional phase of the religious program provided for by student participation in religious worship.   We use the University of Notre Dame as an illustration of an institution which has developed an extensive program. Responsibility for this program is placed definitely on the shoulders of the Prefect of Religion and his assistants, all of whom are administrative officers devoting their entire time to this work.   At their beck and call are more than seventy other priests on the administrative and teaching staffs, rectors of resident halls, and prefects living on the floors with students. With such a corps of workers, so many and so various are the opportunities offered students to take part in religious services we can only list them, with an occasional explanatory comment.

1. *Daily Exercises:* Morning and evening prayers in all hall chapels; daily mass and reception of Holy Communion promoted by rectors and prefects; prayers before and after classes; grace before and after meals in the dining halls.

2. *Weekly Exercises:* Sunday services, mass and sermon, in the College Church at 6, 7, 8:30 and 10:00 o'clock, the 8:30 service, a high mass; confession urged on all students at least once a week, with confessors on hand in every hall after evening prayer every night; confessors also available in the hall chapels every morning and in the chapels next to the Offices of the Prefects of Religion for the reception of the Sacraments and spiritual guidance every morning from 6:30 till noon; Sunday evening, benediction in the college church at 7:00 and 7:30 with confessions.

3. *Occasional Exercises:* Great feasts and Holy Days of Obligation (three of the latter, All Saints', November 1; Feast of the Immaculate Conception, December 8; and Ascension Thursday occur during the school year) observed with solemn high mass and sermon; seasonal devotions in the College Church during Lent; benediction and sermon, Wednesday evenings, Stations of the Cross, Friday evenings; May Devotions in honor of Our Lady, benediction and sermon, Wednesday evenings; student missions: first week of the school year, mission for the freshmen, mass and instruction in the morning, sermon and benediction in the evening; second week, mission for upper classmen, with special facilities during the week for reception of the Sacraments and spiritual guidance on life problems; the same week, mission for the lay faculty; adoration of the Blessed Sacrament on special occasions, during which students are asked to devote one-half hour in silent prayer, with a calendar arranged so that volunteers are on hand for each period throughout the day; May devotions at the grotto each evening during the month of May, students walking from the dining halls to the grotto to join in prayers and singing of hymns in honor of Our Lady, *Notre Dame*, the patroness of the School; academic occasions, such as Founder's Day and commencement, observed with the pageantry of an academic procession, a Pontifical High Mass, and sermon.

With these and other opportunities for participation in religious worship, one can readily realize that the so-called religious atmosphere of the campus is a reality. There are material aids to this end, however, which should not be overlooked: dominating the campus, the gilded dome, surmounted by a statue of Our Lady, and the college church, with its spire towering over the other buildings, are in the very center; the interior of the church is inspiring, with its gothic lines and mural decorations; behind the library is the log chapel, a replica of the chapel used by the Indian missionaries who lived and labored on this spot before Notre Dame was founded, the favorite chapel when students return to the campus to be married. Each resident hall has its own chapel, with the Blessed Sacrament reserved night and day; each classroom has a crucifix on the wall behind the teacher's desk. The grotto, a replica of the famous Notre Dame shrine of Lourdes, France, and an outdoor stations of the cross along the shore of one of the lakes leading to the shrine, Calvary, are beauty spots of the campus.

Without doubt, however, the greatest agencies in developing the religious program at Notre Dame have been the Religious Bulletin and the Religious Surveys. The Bulletin, mimeographed or printed, is placed at every student's door on the campus, every day except Sunday. It contains announcements of coming events, requests for prayers for the sick, the dying, or the departed, discussions of moral issues in student vernacular, reprints of cartoons from metropolitan dailies, anything, in fact, directly or indirectly connected with religion, which may be of interest to students. The Surveys are summaries of questionnaires sent out in alternating years to students and alumni, which give real insight into what students, present and past, are thinking, saying, and doing about religion, intensely interesting documents of great assistance in planning the program of religious activities from year to year.

But after all, atmosphere is created by personalities more than by any other single influence, and Notre Dame is peculiarly fortunate in this respect. More than seventy priests are on the teaching staff, others on the administrative staff, with brothers as teachers, prefects and office workers and sisters in the laundry, all wearing the religious habit. Priests, seminarians, and brothers are in regular attendance at class, also wearing the religious garb. The majority of the lay members of the faculty, and more than ninety two per cent of the student body, are Catholics, giving a solidarity to the group which, perhaps, could not be duplicated in any institution of similar size in the world.   This is what creates atmosphere.

(c)   PRACTICAL PHASE—SERVE GOD!

That is practical which translates itself into practice in every day life.   So interpreted, the word has deep implications for the program of religious education conducted by any college. Conduct is the final test.   The difficulty here is, that as soon as the words "conduct" or "behavior" are mentioned, we are prone to think only of repressive measures in student discipline. If this is the case, we are enrolling ourselves in what we may call "the compulsion school," the fallacy of which has been so aptly described by Newman in "The Tamworth Reading Room."

> Those who have to do with our colleges give us their experience, that in the case of the young committed to their care, external discipline may change the fashionable excess, but cannot allay the principles of sinning.   Stop cigars, they will take to drinking parties; stop drinking, they gamble; stop gambling and a worse license follows.   You do not get rid of vice by human expedients; you can but use them according to circumstance, and in their place, as making the best of a bad matter.   You must go to a higher source for renovation of the heart and of the will. You do but play a sort of "hunt the slipper" with the fault of our nature, till you go to Christianity.[1]

No, the "renovation of heart and will" is fundamentally a matter of self-mastery, but self-restraint which has religion for its motivation is, through the influence of divine grace, the most powerful influence to bring it about.

For discipline is not merely a negative thing.   It has its

[1] John Henry Newman, *Discussions and Arguments*, Chapter IV, "The Tamworth Reading Room," pp. 270–271.

positive side also. Students are not to be led merely to refrain from misconduct, but rather they must be led into a way of life in which religion is the supreme motivation. Many campus activities are closely linked with religion. The most frequent association is perhaps when clubs attend a special mass offered for their special intention. They also sponsor activities, dramatics, boxing bouts, etc., the proceeds from which are devoted to religious purposes. Some clubs, however, like the Servers Club, are distinctly religious in purposes. Another such, is the St. Vincent de Paul Society. This society is established in practically all parishes and for students to take an active part in its activities in college is specific preparation for continuing this activity when they return to their home parishes. Among the activities of this society during the school year are the following: serving as "big brothers" for underprivileged boys; collection and distribution of old clothes, shoes, and magazines; doing clerical work in the offices of understaffed social agencies; visitation of institutions—the County Infirmary, hospitals, Mission for Men, etc.; financing Christmas baskets for the poor, giving financial aid to the negro parish, etc. In the words of St. James, this is "Religion clean and undefiled."[1]

Such, in brief, is one aspect of the educational program which Notre Dame is attempting to carry out. The ideal aimed at is stated in the quotation from Newman on the back of the title page of the University Bulletin:

Here then, I conceive, is the object of the Holy See and the Catholic Church in setting up Universities; it is to reunite things which were in the beginning joined together by God, and have been put asunder by man. Some persons will say that I am thinking of confining, distorting, and stunting the growth of intellect by ecclesiastical supervision. I have no such thought. Nor have I any thought of a compromise, as if religion must give

[1] Epistle of St. James, I, 27.

up something, and science something. I wish the intellect to range with the utmost freedom, and religion to enjoy an equal freedom; but what I am stipulating for is, that they should be found in one and the same place, and exemplified in the same persons. I want to destroy that diversity of centres, which puts everything into confusion by creating contrariety of influences. I wish the same spots and the same individuals to be at once oracles of philosophy and shrines of devotion. It will not satisfy me, what has satisfied so many, to have two independent systems, intellectual and religious, going at once side by side, by a sort of division of labor, and only accidentally brought together. It will not satisfy me, if religion is here, and science there, and young men converse with science all day, and lodge with religion in the evening. It is not touching the evil, to which these remarks have been directed, if the young man eat and drink and sleep in one place, and think in another: I want the same roof to contain both the intellectual and moral discipline. Devotion is not a sort of finish given to the sciences; nor is science a sort of feather in the cap, if I may so express myself, an ornament and set-off to devotion. I want the intellectual layman to be religious and the devout ecclesiastic to be intellectual.

This is not matter of terms, nor of subtle distinctions. Sanctity has its influence; intellect has its influence; the influence of sanctity is the greater in the long run; the influence of intellect is the greater at the moment. Therefore, in the case of the young, whose education lasts a few years, where the intellect is, there is the influence. Their literary, their scientific teachers really have the forming of them. Let both influences act freely. As a general rule, no system of mere religious guardianship which neglects the reason, will in matter of fact succeed against the school. Youths need a masculine religion, if it is to carry captive their restless imaginations, and their wild intellects, as well as to touch their susceptible hearts.[1]

We say, then, that the ultimate aim of education in the philosophy of Supernaturalism is twofold: Christian perfection in this life and eternal salvation in the next, that is, life with

[1] John Henry Newman, *Sermons on Various occasions.* Sermon I. "Intellect, the Instrument of Religious Training."

God. Life with God in the next life is what we mean by heaven. Heaven as the ultimate end of all living is often ridiculed by moderns, particularly out-and-out naturalists. Life is its own reward, they say, and it is childish to offer a prize for leading a good life. It is like offering a piece of candy to a child for good behavior. These shallow-minded critics have missed the meaning of the supernatural life entirely. Look at the etymology of the word, *"super naturam,"* the two Latin words literally translated meaning "above nature." For those accepting revelation, why are we asked to live a life above nature? What is the purpose of this life *above nature?* An analogy may help us understand this purpose. Suppose a student after a period of arduous application to study wins a prize. The prize itself may be totally unrelated to the period of study, for example, membership in an exclusive golf club with an elaborate set of golf sticks. Or it may be closely related to his period of study, a scholarship which makes it possible for him to continue his studies. Heaven is of the latter type, for preparation must be made for life in heaven in the same way that preparation must be made for advanced study. Sheed explains this with admirable clearness:

> This life is not only a test which a man must pass in order to obtain the reward of heaven, it is a preparation which man must successfully undergo in order to live the life of heaven.
>
> From this it follows that whatever is necessary to enable a man to live the life of heaven must, in some way or other, be acquired by man in this life: otherwise this life would not be a preparation for heaven. And this consideration brings us to the most important point in the whole of Catholic teaching, the doctrine to which all others whatsoever are related, an understanding of which is necessary if Catholicism is to be understood at all. We may approach it in this way. If we were offered a journey to another planet, we should be wise to refuse, because the breathing apparatus which we have by nature, was made for the atmosphere of this world. In our atmosphere it works: in a totally

different atmosphere it would not work, and we should die of suffocation. This illustration points the way to the truth, namely, that the equipment which is adequate to life in one world, may not be at all adequate to life in another. And God has told us that our human nature, while adequate to the ordinary life of this world, is not adequate to the life of the world to come. If we were to enter heaven with only the powers of our human nature, we should no more be able to live there than, in the illustration I have given, we should be able to live on another planet with no powers beyond those of our nature.

And just as we should need some extra powers of breathing, not contained in our nature, to live on another planet, so we need extra powers in our soul, not contained in our nature, in order that we may live the life of heaven. These powers which are not ours by nature, are what is called in Catholic teaching, the Supernatural Life.[1]

In Chapter I, at the conclusion of Section 1, "What Is Education?", we formulated a definition of education which threw into relief the three changes into which we had analyzed the educative process (p. 9). Insofar as that analysis is correct, this definition is acceptable to all educational theorists, since it is merely breaking down into its elements the natural process of learning, no matter what may be their philosophy, whether they are Materialists, Idealists, Humanists, or Supernaturalists, as defined in Chapter II.

We are now prepared to formulate a definition of Christian Education. We have explained in this chapter the meaning of Supernaturalism as it has been interpreted traditionally by historical Christianity, which means the Catholic Church. The ultimate aim of all education in this philosophy is the perfection of the human person in his individual and social life on earth after the model of Christ, and his eternal salvation with God in the life to come. The means at his disposal for the achievement of that aim are self-discipline in all the areas

[1] Francis J. Sheed, *The Map of Life*, Sheed & Ward, 1933, pp. 34–35.

of life (self-help) and grace, which means the help God gives all men of good will to work out their eternal destiny. Christian Education adds something to each of the three parts into which our definition is divided. Knowledge of the fallen nature of man and of the means at his disposal to achieve his destiny which comes to us through revelation is an essential part of the social inheritance. The life ideal of the Christian is no vague and nebulous ideal of goodness or righteousness; it is a concrete ideal in the person of Jesus Christ, who, as the second Person of the Blessed Trinity, true God, became man "and dwelt amongst us" on earth. The abilities which man possesses of his very nature to advance his own perfection are lifted up to the plane of the supernatural through the influence of divine grace, which is his for the asking. Christian Education, therefore, may be defined as follows: the process of growth and development whereby the natural man (1) assimilates a body of knowledge derived from human effort *and divine revelation*, (2) makes his life ideal *the person of Jesus Christ* and (3) develops the ability, *with the aid of divine grace*, to use that knowledge in pursuit of this ideal.

How this dual aim of the philosophy of Supernaturalism, Christian perfection here below and eternal salvation with God hereafter, is integrated with the social objectives of education as presented in Chapter VI., "The Universal Human Needs," and with the psychological objectives presented in Chapters III. to V. will be the subject matter of the succeeding Chapter VIII., under the title, "The Hierarchy of Educational Objectives."

SUGGESTED READINGS

I. THE MEANING OF THE SUPERNATURAL

Anger, Joseph and John J. Burke, *The Doctrine of the Mystical Body of Christ*, Benziger, 1931.

Benson, Robert H., *Christ in the Church*, Herder, 1911.

Cuthbert, Hess, *God and the Supernatural*, Longmans Green, 1920.

Eby, Frederick, *Early Protestant Reformers*, McGraw-Hill, 1931, Calvin's "View on Human Nature" and original sin, pp. 236–240.

Myers, Edward, *The Mystical Body of Christ*, Macmillan, 1931.

Pohle, Joseph, *Grace, Actual and Habitual*, Herder, 1924.

——, and Arthur Preuss, *God the Author of Nature and the Supernatural*, Herder, rev. 1919.

Sheed, Francis J., *A Map of Life*, Sheed & Ward, 1933, is fresh and stimulating on the Supernatural.

Sheen, Fulton J., *The Mystical Body of Christ*, Sheed & Ward, 1935.

2. ASCETICISM AND THE SUPERNATURAL

Foerster, Friedrich W., *Marriage and the Sex Problem*, Stokes, 1936, has an excellent chapter on the place of asceticism in the life of the Christian.

James, William, *Psychology*, Holt, 1920, Vol. II, the Chapter on "Habit" as quoted in Chapter V., is a classic, pp. 57–58.

Maturin, B. W., *Self-Knowledge and Self-Discipline*, Longmans Green, 1915, see section "Mortification and the Supernatural," pp. 253–282.

3. EDUCATION AND THE SUPERNATURAL

De Hovre, Franz and Edward B. Jordan, *Catholicism in Education*, Benziger, 1934, the first part is entitled Part I. "Catholic Philosophy and Catholic Education," pp. 3–161. A bibliography is given on pp. 161–162.

McGucken, William J., *The Catholic Way in Education*, Bruce, 1934, has an excellent chapter III, "The Supernatural and Education" but does not discuss the religious education program of the school, pp. 27–36.

Newman, John Henry, *Idea of a University*, is the classic presentation of the bearing of Theology on other knowledge; see also his sermons, particularly the one quoted in this chapter,

——, *Sermons on Various Occasions*, Sermon I. "Intellect, the Instrument of Religious Training."

——, *Discussions and Arguments*, Chapter IV, should also be read.

Shields, Thomas E., *Philosophy of Education*, Catholic Education Press, 1917, Chapter X. "The Ultimate Aim of Christian Education," is excellent.

A HIERARCHY OF EDUCATIONAL OBJECTIVES

The teacher should have a hierarchy of objectives. He should have a general, or ultimate aim, under which should be arranged in a descending order proximate aims, terminating in the specific aims of the immediate lesson that is to be taught for the day. The ultimate and the more general proximate aims are not the objectives to be kept in the focus of attention. The aim before the teacher, which determines the method that is to be employed in each specific lesson, must be related to the "higher" proximate aims and to the ultimate aim, but they cannot be substituted for it.

> Stephen Sheldon Colvin, *An Introduction to High School Teaching*, Macmillan, 1917, pp. 335–336

The basic difficulty in applying many formulations of educational objectives is due to the fact that the aim of education may be considered from several points of view, which tend to form a sequence. The immediate objective of the teacher is to stimulate and direct his students so that they will acquire certain abilities, such as ability to solve quadratic equations of a specified type; ability to translate certain passages of a foreign language; ability to apply principles of physics in solving certain types of problems; ability to plan and construct a table or chair in the shop; ability to organize information relating to a topic and present it effectively; and the like . . .

Abilities are engendered by the school in order that the students may be equipped with controls of conduct for performing the duties of adult life. Hence the desired kinds of future behavior or conduct may be considered as the *ultimate* objectives of education.

> Walter S. Monroe, *Directing Learning in the High School*, Doubleday Page, 1927, pp. 54–55.

CHAPTER VIII

THE HIERARCHY OF EDUCATIONAL OBJECTIVES

We bring to a close now our discussion of educational aims, or, in the present-day terminology, educational objectives. We have distinguished three groups of aims or objectives, namely, the psychological, the sociological, and last of all, the philosophical, which for a philosopher of the school of supernaturalism are predominantly religious in nature. Our task in this part of our study is to integrate these groups of aims, *i.e.*, to develop their interrelations, showing how they flow one into the other and, properly interpreted, make one complete whole.

1. THE HIERARCHY OF OBJECTIVES

The first group of objectives which we analyzed, we called psychological objectives. This group carries this name because it is an analysis of mind. We began our discussion of education in Chapter I by defining it as a process in which three types of changes are brought about, changes whereby the human infant, born into the world differing only slightly in his inherited tendencies from the young of the higher animals, is transformed into a civilized being, that is, a human personality with an informed cultured, disciplined mind, qualities which

267

make him human and mark him off from the rest of the animal kingdom.

These three changes are brought about through the achievement of the learning outcomes. Many words are used to label these outcomes but we rather arbitrarily have agreed to speak of them under these terms: (1) knowledge, (2) attitudes, and (3) abilities, thus indicating the three lines of development aimed at in the exercise of the three fundamental mental functions, cognition (knowing), affection (feeling), and conation (doing). But this arbitrary labelling of these groups of learning outcomes does not bring us very far in our analysis of the problems of education. It is all very well to emphasize, as we will do when we discuss the problem of the teacher that every time a teacher walks into a class room and begins to carry on any teaching procedure he is aiming or should be aiming primarily at one of these learning outcomes with his teaching procedures adapted accordingly. Hence we speak of these learning outcomes as teacher objectives. From the teacher's point of view they are the objectives which he aims to realize in the development of the pupil. From the pupil's point of view they are outcomes which will result from his activities if these activities are diligently carried on under intelligent direction. The direction, of course, is the teacher's primary responsibility but the activities themselves are the pupil's. As we have emphasized so often in the preceding pages—the pupil can learn in no other way, i.e., only *through his own activities*.

These three learning outcomes, (1) growth in knowledge, (2) setting up of desirable attitudes and (3) the development of abilities, are the immediate goals, the direct point of attack for the teacher in planning his activities. But the question immediately arises, Which knowledges, which attitudes, and which abilities are to be aimed at in the process of transforming this "child of the flesh, into a child of God"?   (See p. 21 for Shield's definition of education.)

The answer to this question must be given in terms of the kind of society we hope to establish on earth and to prepare for in heaven.   We need not enter here into the controversy over the question whether education should be preparation for complete living (Spencer) or participation in present living (Dewey).   It must, of course, be both.   If the curriculum is not built up in relation to adult needs it is of no value; if it is not presented in terms of pupil interest, no learning will result.   But just as pupil interests must be the primary determining factor in the question of method, so pupil needs must be the primary consideration in determining the content of instruction.

We turn then to an analysis of society to develop insight into the problem of curriculum content, although in the presentation of the curriculum on the lower levels of the educational ladder the problem of method will always be to the fore.   What does man need to live adequately in society as we envision it at its best?   In Part I, Section B, "Sociological and Theological Foundations," we have analyzed the fundamental human needs as sevenfold.   One of those needs was analyzed in detail in Section A, "Biological and Psychological Foundations," namely, the need, education.   With society as complex as it has become today, not merely education but *formal* education within the school is necessary for the abundant life.   Knowledge and ability are necessary, of course, but unless, along with these, the attitudes of the civilized human being are developed, it would be better for society and for the individual himself if he had never received any education at all, since with antisocial attitudes acquired, he becomes an enemy to society and an obstacle to his own welfare.

But knowledge, attitudes, and abilities cannot function in a vacuum. Knowledge is knowledge of something; attitudes are relative to something, to somebody, or to some situation; and ability is ability to do something. And so to the question, which knowledges, attitudes, and abilities are to be the immediate objectives of teaching, the answer is, those knowledges, attitudes, and abilities which make for enriched living in the other six fields of social living wherein are located the six fundamental human needs other than education.

What are these fundamental human needs besides education? If a human need is experienced universally by man in society it is to be expected that society would make provision for the satisfaction of that need. This we find to be the case in regard to these universal human needs which we have identified. In the case of four of these needs, the social institution is a distinct agency housed in a building which has become the symbol of that agency: for civic security, that is, government, the state capital; for human companionship provided for by the family, the home; for divine security through religion, the church; for education, the school. For economic security after our experience in 1932 we would hardly use the bank as an adequate symbol. In the case of the remaining two, namely, health and leisure, there is no distinct agency, but there is a multitude of agencies all concerned with providing for these needs: for health, hospitals, clinics, the medical profession, etc.; for leisure, playgrounds, parks, libraries, theatres, newspapers, etc. From the purely natural point of view the achievement of satisfactions in these six fields of social living is the end of all living. From this point of view these become the *ultimate* objectives of education. But from the point of view of Supernaturalism they are not ultimate. Rather they are mediate, that is, through the mediation of these as means we achieve the ultimate ends of education as viewed by Supernaturalism.

What are these ultimate aims? They are two, one in terms of this life, the other in terms of the life to come. From the purely natural point of view these seven aims might be subsumed under one inclusive of them all. If this were done (though not commonly done in educational literature today) it would be worded in some such phrase as "complete personality." For the humanist complete personality would be interpreted primarily in terms of the rational part of man's nature. But for the supernaturalist it is much more definite than this. From this point of view there has been in the world One Complete Personality, complete in the fullest sense of the word, namely, the personality of Jesus Christ, true God and true man. Man's aim in life is to become as much like Him, the divine model, as it is possible to become. Man's model is perfect, therefore perfection is his goal. Though man knows he will never achieve that goal in all its completeness, it is nevertheless the source of his inspiration; and in the divine economy through the help from on high which we call grace, man is enabled to make great progress toward that perfection. The lives of the saints are our evidence for this. To become like Christ, that is, to achieve Christian perfection, is our goal here below.

Now Christian perfection means the perfect performance of all duties encumbent upon man. What are these duties? One analysis is the duties arising from the obligations which man has living his life as a member of society. He has duties (1) of being a good member of society, either as a child or as a parent; (2) of being a good citizen; (3) of being an honest, faithful worker; (4) of taking care of his health; (5) of advancing his perfection through education; (6) of making the proper use of his leisure time. Finally, there are (7) duties relative to God, faith, worship, and good works. And the performance of these duties is the road he must travel toward his eternal goal, the salvation of his soul. This means life with God hereafter, but it is achieved only through the right kind of life with his fellow man here below. This is the supreme paradox that Christ was continually preaching, "He that will save his life shall lose it: and he that shall lose his life for my sake, shall find it"; [1] lose it in working for others, find it in terms of gaining life everlasting with God through living his life here below with and for his fellow man.

Here then are the ultimate ends of education for the supernaturalist. Properly understood, they give meaning to the other educational aims on the two levels below. (Figure 16, p. 273.) We may phrase the philosophical objectives, therefore, which are a unification of all three levels in some such formula as this: Christian perfection in this life, that is, complete personality developed on the model of Jesus Christ through activities that result in knowledges, attitudes, and abilities in the other six fields of social living, (1) as a body-mind organism, (2) a member of the family, (3) of the state, (4) of the economic order, (5) of leisure time groups, and finally (6) of the church—leading to life with God hereafter, that is, eternal salvation. (Figure 16, p. 273.)

2. THE EMERGENCE OF PERSONALITY THROUGH EDUCATION

In the formulation of the objectives of education in the philosophy of Supernaturalism just given, the attempt has been made to state all three groups of objectives, the psychological, the sociological, and the philosophical, in a formulation which presents them as an integrated whole. The key phrase in this statement is "complete personality." What do we mean by personality, and what part does education play in its complete development? According to the dictionary, personality

---

[1] Matt. XVI, 25; Mark VIII, 35; Luke IX, 24.

FIGURE 16.—THE HIERARCHY OF EDUCATIONAL OBJECTIVES

	ULTIMATE OBJECTIVES		PHILOSOPHICAL ANALYSIS	
PHILOSOPHER'S LEVEL	ETERNAL SALVATION		NEXT LIFE	
	CHRISTIAN PERFECTION		THIS LIFE	
	HUMAN NEEDS	MEDIATE OBJECTIVES	SOCIAL ANALYSIS	SOCIAL AGENCIES
SOCIOLOGIST'S LEVEL	7 DIVINE SECURITY (RELIGIOUS LIFE)			7 CHURCH
	6 CIVIC SECURITY (CIVIC LIFE)			6 STATE
	5 LEISURE (LEISURE LIFE)			5 LEISURE TIME AGENCIES
	4 ECONOMIC SECURITY (ECONOMIC LIFE)			4 ECONOMIC ORDER
	3 HUMAN COMPANIONSHIP (FAMILY LIFE)			3 HOME
	2 HEALTH (ORGANIC LIFE)			2 HEALTH CONSERVING AGENCIES
	IMMEDIATE OBJECTIVES	PSYCHOLOGICAL ANALYSIS		
TEACHER'S LEVEL	1 EDUCATION (MENTAL LIFE)	KNOWLEDGES (FACTS AND MEANINGS) / ATTITUDES (IDEALS AND APPRECIATIONS) / ABILITIES (HABITS AND SKILLS)		1 SCHOOL

means simply "being a person." (*Webster's Secondary School Dictionary*) Philosophically defined, a person is *an individual rational nature conceived as a complete being subsisting in itself,* or more simply, *"an individual and incommunicable substance of a rational nature."* [1] A stone is an individual substance but it is not a person since it is not rational. A dog has sentient life but again since it has no rational life (intellect and will) it is not a person. God is a person. Pantheism identifies the universe and God, denying His *individuality*, hence His personality. Atheism denies His *substantiality*. Theism holds to all three attributes in God, substantiality, individuality, and rationality; hence He is a person. So, too, with man. He is a person not because he has a mind nor because he has a body but because he subsists through both, which constitute his individuality, incommunicable to any other person. As Maher states it "the true human person is neither consciousness, nor soul, nor body, but the complete Ego—the living rational being arising out of the substantial union of both principles," soul and body.[2]

But we have the two terms, "person" and "personality," hence there must be some distinction in their meaning. The newly born human infant is a person but his personality is still in the forming. This latter term refers to all those traits which come to characterize the individual as he grows and develops, particularly those traits which manifest themselves in his dealing with others. Thus we say of a particular person that he has a likable or disagreeable personality.

As the life history of each individual unfolds, what are the factors which influence the development of personality? The preceding chapters have been our attempt to analyze these factors, to show the importance of each, and to point out how the school must work with them to help the pupil evolve a worthy personality. There was first of all the factor of *heredity*. In the discussion of personality it is customary to say temperament is what we are by birth (heredity), character is what we

---

[1] Michael Maher, S. J., *Psychology*, Longmans, Green, 1909, p. 558.
[2] *Ibid.*, p. 559.

make ourselves to be. This latter brings forward a second factor in the formation of personality, the *self*. Is man responsible for his own acts? If he is, he is responsible in major part at least for the development of his own personality. This development will be conditioned, of course, by his surroundings, the circumstances under which he is compelled to live his life. Here we have a third factor, *environment*, pressing upon man and determining to a great extent the development of his personality. Watson would have us believe that this factor is prepotent in the life of man. But humanists and supernaturalists, believing in the dual nature of man (matter and spirit) and believing that the problem of life for each individual is to bring it about that the spiritual within him shall dominate over the material, see the self as the prepotent factor in the formation of personality. Heredity plays a part, environment plays a part, and Providence plays a part (here is the fourth factor, *grace*, help from God to achieve the good life), but man cannot shirk the responsibility for his own development. Since this factor, his own self, exerts more influence than any other factor, man's destiny lies in his own hands and he alone is held responsible for his own development. If that development proceeds harmoniously, man achieves what we call an integrated personality. If it does not proceed harmoniously, disintegration is the outcome.

What is the source of this disintegration in the life of man? Some would find it in the factor heredity. "Man has been denied his birthright." Others would locate this source of disintegration in his environment. "This individual never had a chance. Opportunity for development was denied him." Others in history have located the cause of the conflict in the life of man in the struggle between a good and an evil spirit, each seeking to gain the mastery over man. But Supernaturalism has the simplest and yet the most satisfactory answer ex-

plaining the conflict in the life of man which only too often de-
stroys the possibility of an integrated personality. Supernaturalism says man was made to the image and likeness of God
but through rebellion he fell from this high estate. The spiritual element within him succumbed to the material element,
and he can never find rest until the spiritual is again in complete
control. Since man was made to the image of God, this ideal is
ever before him. He is ever seeking after God, striving to be
Godlike. Even the saints are ever conscious of this conflict between the lower and higher elements in man's nature. St.
Augustine in his *Confessions* tells the story of the conflict in
his own life and in that story utters the poignant cry: "Thou
hast made us for Thyself, O Lord, and our heart is restless
until it rests in Thee." (Book I, Chapter I.)

But there is a second part to the answer of Supernaturalism.
It is *restoration* through Jesus Christ, Our Lord. Perfect rest
is not promised to man in this life. Rather, struggle and conflict. But perfect rest *is* the promise of future life for those
who, with the help offered them through the merits of Jesus
Christ, submit themselves to a continued regimen of self-discipline that the spiritual in their natures may dominate over the
material. Maturin has expressed this thought in a masterful
fashion:

> This dualism that rends and tortures you is not of God's making
> but your own. It had a beginning and it will have an end. It
> is the penalty of that act of disobedience whereby Adam sacri-
> ficed the supernatural union with God which held the body sub-
> ject to the soul. The soul unaided is not able to keep the whole
> nature in harmonious order. Man's nature was never intended
> to be complete in itself, it was created so that it could only fulfil
> itself and its destiny by union with God. That union was lost by
> sin. Then began the conflict, "the flesh lusting against the spirit
> and the spirit against the flesh." But the body however rebel-
> lious is an integral part of man's nature. He must be saved body

and soul, or he cannot be saved at all. Men must pay the penalty of the Fall, that inner conflict which ends only in the separation of soul and body in death. . . .

The answer then of Christian Revelation to man's perplexity lies in disclosing the past and the future, the Fall and the Resurrection. And between these, the dispensation of Christ, wherein He bestows upon man the supernatural gift of grace by which once more he is restored to union with God. And this gift does not indeed establish that inner harmony which was forfeited once for all by the Fall, but it bestows upon him a power by which he can gain control over the flesh to discipline and train it, to check its rebellions and teach it to take its place of subordination as the soul's servant and not his master.[1]

The great failures in life are not failures in knowledge and skill necessary for the successful pursuit of any life calling. The average individual with ordinary opportunity can adequately prepare himself, as far as technical knowledge and skill are concerned, for the successful pursuit of the vocation he has set his heart on. Knowledge comes through study; skill comes through practice; and these within limits can be acquired by all. But failure comes, particularly those tragic failures which wreck lives, because of some defect in personality. The doctor, the lawyer, the clergyman, the teacher, all may have the knowledge and technical skill necessary for success, but if their personalities are such as repel people instead of attracting them, how can they expect to hold the esteem, the confidence, and therefore the patronage of those whom they would serve? The same is true of persons on the lower occupational levels. The man who cannot hold a job, the floater who tries one occupation after another, never making himself expert in any small field, has some fundamental defect in his personality.

We live most of our time in contact with others. We should

[1] B. W. Maturin, *Self-knowledge and Self-discipline*, Longmans, Green, 1915, pp. 224–230.

live all of our time with and for God through serving fellow man. But whether or not we succeed in these fields, we must live all of our time with ourselves. No one can get away from himself. Conscience may be silenced for a short period but if it is, it will return to destroy the peace of the mind that has failed to live up to its recognized obligations. This is one of life's fundamental lessons, which man must learn early in life if it is to be lived in peace and contentment, namely, that, first of all, man must live with himself. If here he is a success, if, instead of being torn this way and that by conflicting desires, he recognizes that not all desires can be satisfied and chooses those which give greatest promise of being satisfied, he has prospects of living at peace with himself. At peace with himself, he has made the proper approach for living at peace with others.

In the light of this fact we can see the truth in the statement that all education is self-education. The integrated personality, the personality that is in any degree *at one with itself* is a product of self-discipline. We see further that education is a much larger word than "schooling." Every experience which an individual goes through insofar as it works a change in his personality is an element in his education. But it is his reaction to the experience which effects the change, and he alone is responsible for this reaction.

Our major concern, however, is with the influences which the school can bring to bear upon its pupils in helping them to achieve the objectives of education as analyzed above. This means helping them develop worthy personalities. What means does the school have at its disposal for working towards this goal? These means are three. We now turn in Part II. "Means in Education," to the discussion of these three means within the school, namely, 1. the curriculum (materials) 2. the teacher (method) 3. the institution (administration). This brings before us the three remaining problems of the four which we are listing as *the pivotal problems of education.*

SUGGESTED READINGS

1. THE HIERARCHY OF OBJECTIVES

Cox, Philip; Peters, Charles and Sneeden, David, "prepared by" *Objectives of Education,* Second Year Book, Nat. Society for the Study of Educational Sociology, Bureau of Publications, Teachers College, Columbia Univ., 1929.

Douglas, Aubrey, *Secondary Education,* Houghton Mifflin, 1927, on page 363 speaks of a "hierarchy of objectives"; See Figure 13, "Educational Aims and Objectives."

Englehart, Fred, and Alfred Overn, *Secondary Education, Principles and Practices,* Appleton-Century, 1937, Chapter VII, concludes with a brief section entitled "Current Modification of Aims," pp. 188–218.

Wilson, H. B., *The Course of Study in the Work of the Modern School,* a monograph by the Superintendent of Public Schools, Berkeley, Calif., contains a diagram entitled "Social Efficiency" somewhat similar to Figure 16.

2. THE EMERGENCY OF PERSONALITY

Allport, Gordon W., *Personality a Psychological Interpretation,* Henry Holt, 1937, excellent.

Chapman, J. Crosby and George S. Counts, *Principles of Education,* Houghton Mifflin, 1924, Problem 9 "How Does Personality Emerge through Education?" pp. 123–154.

Murchison, Carl A., (editor) *Psychologies of 1925,* Clark Univ. Press, 1926, chapter by Morton Prince entitled "The Problem of Personality."

Wheeler, Raymond and Francis Perkins, *Principles of Mental Development,* Crowell, 1932, Chapter XII, "The Development of Personality."

Woodworth, Robert S., *Psychology* (fourth edition), Henry Holt, 1939, Chapter V "Personality" shows the psychologist's method of appraising personality traits; VI, "Factors in Personality," how personality can be improved.

THE SPIRITUAL INHERITANCE

If education cannot be identified with mere instruction, what is it? What does the term mean? I answer, it must mean a gradual adjustment to the spiritual possessions of the race, with a view to realizing one's own potentialities and to assisting in carrying forward that complex of ideas, acts, and institutions which we call civilization. Those spiritual possessions may be variously classified, but they certainly are at least fivefold. The child is entitled to his scientific inheritance, to his literary inheritance, to his aesthetic inheritance, to his institutional inheritance, and to his religious inheritance. Without them all he cannot become a truly educated or a truly cultivated man.

Nicholas Murray Butler, *The Meaning of Education*, Scribners, 1915 (rev.) pp. 25–26

CHAPTER IX

THE PHILOSOPHY OF THE CURRICULUM

President Hutchins, in his book, *No Friendly Voice*, makes this statement:

> Wherever I have met with educational people, from Hawaii to Rhode Island and from Minnesota to Texas, I have been struck by their unwillingness to discuss the only important question about education and research, and that is the question of content. They want to talk about methods, the size of classes, organization, administration, student supervision, degrees, and buildings.[1]

The question of content in education is the question of the curriculum. The acceptance of the elective system in American education introduced the fallacy of the equivalence of studies: any study is as good as any other study, provided it is taught as well and studied as hard. That this view is fallacious it will be our purpose to show in formulating principles for building the curriculum.

The curriculum is the tool in the hands of the artist (the teacher) to mold his material (the pupil) according to his ideal (objective) in his studio (the school). This analogy brings to the fore what we are calling *The Pivotal Problems of Education* (since the teacher's ideal is the same problem as pupil nature

[1] Robert Maynard Hutchins, *No Friendly Voice*, Univ. of Chicago Press, 1936, p. 170.

and pupil needs), but like all analogies, it limps. This analogy is particularly defective in one of its specifications. The material which the sculptor uses to chisel his ideal into concrete form, *e.g.*, marble, is an inert mass. Not so the pupil, the material with which the teacher works. On the contrary, the outstanding feature of the pupil is self-activity. As Hamilton states it: "the primary principle of all education is the determination of the pupil to *self-activity*." In no true sense of the word, therefore, is it the teacher's task to mold an inert mass of material after a certain pattern. On the contrary, since all learning is through self-activity, the teacher's task is threefold: first, to provide and explain to the pupil a pattern for his study and imitation (*instruction*), second, to arouse him to activity (*motivation*) and third, to demand a high quality of achievement giving him guidance so that his activity may carry him forward to the realization of the fullest development of which he is capable (*discipline*). The curriculum, therefore, is not inert material to be poured into the pupil. Rather, it is a series of activities the older generation plans for the younger generation, with the hope that through carrying on these activities young people will grow into the kind of men and women that society, of which they are to be members, holds as its ideal.

1. EDUCATION A DUAL PROCESS

Once this concept of the curriculum as the tool in the hands of the teacher to be used in the realization of educational aims is accepted, the question immediately arises, "Is this a perfect tool, or is it subject to continued improvement?" In other words, is it to be expected that the curriculum will be constantly undergoing changes; or, on the contrary, can we ever expect that some day it will reach perfection, and the only task of the teacher will be to improve his technique in its use? In answering this question there are two principles which give us guidance, one which we may call the principle of *permanence*, the other the principle of *change*. The principle of permanence arises from the nature of man; the principle of change, from the nature of society. No one questions that society is constantly undergoing changes. These changes during the last half century have been so manifold and so important, that we could hardly expect the curriculum of the school to keep up with them, even if it were thought desirable that all social changes should be immediately reflected by changes in the curriculum. Any school that tries to keep up with all social changes, introducing them before they have proved their worth for the betterment of social living, would be so lacking in stability that it would be ruinous for the lives of the individual pupils who form its clientele and for the welfare of the society in which they are soon to be the adult members. We have the other principle, however, to offset the inherent dissipating tendencies of the principle of change, and this is the principle of permanence. As said above, it arises from the nature of man. In spite of the statement of some psychologists so-called, who tell us that human nature is constantly undergoing changes, and that the business of the new education is to accelerate these changes, we contend that just the contrary is the true statement of the case. Psychologically, the forces resident within man are the same today as they have been from the beginning, and the same as they will be tomorrow. It is the forces outside of man that are constantly undergoing changes. On this principle, there are certain elements within the curriculum, if it is to be an instrument for the perfection of man's nature as it unfolds through childhood and adolescence into adulthood, which will always remain substantially the same. Thus, language study will always remain the core of the curriculum of general education, though, of course, the particular language that constitutes that core will change from people to people. In China it will be Chinese, but in the United States of America it will be English; and language study, taught either formally in language classes or informally in other classes in which it is the medium of instruction, will always be one of the essential elements of the curriculum in general education.

The reason for this is obvious. In our concept of the nature of man there is a duality. Man is matter and spirit, united in substantial union to form the being we call man. On this basis, man, therefore, is an animal carrying on many activities in common with the members of brute creation, but the matter of chief concern to the school is that he is a *rational* animal. From this rationality arises two powers which mark man off from animals of the lower orders, namely, the power of thought and the power of expression. When we say the power of thought, we mean, of course, the ability to do abstract thinking. Thinking in the concrete may be ascribed to animals of the lower order. After all, a dog knows his master; and knowing, even on this level, is a kind of thinking. But conceptual thought, abstract thinking, is an entirely different affair, and this is peculiarly characteristic of man. In the same way, expression on a very low level is characteristic of the lower animals, but only in a metaphorical sense can they be said to have a language; and nowhere do we find even the slightest trace of anything resembling a written language. Perhaps even more important for human kind is the fact that language is not only a tool for communication; it is a tool for thinking. Words are labels for ideas, and as labels they are of particular importance in the realm of abstract thinking. Without such labels it is hard to see how the mind could hold ideas before it, comparing one with another, discovering relationships between ideas, that is, making inferences, and this is the very nature of abstract thinking. Hence we repeat: on the level of general education, language must

always be the core of the curriculum. This is true even in vocational education, particularly on the professional level.
When, for example, the student enters a medical school, one
of his chief tasks is learning the technical vocabulary of that
profession so that he can grasp and hold in mind the ideas which
make up the sciences basic to that calling. These ideas in turn
lead to the development of techniques and skills, that is, procedures resulting in the outcome the profession is aiming at, in
this case, health.

This concept of the two principles, the one of permanence
and the other of change, calls our attention again to the fact
that education is both an individual and a social process. It is
a process through which the race hands over to each succeeding
generation its accumulated treasures, the so-called social inheritance. But it is also a process in which the individual, in his
efforts to assimilate that social inheritance, advances his own
development. The two phases of the process, that is, the social
phase and the individual phase, are not conflicting; rather, they
are complementary. One cannot go on without the other. The
individual in his efforts to assimilate the social inheritance inevitably promotes his own growth and development. This inter-
relationship of these two phases of the educative process, that
is, *social transmission* on the one hand and *individual development* on the other, has been well stated by Durant as follows:

> Two processes constitute education and unite with it; in the one,
> the race transmits to the growing individual its profuse and accu-
> mulated heritage of knowledge, technics, morals, and art; in the
> other, the individual applies this inheritance to the development
> of his capacities and the adornment of his life. In proportion as
> he absorbs this legacy he is transformed from an animal into a
> man, from a savage into a citizen; perhaps, . . . from a simple-
> ton into a sage. Education is the perfecting of life—the enrich-
> ment of the individual by the heritage of the race. Let this vital
> process of transmission and absorption be interrupted for half a

century, and civilization would end; our grandchildren would be more primitive than savages.[1]

BUILDING THE CURRICULUM

The curriculum of the school, then, is the social inheritance organized for its rapid assimilation by immature minds. Not all of the social inheritance can be handed over to the pupil through the school. Its very magnitude makes this impossible. Hence it must be selected. In the second place, some portions of it, the product of the mature minds of the race, would be meaningless to the immature mind of the child. Hence it must be graded. In this selecting and grading process, what is the best approach for building the curriculum?

One might think that we have already answered this question in the preceding chapter when we analyzed the aims of the school under the title, "The Hierarchy of Educational Objectives." Having determined the outcomes of learning as knowledges, attitudes, and abilities, we are inevitably led to ask, what knowledges, what attitudes, and what abilities do we want to develop within the pupil? Proceeding to the next level of the hierarchy it is easy to answer that we wish to develop those knowledges, attitudes, and abilities which will make for enriched living in the other six fields of social living. Then we might proceed according to the technique of job analysis and break down the things people do in a well-ordered society and plan a curriculum that would include, at least, all the fundamental activities which our analysis has brought forth. Such a procedure would probably be accepted as scientific technique in curriculum building. We doubt, however, the wisdom of any such approach. The psychological objectives are of great help to the teacher setting up goals for which teaching procedures

[1] Will Durant, "What Education Is of Most Worth?" *Saturday Evening Post*, April 11, 1936, p. 14.

may be definitely planned. So, too, the sociological objectives are well worth while setting forth in order to deepen the teacher's understanding of the problems of life and the school's part in helping pupils prepare for living in the society of which these social objectives are an analysis. But there are some things which must be learned and cannot be taught. That is, they cannot be taught by any method of direct instruction in the classroom. Patriotism, for example, is an ideal which we hope to implant in the minds of every pupil, but the writer has never heard of any school offering a course in Patriotism. What the school can do through direct instruction is to teach the science of government so that an understanding of the part it plays in society will become the possession of the pupil. Such courses, if handled by teachers who themselves are imbued with patriotism, members of a staff in which this ideal is evident to pupils as a fundamental attitude in their lives, together with loyalty to the school community characterizing the atmosphere of the school, these three factors we believe will provide specific training leading on to a loyalty to that larger community in which the child will live his adult life. In such a situation we have some hope that patriotism will be a possession of the pupil sharing the life of this community.

Similarly, in character building. It is well for the teacher to see that one of the social objectives of the school is ethical character (Seven Cardinal Principles), or in the Catholic school, Christian character. It does not follow from this that schools should set up within the curriculum courses in Character. Such courses in all probability would not only fail to achieve their objective, building character in pupils, but they probably would set up inhibitions which would defeat the very purpose of the course. President Wilson has stated this truth forcibly:

There is nothing that makes a man so hateful to his fellows as the conscious cultivation of character. Character is a by-product.

Socrates may have said that knowledge is virtue. But as an offset to this mistaken view we have Aristotle, who stresses habit formation as the essence of virtue. As President Hutchins has stated it:

> The moral virtues are habits. The environment of education should be favorable to them. But only a diffused sentimentality will result from the attempt to make instruction in the moral virtues the object of education.[1]

The same may be said about the social objective, family life. The vast majority of individuals will, some day, "leave the home of their childhood to enter the home of their choice;" and this choice is undoubtedly one of the most momentous decisions they will ever make. But it does not follow from this, that the school should set up in the curriculum courses in Choosing a Mate. Herbert Spencer made this attack upon the curriculum of the schools of his day in his famous *Essay on Education:*

> If by some strange chance not a vestige of us descended to the remote future save a pile of our school-books or some college examination papers, we may imagine how puzzled an antiquary of the period would be on finding in them no indication that the learners were ever likely to be parents. "This must have been the *curriculum* for their celibates," we may fancy him concluding. "I perceive here an elaborate preparation for many things; especially for reading the books of extinct nations and of co-existing nations (from which indeed it seems clear that these people had very little worth reading in their own tongue); but I find no reference whatever to the bringing up of children. They could not have been so absurd as to omit all training for this gravest of responsibilities. Evidently then, this was the school course of one of their monastic orders." [2]

[1] Robert Maynard Hutchins, *No Friendly Voice*, Univ. of Chicago Press, 1936, p. 130.
[2] Herbert Spencer, *Education*, pp. 54–55.

The sane policy in this problem is the same as in the preceding: some things must be learned, but they cannot be taught by direct instruction. They are learned through living. The child begins his learning as well as his living in the home. The problems of family life are early a reality to him and continue through childhood and adolescence. If he is intelligent he will learn the solutions of many of these problems, insofar as they can be learned by any human being, since they are never the same for any two individuals, but that he should have a course in Marriage before he enters the home of his choice is another matter. Spencer continues:

> Thus we see that for regulating the third great division of human activities, a knowledge of the laws of life is the one thing needful. Some acquaintance with the first principles of physiology and the elementary truths of psychology is indispensable for the right bringing up of children . . . Judge, then, whether all who may one day be parents, should not strive with some anxiety to learn what these laws are.[1]

This is hardly what one would expect after the attack on the school curriculum quoted above. Here we are in entire agreement with Spencer. This is what the curriculum of the school can do preparing youth for marriage. The school, through its curriculum, can teach physiology, psychology, and we would add sociology, with particular reference to the place of the family as the foundation of all social living. If such courses are given by instructors who are living the family life, in a way that sets an example for students, we have the ideal situation. In the Catholic school the ideal would seem to be to have the staff equally divided among those living the family life in the world and those living the communal life, that is, the life of the spiritual family in religion. These by their example say to the pupils,

[1] *Ibid.*, p. 63–64.

if we can live the communal life, the family life of the spirit according to the vows, you can live the family life in the world according to the commandments. Instruction in religion, classes on the sacrament of matrimony, and, in philosophy, the course in ethics, will together give the student an understanding of the importance of the family in society and a clear knowledge of the obligations resting upon those who choose this life; but it is the life of the school which is going to do more than anything else to give them training in those virtues controlling the give and take of social living basic to a wholesome and truly Christian family life.

In regard to the next level of the hierarchy, that is, the philosophical or ultimate objectives, Christian perfection, means the performance of all duties in all seven fields of social living. With such performance we have the best guarantee for the achievement of the ultimate end of man in future life, that is, life with God, our eternal salvation. But again, these concepts are hardly helpful for building the curriculum; not because they are so specific like the social objectives, but because they are so general. They deserve our attention because once these concepts are grasped, they deepen our understanding of the function of the school; but they do not solve for us the problem of curriculum construction.

2. THE TWO HUMAN ABILITIES

If the above analysis is sound, it is evident that the basis for building the curriculum is not primarily the nature of society; rather, it is the nature of man. And again we return to our statement on the nature of man: he is a *rational* animal. We see that man as a rational animal has two abilities distinctly human which mark him off from the lower orders of the animal kingdom, the power of thought and the power of expression. Man, in the exercise of these two powers, through the ages has accumulated what we call the social inheritance. It is well for the school to say that its primary task is to train the pupil in thinking and in the expression of thought. But the only way to train the pupil in thinking is to bring him in contact with the best that has been thought by man, and is left to us in the written record, the literatures of the ages. In fact, this is Matthew Arnold's definition of culture: "pursuit of our total perfection by means of getting to know, on all matters which most concern us, the best which has been said in the world." [1]

(A) THE POWER OF THOUGHT

What are the fields into which the thought of man logically divides itself? Or, in other words, what are the fields of knowledge with which we wish, through the curriculum, to bring the pupil in continued contact? We submit that there are three worlds in which man lives, and the process of education consists in becoming acquainted with all three of these worlds. There is first of all the material world, that is the physical universe. Antithetical to this we have the world of spirit, which, in the Christian concept, means the world of God, the eternal Spirit. Intermediate between these we have that combination of matter and spirit, which is man, the human world. These three worlds, then, the material world, the spiritual world and the human world, are the worlds with which the educated man must become acquainted. We repeat again that in the act of becoming acquainted with these three worlds he will be developing his power of thought as well as his power of expression. Now the bodies of knowledge which represent man's thought about these three worlds are the sciences. We have first of all the natural sciences dealing with the world of nature, which may be divided into the physical sciences, physics, chemistry,

[1] Matthew Arnold, *Culture and Anarchy*, preface.

etc., and the biological sciences dealing with living matter. On the other extreme we have what we may call (to use President Hutchins' word), the metaphysical sciences, philosophy and theology. Philosophy deals with God, and with man and the physical universe relating them to God for, their origin, but it is studied through the unaided light of human reason. Theology, on the other hand, as commonly understood, deals with God as made known to us through revelation and man's relations to God, again studied through the light of revelation. In the third place, we have that group of sciences dealing specifically with the world of man, commonly called the "social sciences." A much better label for this group, is the "humanistic sciences," since it includes general psychology, dealing with man as an individual, as well as social psychology, sociology, economics, politics, and history, the latter tracing man's thought and action in all these fields through the ages. Here then are three bodies of knowledge which must be handed over to the pupil by the teacher through the curriculum. They are constantly growing, and from this point of view, we must expect that the curriculum will constantly be undergoing change. Less than a century ago, one of the subjects in the curriculum of general education was Natural Philosophy. Looking into the content of one of those old texts carrying that title, we see that it was made up of the knowledge man then had of what we now call physics and chemistry. But today we no longer teach "Natural Philosophy," so-called. We teach the sciences, physics and chemistry, since the knowledge which has grown up in these fields is so great that they have justified their right to separate themselves off from the house of philosophy and set up housekeeping for themselves. Similarly, we are now confronted with the same situation in the humanistic sciences. The problems of private property, of marriage, and of government were once taught only as part of social ethics. But now, with the great *still part f ethic*

increase in knowledge in these three fields, we have the three separate sciences, economics, sociology, and politics. In the realm of the metaphysical sciences, that is, theology and philosophy, a change, too, is continually going on, since, although the principles formulating these sciences are permanent, the application of these principles to the business of living is subject to constant change. Usury was one problem during the Middle Ages, but today interest as a problem under justice and right finds itself in an entirely different setting in the greatly complex economic, social, and political situation in which we are living today.

(B)   THE POWER OF EXPRESSION

The second human ability which makes man man is the power of expression. Expression occurs most commonly through language, oral and written, but it is not confined to this. Expression includes all those ways which man has invented to register his thought in some concrete embodiment for his own satisfaction or for the satisfaction of others, which means the communication of his thought to others. All the arts are means of expression, but it is the linguistic arts which are preëminent in serving this function, expression through words as symbols, that is, words serving as labels for ideas. Here we repeat that language is not merely a means of communication; it is also a tool for thinking. This is no place to discuss whether thought is possible without words. Our affective life, the feelings and emotions, is often at a loss for words to express itself adequately. But this does not deny the fact that we search for words and other means by which to give expression in some form to our deepest feelings. The poet is one who has special facility in this art, and that very power of expressing emotional life in words with rhythmic cadence is what makes him a poet. With words as labels for ideas we can hold ideas in the mind and compare them one with another, seeking out relationships. Such perception of relationships is thinking in the higher reaches of the intellectual life. This twofold function of language, that is, as a means of communication and as a tool for thought, is so important in the development of the pupil that we can say without fear of disagreement by anyone who has given careful consideration to the problem, that language must always form the core of the curriculum on all levels of general education. It may be taught formally in language classes or informally through use in the study of other subjects, but taught it must be, if the pupil is to come into his intellectual heritage in all its richness without loss of time and effectiveness.

Language, however, is not the only medium for the expression of thought. Words are not the only symbols in which man registers his mental life and communicates it to others. On the contrary, all the arts are means of expression. The fine arts in particular have their place in the life of man for the development of his intellectual life while the practical arts, on the other hand aim specifically toward making this world of ours a more comfortable place to live in. Since we are now speaking of general education in contrast with vocational education, we leave this question and turn our attention to the place of the fine arts as a medium for the expression of man's mental life in symbolic representation or through imitation.

To understand the place of the fine arts in general education for all students on all levels of the educational ladder, it is necessary to determine the function of art in the life of man as contrasted for example with the sciences; and with this determined, to distinguish the different ways in which that function may be performed for various groups of individuals. Again we lay down the principle that what makes man man is his mental life. He is a rational animal. In the operation of his reason the intellect has for its object truth, and the sciences in all fields of knowledge are the repository of the accumulations of the intellect of man throughout history. The means for their preservation and improvement are the intellectual virtues. The object of the will is the good, and the means for its realization are the moral virtues. The object of the emotions is the beautiful and the means for its realization in the life of man, if we may coin a phrase, are the "emotional virtues." We mean by this appreciation or taste, the power of discerning order, symmetry, proportion, and beauty and finding pleasure in these perceptions.

In the arts this quality of appreciation functions on three different levels. We will illustrate from music. There is at the top the creative artist. He has the ability, the genius, we are inclined to say, not merely to enjoy, *i.e.*, to appreciate, the works of the masters which have been preserved for us, but to add to this store of treasures through his own creations. On the second level we have what may be called the reproductive artist. He may not have the ability to create any thing of lasting worth, but he does have the ability of performance, and through skillful performance not only gives expression to the artistic urge within himself, thereby enriching his own emotional life, but in addition he enriches the lives of those who are privileged to enjoy his skillful performance. This last situation brings us to the third level, the level of appreciation without the ability either of creation or performance. On this third level all are called to be artists in the sense that taste should be cultivated so that a love for music will manifest itself in domestic life, civic life, religious life, and leisure life in general. The phonograph and the radio are great aids to the school in this task of elevating the taste of pupils and through them reaching back into the homes to improve the taste of the generation that was denied this experience during their school days.

But there are other ways besides words and musical sounds

through which man expresses his mental life. The pictorial and plastic arts have design and color, shape and form, giving us the arts of drawing, painting, sculpture, and architecture and the lesser arts like ceramics, etc. Another type is through motion in the dance. Perhaps no art has been so neglected by the school as this one. Yet if we could develop in the minds of youth an understanding of the principles directive of the expression of beauty through motion, perhaps no influence would be so helpful in elevating the tone of social dancing which plays so conspicuous a role in the activities of students outside the classroom.

Any distinction between the literary and the fine arts is evidently quite arbitrary. This is well illustrated by poetry. We may say it is "the finest of the fine arts" meaning by that, that it offers the best medium for the expression of the emotional life of man at its deepest. It is a combination of sound and word symbol. To a certain extent all literature partakes of this characteristic as illustrated through the cadence of beautiful prose. Literature is the written record of the race, the story of the part that truth, beauty, and goodness have played and are playing in the life of man, and of their opposites—the false, the ugly, and the evil. This is one of the fine arts which has won a respectable position in the curriculum.

What may be called the language arts, notably the three R's are taught better. The reason for this is that they are made up of specific skills, and these skills can be developed in any normal individual through practice intelligently directed. Literary art, however, is another matter. As Bliss Perry has expressed it:

> The mechanics of English composition can be taught. They are taught well in hundreds of schools, and may if necessary be imparted to such college students as have failed to receive proper

instruction. Beyond this field of mechanical correctness lies the domain of literary art, and art in writing is mainly a matter of self-discipline, although the practitioner may be helped by expert criticism . . . From youths one should not expect immediate triumphs. One cannot make bricks without straw or a work of art without materials, and very few undergraduates have read enough, experienced enough, pondered enough, to have even the raw material for a literary masterpiece.[1]

It would be of some interest to know how it happened that the trivium of medieval education (grammar, logic, and rhetoric) broke up into separate subjects in the curriculum of the modern school, when by their very nature these subjects should be taught as a single discipline by the same teacher. An interesting experiment is being carried on by St. Mary's College, Notre Dame, in an attempt to reëstablish this unity in the curriculum. Freshman Rhetoric and Sophomore Logic have been done away with and both are taught in a single course meeting five times a week throughout the whole of the freshman year. It begins with grammar, not English grammar, however; rather, general grammar, the science of language which means elementary logic. Rhetoric, the art of language, is the work done outside of class, guided first by specific directions on mimeographed sheets for the student's reading in which he has his models, and then writing exercises with individual conference with the instructor for critical evaluation of his written work. Logic, as commonly understood, follows grammar in class. It is taught both as a science, the science of language beyond grammar, and as an art, basic to rhetoric in its highly developed forms of description and narration, exposition and argumentation. It is felt that with this approach the student will have a deepened understanding of the relationship between lan-

---

[1] Bliss Perry, *And Gladly Teach*, Houghton Mifflin, 1935, pp. 254–255.

guage and thought and an improved skill in expressing thought in language.[1]

3. THE FIVE FIELDS OF KNOWLEDGE

With the trivium of the medieval schoolmen reëstablished in the curriculum of the modern school through a unified training in the language arts, the other four fields of knowledge become the modern quadrivium. Figure 17. "Analysis of the Curriculum" reveals that our analysis based on the two powers of man giving us five fields of knowledge is identical with Nicholas Murray Butler's analysis of the "spiritual inheritance," also fivefold. (See quotation introducing this Chapter, p. 280.)

FIGURE 17.—ANALYSIS OF THE CURRICULUM

THE TWO HUMAN ABILITIES	THE FIVE FIELDS OF KNOWLEDGE	THE ARTS AND SCIENCES	BUTLER'S "SPIRITUAL INHERITANCE"	HUTCHINS' "ACCUMULATED WISDOM"
I Thought about the	1. Material world	Natural sciences	Scientific inheritance	1. Scientific
	2. Human world	Humanistic sciences	Institutional inheritance	2. Political
	3. Spiritual world	Metaphysical sciences	Religious inheritance	3. Philosophical (ethical)
II Expression through	4. The arts	Fine arts	Aesthetic inheritance	4. Artistic
	5. Language	Language arts	Literary inheritance	5. Literacy

That this analysis is not followed universally today is evident from what happened at Chicago University in 1932 when in relation to the first two college years it discontinued its seventy odd departments and reorganized their work under four "Divisions." These divisions are Physical Sciences, Biological Sci-

[1] The text used in this course is: *The Trivium, Integrated with College Composition*, Sister Miriam Joseph, C.S.C., Burgess, Minneapolis, 1937 (planographed edition).

ences, Social Sciences, and the Humanities. This is typical of
the presentday trend to overemphasize the sciences, splitting
the natural sciences into two, the physical and the biological,
and lumping what we call in our analysis the Metaphysical
Sciences (theology and philosophy), the Fine Arts and the
Language Arts into one division, the Humanities. Undoubtedly, as Dean Boucher says, the new university president, Dr.
Hutchins, was in sympathy with the "objectives" of this reorganization.[1] But that he does not see this fourfold divisional
arrangement as an adequate analysis of the content of general
education is evident from the following statement:

> I take it to be self-evident that every American citizen should
> know how to read, write, reckon, and speak . . . (and) should
> have a chance to master the accumulated wisdom of the race. . . .
> The accumulated wisdom of the race is ethical, political, artistic,
> philosophical, and scientific. Without it education loses the name
> and becomes merely a prolonged pause between birth and going
> to work.[2]

At first sight this looks like a sixfold analysis of the "accumulated wisdom of the race," since literacy, the ability to assimilate and communicate that wisdom is an essential part of it, but
when "ethical" wisdom is grouped as a part of "philosophical"
wisdom, which it is (See Diagram 1, "Outline of Philosophy,"
p. 11), we see that Hutchins' analysis is the same as Butler's,
and therefore the same as ours. (Figure 17, "Analysis of the
Curriculum," p. 298, 5th column.)

Our contention is that this fivefold division should form the
basis for building the curriculum on all levels of general education from the primary grades through the college. On the

[1] Chauncey Samuel Boucher, *The Chicago Plan*, Univ. of Chicago Press, 1935,
p. 7.
[2] Robert M. Hutchins, "Vital Education," *The New York Times*, *World's
Fair Section*, March 5, 1939, p. 50.

elementary level the organization and presentation of these materials will be psychological rather than logical.   By psychological we mean organization and presentation from the point
of view of the pupil's nature and needs.   The approach to the
immature mind of the child will be through Nature Study, not
the logically organized sciences of physics, chemistry, and biology.   Nevertheless the aim is the same, an acquaintance with
and understanding of the material world which forms part of
the environment in which man lives.   Similarly with man's
social environment.   Study of community life will be part of
the work of the elementary grades, although the approach will
not be through the highly organized sciences of sociology,
politics, and economics.   This approach is proper on the college
level when the minds of students have matured.

But even on the college level the problem is not free from
controversy.   Should the student be offered a survey course
covering a wide field through lecture and demonstrations, say,
in the Natural Sciences, or would it be more to his benefit to
follow one of the so-called "sample courses" in one of the special
sciences, *e.g.*, chemistry, or biology?   This introduces us to the
difficult problem of values.   The question as stated resolves itself into this: is a subject of value primarily because of its content or because of the procedures the assimilation of its content
involves?   Those who answer this question in terms of procedures subscribe to the theory of discipline.   The possession
of truth is, of course, a perfection of the mind, therefore to be
desired and to be aimed at.   But the emphasis running all
through the educational theory we are presenting here is that
if the mind is to continue its growth and development, it is the
pursuit of truth which is most significant, not its possession.
As Von Muller puts it "Truth is the property of God; the pursuit of truth is what belongs to man."

If this point of view is accepted, we see the fallacy of the pres-

ent trend in survey courses. If their justification is that they
present to students "knowledge which they cannot afford to be
ignorant of," they are following a false scent. The value of all
knowledge of things mundane is relative to the needs of the
individual—to a particular individual at a particular time in a
particular situation. The individual grows in knowledge only
in response to a felt need. If, on the other hand, a survey course
makes the individual conscious of needs, of certain gaps in his
apprehension and comprehension of the material, the spiritual
and human world, *i.e.*, if it stimulates interests which will result
in arousing activities that will mean the carrying on and the
carrying forward of his own self-education, then they have a
right to a place in the curriculum of general education. Will
they nullify the disciplines which are the chief value of activities in these various fields? Will a survey course in the Natural
Sciences, *e.g.*, through lecture and demonstration, rob the student of all personal contact with the discipline of precision characteristic of the scientific method? If it would, then such a survey course should be abolished. It does not seem impossible,
however, that both these values can be achieved during the
extensive number of years devoted to general education. Certainly the student on the college level should have the experience of using the scientific method in some field, *e.g.*, chemistry,
if he is ever to have any adequate comprehension of what it
really is, what it costs in effort, and what it achieves in outcomes. But, on the other hand, it is altogether possible that
this same student, through a short series of lectures on astronomy with slides given as part of a survey course, might have his
interest aroused in astronomy, with the outcome of an intellectual hobby that will do more to enrich his life, if not his pocket-
book, than any other single experience he may have during the
whole period he devotes to general education. The point we
wish to emphasize is that all true education is self-education.

In the early stages the curriculum must be within the capacities of the pupil. We do not teach calculus to kindergartners. Subject matter must not only be within the capacities of the learner, but, as far as possible, it should be within the range of his interests, present or to be aroused. We do not mean by this latter statement that we subscribe to the theory of the ultra-progressives with their so-called "child-centered school," that is, a school in which the child's interests determine the curriculum. Chapman and Counts state:

> The factor of interest must always be considered by those who control the studies and methods of the school; but interest as the major criterion for the selection of subject matter is a pernicious guide. . . . Any system of education which sets up child or student interests as its guiding star is doomed to failure. In the determination of the nature of the activities, not the temporary and often misguided interest of a relatively ignorant pupil, but the requirements of a well-conceived society constitute the final standard of value.[1]

Interest is the key to method, but the pupil's needs, as an individual and as a member of society, is the key to content. And the content must be graded progressively, passing from the simple to the more complex as the pupil progresses in capacity so that it always constitutes a challenge to call forth his best efforts.

The question of values in planning a curriculum is of such importance that we will devote the succeeding chapter to its consideration. Content values, interest values, and procedure values will be discussed under the traditional labels for these three aspects of this difficult problem, namely, utilitarian values, cultural values, and disciplinary values.

[1] *Op. cit.*, pp. 376–377.

SUGGESTED READINGS

Bobbitt, J. F., *How to Make a Curriculum*, Houghton Mifflin, 1924.

Bode, B. H., "Determining Principles of Curriculum Construction," *Educational Administration and Supervision*, Vol. XII, Apr. 1926, pp. 217–228.

Briggs, T. H., *Curriculum Problems*, Macmillan, 1923.

Chapman, J. Crosby and George S. Counts, *Principles of Education*, Houghton Mifflin, 1924, Problems 19, 20, and 21, constitute one of the best presentations from the naturalist's point of view.

Charters, W. W., *Curriculum Construction*, Macmillan, 1923.

Foerster, Norman, *The Future of the Liberal College*, D. Appleton-Century, 1938, Chap. IV, "The College Curriculum of the Future" a caustic criticism of four present day theories of curriculum making.

Harap, Henry, *The Technique of Curriculum Making*, Macmillan, 1928.

Hopkins, L. T., *Curriculum Principles and Practices*, Sanborn, 1929.

Inglis, Alexander, *Principles of Secondary Education*, Houghton Mifflin, 1928, "Part III Means and Materials of Secondary Education" Chapters XI–XX, though one of the oldest books is one of the best on the secondary school curriculum.

McMurry, C. A., *How to Organize the Curriculum*, Macmillan, 1923.

Rugg, H. A., "Curriculum Making: What Should Constitute the Procedure of National Committees?" *Journal of Educational Psychology*, 1924, pp. 23–42.

Schwitalla, Alphonse M., "The Curriculum in the Liberal Arts College," *North Central Association Quarterly*, Jan. 1940, pp. 239–252, an excellent presentation.

Shields, Thomas E., *Philosophy of Education*, Catholic Education Press, 1917, Chap. XXII, "The Curriculum," pp. 397–412.

Willman, Otto, "Seven Liberal Arts," Vol. I, *Catholic Encyclopedia*, pp. 760–764.

Whipple, Guy Montrose (editor), *Twenty Six Year Book, 1926*, National Society for the Study of Education, Part I. "Curriculum Making Past and Present," Part II. "Foundations of Curriculum Making," Public School Pub. Co., Bloomington, Ill.

UTILITARIAN AND CULTURAL VALUES

As to their studies, it would be well if they could be taught everything that is useful and everything that is ornamental. But art is long and their time is short. It is proposed therefore that they be taught those things that are likely to be *most useful* and *most ornamental.*

Benjamin Franklin, *Proposals Relating to the Education of Youth in Pennsylvania, 1749.*

DISCIPLINARY VALUES

Until about 1890 the ruling notion in American education was that there existed such a thing as *general discipline,* general knowledge, and general capacity, all of which should be developed and made the most of by cooperation between home and school. As a result of a few hopelessly superficial and irrelevant experiments, it was one day announced from various psychological laboratories that there was no such thing as *general discipline* and general capacity, but that all disciplines were particular and that all capacities were specific. The arrant nonsense of this and the flat contradiction given to it by human observation and human experience went for nothing, and this new notion spread abroad among the homes and schools of the United States to the undoing of the effectiveness of our American education.

. Nicholas Murray Butler, President, Columbia University, *Tracts for Today, Law and Lawlessness,* pp. 6–7.

CHAPTER X

VALUES AND THE DISCIPLINES IN SCHOOL ACTIVITIES

The title of this chapter has been chosen advisedly. We speak here of school "activities" not school "subjects." Our reason for this is to recall to the student's mind that we formulated in Chapter V, "Theories of Learning," as the primary principle of education, *the pupil learns only through his own activity.* School subjects, therefore, if they are to be the medium through which learning is to take place, must be activities. The curriculum is the group of activities planned by the school for pupils, through which, under the stimulation and guidance of teachers, learning will take place. Since no curriculum can possibly contain all there is to be learned in life, selection must be made. And the basis for this selection must be in terms of value for the pupil. No activity the carrying on of which does not make a real contribution to worth-while learning for the pupil, must be allowed to take up any of the time of the curriculum. Worth-while learnings are those which make a contribution in terms of enriched living in one or more of the seven fields of social living which we analyzed in Chapter VI, "The Universal Human Needs." Unless it can be demonstrated that an activity (or a subject) has value for one or more of these areas of life, it has no place in the program of the school. What are the pos-

sible values an activity may have in terms of worth-while learnings?

Traditionally, the possible values of a school study have
been classified as threefold. A subject is entitled to a place in
the curriculum because it has *utilitarian* value or *cultural* value
or *disciplinary* value or, in the case of particular subjects,
some combination of these. Of late years, however, these
terms have become outmoded in educational literature and
other terms have been employed to label the same ideas. Thus,
in Chapman and Counts, *Principles of Education*, we read:

> In weighing the merits of a particular study, there are three con-
> siderations that must be borne in mind: (1) interest value; (2)
> content value; (3) procedure value. The values are so inter-
> related that convenience of thought alone justifies their separate
> discussion. By interest value is meant the power that study has
> of awakening agreeable responses in the student. Interest is evi-
> dence that there is a voluntary identification of the self with the
> activity. The degree of interest is a measure of the felt signifi-
> cance of the study to the total life experience. The content of a
> subject is the factual basis. The content value of a study is meas-
> ured in terms of the contribution which it makes to the furthering
> of the purposes of the individual. The procedure value of a study
> is measured in terms of the contribution which it makes in form-
> ing sound habits such as we have illustrated in a limited intellec-
> tual realm,—habits which may have a somewhat wide range of
> application. (p. 395)

This is a clear statement of the possible values that a school
activity may have for the learner. These words, "content,"
"interest" and "procedure," have certain connotations which
help bring out the real meaning of the terms "utilitarian,"
"cultural" and "disciplinary" and we will use them from time
to time in this discussion for purposes of clarification; but the
older terms have rich connotations also, and so as not to lose

them, we will adopt these terms as headings for our treatment of this difficult problem.

Here we call attention to the fact that we have not used the word "practical" in our classification of values. The reason for this is that anything learned through a school activity is "practical" if it translates itself into *practice* in some other activity, either in school or in life outside of school. Take, for example, a pupil who, through rigorous and sustained application to the study of mathematics in school, has learned to apply himself to a difficult and disagreeable task. Suppose then that in his first employment outside of school he finds himself confronting a similar situation in a difficult and disagreeable job and carries over the attitude of application from school and puts it in practice in the new situation. Surely nothing could be more "practical" for him than his study of mathematics, although none of the content of the course functions in the slightest degree. To make "practical" synonymous with utilitarian is an unwarranted restriction of the term. Utilitarian, cultural, and disciplinary values are practical if they translate themselves into practice in life outside of school. If they do not, they are not values at all, and, as far as the school is concerned, may be ignored.

The real problem in this whole discussion is in determining the proper place of utilitarian and disciplinary values in planning a school program. Cultural values are much simpler to handle. We will begin our discussion, therefore, with these, reserving the other two values to Section 2, "Utilitarian and Disciplinary Values."

1. CULTURAL VALUES

What do we mean by culture? Some may object to Matthew Arnold's famous definition, "pursuit of our total perfection by means of getting to know, on all matters that most concern us, the best which has been thought and said in the world," (*Culture and Anarchy*, Preface) as too narrow for this all-inclusive term, culture. Taken literally, it seems to put the emphasis on science and on literature to the neglect of the other fine arts. But music with the pictorial and plastic arts, as well as the other arts, are avenues for the expression of man's intellectual and emotional life, and as such may be thought of as included under the word "said" interpreted largely. Surely getting to know the best thought that has been expressed through the arts is a part of culture. Adopting this broad interpretation we have here a working definition of culture.

But more important for our purposes in thinking through the problem of the school, is an adequate description of the cultured person. Here we probably could do no better than to select one of the descriptions of the gentlemen from Newman's *Idea of a University*. Here is one taken from Discourse VIII. "Knowledge Viewed in Relation to Religious Duty," Section 10:

> The true gentleman . . . carefully avoids whatever may cause a jar or jolt in the minds of those with whom he is cast;—all clashing of opinion, or collision of feeling, all restraint, or suspicion, or gloom or resentment; his great concern being to make every one at his ease and at home. He has his eyes on all his company; he is tender towards the bashful, gentle towards the distant, and merciful towards the absurd; he can recollect to whom he is speaking; he guards against unseasonable allusions, or topics which may irritate; he is seldom prominent in conversation, and never wearisome. He makes light of favours while he does them, and seems to be receiving when he is conferring. He never speaks of himself except when compelled, never defends himself by a mere retort, he has no ears for slander or gossip, is scrupulous in imputing motives to those who interfere with him, and interprets every thing for the best. He is never mean or little in his disputes, never takes unfair advantage, never mistakes

personalities or sharp sayings for arguments, or insinuates evil which he dare not say out. From a long-sighted prudence, he observes the maxim of the ancient sage, that we should ever conduct ourselves towards our enemy as if he were one day to be our friend. He has too much good sense to be confronted at insults, he is too well employed to remember injuries, and too indolent to bear malice. He is patient, forbearing, and resigned, on philosophical principles he submits to pain, because it is inevitable, to bereavement, because it is irreparable, and to death, because it is his destiny. If he engages in controversy of any kind, his disciplined intellect preserves him from the blundering discourtesy of better, perhaps, but less educated minds; who, like blunt weapons, tear and hack instead of cutting clean, who mistake the point in argument, waste their strength on trifles, misconceive their adversary, and leave the question more involved than when they find it. He may be right or wrong in his opinion, but he is too clear-headed to be unjust; he is as simple as he is forcible, and as brief as he is decisive. Nowhere shall we find greater candour, consideration, indulgence: he throws himself into the minds of his opponents, he accounts for their mistakes. He knows the weakness of human reason as well as its strength, its province, and its limits. If he be an unbeliever, he will be too profound and large-minded to ridicule religion or to act against it; he is too wise to be dogmatist or fanatic in his infidelity. He respects piety and devotion; he even supports institutions as venerable, beautiful, or useful, to which he does not assent; he honours the ministers of religion, and it contents him to decline its mysteries without assailing or denouncing them. He is a friend of religious toleration, and that, not only because his philosophy has taught him to look on all forms of faith with an impartial eye, but also from the gentleness and effeminacy of feeling, which is the attendant on civilization.

The school that plays a prominent part in developing personalities such as that just described has great cultural value for its pupils. We realize that such an outcome is not primarily the result of the curriculum. Rather, it will be brought about by personal contact with teachers who themselves are cultured persons. The learning outcome here is what we call "attitudes." Every attitude is an idea fringed with emotion. The emotion is the driving power of the attitude, inspiring the learner to strive for the realization of the idea in his own self. Looked at from this angle, we think of attitudes under two headings. There are the attitudes which we call *ideals*, functioning as the driving forces in the realm of human conduct; and the attitudes we call *appreciations*, functioning as the drive in the pursuit of the beautiful. What is an ideal? Taking the word apart we see that the first four letters give us the word "idea." Every ideal has as its basis an idea, that is, knowledge. The ideal of patriotism, for example, rests upon the foundation of a knowledge of one's country and the value for the individual in belonging to it. What does "l" stand for? This we may interpret as standing for loyalty. An ideal, in this analysis, is an idea to which a person is loyal or, at least, to which he promises himself he will be loyal. If there is no such implicit promise, a person cannot be said to have the ideal.

Appreciations are similar drives but directed to objects other than those which are the aim in the field of conduct. An appreciation of music, for example, means that one who has the appreciation finds value in music for his own living. Here we see the appropriateness of Chapman and Counts' term for this value, namely, "interest value." What is it that differentiates the savage from the sage? Is it not primarily a difference of interests? The savage has few interests and they are for the most part on a low level, hunting, fighting, eating, and procreation. The sage, on the other hand, has many interests, and they are concerned for the most part with the achievements of civilization, the higher things in the life of man.

Here then is the task of the school if it would minister to the pupil by making it possible for him to achieve the cultural values of life. It must implant ideals of worthy living and develop appreciations of the beautiful in life. As we said above, worthy ideals will become the possession of the pupil largely through the silent operation of inspiring example on the part of teachers whose own lives are regulated by these ideals. But appreciations are subjects for direct attack through the curriculum. Just how this approach must be made, if there is to be any hope that these learning outcomes will be realized, is a subject for discussion in Chapter XIII, "The Technique of Teaching."

2. UTILITARIAN AND DISCIPLINARY VALUES

The discussion upon which we are entering brings before us the most difficult and at the same time the most important problem in the whole field of education. It is the most difficult because it is the most abstract, throwing us, as it does, into the realm of metaphysics in our efforts to arrive at a clear concept of the nature of mind; and it is the most important because whatever answer we give to the question on the nature of mind determines the answers that will be given to the two practical problems in education: *what* shall we put into the curriculum and *how* shall we put over what we put in; the problems of the curriculum and method. To place the matter squarely before us we quote the words a great teacher pronounced in his classroom in 1836:

> Considered as ends, and in relation to each other, the knowledge of truths is not supreme, but subordinate to the cultivation of the knowing mind. The question—Is Truth, or is the Mental Exercise in the pursuit of truth, the superior end?—this is perhaps the most curious theoretical, and certainly the most important practical, problem in the whole compass of philosophy. For, according to the solution at which we arrive, must we accord the higher or the lower rank to certain great departments of study: and, what is of more importance, the character of its solution, as it de-

termines the aim, regulates from the first to last the method, which an enlightened science of education must adopt.[1]

It is something of a surprise to come across this phrase "the science of education" in a lecture delivered more than one hundred years ago. It is still more surprising to find it used by a professor of philosophy and it is nothing less than shocking to find it in a volume carrying the title, *Lectures on Metaphysics and Logic*, by Sir William Hamilton, the eminent Scottish philosopher of the first half of the 19th Century. Knowledge, of course, is a perfection of the human mind, but the problem which these words from Hamilton place before us, the problem, namely, whether in the process of education it is *the pursuit* of knowledge or its *possession* that best advances that perfection, has divided educational theorists ever since it was first discussed in Greece twenty-five hundred years ago.

THE TWO SCHOOLS OF THOUGHT

Going back to the Greeks, we have first the sophists, who claimed, as their name signifies, that they possessed knowledge and were ready to pass it on to others provided they were paid for it. Opposed to the sophists were the philosophers. They, as their name signifies, were in pursuit of knowledge, but they made no claim that they were in possession of it. Monroe describes the situation in Greece during the fifth century B.C. in these words:

> To both Socrates and Plato little mental improvement comes from the direct impartation of knowledge. Against the popular methods of the sophists, which aimed to disseminate information through the formal lecture, these philosophers opposed the dialectic or conversational method, the object of which was to generate the *power* of thinking. Their aim was to create minds capa-

[1] William Hamilton, *Lectures on Metaphysics and Logic*, p. 6.

ble of forming correct conclusions, of formulating the truth for themselves, rather than to give them the conclusions already elaborated.[1]

Plato defines man as "the hunter of truth." Always with him the emphasis is on the pursuit, not the possession of knowledge. So Aristotle in one passage says, "The intellect is perfected not by knowledge but by activity," and in another, "The arts and sciences are powers, but every power exists only for the sake of action; the end of philosophy, therefore, is not knowledge, but the energy conversant about knowledge."

This tradition established by the philosophers of Greece with its emphasis on the pursuit of knowledge rather than its possession as the very heart of the educative process dominated thought well down into modern times. Thus St. Thomas, the greatest of schoolmen, says, "The intellect commences in operation and in operation it ends," and Scotus even declares that a man's knowledge is measured by the amount of his mental activity. The implication of this, of course, is that those who place the emphasis on the pursuit of knowledge, rather than on its possession, in the long run arrive at its possession more fully than those who set possession as the goal. The reason for this is, of course, that coming into possession of knowledge presents no obstacle to the cultivated intellect, once the need for knowledge in any particular field arises. Quoting Hamilton again:

The profoundest thinkers of modern times have emphatically testified to the same great principle. "If," says Malebranche, "I held truth captive in my hand, I should open my hand and let it fly, in order that I might again pursue and capture it." "Did the Almighty," says Lessing, "holding in his right hand *Truth,* and in his left *Search after Truth,* deign to tender me the one I might prefer—in all humility, but without hesitation, I should request *Search after Truth.*" "Truth," says Von Muller, "is the property

[1] Paul Monroe, *History of Education,* Macmillan, 1925, p. 128.

of God, the pursuit of truth is what belongs to man;" and Jean Paul Richter: "It is not the goal, but the course, which makes us happy." [1]

The break in this tradition came in the 17th century. This is the century of the scientific revolution when Galileo and Newton made their great contributions in the field of the physical sciences. Science means knowledge. No wonder that once again in education the emphasis is placed on the *possession* of knowledge rather than on its *pursuit*. In the history of education the scientific movement is reflected in the movement called realism. Education is now to be concerned with the realities of life. The greatest of the realists was Comenius. To what extent he placed the emphasis on knowledge is indicated by the fact that the curriculum he advocated was pansophic, that is, embracing all knowledge. His exaggerations in this respect are revealed in this quotation from Laurie's *Life of Comenius:*

> There is nothing in Heaven or Earth, or in the Waters, nothing in the Abyss under the earth, nothing in the Human body, nothing in the Soul, nothing in the Holy Writ, nothing in the Arts, nothing in the Economy, nothing in Polity, nothing in the Church of which the little candidates of Wisdom shall be wholly ignorant.

But Comenius in the 17th century was not the only educational theorist of prominence in Europe. John Locke in England is often classified as the leader of the other school. For Locke it is the process of learning that is all-important, not the possession of the thing learned. Here the fundamental principle is: *self-development through self-discipline*. Locke applies this principle in the three fields: (1) physical education with his hardening process, (2) moral education with emphasis on training in habits, and (3) intellectual education.

[1] *Op. cit.,* p. 9.

We may now say that the two camps are definitely formed. In the one camp we have the disciplinarians under the leadership of Locke, and in the other the utilitarians (knowledge for use) under the leadership of Comenius. With the advance of the natural sciences in both their pure and applied aspects during the modern era, the utilitarians gained the ascendancy. In the middle of the last century Spencer in England with his famous essay proved to his own satisfaction, and that of many others, that the knowledge of most worth is science. Huxley popularized this idea in his lectures at the same time ridiculing the discipline theory still operative in the English Public School. A little later came the break with tradition in the United States when Eliot introduced the elective system at Harvard. The theory back of this innovation was what we may call the fallacy of the equivalence of studies; that is, any subject of study is as worth while as any other subject, provided it is taught as well and studied as seriously. Carried to its logical absurdities, this means that ping pong has as much value for the student as mathematics, provided it is taught as well and the student applies himself to it as seriously. The only criterion for the choice of studies is use. No one should study mathematics beyond the elements of arithmetic unless he is going to use this mathematics; in the same way no one should study ping pong unless he is going to use ping pong in some life activity.

The utilitarians had now gained the day and the elective system spread over the country like a prairie fire. Early in this century most high schools and colleges had adopted it in some more or less modified form. The chaos resulting brought forth the system of required subjects in high school and in college, majors and minors as provisions for insuring general education. Today in college the popular terms are distribution in the first two years, and concentration in the last two years. Now I suppose we can say that the leadership of this school has passed from Harvard to Chicago University with the organization of what they call the "college," that is, the first two years after high school, into four divisions, with a curriculum of which the core is four introductory courses, one in each of the four divisions, (1) physical science, (2) biological science, (3) social science, and (4) the humanities. Notice that three of the four divisions carry the word "science" in their titles. Again the emphasis is on knowledge. There is no recognition here that education is primarily a process of inner development; what President Wriston in an address before the Association of American Colleges in 1936 called "maturation." No, a student is granted his B.A. degree as soon as he is able to pass comprehensive examinations in these four fields of knowledge with special examinations in one of them; and one student is reported to have accomplished this in eight and one half months after high school.

MECHANISTIC PSYCHOLOGY

With this emphasis in practice on knowledge as the supreme goal in education it would have been strange, indeed, if back of it there was no educational theory justifying the practice. Herbart began the attack here. First he eliminated faculties. With these gone education became a matter of storing the mind with knowledge, in the technical jargon of his school, "apperceptive masses." Herbartianism came to this country in the Gay Nineties following the return of a group of American students from the University of Jena. The heart of the theory was the denial of faculties. Totally ignorant of the Aristotelian concept of faculties, these theorists seemed to have conceived them as little imps, little jack-in-the-boxes; press one button and one little jack would jump out to do his stuff; press another button and another little jack would jump out.

Since obviously there were no little imps in the mind—and therefore no faculties—it was absurd to speak of training the faculties. How, then, did learning take place? Thorndike came to the rescue here with his theory of S-R bonds. Learning was simply the establishment of a bond in the nervous system between a stimulus or a situation and a response. Since the situations of life are multitudinous, the business of education consists in establishing multitudinous bonds. The theory is summed up in the statement: *all learning is specific.* And following this theory of learning came the job-analysis technique of building the curriculum. This is not quite the pansophic curriculum of Comenius, since there is selection, but it should be noticed that the utilitarian emphasis is the very basis of this selection. To make clear to what a pass this theory of learning has brought American education, we quote a statement by one of the leaders among the moderns, George S. Counts, who says:

> The principle of practical utility has received quite unexpected support from a long series of learning experiments conducted by American psychologists since the Nineties of the last century. These investigations have been interpreted as proving that learning is specific rather than general, that the development of facility in one field of endeavor is of little value in another, and that, in a word, all talk about training the mind should be regarded on the same plane as belief in witchcraft. . . .
>
> Being convinced that education should prepare for the real activities of life and being convinced further now that the only sound method of preparation is through direct participation in these activities, they (the Americans) were forced to turn for guidance to an examination of contemporary society. The logical result was the development of the technique of job or activity analysis. According to this method life as it is lived today in America should be analyzed into its separate activities and the school program should be compounded in some fashion from the findings. The underlying assumption is that learning is specific

and that faith in the development of general intellectual powers is educational superstition.

At the present time, however, the Americans find themselves in a serious dilemma. They have come to realize that they are living in the most dynamic civilization of history and that the world about them is undergoing constant transformation. Obviously the doctrine of specific training, the doctrine of psychological mechanism, the doctrine that all learning is essentially the formation within the nervous system of bonds between particular situations and particular responses, the doctrine which was welcomed half a generation ago as the sure road to educational salvation, makes no provision for adjustment to a changing civilization. As a consequence, educators find themselves constrained to prepare the coming generation for the rapidly shifting scenes of industrialism with a psychology which implies that this is impossible. They are therefore turning to the reëxamination of theories once discarded and the formulation of a new theory of learning.[1]

But an apt reply to Thorndike's atomistic theory of learning with its contention that all learning is specific and its explanation in terms of isolated stimuli, specific reactions, and S-R bonds between them, appears to have been given by the Gestalt psychologists. In this theory learning is explained in terms of insight. Insight operates on "Gestalts," in English, configurations, or patterns, that is, on *wholes*, and dynamic organization takes the place of the S-R bonds. In a letter which the writer received from a graduate student of education at Leland Stanford University, in 1937, this statement was made: "All curricula and courses of study in the public schools are now being revised in the light of the implications of Gestalt psychology." This, we can well imagine, is an overstatement of the facts made in a moment of enthusiasm. In education, as in all fields of human endeavor, practice lags

[1] George S. Counts, *The American Road to Culture*, John Day, 1930, pp. 166–168.

behind theory. But one thing is evident. What someone has called the "muscle-twitch" psychology has had its day, and mind re-enters the house of psychology from which it has been banished by the materialistic mechanists. With the return of mind to psychology, will mental discipline be welcomed back by American educators; and if so, what interpretation will be given to the term? This we will discuss in the final section of this chapter, 3. "The Disciplines in School Activities."

VOCATIONAL VERSUS GENERAL EDUCATION

When the problem of values is presented in this light, the sharp contrast between vocational and general education is immediately apparent. In vocational education the values of supreme moment are utilitarian. All subjects are introduced into the curriculum of the vocational school, whether on the level of secondary or higher education, because it is believed they have a definite contribution to make in preparing the student to carry on that vocation effectively. In the elementary school the teaching of the tool subjects has the same practical importance. The tools will continue to be *used* by every pupil all his life long as he carries on the social processes of communication and exchange. But on the levels of secondary and collegiate education there is a definite shift in relative importance. On these two levels it is the cultural and disciplinary values that are supreme. But in general we may say that only insofar as a subject or activity has one or more of these values in some appreciable degree, is it entitled to a place in the curriculum. In what is perhaps the most famous quotation in the history of American education, Benjamin Franklin, 1749, in his tract on the Academy names two of the values, if we interpret his word "ornamental" as equivalent to "cultural":

As to their studies, it would be well if they could be taught everything that is useful and everything that is ornamental. But art is long and their time is short. It is proposed therefore that they be taught those things that are likely to be *most useful* and *most ornamental;* regard being had to the several professions for which they are intended.

But it must be remembered that his proposal of the Academy was a protest against the Latin Grammar School, in which the disciplinary values were supreme. It is only now, after almost two hundred years, that the bias given to American education by Franklin in favor of utilitarian values is giving way to a more balanced point of view revealed in the current discussions of "general education" in which all three values have their part to play.

We remind the student again, that this distinction in values is a logical distinction, the same as the distinction between mental functions which we developed in Chapter III, "The Nature of Man." This distinction is made for purposes of study that we may deepen our understanding of the school problem, but it is founded on the facts of experience and it is valid. We cannot separate these values into three logic-tight compartments. They all inter-penetrate one with another. It is a simple matter to set up a diagram as we do here (Figure 18), showing the relationship between the three values and the three outcomes of learning. Similarly in the same diagram we can divide the subjects in the curriculum on the basis of their contribution in terms of the learning outcomes, into Science subjects, Appreciation subjects and Arts subjects (emphasizing doing) and in this way make a primary association for each one of the subject groups with one of the values. But it would be a fatal error for the student to interpret this diagram as meaning that any subject in the curriculum can make a contribution to the growth and development of the pupil in

terms of one of these three values only. Just the contrary is
the case. Any subject in the curriculum will make some
contribution in terms of all three values, but its *primary*
contribution is in terms of one of the learning outcomes, and

FIGURE 18.—VALUES OF A SCHOOL ACTIVITY

LEARNING OUTCOMES	TYPES OF SUBJECTS	TRADITIONAL LABELS	CHAPMAN AND COUNTS' LABELS	THE PRODUCT, A MIND
Knowledge (facts and meanings)	Science subjects	Utilitarian values	Content values	Informed
Attitudes (ideals and appreciations)	Appreciation subjects	Cultural values	Interest values	Cultured
Abilities (habits and skills)	Arts subjects	Disciplinary values	Procedure values	Disciplined

this should determine the direct attack of the teacher. The
other outcomes will be realized to some extent and insofar as
this is the case the other values will come to the pupil also.
But these other values will be realized largely by a process of
indirection. Thus, in the professional course in Education
for which this text is written, the aim is *knowledge,* a deeper
understanding of the problem of the school as a social agency
for forwarding the development of the pupil. This is a *science*
course, using that word in the larger sense inclusive of the
natural, the humanistic, and the metaphysical sciences, in their
pure and applied aspects. But if this outcome of deepened
knowledge and understanding of the school's problem is realized in any adequate degree at all, it would be strange, indeed,
if certain attitudes were not set up in the minds of the prospective teachers who have been carrying on this study. Further,

technical teaching skill is certainly not the primary objective of a work such as this. That is the purpose of courses in student teaching. Nevertheless, if the student, in his search for the relationship between ideas, has been aided by the diagrams and figures, similar to the one we have just referred to (Figure 18), if this visual presentation of these relationships in diagrams has aided him in his efforts at clear thinking, surely we may expect that he, too, will develop a technique of teaching that will include a presentation of the abstract in terms of the concrete by diagrams on the blackboard, using visual presentation to supplement oral presentation, at the same time urging his pupils to do the same in their study activities. Here is an instance of transfer which any intelligent student will make when he begins teaching. It is only through teaching of this type that we may expect that all the values of the various subjects will be realized for pupils in any adequate degree.

TRANSFER OF TRAINING

Locke seems to have been the first to use the word "transfer" in this connection.

> Would you have a man reason well, you must . . . exercise his mind. . . . Nothing does this better than mathematics, which, therefore, I think should be taught to all those who have the time and opportunity; not so much to make them mathematicians, as to make them reasonable creatures . . . that having got the way of reasoning, which that study necessarily brings the mind to, they might be able to *transfer* it to other parts of knowledge, as they shall have occasion.[1]

Utilitarian values are those in which the transfer is obvious. A child, for example, who in school has learned to multiply 2 times 5 and knows that this makes 10, knows that, if he wishes to buy two five-cent candy bars, he must have ten cents when

[1] John Locke, *Conduct of the Understanding*, pp. 6–7.

he goes to the store to make the purchase.   Here is a typical example of a utilitarian value of a school activity, arithmetic. But when we consider the other two values, cultural and disciplinary, the problem is not nearly so simple.   Libraries have been filled with books during the past fifty years attacking this problem from different points of view.   In the case of disciplinary values, the attack, for the most part, has been to explain belief in the value of mental discipline as resting upon a false theory of "faculty psychology."   This false theory is supposed to be an inheritance from the medieval scholastics foisted upon modern education by John Locke.   It is apparent that those who hold this view never read Locke.   Here is what he says about faculties:

6. Faculties.—These powers of the mind, viz., of perceiving, and of preferring, are usually called by another name: and the ordinary way of speaking, is, that the understanding and will are two faculties of the mind; a word proper enough, if it be used, as all words should be, so as not to breed any confusion in man's thoughts, by being supposed (as I suspect it has been) to stand for some real beings in the soul that performed those actions of understanding and volition.   For when we say the will is the commanding and superior faculty of the soul; that it is or is not free; that it determines the inferior faculties; that it follows the dictates of the understanding, etc.; though these and the like expressions, by those that carefully attend to their own ideas, and conduct their thoughts more by the evidence of things than the sound of words may be understood in a clear and distant sense; yet I suspect, I say, that this way of speaking of faculties has misled many into a confused notion of so many distinct agents in us, which had their several provinces and authorities, and did command, obey, and perform several actions, as so many distinct beings: which has been no small occasion of wrangling, obscurity, and uncertainty, in questions relating to them. . . .
19 . . . But in all these it is not one power that operates on another; but it is the mind that operates, and exerts these powers;

it is the man that does the action, it is the agent that has power, or is able to do. . . .

20 . . . But the fault has been, that faculties have been spoken of and represented as so many distinct agents.[1]

If the critics of faculty psychology had any acquaintance with the Aris-thomistic philosophy they would know that in this view the mind is a spiritual entity. As spiritual it is nonmaterial and, therefore, can have no parts. Unity is its prime characteristic and this unity is not a discovery of modern psychology. The question of the distinction between the mind (or soul) and its faculties and the distinction among the faculties themselves was always controverted and probably always will be. These are philosophical concepts, and even if agreement could be reached as to their meaning, we could not expect much light therefrom for the science of education. As Kane states it:

> The violent quarrel in psychology about "faculties" has simply no significance in the field of education. It is immediately evident as a matter of fact that the process of adding two and two differs from the process of recalling an historical event or the process of "giving to airy nothings a local habitation and a name." Whether we demand that these processes originate in distinct powers or faculties of the mind, or consider them diverse modes of functioning of a single central power, does not affect in the least the practical business of training the mind in these processes. In this connection, it is amusing to note how many writers on education, who get quite worked up over what they consider the absurdity of classifying the activities of a single human being by "faculties," blandly venture to classify whole groups of men as "realists," "humanists," "naturalists," and the like. Logic and common sense are not always conspicuous in violent quarrels.[2]

[1] John Locke, *An Essay Concerning Human Understanding*, Book II, Chapter XXI, Of Power. Sections 6, 19 and 20.

[2] W. Kane, S.J., *A History of Education*, Loyola Univ. Press, 1935, pp. 333–334.

To substitute capacities, abilities, powers, etc., for "faculties" as the modern do, does not add much light to the problem. In this presentation, to keep free from this controversy, we have consistently used the phrase "mental functions" rather than "mental faculties." After all, the mind does things, and if we are to study what it does we must classify its activities. The threefold classification of cognition, affection, and conation gives us our basis for the outcomes of learning, knowledge, attitudes, and abilities. Insofar as these outcomes are realized in the case of any individual pupil we may say that he has an informed, cultured, disciplined mind (see Figure 18, Column 5, p. 321).

THE WEAKNESS OF THE MENTAL DISCIPLINE THEORY

No doubt some of the proponents of the theory of mental discipline in their enthusiasm have been guilty of reifying faculties, though this cannot be said of authorities like Aristotle and St. Thomas. That is, they have never made them out to be things like two blades of a jack-knife, for example, either of which could be sharpened by application to a whet-stone. Nevertheless, it is correct to say that faculties or powers are sharpened by exercise, since in the analogy, sharpening means learning, and learning, as we have emphasized all through this treatise, takes place only through activity. The weakness of the theory of mental discipline is made evident when it is naïvely assumed that training gained in one field will automatically carry over into another, and that this transfer will be made without loss of effectiveness. For example, even such a general thing as the habit of hard work learned through application to Latin in school, may not carry over into the business world. Motivation (interest) is the all-important factor. The son of a banker with the academic type of mind will work hours over his

Latin with supreme enjoyment, but if his father insists on his going into the bank when every inclination of his mind rebels against it, what hope is there that he will work hard at learning the banking business? From this two things follow: First, teachers must teach transfer; they must demonstrate to their pupils how transfer can be made. The coach, teaching team work—"All for one and one for all."—must show how this will work for success in a business organization. "All for one and one for all" is a universal principle, but application must be made consciously, and teachers should point out how the application can be made. A second important point follows from this: the pupil must plan transfer. He must anticipate occasions when he can carry over what he has learned through curricular activities, or those that are co-curricular, into life situations.

Only too often the loudest proponents of the mental-discipline theory are living examples of this failure in their own lives. The professor who is meticulous in the correction of language themes and is slovenly in his dress, or neglectful in the matter of shaving, for example—where is the transfer of the habit of neatness? An insistence on the niceties of language expression is one thing. But only too often the instructor who makes most of this insistence is utterly neglectful of the fact that habits of dress and personal cleanliness are modes in which he expresses his own personality. Hence the important thing in education is:

> First, teachers must *teach transfer; i.e.*, they must make clear to students how the effect of training can be carried over into fields other than the one in which it was developed, and
> Second, students must *study transfer; i.e.*, they must anticipate those life situations in which training received in one field can and should be carried over into the new field they plan to enter.

3. THE DISCIPLINES IN SCHOOL ACTIVITIES

The thesis which we have been developing throughout this entire treatise is that all true education is a process of *self-development through self-discipline*. The word "discipline" has many meanings. Too often it is used to refer to the order or regulatory system superimposed from above down by some external authority more or less accepted or resented by those upon whom it is imposed. This is the kind of discipline in vogue in those countries in Europe today under a dictator. The discipline of a democracy as a political system, of an army recruited from volunteers, of the church, or of a religious community living under the vows according to a rule—all of these have certain characteristics of an authority above, ruling those in the ranks, but in all these cases membership in the organization means acknowledgment of the right of authority to rule, to impose a discipline upon the whole organization for the good of the entire group. Here, as in Heaven, order is the first law.

The same is true of education as it is operative in the life of the child. A rigid discipline is superimposed upon the infant and is aimed at the development of physical habits that will put him in control of the body processes, regular periods for sleep and play, for feeding and excretion, etc. The same must be true of the growing child, and in a particular manner of the growing adolescent, only now the discipline is extended to include mental and moral habits. The child who has not learned implicit obedience at home is poor material for the school to work upon. As Ella Frances Lynch states it: "Men and women are what they are because the home either trained them in the right way or failed in that responsibility. The school cannot remodel the child who has been given a wrong start at home." [1]   But as childhood advances and as adolescence proceeds, this discipline which in the beginning was superimposed by parent and teacher must give way to a discipline that is self-imposed until when the level of higher education has been reached the student manifests that maturity of mind that is characterized by a self-imposed discipline.

In Chapter VI, "The Universal Human Needs," we have stressed the point in Section 1, "Education," that the school is an intellectual agency.   Its primary responsibility is, therefore, the cultivation of the intellectual virtues.   In addition it will help the home and the church develop the moral virtues, but these are not subject to direct attack through formal instruction in the classroom.   The intellectual virtues are the product of a discipline that is intellectual, that is, which is concerned with things of the mind.   The most helpful sign in American education today is the restored prestige which the word "discipline" now carries in the current literature.   But it is significant that we no longer speak of "general mental discipline."   Rather we use the word in the plural, "disciplines."   It is now recognized that there are many disciplines in the process of education.   Though we now speak of the "disciplines" in the plural, the idea is the same it has always been.   It is usually assumed that the etymological basis of the word "discipline" is the Latin "discere," to learn.   However, the word is actually derived from "dis-capere," meaning to "take apart, to isolate," and as used in its strict etymological meaning it provides suggestions of some significance to the teacher.   "Discipline" stands in antithesis to "doctrine." [2]   Doctrine is from the point of view of the teacher; it is what he possesses in a given field of knowledge, and tends

---

[1] Ella Frances Lynch, *Bookless Lesson for the Teacher-Mother*, Nat. League of Teacher-Mother, Minerva-in-the-Adirondacks, 1931, p. 2.

[2] *Shorter Oxford English Dictionary*, Vol. III, p. 519.

to be more abstract and theoretical. It makes little difference whether the teacher comes into possession of a given body of facts by means of original research, or whether he expounds and interprets facts discovered by other researchers. In any case, the business of the teacher is the organization and presentation of a systematic body of knowledge. Discipline, on the other hand, is from the point of view of the learner; it tends to be more concrete and practical, because the individual student isolates and appropriates from the general body of doctrine that portion of it which best serves his own particular needs. The uses to which a set of facts can be put are as wide as the range of human interests themselves. Nevertheless, each subject possesses one or more general applications, and the distinction and enumeration of these general values is implied in the use of the word in the plural, as "disciplines."

When we attack the problem of differentiating the several disciplines that are of primary concern in general education we may well adopt the definition of a discipline in this field given by President Wriston: "Discipline, as I define it in this connection, is the essential mode of thought in a field of study." [1] Since in Chapter IX, "The Philosophy of the Curriculum," we have analyzed man's intellectual world into five fields of knowledge, we will now speak briefly of the "essential mode of thought," that is, the discipline characteristic of each field as analyzed in Figure 19, p. 330.

(A) THE DISCIPLINE OF PRECISION

The first of the fields of knowledge analyzed in Figure 19, is that of the Natural Sciences dealing with the physical universe. The characteristic trait of thought in this field is precision, exactness. Precision is achieved through measure-

---

[1] Henry M. Wriston, *The Nature of the Liberal College*, Lawrence College Press, 1937, p. 146.

ment, one of the chief functions of mathematics in the life of man. When the child has learned that 2 plus 2 makes 4, and that they can never add up to anything else, he had had an experience that is in sharp contrast to that which he will have in other fields of knowledge where mere opinion will be pre-eminent. The physical sciences dealing with nonliving matter, and the biological sciences with living matter, both carry forward this thirst for precision in their use of the experimental method. Here then is their contribution to the general education of the student. Working in this field he will assimilate a body of knowledge of the physical universe in which he is immersed, but more important than the amount of knowledge he assimilates is the passion for precision which study in this field should develop within him.

FIGURE 19.—THE DISCIPLINES IN SCHOOL ACTIVITIES

THE TWO HUMAN ABILITIES	MAN'S WORLDS AND THE ARTS	THE SCIENCES AND THE ARTS	THE DISCIPLINES OF	COLLEGE ACADEMIC GROUPS
I *Thought* about the	1. Material world	1. Natural sciences	a. Precision	1. Mathematics and natural sciences
	2. Human world	2. Humanistic sciences	b. Tolerance	2. History and humanistic sciences
	3. Spiritual world	3. Metaphysical sciences	c. Unification	3. Theology and philosophy
II *Expression* through	The arts	1. Fine arts	d. Appreciation	4. Music and fine arts
		2. Language arts	e. Expression	5. Language and literature

If this *discipline of precision* is the heart of the educative process in this field, the question of introductory survey courses in the natural sciences for the general student takes on a new aspect. Would even the most ardent advocate of a survey course in the natural sciences claim that students in such a course experience the discipline of precision to the same degree as do students following a laboratory course in any one of the sciences? Or, to put it another way, does anyone believe that students following a lecture course in the natural sciences, even with a well-constructed syllabus, richly supplied with reading references and an adequate library at hand in which these references are available, does anyone believe that these students will develop an adequate concept of scientific method, as compared with students who go into the laboratory and have first-hand personal experience of scientific method by carrying it on for a year in a course in chemistry or biology? If this is a fair statement of relative values, then a survey course in the natural sciences must justify its place in the curriculum on the basis of some discipline other than that of precision, some discipline which it provides better than any sample course can do.

To say that here is knowledge no educated person can afford to be ignorant of is a return to the theory of erudition advocated by Comenius. Knowledge has grown so great in all fields that no one person can assimilate it all in any field. As a matter of fact, there is no knowledge, except that which an individual cannot help learning by living in civilized society, which is absolutely necessary for anyone today. Knowledge has become so highly specialized in all fields that when one encounters a problem for the solution of which he has no knowledge, the intelligent thing to do is to hire an expert to do his thinking for him in that field, until he has assimilated the knowledge necessary to meet his need. The important thing is that he learn the "essential mode of thought" in the field. With this learned, he can soon assimilate the knowledge necessary for any of the ordinary exigencies of life.

(B) THE DISCIPLINE OF TOLERANCE

In sharp contrast to the discipline of precision characteristic of observation and reflective thinking in the Natural Sciences is the discipline characteristic of what we are calling the Humanistic Sciences. It is very difficult to select a name for the essential mode of thought in this field of human relations. President Wriston in his admirable presentation of this difficult problem delivered at the Institute for Administrative Officers of Higher Institutions has two names for the discipline characteristic of this field of knowledge. The paragraph title reads "The Discipline of Hypothesis," but the opening sentence says the basic discipline here is that of "opinionation." [1] We have thought sometimes that a more appropriate name would be suspended judgment. The natural sciences, of course, carry this discipline also, but it is of particular importance in the sciences dealing with man's social life. If we ask a German what were the causes of the World War, we will get one answer. The same question put to a Frenchman will call forth another answer. These are opinions, as President Wriston calls them. But they rest on knowledge, though this knowledge lacks the precision characteristic of the natural sciences. But no one should determine his own opinion until he has in his possession all the important facts bearing on the problem. This means he should suspend his judgment until he knows these facts. The recognition that much can be said on both sides of most of the problems arising within the field of human relations is so important that we have decided that a good name for the discipline characteristic of this field is *the discipline of tolerance*.

A dictionary definition of toleration is "recognition of, or disposition to recognize, the right of individual judgment."

[1] Henry M. Wriston, "Nature, Scope and Essential Elements in General Education," in *General Education* (Gray, editor), Chicago Univ. Press, 1934, p. 11.

We are reminded here of Newman's definition of the gentleman which we quoted in Section 1, "Cultural Values" (p. 308). If the student will reread this description, he will see that the person so described has developed the essential mode of thought characteristic of this field, and he may profitably reflect that insofar as he himself has done so, he is on the way towards becoming an educated person.

(c) THE DISCIPLINE OF UNIFICATION

The third field of knowledge is that of the spiritual world in which man lives, and the sciences dealing with it are the metaphysical sciences, theology and philosophy. On the lower levels of the educational ladder, the elementary and the secondary, theology is taught under the name, Religion. Philosophy is confined to the college level, but Catholic students who have had twelve years of training in the lower schools are ready when they enter college for theology in the strict meaning of the term, the science of God and of man's relations to God which contitute the spiritual universe in which he lives. In Matthew Arnold's fine phrase, the cultured individual "sees life steadily and sees it whole." Religion, particularly for those with faith in a revealed religion, is the influence that enables man to see life *steadily* in terms of his eternal destiny, life with God hereafter, and it is also the influence that enables him to live it *steadfastly* in terms of service to his fellow man here below. But the very business of philosophy is to train man to see life *whole*. Hence it is called the synoptic science, taking in all reality in one view. The Germans have an expressive word for this, *"Weltanschauung,"* literally a world view. Hamilton phrased the same idea in these words, "The end of philosophy is the detection of unity."

But if this synoptic view of the universe of matter, man and spirit is to be achieved by the student, he must complete a "course" in philosophy. This does not mean merely that he take a history of philosophy, giving an overview of all the philosophical theories the world has known. Rather, it means a course that begins at the beginning, with logic, goes through the middle, the whole field of general and special metaphysics, and comes out at the end in ethics, covering all of the eight departments into which philosophy is divided (see Diagram 1, p. 11). The problem of knowledge is taken up in epistemology, and the problem of being in ontology, the two together constituting general metaphysics. In the three departments of special metaphysics, the three types of being are studied separately and in their relations: material being in cosmology, the philosophy of the physical universe; spiritual being in theodicy, the philosophy of God; and the combination of matter and spirit that is man, the philosophy of mind, which might better be called philosophy of man. These five constitute the great field of speculative philosophy. It surveys all being in all its modes. In normative philosophy the whole of man's mental life is surveyed with the determination of norms to guide man in his search for the true, the beautiful, and the good, in logic, aesthetics and ethics, respectively. Here is a unified course that will challenge the best efforts of the best students any college may be blessed with. Dr. James Walsh, shows that philosophy so interpreted and so taught was the very core of the college curriculum in colonial days.[1] The founders of the republic, did a great work when they wrote the Declaration of Independence and the Constitution and started the new nation on its career with an instrument of government the equal of which has never been known in the life of man. What we need to do today is to take a leaf out of the notebook of the first American colleges of the 17th and 18th centuries

[1] James Walsh, *The Education of the Founding Fathers*, Fordham Univ. Press, 1935.

and on the upper level of general education make philosophy the core of the curriculum again, with its supreme *discipline of unification,* instead of devising new schemes for the so-called "enrichment of the curriculum," which so often result in the impoverishment of the student.

(D) THE DISCIPLINE OF APPRECIATION

The fourth field of knowledge in the analysis in Figure 19 (p. 330), is that of the fine arts. Here the discipline is that of *appreciation.* The business of the school concerned with general education is not to produce professional musicians, or painters, or any other type of professional artist. But every man, as well as every woman, is called to be an amateur artist, that is, an artist on the level of appreciation (cf. p. 295). This means every one should develop the ability to recognize and to enjoy the beautiful in nature and in the products that come from the mind and hand of man. In the past the school did little to develop this ability in all students. It is doing a much better job now. In music, for example, the phonograph and now the radio make it possible to bring into the schoolroom the music of the great masters played by the great artists of the day. But it must be remembered that the learning outcome here is an emotionalized attitude of enjoyment. This cannot be forced, but it can be cultivated. The same is true of the other arts. Beautiful buildings and beautiful campuses and landscaped schoolyards all play their part. We learn to love beauty by living with it, and living with it is one phase of the discipline of appreciation. This explains the case of two college students, science majors headed for medical schools, whom the writer discovered in a college dormitory. They had purchased a book of the operas. During the week they read the story of the opera to be presented each Saturday and then spent Saturday afternoon enjoying the broadcast from the New York Metropolitan.   These students were already realizing returns on the discipline of appreciation which they had been undergoing as members of the choral club.   Here was an interest that gave promise of enriching their leisure throughout their lives.   Both school and college can well afford to direct some of their activities towards bringing this discipline of appreciation into the lives of all their students.

(E)   THE DISCIPLINE OF EXPRESSION

The fifth field of knowledge in the analysis in Figure 19 (p. 330), is that of the Language Arts.   The discipline characteristic of this field is that of *expression*.   It has two phases.   In one the student receives training in expressing his own ideas in speech or in written discourse; in the other the training is directed towards enabling him to grasp and comprehend ideas expressed by others.   This means teaching him to read understandingly.   We ordinarily assume that the reading adaptation is achieved in the elementary school, but high school and college teachers early discover that most of the academic difficulties students encounter arise from their inability to read understandingly.   Teachers of mathematics in college often complain that the difficulties students experience with mathematics arise from the fact that they cannot read the statement of a problem with sufficient comprehension to understand what the problem is.   If this difficulty is so real, what shall we say about students' difficulties in expressing their own ideas in oral and written discourse understandable by others?

The foreign language teacher, particularly the teacher of an ancient language like Latin, has both an opportunity and an obligation here in the matter of helping students reap the fruits of the discipline of expression.   From the very beginning students must be brought to realize that Latin says something;

that it makes sense. In reading Latin, therefore, the student's task is to discover what it says. Once this is accepted as the aim, transverbalization, the literal rendering of word for word, will not be tolerated by either teacher or pupil. Then when the idea expressed by the Latin author has been grasped, the next task is to state the same idea in the king's English. Latin courses conducted in this wise, instead of Latinizing a student's English, will bring him the experience of the discipline of expression in a way that no training in his mother tongue can do.

The value which school activities may have for students are then, utilitarian, cultural, and disciplinary. If the average student carries on these activities with application under the sympathetic guidance of intelligent teachers during the years devoted to general education in this country, we have every assurance that the product will be an *informed, cultured*, and *disciplined* mind (see Figure 18, p. 321). In the American comprehensive high school, including as it does all the children of all the people, there are great differences in pupil ability. Utilitarian values are accessible to pupils of even the lowest ability. Cultural values, also, at least to a certain extent, will be achieved by all pupils. Disciplinary values, when referring to what we call the intellectual disciplines, are another matter. Here the extent of value realized is conditioned so definitely by the intelligence of the pupil that we must recognize that many of the so-called "disciplinary studies" are absolutely valueless for pupils on the lower ability levels in our comprehensive schools. They have already reached their point of intellectual saturation as far as certain studies are concerned, *e.g.*, mathematics. For them, the major consideration must be utilitarian values, if they are to remain in school and continue to profit by the experience. The problem presented by students of variant abilities in American comprehensive secondary schools will be discussed in the next chapter under the title, "The Dilemma of Democratic Education."

SUGGESTED READINGS
I. AND 2. VALUES

Bagley, William C., *Determinism in Education*, Warwick and York, 1925, particularly pp. 145–148.

———, *Educational Values*, Macmillan, 1911, theory of "conscious effort," pp. 193 ff.

Bode, Boyd H., *Conflicting Psychologies of Education*, Heath & Co., 1929, the only present-day writer among the naturalists who has any adequate grasp of the implications of faculty psychology properly understood. See particularly the first four chapters.

Chapman, J. Crosby and George S. Counts, *Principles of Education*, Houghton Mifflin, 1924, Problem 18. "What Constitutes the Value of a School Activity" pp. 367–401, is the best brief discussion of this question of values.

Commins, W. D., *Principles of Educational Psychology*, Ronald Press, 1937, Chapter XIV. "The Transfer of Training," pp. 416–444; best brief discussion of transfer of training; it is from the organismic point of view in psychology, stressing transfer through "patterns of experience."

Douglas, Aubrey, *Secondary Education*, Houghton Mifflin, 1927, discusses Values in Chapter XIII. "The Selection and Validation of Curriculum Materials," pp. 345–392.

Freeman, F. N., *How Children Learn*, Houghton Mifflin, 1917, theory of "development of attitudes," pp. 247 ff.

Hamilton, William, *Lectures on Metaphysics*, 1860; Chap. I gives an excellent discussion of the theory of "discipline" versus the theory of knowledge or "erudition."

Inglis, Alexander, *Principles of Secondary Education*, Houghton Mifflin, 1918, Chap. XI. "The Program of Studies—Criteria of Subject Values," well worth reading.

Judd, Charles Hubbard, *Psychology of High School Subjects*, Ginn & Co., 1915; theory of "generalization" in Chapter XVII.

Locke, John, *Essay Concerning Human Understanding*, Book II. Sec. 6, "Faculties"; see also his essay.

Locke, John, *On the Conduct of the Understanding*.

Monroe, Walter S., James C. DeVoss and George W. Reagan, *Educational Psychology*, Doubleday Doran, 1930, gives a good review in Chap. VII. "Transfer of Training," pp. 225–251.

Mursell, James L., *The Psychology of Secondary School Teaching*, Norton, 1939, Chapter 4. "How to Deal Effectively with the Factor of Transfer," pp. 87–116.

Orata, Pedro T., *The Theory of Identical Elements*, Ohio State Univ. Press, 1928, p. 41.

——, "Transfer of Training and Educational Pseudoscience," *Mathematics Teacher*, XXVIII, 1935, pp. 265–289.

Starch, D., *Educational Psychology*, Macmillan, 1927, gives a review of the experimental evidence on transfer, pp. 220–241.

Thorndike, E. L., "Mental Discipline in High School Studies," *Journal of Educational Psychology*, 15: 1–22, 83–98, January and February, 1924.

3. THE DISCIPLINES

Bagley, William C., "An Essentialist's Platform for the Advancement of American Education" *Educational Administration and Supervision*, April, 1938, pp. 241–256.

——, "The Significance of the Essentialist Movement in Educational Theory," *The Classical Journal*, March, 1939, pp. 326–344.

Gray, William S., (editor) *General Education—Its Nature, Scope and Essential Elements*, Univ. Chicago Press, 1934, Vol. VI., of the Proceedings of the Institute of Offices of Higher Institutions. The first address by President Wriston of Lawrence College, pp. 1–15, treats of four "basic disciplines."

Turley, John P., "Latin on the College Level," *Catholic Educational Review*, Oct. 1937, treats the three disciplines characterizing college Latin, of History, of Literature and of Expression.

McKeon, R. P., "Education & the Disciplines," *International Journal of Ethics*, 1937, pp. 370–381.

Wriston, Henry N., *The Nature of a Liberal College*, Lawrence College Press, 1937, Chapter IX, "A Theory of Disciplines," pp. 142–162.

THE AMERICAN SINGLE SYSTEM

Early in the development of our educational institutions the dual system of education with its two distinct parallel divisions was abandoned. In its place, through the organization of a secondary school that articulated with the elementary school at one end and with the college at the other, a single continuous system was established. This revolutionary change will, in the history of intellectual and social emancipation, be regarded as one of the greatest, if not the greatest, cultural achievement of the American people. The significance of this change is, as yet, hardly realized, and is only just beginning to bear fruit.

J. Crosby Chapman and George S. Counts,
Principles of Education, Houghton Mifflin,
1924, p. 445.

CHAPTER XI

THE DILEMMA OF DEMOCRATIC EDUCATION

The problems that arise in the governing of any group have their origin from two distinct sources: first, those concerned with the leaders of that group; and second, those concerned with the followers, that larger body over whom the former are to exercise their leadership. With regard to the leaders problems arise first, in the matter of their selection; second, in regard to their training and third, in a democracy at least, in regard to their election. This latter problem is, of course, primarily a problem concerning the followers, that is, it is a matter of developing a group of followers with sufficient intelligence and the mental attitude which will result in their choosing the right kind of leadership. This means intelligent voting.

In the older form of government, the monarchical, all of these problems found a very simple solution. The selection of leaders was a matter of birth; they were of the royal family. So also with the second problem, training for leadership. The prince was trained from the very earliest days for the kingship which was in store for him. Finally his promotion was merely a matter of seniority, the first-born son of the king becoming the king when the latter had passed on to his reward.

No such simple solution is present in the democratic form of government. Leaders must be discovered as they arise out of the mass. In the second place they must be trained. Further, they must be trained along with their followers, since in the early stages at least, no one knows who the leaders are going to be. In the third place they must be elected by the followers. As we said above this latter problem is one concerned primarily with the followers rather than with leaders, but again it is a matter of training. Followers must be trained to recognize the true leader when he comes forth and they must be trained also to reject false leadership and to want the right kind that will lead them forward toward achieving those things which are for their own best interests and the interests of the group as a whole. For the solution of these problems a democratic nation can rely only on one thing and that is education.

1. THE DILEMMA STATED

The school, like every social institution, reflects the society from which it springs. But the school from the very purpose of its establishment should also reform society, that is, remake it according to the heart's desire of those who are leaders within that society. Whether or not the school throughout its history has been an agency for reforming society, it always reflects the social *milieu* that has brought it forth. Here is a typical example.

In Prussia before the World War, society was definitely stratified on two levels, the classes and the masses, the leaders and the led. It is not surprising to find therefore in this society two distinct school systems one for the ruling classes and the other for the masses. The latter called the *Volksschule*, that is, the people's school or perhaps more accurately rendered in English, the peasant's school, was an eight-year institution giving a thorough foundation in the elements of education followed by a trade training. According to Curoe 92 per cent of the people were educated in this school system.[1] The other school system for the remaining 8 per cent had for its first unit a *Vorschule* of three years teaching the elements, followed by a nine-year institution, the *Gymnasium* proper, of several varieties but all contrasted with the *Volksschule* by the fact that foreign language was an integral part of the curriculum. This school in turn was followed by a third unit, the university with its various advanced and professional schools. In theory the brighter pupils of the *Volksschule* could transfer to the *Gymnasium* and in this way go on up into the university, but Paulsen says that not one in ten thousand ever did this. Thus membership in the higher professional classes, the holding of the higher civil offices, and advancement as officers within the army was effectually closed to all those who began their education in the *Volksschule*.

Now this arrangement of two separate school systems one for the people, the other for their leaders had certain distinct advantages. In the first place, with a highly centralized government behind it to enforce compulsory school attendance, it practically eliminated illiteracy, something which we in our own country have as yet failed to accomplish. In the second place, the efficient trade training of the lower classes played a prominent part in Germany's threat to capture the world markets, certainly one of the contributing factors that precipitated the World War. In the third place, this school system dealing with a highly selected group of students thoroughly trained in elementary, secondary, and higher education in the university resulted in that thoroughness characteristic of German scholarship and was a factor in producing that super-efficiency characteristic of German organization whether military, governmental, industrial, or commercial. But what price efficiency? The World War was one answer to that question. (See Figure

[1] Philip R. V. Curoe, *History of Education*, Globe Book Co., 1921, p. 178.

20, "Education in the German and American Systems.")

Contrast now with this double track system of Prussia our own educational system as it has evolved up to the present time. The first period of the history of education in this country we call the period of Transplantation. (Figure 21, "Evolution of the American Four Step Educational Ladder," p. 345.)

FIGURE 20.—EDUCATION IN THE GERMAN AND AMERICAN SYSTEMS

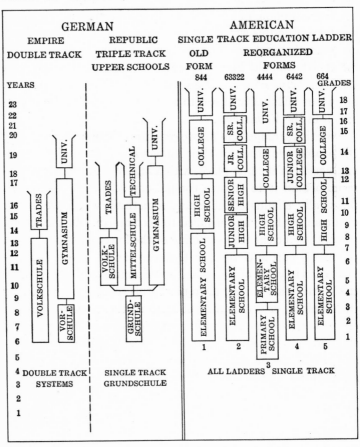

FIGURE 21.—EVOLUTION OF THE AMERICAN FOUR STEP EDUCATIONAL LADDER
PERIODS IN THE HISTORY OF EDUCATION IN THE U. S.

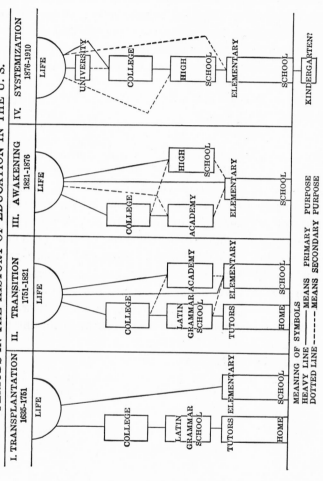

345

That means it was the period when schools characteristic of Europe were brought over to this country and set up here practically without change.   Insofar as there was any system at all during colonial times, it was dual in character.   True, as early as 1647 the Massachusetts school law called for an elementary school in every community of 50 families or more and a secondary school in every community of 100 families or more. These schools established by law, hence tax supported and therefore "public," indicate the democratic spirit at work from the very beginning.   But the ideal of educational opportunity for all had a long time to wait for realization.   In most communities little if any provision was made for elementary education and when such provision was made for the lower classes most commonly it was the type known as "pauper schools." On the other hand the colonial colleges, *e.g.*, Harvard, William and Mary, etc., were early established as training grounds for the leaders of the several communities, with Latin Grammar schools preparatory to them.   Training in the elements leading to the Latin Grammar school was provided for the most part by tutors in the home.   Little or no provision was made for either elementary or secondary education for the people as a whole.   (Figure 21, p. 345.)

Within a hundred years, however, the great democrat Benjamin Franklin, set out to remedy this situation with the establishment of his academy in 1751 and the Transition period had begun.   The academy was an institution designed to be the "peoples college" offering training of a more practical nature than that given in the Latin Grammar schools, whose curriculum as the name indicates was made up largely of Latin and Greek preparatory to the college.   But the academy as it developed, early took over the college preparatory function and eventually became dominated by it.   Three quarters of a century were to pass before another attempt was made to provide secondary training for the people. This came with the establishment of the first high school in Boston in 1821 and the period called the Awakening had opened. The high school also designed to be the "people's college" offered training of a practical nature preparatory to life. But the high school suffered the same fate as the academy. Early in its history it took over the college preparatory function and like the academy eventually became dominated by it.

The first eight-grade elementary school as we know it today was established in Quincy, Mass. in 1848. By this time the Latin Grammar school had disappeared. Following the Civil War the academies were converted into high schools or became distinctly college preparatory schools or else they disappeared entirely. Thus the high school became the dominant secondary institution. Following Harvard, private colleges were rapidly established throughout the country. Some began early to transform themselves into universities. With the passing of the Morrill act in 1862 the state university was on its way to become the characteristic American institution of higher education. Johns Hopkins University was established in 1876 and the period of Systemization had begun. But this institution like the other two which started out to be universities (Clark University and The Catholic University) found it necessary to set up an undergraduate college as part of its university organization. Thus the last quarter of the nineteenth century saw the American four-step educational ladder come into being, comprised of an eight-year elementary school, a four-year high school, a four-year college, and the university of graduate, professional, and technical schools. (Figure 21, p. 345.)

This single system was something new in the history of education. Comenius had visioned such a system of schools offering educational opportunity to all (see page 367), but Europe never accepted the idea and even today is not sympathetic towards it. This was the first great American contribution to education, a single school system offering educational opportunity to every student from the elementary school at the bottom to the university schools at the top, limited only by his ability and his willingness to advance himself within the system. At least this was the theory. Many an individual possessing ability, however, because of economic handicap was unable to take advantage of the opportunity this system in theory afforded to all.

Such a system has one distinct social advantage, namely, it promotes *social solidarity;* all students living and learning together and learning to live together by practicing living together; the only way that any activity can be learned. Such a system must exert a positive influence against the stratification of society. Leaders and led are in the same school, the leaders demonstrating their capacity for leadership, and the led learning to follow by practicing following while still within the learning period. But there is also a distinct disadvantage to such a system. It promotes *social solidarity* but it does not make provision for *individual development*, according to the capacity and the industry of each. The inevitable tendency of such a system is to gear down the pace of the whole institution to bring it within the capacity of the dominating middle group. This pace is too fast for the slow and too slow for the fast. It fits only the great middle group, the average. If the qualities of leadership of the gifted are to be developed, it is recognized that these superior students must be kept working up to capacity. But is this possible in an instutution where the pace is set by the average? Democratic education, therefore, is faced with a dilemma. If through the singleness of its system it makes provision for the development of social solidarity, it holds back the development of the superior mind. If on the other hand through a dual system such as has been characteristic of Europe, it makes provision for the development of the leaders and of the led in two separate systems, it creates a social rift between the two classes. (See Figure 21, "Evolution of the American Four Step Educational Ladder," p. 345.)

Here is one of the major problems that American education is confronted with today. No one familiar with the American temperament believes that we are going to give up the singleness of our system. This, as Chapman and Counts state in the quotation introducing this chapter (p. 340) is the one great contribution that this country has made to democratic education. But this interpretation of an educational system truly democratic in character, creates its own problem. How can we make provision for the different abilities, interests, and needs of the unselected student bodies of our elementary, secondary, and collegiate institutions? Before presenting the attempts to solve this problem now in operation on all levels of the American educational ladder, it will pay us to make a brief excursion into the history of education and review briefly the search for a solution during the nineteenth century,—and its failure.

2. THE SEARCH FOR A SOLUTION

The Political Revolution of the eighteenth century carried over into the nineteenth. Democracy was on the march. democracy applied to education implies equal opportunity for all. Strangely enough it was not a political democracy that first brought education to all the children of all the people. Rather, it was Frederick the Great, one of the benevolent despots, who with a highly centralized monarchical government behind him, by the law of 1763 made universal education a reality in Germany. Here was universal education abolishing illiteracy but it was not democratic education since there were two separate systems one for the classes and one for the masses. The Romantic movement of the nineteenth century presented to the

world the dream of the perfectibility of man and equal education for all as the means for the realization of that dream.
Rousseau was the inspiration here, but the psychologists of the
first half of the nineteenth century were to work out the "universal method" that would make all schools effective instruments for the realization of this dream.

(A)   A UNIVERSAL METHOD

Pestalozzi (1746–1827) contributed enthusiasm for the study
of the child but made little contribution in the field of method.
Even his "object lesson" was nothing but a concrete application of the old scholastic adage that all knowledge begins in
the senses.   Herbart (1776–1841) made two contributions, the
doctrine of abiding interests and the doctrine of apperception,
the latter leading to correlation through the application of the
"formal steps."   Froebel (1782–1852) made two contributions
with his emphasis on the principle of self-activity through
social participation and the introduction of a new school unit,
the kindergarten, in which the principle of self-activity with
social participation was operative in play, handwork, and nature study.

The chief result of all this emphasis on method was to throw
into relief the importance of teacher training.   The Pestaloz-
zian influence came to this country in the first half of the nineteenth century through the reports of Horace Mann, Griscom,
and Stowe.   From 1860 on, the Oswego Movement radiating
from Oswego, New York, emphasized psychological method,
enriched content, and teacher training.   Herbartian influence
was at its height in 1895 when "The National Herbart Society
for the Scientific Study of Education" was organized at the
Denver N.E.A., meeting.   This enthusiasm for Herbartianism
rapidly waned, and in 1902 the scope of the society broadened
and its name changed to the "National Society for the Scienti-

fic Study of Education." The Froebelian influence came to this country with the establishment of the first English-speaking kindergarten in Boston in 1860. This was followed by the establishment of the first training school for kindergartners in the same city in 1868. In 1873 the first kindergarten in a public school system was opened in St. Louis by Susan Blow under William T. Harris. The Office of Education now estimates that kindergartens are now available for almost one third of the nation's five-year-olds.

THE VARIABLES IN A TEACHING SITUATION

Apart from this impetus given to teacher training and the emphasis on the necessity of conformity between "method" as taught to students in training schools and the principles of learning formulated by the psychologists, the search for a "universal method" was a failure. In the very nature of the case this was inevitable. The teaching situation is one that is characterized by variables rather than constants. The number of variables in any teaching situation is almost unlimited but five are of such importance we name them here. There is first of all the personality of the pupils. The "simultaneous method" of St. De la Salle had brought about grading, which was a great improvement over the old individual instruction method, since it increased the amount of time during which each pupil received instruction. But in any group no matter how well graded, no two personalities are identical and instruction must always be adapted to these differences in abilities, interests and needs. In the second place no two teachers are alike in their own personalities. A method which is an efficient tool in the hands of one teacher may be an encumbrance when another attempts to employ it. Third, different subject matters call for different treatment. Skill comes through continued intelligent practice, whereas knowledge and under-

standing are outcomes of observation and reflective thinking.
In the fourth place, no two schools are alike. In one where the
ideal of scholarship is dominant, the teacher need spend little
time arousing students' interests; rather it is his task to give intelligent guidance (sometimes restraint) to the many activities
student interests initiate. In another school where the atmosphere is one of lazy indifference, arousing study activities becomes the teacher's main task. Finally, method itself must
be a variable, as mentioned above when speaking of subject
matter. For a chemistry teacher in his laboratory to despise
the approach a teacher of literature makes to his problem of
developing in students a liking for poetry by reading to them a
poem like Francis Thompson's "Hound of Heaven" and through
interpretive comment developing within them an understanding of its meaning as well as an appreciation of its beauty, is
nothing less than blindness to the chief characteristics of the
teaching situation, its variability. Teaching cannot be cast
in one mold. This is what happened to the Herbartian steps.
They became *formalized*. That is, students in training schools
were taught that if this "method" was mastered, any teacher
could teach any subject, in any school, to any group of pupils.
This was an inherently false interpretation of the "steps."
Certainly it was far from the mind of Herbart. The search for
a "universal method" has now been abandoned and the movement has gone to the other extreme. Today the number of
"methods" presented by authors dealing with this problem is
almost without limit. Here is a partial list of those that fill the
books treating "General Methods:"

Appreciation	Demonstration
Assignment	Development
Book Study	Discovery
Contest	Discussion
Conversation	Dramatics
Deductive Method	Dramatic Appreciation

Dramatic Expression
Drill
Experiment Method
Expressive Method
Inductive Method
Investigation
Laboratory Method
Lecture Method
Object Lesson
Objective Method
Participation Technique
Practice Technique

Problem Technique
Project Method
Recitation
Review
Self-Activity
Showing
Socialized Recitation
Story
Supervised Study
Telling
Topical Report
Unit Plan

(B) THE GRUNDSCHULE IN THE GERMAN REPUBLIC

Before turning our attention to the various solutions of the dilemma now being attempted in this country, it will help us to see the problem more clearly if we review briefly what happened in Germany following the World War. With the passage of the law of 1925 by the Weimar Republic, the old division between the classes and the masses on the level of elementary education, the *Volksschule* for the latter and the *Vorschule* for the former, was wiped away and in the place of these institutions a new school called the *Grundschule* was set up. (See "Single Track Grundschule" in Figure 20, p. 344.) As its name signifies this school is the foundation school. All the children of all the people attend this school for four years. At the end of these four years depending upon the record of the pupil within the school, his achievement in final examinations at the end of the fourth year, the recommendations of his teachers and the desire of his parents, it is determined whether the pupil is to continue his education in the last four years of the old *Volksschule*, or be transferred to the *Gymnasium* to begin secondary education leading to the university. A third alternative is also offered. A pupil may enter a new institution, which was coming into prominence before the war, but later was definitely set up as a part of the national system, the *Mittelschule*, a six-year school leading to training in lower technical schools. Thus the new German system although it was single track on the first level, was a triple track system following that. The policy of segregation was not given up except on the first level. In fact, it was intensified. After completing elementary education in the *Grundschule*, on the basis of their ability and industry, pupils were to be segregated in the *Volkschule*, in the *Mittleschule*, or in one of the various types of *Gymnasia* leading to the university. The single track *Grundschule* makes provision for social solidarity; the triple track system following the *Grundschule* makes provision for individual development. This is in sharp contrast to our American cosmopolitan high school in which those going *out* at the end of the four years and those going *on*, are all congregated in the same institution. The financial difficulties of the late twenty's, however, made it impossible for Germany to carry into effect these elaborate provisions for differentiation among pupils. The *Grundschule* was the one feature that actually came into being and it is still operative. What can be said about the school system of tomorrow under the Nazi regime?

THE GERMAN SYSTEM OF TOMORROW?

If we can believe the reports appearing in the press, there is going to be further differentiation in the new Germany but hardly on a basis that is democratic. Quoting Herman Rauschning, a one time intimate of Hitler, *Time* says that the new Germany will be definitely stratified on three levels: (1) a ruling class, the great hierarchy of the party, (2) an eternally disfranchised serving collective and (3) the subject alien races, "the modern slave class." The educational system to prepare these classes for their respective places in society apparently will be dual on the first level, the *Grundschule* for Germans and, it may be supposed, something corresponding to the old *Volksschule* for the subject alien races. At the age of 12, boys showing qualities of leadership will be selected from the entire German population to be trained for the Party organization. All others will, no doubt, continue in an institution corresponding to the *Mittelschule*. The little *Führers* will spend six years in 32 *Hitlerschulen* receiving a thorough fundamental education with emphasis on languages, history and the development of leadership. There will be no examinations—character being the basis for promotion. Following graduation incipient *Führers* are to be released for seven years of "practical life study," during which time they will serve in labor and military services, learn a trade or profession and continue their practical political work in the Party. At the end of this period, one fourth of each class will be picked for three years of training in three *Ordensburgen* (Citadels of the Nazi Order) specializing in ideology and the theory of leadership. Then the final selection is to be made and those found to possess supreme qualities of leadership will go to the *Führerschule* where they will "imbibe the spiritual understanding and enlightenment necessary for proclaiming to future generations the word which will guide the world." [1] The German university, famous for its scholarship, seems to disappear in this picture.

(c) REORGANIZATION AS A SOLUTION

Returning now to the United States, we review briefly the attempts being made today to solve the problem of the dilemma. In general we may speak of these attempts as phases of what is called the "Reorganization Movement." The movement has two major aspects first, that concerned with the regrouping of grades, *e.g.*, the junior high school and the junior

[1] *Time*, July 8, 1940, p. 25.

college; and second, that concerned with the regrouping of pupils within any grade *e.g.*, ability grouping, or within any number of grades that form a unit in the educational system *e.g.*, "Honors Courses" in college.

The reorganization movement as applied to the regrouping of grades began about 1910. When we reflect that the four steps on the American educational ladder, (1) elementary school, (2) high school, (3) college and (4) university were not planned as parts of a single system each step leading to the one above, it is not surprising that, when in the last half of the 19th century they were fitted together to form a single system, there should be gaps here and overlapping there. The high school established in 1821 was originally planned as a finishing school for that group of secondary-school pupils who wanted a practical curriculum rather than one preparatory to the college. Early in its development, however, the high school suffered the same fate as the academy, college domination. It was sandwiched in between the elementary school below and the college above extending the period of general education in this country to sixteen years, eight in the elementary school, four in the high school, and four in the college. (See Figure 20, American Ladder, Old Form, No. 1, p. 344.) With the appearance of the junior high school, grades 7, 8 and 9, generally were grouped as one institution, leaving grades 10, 11 and 12 as the senior high school. The justification of this regrouping rested upon the theory that the nature and needs of early adolescent pupils (from 12 to 15) could be met better by placing these pupils together in one administrative unit, the junior high school. With the appearance of the junior college about the same time, grades 13 and 14 were split off from the four-year college and the education of adolescent pupils (from 12 to 20) was provided for in three separate units, the junior high, the senior high school, and the junior college. (Figure 20, Ladder

No. 2.) Many educators, however, are agreed that two years is too short a time for any institution giving general education to hold its pupils, if it is going to make a significant contribution to their growth and development. Accordingly ladders characterized by four-year units, typically that of Pasadena, California, took form and today seem to be spreading to other cities notably in California. (Figure 20, Ladders 3 and 4.) In Chapter XIII, "The American Educational Ladder," the reorganization we will advocate is Ladder 5 in Figure 20 a six-year elementary school, a six-year high school, leaving the four-year college intact with the university above it.

It is apparent, however, that no mere regrouping of grades offers a solution of the dilemma. At the beginning of the junior high school movement it was frequently stated that the *raison d'être* of this reorganization was "provision for individual differences." Departmentalization of certain subjects was brought down from the upper years of the high school, and the curriculum became the "constants and variables" type. The constants, *e.g.*, English, are carried by all pupils, whereas the variables allow a certain amount of election, *e.g.*, Foreign Language for the academic pupils or Practical Arts for non-academic pupils. Such a curriculum makes provision to a certain extent for what we may call "group differences" but hardly for individual differences. Further, it is contended by many that the real work of the junior high school is to give to all American boys and girls, while still within the period of compulsory education, continued general education on a level beyond that of the elementary school. But this is done primarily through the constants not through the variables. If individual development is to be provided for a new technique of administering the curriculum must be introduced that goes beyond the freedom offered by restricted variables.

The second phase of the reorganization movement is an at-

tempt to do just this. This phase is characterized by the regrouping of pupils within a grade or within a number of grades
forming a unit within the system, *e.g.*, the high school or the
college. "Plans" are appearing on all levels of the educational
ladder. The measurement movement, the outstanding contribution of educational psychology to date, is making possible
ability grouping in all schools. The Dalton Laboratory Plan
does away with grade rooms entirely, converting them into
"laboratories" one for each subject in the curriculum, presided
over by an expert in his field. In the mathematics laboratory
e.g., this specialist, the teacher, handles all the pupils of all
grades by a system of contracts which must be completed within a certain time limit. A pupil weak in one subject can devote
extra time to that, ignoring for the time being the subjects in
which he is further advanced. The Winnetka Plan makes a
different attack dividing the school day into two portions. One
half is devoted to individual instruction in the tool subjects,
permitting the pupil to progress at his own rate. The other
half is devoted to group activities. Here is definite provision
for individual development and group solidarity. On the college level, ability grouping in the lower biennium, the first
two years, and independent study plans during the upper biennium are now found in all progressive institutions.

No one believes that we are going to give up our single track
system. It is America's contribution to democratic education.
But it creates problems peculiar to itself. Europe says we are
attempting the impossible. On the elementary level the problem of providing for individual differences is not so acute because pupil development is still in its early stages. Since the
college is a selective institution with graduation from high
school as a minimum entrance requirement, it is partially met
there. It is in the secondary school that the problem is acute.
We present now a general outline of the educational program

that must characterize American secondary education if we are to continue the single system.

3. A NEW EDUCATIONAL PROGRAM

From this sketchy review of the various plans which are being tried out to solve the dilemma democratic education is confronting in this country, we can make some generalizations which should give us guidance in working towards a solution. We are confronted with a new situation and we need a new educational program to meet that situation. The first aspect of this new educational program is what we may call the *instructional program*. (See Diagram 6, p. 360.) This refers both to the curriculum and to those co-curricular activities which are now looming so large in the American high school and college. First with regard to the curriculum, it must be a differentiated curriculum, planned to meet the variant needs, interests, and abilities of the heterogeneous mass of students who make up the high-school population. If the American secondary school is to continue as a cosmopolitan school, that is, giving education to all the children of all the people, it must become truly comprehensive in its offerings. We do not like the phrase "provision for individual differences." It is pretentious. No social institution, like the school, handling large groups can make provision for the individual apart from the social group of which he is a member. But provision can be made and must be made for group differences. There is at one extreme the group that is certainly going on to advanced study in college. Their curriculum obviously must be college preparatory. At the other extreme is the group that is certainly *not* going on beyond high school, either through lack of ability or lack of interest or, in most instances, the two combined. Foreign language, and higher mathematics have no place in the curriculum for this group. The larger group in

THE EDUCATIONAL PROGRAM
OF
THE AMERICAN COMPREHENSIVE HIGH SCHOOL

I. The Instructional Program

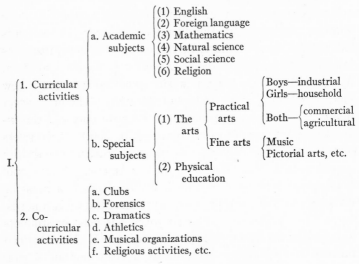

II. The Guidance Program

DIAGRAM 6.

the middle whose probable futures cannot so easily be forecast create a more difficult problem. The chief question is to what extent, if at all, vocationalism should characterize the curriculum for this group. The writer believes it should not characterize it at all except for agriculture in the rural high schools and commercial studies in urban high schools. The commercial studies can be taught in school but for some reason or other the high school does not seem to be able to accomplish in its course of study of two years what the proprietary commercial school does in six months with its intensive training limited to the distinctly commercial subjects. As for the other vocations, preparation for these should be left to technical high schools or to industry itself and not attempted by the comprehensive high school.

In regard to the co-curricular activities, those running along with the curriculum, they should be recognized as having real value. But their values are for the most part social not intellectual, and the latter values are, as we have said, the primary purpose of the school. Since the activities have value, some school men are demanding that they be recognized as part of the curriculum, the same as any academic subject. This we believe would result only in a confusion of values. Students are not to be advanced in school on their success in club activities or in sports. But if these activities are kept under proper control and given sympathetic and intelligent guidance, they may be of great advantage in rounding out the social education of the pupil.

The second phase of the new educational program is what we may call the *guidance program*. (See Diagram 6, p. 360.) In the cosmopolitan high school, with students of variant abilities and several curricula to choose from, educational guidance is of great importance. But no guidance program can be successful unless it is based on accurate information about student ability. This means a testing program including not only the tests or examinations given by teachers in their subjects but also intelligence tests and, from time to time, standard achievement tests which will function not only as a measure of student learnings but also as a measure of the quality of teaching in the school. Tests, however, are of little value if they are of the snapshot variety with little or no permanent record available as a basis for guidance. This means that cumulative records must be introduced which will carry forward the achievement or failure of the pupil from year to year, so that a panoramic view of his academic history is available to those who are to do the guiding. This leads to the third element in the guidance program, namely, counseling. Counseling is difficult work. Not all teachers are suitable for it. To succeed at this, a counselor must have deep sympathy with students, untiring energy, with patience and insight into their problems. If guidance is to go beyond the educational and vocational to include personal problems which often are moral problems, nothing less than wisdom must characterize the counselors who are to carry on this work. In the Catholic school this will be left to the priest in the confessional where no records are made. Because of this fact the student knows that here he can tell the story of any moral problem that is worrying him without its becoming common talk in a personnel office. With such a program as we have just outlined in operation in any school, we have some hope that the solution of the dilemma is under way along with the preservation of the democratic function of our single system, which means equal opportunity for all without segregation of pupils in separate schools.

In the history of education it is evident that provision has long been made for the education of the few but for centuries little has been done for the education of the many. Even up to the end of the 17th century the ability to read and write was a comparatively rare accomplishment. How to bring literacy to the people? De La Salle in France solved that problem. The curriculum was at hand, education in the three R's. A new method was needed and with his invention of the simultaneous method of class instruction and the setting up of normal schools to train teachers to put that method in operation, education was on the way to bring literacy to all.

Now we are aspiring to reach a new level. President Coolidge said a few years ago "Every American citizen is entitled to the elements of a liberal education." This means a liberal education for all in the literal sense of the word "liberal," education for freedom. Bringing secondary education within the period of compulsory education has definitely determined that we have set out to accomplish this fact and this is to be done in a single school system. The objectors say no. If we provide for the education of the great mass in a single institution we must necessarily neglect the favored few, whereas the potential leaders of the future should be our first concern. On the other hand, if we segregate the favored few and educate them for leadership, what becomes of group solidarity? This is the dilemma of democratic education. Several such problems in the history of education have been met and solved. Cannot this one be? Someone has said that education is the oldest of the arts and the youngest of the sciences. As a science it is being challenged today in a way in which it has never been before. What we need is an educational program with differentiated curricula adapted to the varied abilities of the various groups which constitute our school population and a new technique of conducting that curriculum which will make provision for each individual going ahead at his own rate in the direction that his interests lead him and to the extent that his capacities

make possible.   At the same time while all are learning together they will *learn to live together* by *practicing living together*
in the same institution.

SUGGESTED READINGS

Alexander, Thomas and Beryl Parker, *The New Education and the
German Republic*, John Day, 1927, is the best presentation of
the reorganization effected by the Weimar Republic.

Briggs, Thomas H., *Secondary Education*, Macmillan, 1933, Chapter I to III are entitled "Secondary Education in Other Countries," pp. 1–37, IV to VI "Historical Sketch of Secondary
Education in Our Country," pp. 40–108.

Draper, Edgar M., and Alexander C. Roberts, *Principles of Amer-
ican Secondary Education*, Century, 1922, Chapter II. "The
Evolution of American Secondary Education," III, "Secondary
Education in Other Lands," IV, "The Integration of the
Secondary School Units," treats reorganization; VIII and IX,
treat "Guidance and Counseling."

Eby, Frederick and Charles Arrowood, *The Development of Modern
Education*, Prentice-Hall, 1934, excellent, Chapters XVIII,
Pestalozzi; XX, Herbart and XXI, Froebel.

Engelhardt, Fred and Alfred Overn, *Secondary Education*, Appleton-
Century, 1937, Chapter II, "Secondary Education in Foreign
Lands," III, "Development of Secondary Education in the
United States," V, "Relationship to Elementary Education,"
VI, "to Higher Education."

Hamrin, Shirley A., and Clifford E. Erickson, *Guidance in the
Secondary School*, Appleton-Century, 1939.

Inglis, Alexander, *Principles of Secondary Education*, Houghton
Mifflin, 1918, one of the oldest but still one of the best; Chapter V, "Development of Secondary Education in America,"
VI, "Secondary Education in Other Countries," VII, "Relation to Elementary Education," VIII, "to Higher Education."

Jones, Arthur J., *Principles of Guidance*, McGraw-Hill, 1934, one
of the older but one of the best books on guidance.

Kandel, I. L., *Comparative Education*, Houghton Mifflin, 1933, extensive treatment of elementary and secondary education in

England, France, Germany, Italy, Russia and the United States.

—— *History of Secondary Education*, Houghton Mifflin, 1930, Part II "Rise and Development of National Systems of Secondary Education" Chapters VI, "In France," VII, "In Germany," VIII, "In England" and IX, "In the United States."

Kane, W., *History of Education*, Loyola Univ. Press, Chicago, 1935, Chapter XVIII, "Democracy in Education" the 19th century search for a universal method under the leadership of Pestalozzi, Herbart and Froebel.

Knight, Edgar W., *Education in the United States*, Ginn, 1929, Chapter VIII, "The Awakening."

Learned, William, *The Quality of the Education Process in the United States and Europe*, Bulletin No. 20 Carnegie Foundation for the Advancement of Teaching, 1927, a severe indictment of American secondary education in comparison with English, German and French.

McConn, Max, "The Dilemma of Democratic Education," *American School Board Journal*, December, 1935, same title but a different interpretation of the dilemma by the Dean of Lehigh University.

Noble, Stuart G., *A History of American Education*, Farrar and Rinehart, 1938, Chapter XI, "The Advent of New Method (1825–1900)."

ABILITY GROUPING

Adapting the School to Individual Differences, 24th Yearbook, National Society for the Study of Education, 1925.

Brooks, Robert C., *Reading for Honors at Swarthmore*, Oxford Univ. Press, 1927, ability grouping in college.

Burr, Marvin Y., *Homogeneous Grouping*, Teachers College Columbia Univ., 1931.

Corning, Hobart M., *After Testing What?* Scott, Foresman, 1926, a triple track arrangement in the elementary school.

De la Salle, Jean Baptiste, *The Conduct of the Christian Schools* (tr. and intro. by F. de la Fontainarie) McGraw-Hill, 1935; any history of education covering the 17th century gives his introduction of the "simultaneous method" and establishment of normal schools.

Dewey, Evelyn, *The Dalton Laboratory Plan*, Dutton, 1922, a sympathetic description of the plan.

Freeman, Frank S., *Individual Differences*, Holt, 1934.

Gray, William S. (editor) *Provision for the Individual in College Education*, Univ. of Chicago Press, 1932, Vol. IV. Proceedings of the Institute for Administrative Officers of Higher Education, twenty papers describing procedures at different institutions.

Keliher, Alice V., *A Critical Study of Homogenous Grouping*, Teachers College Columbia Univ., 1931.

Kelley, Robert Lincoln, *The Effective College*, Association of American Colleges, 1928, Chapter XII, "Sectioning on the Basis of Ability" by Lucius H. Holt, Acting-Dean, The United States Military Academy; XIV "Honors Course at Swarthmore College" by Robert C. Brooks.

McConn, Max, *College or Kindergarten*, New Republic, 1928, suggests three different colleges for three types of students.

—— *Studies are Not Everything* (A Diary of a Freshman) entertaining story of a "superkindergartner." Viking Press, 1931.

THE EDUCATIONAL LADDER OF COMENIUS

The Ladder	Age Limits	Location	Attended by
College of Light	24 on	Somewhere in the World	Learned men from all nations
University	18 to 24	Every Province (State)	Those who pass a rigid examination
Latin School	12 to 18	Every City	Those who aspire higher than the workshop
Vernacular School	6 to 12	Every Hamlet	All children
School of Mother's Knee	To 6	Every Home	All children

Adapted from Philip R. V. Curoe, *History of Education*, Globe Book Co., 1921, p. 111.

367

THE CURRICULUM AS RACIAL AND INDIVIDUAL
EXPERIENCE

(1) These three elements, viz., the theoretic, the aesthetic, and the volitional, that together constitute the social environment of man, are the products, and the only products of the race's mental life. The mind of the race is the mind of the individual writ large. The divisions of the spiritual environment as given are complete, since based upon the nature of the mind that produces that environment.

(2) What has been here termed the spiritual environment of the pupil is identical with the educational curriculum. The courses of study offered by the school, which men call the curriculum, is neither an invention of some genius nor the discovery of some explorer; it is the accumulated racial experience, the product of human society as a whole living its life in its world. The curriculum of the pupil is the career of human progress. The books he studies are not the reality; they are but the temporary earthen vessels in which the treasures of natural and human truths are kept.

(3) The educated man, so far as he is educated, has reproduced his race's achievements in his own mind, and so has identified his own thinking, feeling, and acting with that of his race. Thus education socializes and humanizes the prospective members of society.

Herman Harrell Horne, *Philosophy of Education*,
Macmillan, 1917, pp. 145–146.

CHAPTER XII

THE AMERICAN EDUCATIONAL LADDER

Looking back over the centuries it is evident that education, as a system serving the needs of the people supporting it, has undergone greater changes during the past one hundred years than have ever taken place in a similar period. In ancient times formal education was the privilege of the few. Thus in Greece, with its achievement of the highest cultural civilization the world has ever known in art, literature, and philosophy, education was only for the citizens of the city-state, less than 20 per cent of a population of which the rest were slaves. During the Middle Ages the great mass of the people were serfs attached to the land using the simple arts of agriculture, learned through imitation, with no formal instruction of any kind except perhaps in religion. In the early modern period organized government changed all this. In Prussia Frederick William I made education compulsory in the school law of 1717. His son Frederick the Great, "the most brilliant of the benevolent despots," made compulsory education a reality by the law of 1763, with the imposition of fines on parents and guardians who did not send their children to school regularly. The tuition for the poor was paid by the civil or church authorities; supervision was in the hands of the local pastors, who visited the schools twice a week, and a carefully devised system

369

of child accounting was introduced.[1] But this establishment of universal education through an eight-year *Volksschule* was anything but democratic, since parallel to this system for the masses was another system for the upper classes, less than 10 per cent of the population, consisting of a three-year *Vorschule* and a nine-year *Gymnasium* or *Oberrealschule*, leading to the university. This dual system with one school for the masses and one for the classes fixed the type for Europe, from which it has not yet freed itself.

Comenius, in *The Great Didactic* (1657), was the first to advocate the idea of an educational system truly democratic in character, that is, a system recognizing education as a natural right of every man and offering each individual the opportunity to advance himself within that system, limited only by his ability and his industry. (See page 367.) Matthew Arnold coined the phrase, the "Educational Ladder" as descriptive of such a system, but it remained for the United States actually to put it into operation. As we have quoted from Chapman and Counts on page 340, introductory to Chapter XI,

> Through the organization of a secondary school that articulated with the elementary school at one end and with the college at the other, a single continuous system was established. This revolutionary change will, in the history of intellectual and social emancipation, be regarded as one of the greatest, if not the greatest, cultural achievement of the American people.

Proud as we are of the democratic character of the American system we do not for one moment entertain the idea that it even approaches perfection. Now we are passing through a period of reorganization. (See Figure 20, page 344.) No one can predict with certainty what the final outcome will be. In all probability there will be different outcomes in different localities, all

---

[1] Frederick Eby and Charles Arrowood, *Development of Modern Education*, Prentice-Hall, 1934, pp. 582–586.

forms of the ladder, however, having this one characteristic in common, namely, a single-track system devoted to general education up to and including the liberal college, with branches off the main line for specialized education at different levels. But with it all there is a growing recognition in this country that we, like Europe, should think of education on three levels, (1) primary or elementary, (2) secondary, and (3) higher education. In the sections that follow we discuss the curriculum of these different levels of the ladder.

1. ELEMENTARY EDUCATION

It is a commonplace among educators that adults ordinarily overestimate the experience of children and underestimate their capacities for growth and development. Yet, a moment's reflection should reveal that experience is the one thing young children have not had and it is this the elementary school must bring into their lives. The elementary school is the school for children. Here all the children of all the people of any given community are gathered together to share a common experience which carries them beyond the family group, and introduces them, under the sympathetic guidance of the teacher, to that larger group life of which they will always be a part. The experiences which they will share in this group life must be carefully selected if they are to prepare pupils for meeting the seven universal human needs we have analyzed in Chapter VI, and they must be graded to pupil capacities and adapted to pupil interests if learning is to take place effectively.

We have laid down the principle in Chapter IX. "The Philosophy of the Curriculum," that it is not the nature of society which gives the basis for building the curriculum throughout the time devoted to general education; rather, it is the nature of man. The school is interested in all four phases of man's development, his physical, mental, social, and religious development; but one of these four is the primary function of the school, its *specific*, *essential* function. Just as man's social development as a citizen is the primary concern of the state, and as his religious development as a child of God is the primary concern of the church, so his mental development as a rational being is the primary concern of the school. The school is an intellectual agency and it must not be diverted from this primary function in its efforts to supplement other agencies in helping them achieve their own specific functions.

Looking at man as a rational being, we have seen that there are two abilities, two powers which through the ages have made it possible for man to raise the level of his existence here on earth. The development of these two abilities is the primary concern of the school, (1) the power of thought and (2) the power of expressing that thought through the language arts chiefly, but through all the arts in varying degrees. What is the child to be led to think about through the ministrations of the school? He must be led to think about the very things that man has always thought about as he evolved a civilization, the three worlds in which his lot is cast, the material world, the spiritual world, and the human world, this latter uniting the other two in the dual nature of man, his material and spiritual nature. Man expresses his thought about these three worlds most adequately in language, but he expresses it also through the other arts, both practical and fine, in his efforts to create the useful and to enjoy the beautiful. Here then is the fivefold spiritual inheritance of the race (see Butler quotation, page 280) and from it must be drawn the content of the curriculum throughout the whole period of general education. On the higher levels, certainly in the liberal college, this fivefold inheritance is presented to the mind of the mature student in the logical organization of the sciences, the physical sciences, the humanistic sciences, and the metaphysical sciences, and the arts, the fine arts and the language arts. (See Figure 19, "The Disciplines in School Activities," p. 330.) But no such organization is possible in the elementary school curriculum. The immature mind of the child must have these experiences brought to it in a way that will make possible their gradual assimilation until later maturity makes possible their logical organization and presentation. On the elementary school level this must be psychological, not logical; that is, it must be made from the point of view of the child's mind, not that of the mature mind, which can best assimilate the deeper meanings of these experiences when organized from the nature of the subject matter itself. But in the elementary school it is the nature of the child mind and his needs that must be the guide. If the curricular materials are not organized and presented with the child's needs in mind they won't do him any good; and if they are not presented from the point of view of his nature, *i.e.*, his capacities and his interests, no learning will take place. Either failure here stultifies the very purpose of the elementary school. How can these two mistakes be avoided in the organization and presentation of the subject matter of the elementary school curriculum?

TYPES OF EXPERIENCE
(A) SENSE EXPERIENCE

The answer to this question is found in the four types of experience which the elementary school should provide for all pupils. There is, first of all, sense experience. All knowledge begins in sense experience. The old Scholastic adage is: *Nihil est in intellectu quod non prius fuerit in sensu.* Here is where the child must begin. This type of experience is concrete and personal. It is obtained through a large variety of activities which are dominant in the kindergarten but occupy less and less of the school day as the child develops the ability to carry on reflective thinking.   Here is a list of activities commonly found in the public school, limiting its program to the secular point of view, which provide this type of experience: working with paper, cardboard, wood, leather, cloth, yarn, clay, sand, and metal, etc.; using the simpler tools, needle, thread, slate, pencil, eraser, crayon, etc.; carrying on simple processes of folding, cutting, pricking, measuring, molding, modeling, pattern-making, etc.; participating in sewing, weaving, printing, painting, drawing, singing, dramatizing, story-telling, plays, games, and outdoor excursions.[1] This list is notable for its omission of a group of activities which will characterize the Catholic school, namely those that bring religion into the life of the child: vocal prayers, attendance at mass, benediction, reception of the sacraments, confession and holy communion, burning vigil lights and making contributions to the collection, offerings for the missions, etc.   These activities and others similar in type will be carried on in a social setting, each pupil acting as a stimulus to the others.

(B)   VICARIOUS EXPERIENCE

The second type of experiences is in sharp contrast to those just listed.   Instead of being concrete and personal, they are abstract and vicarious.   The child cannot have the personal experience of discovering America, of fighting Indians or of being found in the temple by Joseph and Mary, but he can share these experiences of others by being told about them (hence the name "vicarious," in the place of another) and he can live them through in his own imagination.   Later, when the reading adaptation has been achieved, he shares these experiences without the intervention of the teacher.   In this connection, Judd brings

[1] J. Crosby Chapman and George S. Counts, *Principles of Education*, Houghton Mifflin, 1924, pp. 415–416.

out a striking contrast between the American elementary school of today and the older type still characteristic of Europe:

> If one goes to a German *Volksschule*, one finds that instruction is predominately oral. The teacher gives information orally to the children. This information has the stamp of official approval and it is officially safeguarded. The children get what the teacher gives and no more. There is no reference library in any *Volksschule*. Even in such a subject as geography there is no textbook full of facts about all the countries in the world. The most impressive contrast between American schools and those of Europe today is that American schools are reading schools while the schools of Europe are schools where instruction is given orally by the teacher.[1]

The writer recalls very vividly his experience as a child in the early '90's when a library with children's literature was opened in the basement of the church. How proud he was when he brought home his first book for leisure time reading. The next step was the public library, and Castleman, Alger, and Henty were devoured in turn. In those days no elementary school and, in the smaller towns, seldom even a high school could boast of a library. Today any elementary school not provided with a library of children's literature and a trained person in charge is understaffed and without adequate equipment for carrying on its work. The reading habit is one of the most important outcomes of elementary education.

(c) EXPERIENCE WITH THE TOOLS

The mention of reading brings us to the third type of experience the elementary school must bring to the pupil, namely, the tool subjects. They are well spoken of under this title. We have been emphasizing in this treatise that all education is self-

---

[1] Charles Hubbard Judd, *The Evolution of a Democratic School System*, Houghton Mifflin, 1918, p. 27.

education, and it is a process that should continue as long as life lasts. If this ideal is to be realized in any adequate degree, "command of the fundamental processes" must be an early acquisition, for they are the "tools" of education. To the three R's, reading, 'riting, and 'rithmetic, must be added spelling and speaking, one necessary for written communication, the other for oral communication. With the advent of dictating machines and typewriters, penmanship does not have the importance it once had, particularly in the business world. Similarly, the universal need for skill in written composition has lessened through the invention of mechanical means of communication (*e.g.*, the telephone and telegraph). But the elementary school should be a factor in restoring the art of written composition to the important place it holds in the life of the educated person, *e.g.*, in letter writing, at the same time recognizing the growing importance of the speaking voice following the almost universal adoption of the telephone and the radio. With the great emphasis now being placed on silent reading, there is real danger that the art of reading aloud will not receive the attention it merits. No art is of greater value to the mother in advancing the education of her younger children. The speaking arts (including phonetics and public appearance) are entitled to an important place in the program along with the other fundamental language skills, including mathematics, the language of quantity.

(D) EXPERIENCE OF GROUP LIFE

The fourth type of experience the elementary school brings to the child is the intimately personal experience of sharing the life of a larger group than he has ever known before. The kindergarten, where it is established, makes a happy transition for the five-year-olds from the narrow circle of the home to the larger group life of the school. Throughout all the early grades participation in this group life is very real for the young child in the exercises carried on together. Opening exercises, recess and playground, physical training, school and public programs, and religious services all furnish occasions for developing those qualities of personality and character so essential in a democratic society, fair play, respect for the rights and feelings of others, coöperativeness, and many more that might be listed. These occasions are not thought of ordinarily as part of the *in-*

FIGURE 22.—PURPOSES AND PROGRAM OF THE ELEMENTARY SCHOOL

THE EDUCATIONAL PROGRAM			PURPOSES OF ELEMENTARY SCHOOL
Types of Experience		*Learning Activities*	

I. Individual Experience	1. Experience with the Tools	1. Tool Subjects
		  a. Reading
		  b. Writing
		  c. Arithmetic
		  d. Etc.
			1. Mastery of the Tools

	2. Sense Experience	2. Special Subjects
		  a. Arts
		  b. Music
		  c. Physical Training
		  d. Etc.
			2. Introduction to Fivefold Inheritance

II. Social Experience	3. Vicarious Experience	3. Content Subjects
		  a. Geography
		  b. Nature Study
		  c. Religion
		  d. Etc.	

	4. Personal Experience of Group Life	4. Group Activities
		  a. Class room
		  b. Assembly
		  c. Play
		  d. Religious
		  e. Etc.
			3. Adjustment to Group Life

structional program of the school but they are most certainly an important part of the *educational* program of any well-conducted elementary school. (See Figure 22, p. 377.)

These four types of experience which the school brings to the child fall naturally into two larger categories, namely, individual experience and social experience. The tool subjects and most of the special subjects are primarily individual in character, although practically all the experiences of school life will have a social phase since they are all carried on by the group. The personal experience of group life through group activities and the vicarious experience of the content subjects, wherein the pupil lives through in his own imagination the social experience of the race, are primarily social in character. Out of this analysis we distinguish three aims or purposes of the elementary school. There is, first of all, *mastery of the tools*. This is put first advisedly. It always has been and always will remain the chief purpose of the elementary school in spite of the allegations of so-called educators who arrogate to themselves the title "progressive." The reason for ranking the tool subjects first in importance is the simple fact that their mastery conditions all further education. Second in importance is *introduction to the fivefold spiritual inheritance* of the race as analyzed in Figure 17, "Analysis of the Curriculum," p. 298. Notice we say "introduction." The immature mind of the child is not ready for study of the natural, the humanistic, and metaphysical sciences in the highly organized form in which they will be presented to him during secondary education and later, if he continues schooling on the higher levels. But the child is living in man's threefold world and in the elementary school through the content subjects such as Nature Study, Geography, and Religion as well as through the special subjects, the child will begin to assimilate his inheritance and in this process of assimilation make use of the tools insofar as he has acquired facility in their use.   The third purpose of the elementary school is *adjustment to group life* under school conditions.   (See Figure 22, p. 377.)

A glance at Table II, presented on page 380, from Mann's *How Schools Use Their Time*, reveals that the two types of experiences we have listed as (1) Experience with the Tools and (3) Vicarious Experience, are identical with the classifications given there as the Three R's and Content Subjects.   His third classification, Special Subjects, includes the other two types of experience we have listed under the titles (2) Sense Experience and (4) Experience of Group Life.   The tables give the time distribution of subjects in public schools.   The one notable omission is religion.   Since religion is the social science *par excellence*, anyone familiar with the work of the Catholic school will feel assured that it is doing a better piece of work in citizenship training than any school trying to teach the moral virtues without a religious basis.   If religion is added to the list of activities given in the table for forty-four cities, there is a total of twenty-five activities, counting only one for "miscellaneous." It would be absurd to think that each of the twenty-five must have an equal place in the five hours of the school day, with twelve minutes for each.   Granting that all should have a place, the problem is one of integration, that is, conducting a program that will bring all four types of experience to the child, not in logic-tight compartments, but in an integrated program making an appeal to his interests without sacrificing provision for his needs.   Integration is particularly important in the matter of religious training.   In the Catholic school there will be special periods devoted to religious instruction, of course, but of greater importance is the part religion plays in the other activities of the school creating the atmosphere of Christian culture. This point is emphasized by the late Holy Father in his Encyclical, *The Christian Education of Youth*, in these words:

TABLE II.—AVERAGE AMOUNTS OF TIME IN MINUTES PER WEEK AND PERCENTAGES OF TIME IN EACH GRADE ALLOTTED TO THE SUBJECTS BY FORTY-FOUR CITIES IN 1926 [1]

SUBJECT	GRADE 1		GRADE 2		GRADE 3		GRADE 4		GRADE 5		GRADE 6		TOTAL GRADES 1-6	
	Min.	%	Min.	%	Min.	%	Min.	%	Min.	%	Min.	%	Min.	%
Three R's:														
Reading	388	28.8	348	24.3	293	19.1	212	13.4	168	10.4	149	9.2	1558	17.1
Phonics	68	5.0	51	3.6	24	1.6	5	0.3	1	0.1	1	0.1	150	1.6
Literature	22	1.6	21	1.5	35	2.3	25	1.6	26	1.6	27	1.7	157	1.7
Arithmetic	80	5.9	146	10.2	196	12.8	211	13.3	215	13.3	173	13.3	1063	11.6
Language and grammar	86	6.4	104	7.2	136	8.8	158	10.0	169	10.5	173	10.7	826	9.1
Penmanship	74	5.5	80	5.6	84	5.5	85	5.4	82	5.1	79	4.9	484	5.3
Spelling	31	2.3	82	5.7	94	6.1	96	6.1	93	5.8	89	5.5	485	5.3
Total three R's	749	55.5	833	58.1	862	56.2	792	50.1	754	46.8	733	45.4	4723	51.7
Content Subjects:														
Geography	4	0.3	7	0.5	58	3.8	133	8.4	160	9.9	164	10.2	526	5.8
History	8	0.6	11	0.8	26	1.7	57	3.6	94	5.8	113	7.0	309	3.4
Social science	2	0.1	3	0.2	3	0.2	5	0.3	6	0.4	6	0.4	25	0.3
Citizenship and civics	11	0.8	12	0.8	14	0.9	16	1.0	19	1.2	21	1.3	93	1.0
Nature study and elementary science	21	1.6	23	1.6	21	1.4	19	1.2	17	1.0	16	1.0	117	1.3
Total content	46	3.4	56	3.9	122	8.0	230	14.5	296	18.3	320	19.9	1070	11.8
Special Subjects:														
Art and drawing	71	5.3	73	5.1	74	4.8	73	4.6	72	4.5	70	4.3	433	4.7
Music	74	5.5	76	5.3	77	5.0	80	5.1	77	4.9	77	4.8	463	5.1
Household and manual arts	2	0.1	2	0.1	2	0.2	6	0.4	18	1.1	30	1.8	61	0.7
Hand work	30	2.2	22	1.5	13	0.8	9	0.6	6	0.4	5	0.3	85	0.9
Projects and achievements	8	0.6	6	0.4	6	0.4	5	0.3	4	0.2	2	0.1	31	0.3
Health education	30	2.2	31	2.2	37	2.4	44	2.8	51	3.2	52	3.2	245	2.7
Physical training	79	5.9	79	5.5	81	5.3	81	5.1	80	5.0	80	5.0	480	5.3
Recess	111	8.2	112	7.8	109	7.1	103	6.5	97	6.0	92	5.7	624	6.8
Opening exercises	51	3.8	53	3.7	52	3.4	49	3.1	48	3.0	47	2.9	300	3.3
Supervised study	18	1.3	24	1.7	31	2.0	44	2.8	49	3.0	52	3.2	218	2.4
Unassigned and free time	49	3.6	43	3.0	42	2.7	39	2.5	37	2.3	33	2.0	243	2.7
Miscellaneous	29	2.2	25	1.7	26	1.7	26	1.6	22	1.4	22	1.4	150	1.6
Total special	552	40.9	546	38.0	551	35.8	559	35.4	563	35.0	562	34.7	3333	36.5
Total all subjects	1347	99.8	1435	100.0	1535	100.0	1581	100.0	1613	100.0	1615	100.0	9126	100.0

[1] From C. H. Mann, *How Schools Use Their Time*, Columbia Univ. Press, 1928, p. 23.

It is necessary that all the teaching and the whole organization of the school, and its teachers, syllabi and textbooks in every branch be regulated by *the Christian spirit*, . . . so that religion may be in very truth the foundation and crown of the youth's entire training and this in every grade of the school.

In the case of the tool subjects the problem of integration has long been the source of a sharp controversy. The ultra-progressives in the so-called child-centered school would abolish completely all forms of drill, leaving the child free to carry on his activities in response to a felt need. For example, through playing "store" the child discovers his inability to make change and hence is motivated to practice addition, subtraction, division, and multiplication until he can meet this situation with success. Thomas reports the experience the Chicago University Elementary School in this problem as follows:

In this school, for a number of years prior to 1908, major emphasis was given to supplying the pupils with interesting experiences and materials, with only incidental attention to practice on fundamental skills. In that year Stone tested the sixth-grade pupils on their mastery of the arithmetical processes and found them distinctly below the standard of other city schools. Similarly the test of the handwriting of pupils in this school, conducted by Freeman in 1912, showed correspondingly unsatisfactory quality. As a result of these revelations, those in charge of the school introduced brief periods of systematic drill without, however, very materially reducing the attractive activities and content of the curriculum. The pupils engaged willingly in these short, lively drill periods. Subsequent tests showed a marked improvement, which had been secured at no apparent loss in general interest and initiative on the part of the pupils.[1]

Kandel brings more recent evidence from the schools of the Soviet Republics in Russia pointing in the same direction:

[1] Frank W. Thomas, *Principles and Technique of Teaching*, Houghton Mifflin, 1927, pp. 169–170.

The method of organization of the course of study is that known as the complex (*Gesamtunterricht* in Germany, integrated instruction in the United States), but differing from the German and American practices in being directly related to those major phases of human life—nature, labor, and society. In other words, instead of organizing the curriculum in the traditional fashion, by subjects, the course of study is developed round central themes related to the phases indicated. . . .

In the earlier suggestions for carrying out the work of the unified school on the basis of the complex, it was intended that the so-called fundamental subjects—reading, writing, and arithmetic—be taught incidentally. As it was proved in practice that this could not be done or that these subjects were taught surreptitiously, the time-schedules were modified and special lessons in them were introduced.[1]

The ultraconservatives still continue to make drill the major part of the school day. The distribution of time in Table II on page 380 gives today's actual practice and what many consider to be the optimum practice in this problem. With such a distribution of time, about 50 per cent to the Three R's, it would seem not impossible to provide sufficient practice in the needed skills that will be interesting to the pupil, since it makes possible success in the other activities. This is the meaning of the integrated program in the best sense of the word. The experiences of the child are not isolated one from another. All activities in the curriculum constitute a *whole*, bringing about his growth and development.

For how many years shall these experiences of the elementary school continue? As we have said above, the elementary school is the school for childhood. When childhood is over, therefore, the work of the elementary school, mastery of the tools, introduction to the social inheritance, and adjustment to group life under school conditions, should be completed. This does not

[1] I. L. Kandel, *Comparative Education*, Houghton Mifflin, 1933, pp. 482–485.

mean that there should occur a sharp break with the transition to the secondary school. Just the contrary. Both in subject matter and method each year of the elementary school will approach the secondary school until the child at the average age of twelve will be ready to enter the secondary school. In city

FIGURE 23.—THE AMERICAN EDUCATIONAL LADDER

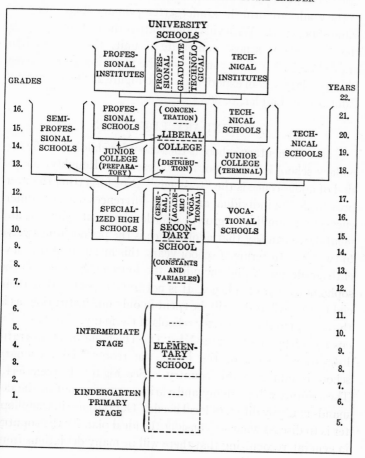

systems which have the necessary funds, the kindergarten will make the transition from the home to the school when the child is about five. In spite of the depression the United States Office of Education reported on the occasion of the Froebelian Centenary (1937) that kindergartens are now available to 30 per cent of the nation's five-year-olds. Where it is established the practice is growing of uniting it with the first and second years of the grades to form the kindergarten-primary stage under the same supervisor. With this organization the last four years of the elementary school constitute a unit, the intermediate grades, and with their completion the pupil is ready to begin his secondary school experience. (See Figure 23, The American Educational Ladder, p. 383.)

2. SECONDARY EDUCATION

As the elementary school is the school for childhood, the secondary school is the school for adolescents. Roughly, the period of adolescence is the "teen age." Not forgetting the ever-present fact of individual and group differences (*e.g.*, sex differences) as it applies to growth and development, physical and mental, we can say that adolescence is the period from twelve to twenty. In terms of school years, this means from the seventh grade up to and including the fourteenth, which is the sophomore year of college. It is not to be expected that these eight years will ordinarily be spent in only one institution, as is the custom in the secondary schools of Germany. We have discussed briefly the Chapter XI, "The Dilemma of Democratic Education," some of the forms the reorganized secondary school is taking in this country. (See Figure 20, page 344.) These forms will be many and various, growing out of the demands made by different local needs. Our purpose in this chapter is to discuss what we consider the ideal plan for the country in general, recognizing that there will be many deviations from it in different geographical areas. That ideal plan is an elementary school of six years, a high school of six years, followed by the four-year college and the university (Figure 23, page 383).

THE SIX-YEAR HIGH SCHOOL

Two words are used today to describe the American high school. It is said to be *cosmopolitan* and *comprehensive*. Unhappily, it cannot be said that these words are always used with definite meanings, each clearly distinguished from the other. Draper and Roberts make them synonymous in this statement: "7. *The high school is cosmopolitan or comprehensive, not specialized.*" [1] The etymology of the word "cosmopolitan" gives us the real meaning of this term. A cosmopolite is a citizen of the world (from the two Greek words, *cosmos*, world, and *polites*, citizen). The cosmopolitan high school is one therefore, that takes in all the citizens of the little world, the community, it is endeavoring to serve. The term applies to the student population and indicates that it is unselected except for the fact that those entering this school have completed the work of the intermediate grades, thus establishing their right to be treated as normal early adolescents. In this country this means they will not be shunted off to some vocational school but instead will begin the second phase of their general education, that is, secondary education. Homer P. Rainey, director of the American Youth Commission, (1937) recently said: "There are more students enrolled in secondary schools in this country than in all the other countries of the world put together." The explanation of this fact is that not content with mere literacy we are committed to an educational program in which the elements of a liberal education are to be brought to all American youth.

[1] Edgar M. Draper and Alexander C. Roberts, *Principles of American Secondary Education*, Century, 1932, p. 14.

But a school that is to receive all the early adolescents of the community it is endeavoring to serve, if it is to meet the needs of all the pupils, must offer a curriculum that presents choices to this unselected student body. The word "comprehensive," strictly speaking, refers to this curriculum of varied offerings. As commonly used today, however, "comprehensive" refers both to the unselected student body and to the curriculum of varied offerings. Such a curriculum indicates a definite change from the curriculum of the elementary school. The elementary school is the school for all and *for all alike*, though even here, of course, there will be differences of rate in the assimilation of subject matter by pupils of variant abilities. But the subjects of study are the same for all. The comprehensive secondary school, however, although it is the school for all, *cannot* be for all alike, since by this time differences in pupil capacities are so great that the curriculum must be planned with these differences in mind. Some years ago the writer was present with a group of educators discussing the junior high school. A professor of secondary education in one of the large eastern universities made the statement that the significance of this rung on the reorganized ladder could be stated in four words: "provision for individual differences." In our opinion this is a false interpretation of the American philosophy of secondary education. On the contrary, the primary purpose of the first cycle of secondary education (the junior high school, if this term is preferred) is to continue *common integrating education* on the secondary level as the basis for realizing the social outcome, group solidarity.

Nevertheless, as we said above, the fact of individual and group differences must be faced and provided for in the comprehensive high school. We are recommending the six-year high school as the institution of the future. In Bulletin 1935, No. 2, of the Office of Education, *Statistics of Public High*

Schools 1933–34, 1412 such six-year institutions are listed as "undivided" (pp. 51–2). This does not appear to be a large number, compared with the 23,614 high schools from which reports were received. But when it is remembered that the policy of conducting the six high school years under one administration is a recent development, the fact that it has already reached such proportions in the public school systems of the country holds much promise for the future. Among the high schools of Indiana accredited by the North Central Association, thirty-one are listed as six-year institutions. This is slightly more than 25 per cent of the total number, 122, holding membership in the Association. There seems little doubt that the six-year high school will continue to spread, the complement of a six-year elementary school.

THE FIRST CYCLE OF SECONDARY EDUCATION

In those institutions in which this six-year organization is effected, the curriculum will ordinarily be organized in two cycles. The cycle concept as applied to grade organization means grouping two or more years as a unit. The idea is presented graphically by concentric circles as in Figure 24. (See page 389.) The center cycle, the elementary school, is the foundation of all later education. Each succeeding cycle is built upon the work of the preceding cycle, but goes beyond it, adding material to that already covered. With the completion of the collegiate cycle the student, having finished his general education, goes out into life or enters the specialized schools of the university, professional, technological, or graduate. The first cycle of secondary education takes care of the first three years of this period, grades 7 to 9 inclusive; the second cycle, of the last three years, grades 10 to 12 inclusive. (See Diagram 7, page 389.) The curriculum of the first cycle of secondary education, stressing common integrating education, is of the "constants and variables" type. The constants, *i.e.*, subjects carried by all students, English, Social Studies, Physical Education (and in the Catholic school, Religion), etc., will be the integrating factor; the variables, not carried by all students, Foreign Language, Algebra, etc., are the factor making provision for individual and group differences. Mathematics is a qualified constant insofar as all students will carry it, but it is a variable in the sense that different groups of students take mathematics of different types, *e.g.*, commercial arithmetic, unified mathematics, or algebra. Why the variable subject, foreign language, is so slow in making its way down into the seventh grade for the brighter students is difficult to explain. In Europe pupils begin foreign language study seldom later than their tenth year after three or four years of elementary schooling. Surely carefully selected American pupils can begin it with profit when they are twelve. The writer remembers the dreary experience of his seventh and eighth grade years in the 'nineties filled up by "reviews," etc., with only one pleasurable thrill, the introduction of algebra in the eighth grade. No doubt, not all of the pupils in that eighth grade were ready for algebra, but certainly some of them were. This is the type of differentiation that should be made during these years. The Boston Public Latin School is a six-year school beginning Latin in the seventh grade.

THE SECOND CYCLE OF SECONDARY EDUCATION

The first cycle of secondary education will commonly come to a close with the completion of the period of compulsory education. Thirty-one states now have compulsory education laws requiring attendance up to the age of sixteen. Those pupils who drop out as soon as the law allows them to are, for the most part, the retarded type. This means that many of them will be sixteen with the completion of the ninth grade. In those states

THE AMERICAN EDUCATIONAL LADDER   389

FIGURE 24.—THE CYCLE CONCEPT APPLIED TO ORGANIZATION BY
GRADES DURING THE PERIOD OF GENERAL EDUCATION

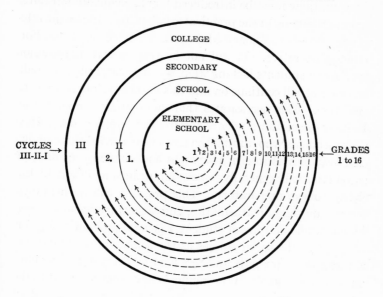

		YEARS		GRADES
		6		1
		7		2
	Cycle I. The Elementary School	8		3
		9		4
		10		5
		11		6
The Cycles in General Education		12	1st. Cycle	7
	Cycle II. The Secondary School	13		8
		14		9
		15	2nd. Cycle	10
		16		11
		17		12
		18		13
	Cycle III. The College	19		14
		20		15
		21		16

DIAGRAM 7.

where the period of compulsory education has been extended to eighteen, there must be introduced for the manually minded a period of training in the practical arts. With entrance into the second cycle of secondary education, the principle of selection becomes operative. It will not be rigid selection, however, since many students lacking what is commonly called the academic mind will continue on into this second cycle of secondary education. This necessitates that differentiated programs of study be offered for students of variant interests and abilities. Those students who, during the first cycle, carried successfully such variables as foreign languages and mathematics beyond arithmetic, will generally follow an Academic Program distinctly college preparatory. This program will be heavy in foreign languages, mathematics, and laboratory sciences. For the nonacademic type of student a general program will offer English and the social studies as the solids, supplemented by household arts for girls and practical arts for boys. A third program will commonly be found in the comprehensive high school distinctly vocational in character. In the larger cities this program will offer training in commercial subjects with emphasis on typewriting and stenography as essential skills for securing employment in the business world. In rural communities the vocational program will offer training in the sciences and arts related to agriculture. Such are the offerings of the typical American comprehensive high school today. These three types of programs, academic, general and vocational (see Figure 23, p. 383) will have a common core, made up of English and physical education (and in the Catholic high school, religion), with social studies. All other subjects, for the most part, will be found only in one of the three programs. Where the curriculum core forms the greater part of student programs in the last three years, the curriculum is often considered to be of the constants and variables type, rather than one offering separate programs.   The academic program will lead on to college; the vocational program will offer specific training leading to employment immediately after high school; while the general program, less severe in its demands on student ability and application, will be offered to that large nondescript group of high school students who must be kept out of the labor market and off the streets until they are about eighteen years of age.   For them, being "graduated from high school" carries a certain social distinction in the local community signifying that they have completed their general education as far as the ministrations of the school are concerned.   So many possible choices emphasize the point we made in the last chapter that a carefully conducted guidance program must be part of the educational program of the adequately administered comprehensive high school.   (See Diagram 6, p. 360)

TRAINING VERSUS EDUCATION

Such is the picture presented by the comprehensive high school (within both the public and the Catholic school systems), the dominant type of educational institution in the American scene today.   How effective is it in realizing the three distinct purposes which the three programs, commonly found within it, aim to accomplish?   If there is any truth in the judgment expressed in Bulletin 20 of the Carnegie Foundation for the Advancement of Teaching, by William S. Learned, *The Quality of the Educational Process in the United States and Europe*, we must admit that up to the present at least the product of the American high school, when compared on any academic standard with the product of the secondary schools of Europe, is a sorry second.   Must this necessarily be the case as long as we retain our single system, congregating all types of students in the same institution?   There is a growing sentiment among educators throughout the country (though not among those actively engaged in high school administration) that this is the unwelcome fact which we must face, if there is to be any improvement of American secondary education. Among those who hold this view is one who is perhaps the severest critic of the American system, Albert Jay Nock. He speaks contemptuously of the American theory of education as "equalitarian" and "pseudo-democratic," resting as it does upon a false foundation in its failure to distinguish between instrumental knowledge and formative knowledge, which is the basis for the distinction between *training* and *education*. Instrumental knowledge has its place in a training school preparing for some specific occupation, while formative knowledge is the material through which an educational institution produces the disciplined mind. On this distinction not all persons are educable. In fact, Nock claims comparatively few persons are educable in any true meaning of the term. "The vast majority of mankind have neither the force of intellect to apprehend the process of education, nor the force of character to make an educational discipline prevail in their lives." [1]

GRESHAM'S LAW IN EDUCATION

Some high school administrators accept this distinction between training and education and point to their vocational and academic programs as separate provisions for each; both going on in the same institution. The general program is a combination of both insofar as those students following this program are capable of either. For Nock this creates an impossible situation:

> One is . . . reminded of the formula known in economics as Gresham's law, that "bad money drives out good"; the two cannot exist in circulation side by side, and it is always the good

[1] Albert Jay Nock, *The Theory of Education in the United States*, Harcourt Brace, 1932, p. 55.

money that is forced out. I do not mean to imply that the work of the training-school is bad money; on the contrary, I have taken pains to express my great respect for it, my appreciation of the need of it, and my wish that it could be extended. I mean only that it is in all respects so different from the work of an educational institution that the attempt to compass both under the same general direction is bound to be ineffectual, and that the mere force of volume would always tend to drive the latter out.[1]

What is to be thought of this argument? The first thing to be said in reply to it is that the argument is only an analogy. Gresham's law may be inexorable in the field of economics, but to claim that there is a similar law in the field of education calls for proof. It is as illogical to transfer theories from one field to another as it is to transfer authorities. If the inferior product of the American secondary school is advanced as sufficient evidence, we reply that even granting the fact (which many Americans will not grant), there are, no doubt, many factors contributing to that inferiority, chief among which is our failure thus far to work out a technique of administration whereby in the same institution general education in the academic field may be carried on side by side with special training for specific life callings. In the previous chapter, XI, "The Dilemma of Democratic Education," we showed that American educators are now conscious of the stupendous task which the American theory of democratic education, that is, equal opportunity for all limited only by capacity and industry, has set for itself. The single system with all the children of all the people in the same institution does promote social solidarity. This is a great boon. At the same time it creates grave problems. But who will say that these problems are unsolvable? On all levels of the ladder, attempts are now being made through various forms of ability grouping to make provisions for individuals and for groups to

[1] *Ibid.*, pp. 140–141.

progress at their own rate, in the direction their talents lead them.   This problem is undoubtedly one of the major problems confronting American Education today.   Study of this problem and experimentation working towards its solution will continue to be carried on, but this continuance must be in the only type of institution where it is possible, that is, in an institution accepting all the children of all the people.   Every child is entitled to pursue a curriculum from which he can derive profit. Whether that curriculum be continued general education or special training, is a matter that must be decided in each individual case.

THE SPECIALIZED HIGH SCHOOL

While this study of the problem of the comprehensive institution, whether on the secondary or collegiate level, is being carried on, there is another type of secondary school, the extension and development of which merits particular attention, namely, the specialized high school.   We mean by this the high school that has chosen for itself one definite aim; that has a student body striving to realize that aim in their own growth and development; that has a teaching and administrative staff which sees this aim clearly, is specially trained to achieve it, and plans and conducts a curriculum that gives some promise that the achievement of the aim will be the outcome of students and staff working harmoniously together.   When this type of institution is mentioned we commonly think of the commercial high schools found more commonly in the larger cities of the Atlantic seaboard.   But this is not the only example of the specialized high school.   In Boston, for example, the oldest secondary school in the country, which celebrated its three-hundredth anniversary in 1936, the Boston Public Latin School, still carries on the classical curriculum preparing 2500 boys for college. Yet just across the street is another large institution, admin-

istering another curriculum for 1500 boys just as specific in purpose as the Public Latin School.   This other high school is the
Commercial High School.   Here is realism rather than sentimentality.   Here there is no falling back on some vague theory
of democracy, so often the justification of the comprehensive
high school.   Again in Cincinnati, the Walnut Hills High School
is a unit in the public school system which is a response to the
demands of parents who wish their children prepared for the
eastern colleges.   To enter this institution pupils must pass a
severe scholastic test, but when they are entered they know
where they are going; the course of study is definitely planned
to carry them there, and they have a well-trained staff of teachers to act as their guides along the road.   Again, this is realism,
not sentimentality.   In Figure 23, p. 383, "The American Educational Ladder," we have presented the six-year high school in
the center as one unit of the main ladder, but we have also presented specialized high schools and vocational schools as step-
ladders on the level of the second cycle.   Vocational schools are
technical high schools for either boys or girls or both.   They are
found in some of our larger cities and offer several programs,
all distinctly vocational in character.   In Figure 23, the arrow
pointing to the right from the specialized high schools indicates
the type that is distinctly college preparatory.   Most of the private secondary schools throughout the country charging high
tuition are of this type.

THE SIX-YEAR HIGH SCHOOL IN THE CATHOLIC SCHOOL SYSTEM

We have been describing the six-year elementary school and
the six-year high school of the American system as the goal to
be striven for.   To what extent is such a plan practical in the
American Catholic system?   There is no problem relative to
the elementary school.   All admit that its work can be finished

with the completion of the sixth grade. But the Catholic system in its foundation schools is a parochial system and it will remain such. Its future development must mean the extension of the parochial school to a nine-year school, with the last three years organized as the first cycle of secondary education. When this is accomplished in any city, the Catholic Central High School can confine itself to grades ten, eleven and twelve, offering the three programs we have described above. Pupils then, on completing the nine-year parochial school, will enter the second cycle in the Central High School or transfer to a vocational school, commonly a public school since there is no possibility of the Catholic system entering on a program of separate vocational schools. Those pupils who do transfer to public vocational schools will at least have had one more year of schooling under Catholic auspices than they are now receiving in the traditional eight-year school, and the last three years of this experience will have been definitely organized on a secondary basis. The Catholic Central High School in many instances will be a six-year school, the first cycle serving the immediate neighborhood, with the second cycle fed by pupils entering from distant nine-year parochial schools. In addition there will be many private six-year high schools conducted by religious communities, separate schools for boys and girls, but if their contribution is to be what it ought to be, the selection which determines their student bodies should be based on an aristocracy of student talent, not on the ability of parents to pay high tuition fees.

The N.C.W.C. Directory of High Schools and Academies, 1936, states that there are fifty-six Catholic high schools organized on the six-year plan, grades seven to twelve inclusive. This, we feel, is the next step forward in the organization of our Catholic system. There is one serious obstacle preventing the realization of the nine grade parochial school, namely, properly prepared teachers and administrators who will make the old seventh and eighth grades and the added ninth grade truly secondary in character. These teachers must be trained as secondary school teachers, which means a college degree as a minimum, with collegiate training in their teaching fields. Until we have such teachers available, and administrators with still more advanced training, it is worse than useless to attempt the reorganization.

THE JUNIOR COLLEGE MOVEMENT

The final phase of secondary education that merits brief treatment here is the junior college movement. This means the addition of two more years of schooling beyond the present high school. Beginning a generation ago, this development progressed slowly at first, but during the last decade has made rapid strides so that now it is estimated there are at least five hundred private and public junior colleges distributed throughout all but five of the forty-eight states. In the beginning most of the junior colleges were private institutions limiting themselves to duplicating the work of the first two years of the four-year liberal college. During the past decade, however, it is the public junior colleges, part of city school systems, that have grown with great rapidity so that in 1930, although they were only 38 per cent of the total number established, they accounted for 56 per cent of the 70,000 students enrolled.

In organization the dominant type is the two-year institution. Eells lists nine institutions organized as four-year institutions including the two top years of high school, seven of which are public institutions and two private.[1] For the most part, these are units in a 6–4–4 plan (see Figure 20, p. 344, Ladder 4), though two in Texas have a five-year elementary school as the first unit.

[1] Walter Crosby Eells, *The Junior College*, Houghton Mifflin, 1931, p. 666.

TERMINAL AND PREPARATORY PROGRAMS

The educational programs of the junior college are of two varieties, those that are terminal and those that are preparatory to still further education. Each of these types of programs is of two varieties. For the most part, the terminal programs are vocational in response to some local need. The most striking illustration of this type of program is that of the junior college in Rochester, Minnesota. In this medical center is located the Mayo Clinic surrounded by hospitals. A need was felt for young women trained to act as medical secretaries. In 1928 the junior college introduced a two-year program giving training combining secretarial work with academic work basic to this field, zoology, psychology, and German, with stress on the meaning of medical terminology and medical dictation. Pathological indexing and manuscript writing are included in the Office Practice Course. The other type of terminal program simply continues general education two years beyond the high school for the student not planning to go on for the bachelor degree in college.

The preparatory programs are also of two varieties, those offering the same subjects as the first two years of the liberal college preparing students to enter the college as juniors so that they can complete the work for the bachelor degree in two more years. The other variety of preparatory program offers subjects making it possible for students to enter professional schools, notably law schools and medical schools and lately schools of nursing that have adopted a four- or five-year program leading to the degree Bachelor of Science in Nursing.

There is no doubt that the junior college, particularly in the public systems of the larger cities, is the institution that will undergo the greatest development in American education during the next generation. In fact, President Hutchins predicts that: "The public junior college will become the characteristic educational institution of the United States, just as the public high school has been up to now." [1] This will mean education that is tax-supported and free for American youth up to the twentieth year of age. But does this mean that the four-year liberal college is doomed to disappear, the first two years taken over by the junior college and the last two years by the university? Prophets of the school of vocationalism and anti-intellectualism together with some others have been predicting this for some time. They forget in making these predictions that the school is one of the three great conservative social institutions, of which the other two are the Church and the Law (government). They further forget that, although the reorganization movement was advocated fifty years ago and has now been in progress for a generation, of the 23,614 high schools reporting to the U.S. Office of Education in 1934, 71.4 per cent were of the traditional four-year type, leaving only 28.6 per cent as reorganized. Nevertheless, this indicates a steady progress in this direction from 1922, when only 11.1 per cent were reported as reorganized. We may well anticipate that the junior college reorganization will continue at an accelerated pace, particularly in the city public systems. Undoubtedly many of the weaker four-year colleges will become junior colleges, discontinuing their two last years but continuing with academy departments to conduct an institution of 8, 6 or 4 years in length. The new accrediting procedure of the North Central Association of Colleges and Secondary Schools now permits such institutions to be accredited as junior colleges. Here is an opportunity for many units in the present Catholic system. The

---

[1] Robert Maynard Hutchins, *The Higher Learning in America*, Yale Univ. Press, 1936, p. 16.

last two college years impose the heaviest financial burden upon the traditional four-year college in salaries for highly trained instructors, extensive libraries, and expensive laboratories. At the same time they are the source of least income because of the small number of students compared with the first two years. Conducting an eight- or six-year secondary school organized in two cycles of four or three years each would be a return to the traditional system of Europe, which many of the teaching orders are familiar with. We may look forward hopefully to this development in the Catholic system.[1]

But the junior college development is no threat to the strong four-year colleges. Babbitt, in *Literature and the American College*, quotes Paulsen, the well-known German educator as envious of the American college, forming as it does the transition from secondary education to university education. The American scene with its emphasis on making a living rather than enriching a life, with its cult of vocationalism, never needed the influence of the liberal college as it does today. It must serve as the training ground for the leadership that is to solve the many problems with which the new era we are now entering is confronting us. Dean McConn of Lehigh University sees the junior college movement "as the thing which will eventually give the four-year colleges both the opportunity and the necessary stimulus to confine themselves to their own proper work . . . (to) differentiate themselves from the competing junior colleges by offering *superior training to the superior few*."[2]

3. HIGHER EDUCATION

We are advocating that American educators like European should recognize three levels in the educational system,

---

[1] James Burns, *Catholic Education*, Benziger Bros., 1917, pp. 136–141.
[2] Max McConn, "College or Kindergarten," *The New Republic*, 1928, p. 1274.

namely, (1) primary or elementary, (2) secondary, and (3) higher education. This does not mean that there should be sharp breaks within the system marking off one level from the other. Just the contrary. The very business of school administrators is to bring it about that as the child enters the system his passage from the lower levels to the higher will be as continuous as possible. Here we must face the everpresent fact of individual differences. This fact results in the situation that no two pupils are precisely at the same stage of growth and development when they pass from one grade to another within any level of the system. Just as the kindergarten, where established, makes the transition from the home introducing the child to the larger group of the school; so, too, the college forms the transition from the secondary school where study commonly is carried on under the "constant tutorial presence of the teacher" [1] to the level of university education where self-dependent study is the characteristic activity. Here the student uses the teacher as he uses the library or laboratory when he has need for them in carrying forward his inquiries in his search for knowledge and the development of his abilities. The university proper with its graduate, professional, and technological schools beyond the liberal college (see Figure 23, p. 383) is formal education at its highest. We will treat the subject of higher education under two headings: (a) the liberal college; and (b) the university proper, *i.e.*, the graduate and professional schools.

(A) THE LIBERAL COLLEGE

Three times in the history of higher education in the United States the attempt was made in the last quarter of the last century to establish and conduct a university on the European

---

[1] Henry C. Morrison, *The Practise of Teaching in the Secondary School*, Univ. of Chicago Press, 2nd edition, 1931, p. 7.

model; Johns Hopkins, Clark University, and the Catholic University. All three attempts failed and ended in the establishment of an undergraduate college as part of the university organization. The reason for this is not far to seek. In Europe the universities have always been fed by the great secondary schools—the German *Gymnasium*, the French *lycée*, the Italian *liceo*, and the English *Public School*. No such system of secondary schools exists in this country. Rather, beginning in the last quarter of the last century the American high school has taken on two characteristics that make it *cosmopolitan* on the one hand (all the children of all the people), and *comprehensive* on the other (varied curricula to meet the needs of the heterogeneous student body it is endeavoring to serve).

Hence, if the university proper, the professional schools, and the research scholars in the graduate school are to receive any students who will carry on in their tradition, there must be a unit in the school system which will select these potential scholars from among high school graduates and give them training that will prepare them to enter the graduate and professional schools. This is one of the major functions the liberal college has been carrying on in this country. The other major function (its primary function) is training a goodly number of men and women with informed, cultured, and disciplined minds among whom the leaders in civic life will be found. There is general agreement that the American college has achieved notable success in the performance of *neither* of these functions, but it is in the second, that is, the training transitional from secondary education to higher education, of the potential scholars and professional leaders, that its failure is most outstanding.

When we look at the college from the point of view of this second major function, we see the meaning of the statement that the liberal college is *the heart of the university*. From the college comes the very life blood of the university, that is, those better minds who will enter its graduate and professional schools and following their training in these schools (particularly the graduate schools) will carry on its work as university teachers and administrators. The recent history of the liberal college, however, reveals that its general purpose which may be stated—*to preserve and propagate the intellectual tradition*—is threatened with nullification. The great increase in enrollment since the World War has meant that the selective quality of its student body has steadily declined. With this inrush of students there has gone on a diversification of the curriculum, to meet the variant needs of this unselected student body, that has worked havoc with the "intellectual tradition." Here is a graphic description of what happened:

> There came during the last century vast social changes, and these were mirrored in its higher education . . . This new society, like the older one it had succeeded, was, as I have said, mirrored in a changed college. The curriculum was invaded by new studies, notably modern languages, history, and the social sciences, which drew away the college from its old strict allegiance to the classical tradition. Also, under pressure of democratic demand, many higher institutions added whole new schools which not only competed with the liberal arts college but showed a strong tendency to exert a shaping influence on its curriculum. Courses of study multiplied, rising in number like a tidal wave, until in our own times the thing got badly out of hand, especially in our state institutions which, like public secondary schools, had to yield before educator-politicians and the pressure of ambitious special interests.
> Yet there was in all this no absolutely necessary engulfment of the liberal arts college in educational chaos. An adjustment to meet the new age was possible through curricular changes involving no abandonment of clear and definite aim and reason for existence, namely, *provision of an intellectual discipline suited to*

men and women as rational and moral beings. It was entirely possible to move with the times, neither dropping old and permanent values nor changing essential purposes. But unfortunately there was a general failure to effect positive reform toward this end, and the result was penetration of the college by those doctrines of individualism and *laissez-faire* which were permeating our whole society. The sign of their arrival was the now much-derided elective system, which, like Liberalism in its early stages, seemed at first to make for a healthy freedom and progress, but ultimately worked to destroy unity, order, and purpose, and delivered over the college to aimless drifting. Each faculty department showed an increasing disposition to emphasize its own special importance at the expense of the curriculum as a whole, and of course to resist efforts at centralized reform and coordination; in which situation lay a strong tendency for studies to become over specialized, unrelated one to another, and irrelevant not only to life but to any rational end of college education. That has been, and is, the condition of the college which numerous experimenting reformers are attacking today. They want to overcome anarchy, irrelevance, and aimlessness, and to close the divorce between related disciplines by a new integral coordination and purpose.[1]

As this development has gone on, many colleges which in their foundation were definitely "liberal" have capitulated to the *zeitgeist* and become "servile" institutions, trading their birthright for vocationalism. Foerster places the greatest blame for this on the state university, subject, as it is, to what Hoffman calls the "educator-politicians." [2] But few, if any, liberal colleges have escaped entirely from inroads by the spirit of vocationalism. In fact, Foerster suggests that "the liberal college has already been damaged beyond repair." [3]

[1] R. J. S. Hoffman, "Education and the Attack on History," *The American Review;* January, 1936, pp. 258–260.
[2] Norman Foerster, *The American State University,* Univ. of North Carolina Press, 1937, entire.
[3] *Ibid.,* p. 185.

To the more optimistic, however, particularly to those aware of the rhythmic movement in human life and human institutions, the wave has reached its crest and recession is already in evidence. The widespread interest in the current discussion on "general education" precipitated by President Hutchins of Chicago University is evidence of this. True enough, President Hutchins is advocating and Chicago University is effecting a splitting of the four-year college in two, relegating the first two years to secondary education and the last two to university education. But the school is one of the three great conservative human institutions along with the church and the state. Further, that unit in our educational system which we call the "college" is the only unit reaching back continuously throughout our whole history (Harvard was founded in 1636), and there is little likelihood that it will disappear at this juncture. Its purpose is still one of the great concerns of man as a rational being, *to preserve and progagate the intellectual tradition.* Its devices may be in need of repair and adaptation to the present American scene, but its purpose is still supreme. Babbit, in *Literature and the American College,* quotes Paulsen, the great German educator, as saying that early in the modern period Germany came near to developing an institution that would have been the German parallel to the American college, but unhappily this development never took place. The fact that the American college is the envy of our European neighbors should give us pause in taking too seriously attacks made upon it by vocationalists and anti-intellectualists and even out-and-out intellectualists such as Hutchins.

The first principle that must be operative, if the liberal college is to achieve its purposes, is that it serve a selected student body. High school graduation should be a definite stopping place for a large group of students as far as general

education is concerned. For many of these, vocational training may offer additional values from continued school experience, but from the point of view of intellectual development
through academic study they have reached the saturation
point. Public junior colleges and new units within the state
universities, like the General College of the University of
Minnesota, may well offer two more years of continued training to the next higher group who have no prospect of becoming
candidates for the bachelor degree. But the liberal college,
whether independent or part of a university organization,
should concern itself with a selected group of high school
graduates. Only such a group is capable of playing a part
in the preservation and propagation of the intellectual tradition, the work of the liberal college.

THE INTELLECTUAL TRADITION

What is the content of this intellectual tradition? Since
it is man's creation, it must arise out of the nature of man.
Looking at man we see that he is possessed of two powers,
intellectual in nature, which have enabled him to build
civilization. These are the power of thought and the power of
expressing that thought so that it may be shared with his
fellow man. The thought of man through the ages is contained
in those great bodies of knowledge we call the "sciences,"
each group dealing with one of the three worlds in which man
lives, the physical world (the natural sciences), the spiritual
world (the metaphysical sciences) and the human world (the
humanistic sciences), now more commonly spoken of as the
social sciences. Man's thought is expressed through the arts.
The arts also admit of a threefold classification, the linguistic,
the fine arts and the practical arts. But the practical arts in
the narrow meaning of the term are not part of the intellectual
tradition and belong to vocational education rather than

general education. Here then are the five bodies of knowledge that constitute what Butler calls the "spiritual inheritance" of mankind. (See quotation introducing Chapter IX, "The Philosophy of the Curriculum," p. 280.) These determine the content of the curriculum on all levels of the educational ladder devoted to general education. In the liberal college, for the first time, they fall into the logical organization now spoken of as the "academic groups," each group the repository of one of these great bodies of knowledge. (For the relationship between the two supreme human abilities and the Academic Groups see Figure 19, p. 330.

With this logical organization as a basis, the ordinary requirement within the college is for the student to take one or more courses in each group during the first two years, the function spoken of as "distribution." But if the college is to form the transition from secondary education characterized by dependent study to higher education, the period of independent study, the responsibility here must be placed upon the student. The ordinary device for doing this is comprehensive examinations in all five fields at the end of the sophomore year, satisfactory performance on which is a condition for entering the upper biennium, the junior and senior years. Chicago University has adopted this procedure with the abolition of all class grades and course credits.

Another device now being used to insure distribution is the survey course covering the high lights in these fields of knowledge. The advocates of this procedure seem to be working on the assumption that there are certain knowledges that the educated person cannot afford to be ignorant of. They put the emphasis on the amassing of information rather than on the intellectual disciplines which the student experiences in his pursuit of knowledge. What do we mean by these disciplines? In President Wriston's words, a discipline is "the essential mode of thought in a field of study." [1] We might distinguish, therefore, as many disciplines as there are modes of thinking in any field of knowledge. In Chapter X, "Values and the Disciplines in School Activities," Section 3, "The Disciplines in School Activities" (p. 327), we have suggested five labels for the chief disciplines characteristic of these five fields of knowledge, namely, Natural Sciences (Precision), Humanistic Sciences (Tolerance), Metaphysical Sciences (Unification), Fine Arts (Appreciation), and Language Arts (Expression). The question is, would a student receive greater value from pursuing a survey course in the natural sciences, for example, covering the physical and biological sciences with some mathematics, than he would by devoting his time to an intensive study of any one of them, *e.g.*, mathematics, chemistry, or biology? Anyone who believes in the college experience as an intellectual enterprise sees at once that first-hand contact with scientific method in the laboratory will do more towards developing the discipline of precision characteristic of the natural sciences than a survey course could ever do, concerned as it must be with generalities without time to go into the details which make these generalities rational conclusions. It would seem administratively possible, however, to have general courses running through the year to which students could have access to fill up the *lacunae* in their general knowledge never filled by sample courses either in high school or in college, *e.g.*, biology, astronomy, etc. (See Figure 25, p. 409.)

THE FUNCTION, CONCENTRATION

What now of the last two years? Robert L. Kelly makes this statement: "It is a period of specialization." [2] We protest

---

[1] Henry M. Wriston, *The Nature of the Liberal College*, Lawrence College Press, 1937, p. 146.

[2] Robert L. Kelly, "The Extent of the Divisional Development of the Curriculum," *Bulletin, Association of American Colleges*, December, 1933, p. 419.

FIGURE 25.—STRUCTURE AND FUNCTION IN THE
LIBERAL COLLEGE CURRICULUM

(1. Unification, all four years)

Upper Biennium
(2. Concentration)

	(Comprehensive exam. in field of concentration)			
Senior year	I Language and	II Mathematics and	III History and	IV Music and	V Theology and
Junior year	Literature group	Natural sciences group	Humanistic sciences group	Fine arts group	Philosophy group
	Lower Biennium (3. Distribution)				
	(Comprehensive exams. covering all five fields)				
Soph. year					
Fresh. year	(One required course in each of five fields during Freshman and Sophomore years)				

The Three Functions

1. Unification: lower biennium, through Theology; upper biennium, through Philosophy.
2. Concentration: upper biennium, more than one half of students' time concentrated in one field.
3. Distribution: lower biennium, students' time distributed over the five fields.

against the use of this term to label the specific function of these two years. "Specialization" is the specific function of the professional school, but not of the liberal college either in whole or in part. Rather, "concentration" is the term for the specific function of these two years. In Richardson's words:

> At the heart of the suggested system is . . . an enlarged provision for concentration which would constitute, more than it now does, the center of the college work. . . . The student should devote at least half his attention in the last two years to this field, and in the senior year it might profitably be more. . . . We should reject the idea of building the provision for concentration by adding together separate courses, . . . it should be carefully planned as a coherent whole, . . . The student should be put upon his own resources more than he is now; he should be placed in the attitude of one who must master a wide field, the material being before him, largely by his own initiative. . . . No pretentious spirit of research should invade the course; it is to be planned, not for the professional scholar, but for the intelligent man of the world.[1]

If this ideal is realized in any college, we may well ask what contribution it makes in the education of the student that has never been made before. What new experience would this be for him which he has never had during the elementary school, the high school, or the first two years of college? It is refreshing to find an answer to this question in an educational classic of the seventeenth century, Locke's essay, *The Conduct of the Understanding*. In Section 44 entitled "Bottoming," Locke says:

> Another thing in the conduct of the understanding that is no less necessary is to accustom ourselves in any question proposed, to examine and find out upon what it bottoms. Most of the difficulties that come in our way, when well considered and traced, lead us to some proposition which, known to be true, clears the doubt and gives an easy solution to the question; whilst topical

[1] Leon B. Richardson, *A Study of the Liberal College*, A Report to the President of Dartmouth College, 1924, pp. 176–177.

and superficial arguments, of which there is store to be found on both sides, filling the head with variety of thoughts, and the mouth with copious discourse, serve only to amuse the understanding, and entertain company, without coming to the bottom of the question, the only place of rest and stability for an inquisitive mind whose tendency is only to knowledge and "truth."

This is the specific function of the provision for concentration, that the student may have the experience of "bottoming" one field of knowledge not with the purpose of producing the erudite scholar; rather, with the purpose of putting the student through a severe intellectual discipline in one field of knowledge with confidence that such an experience is the best possible preparation for thinking through to the bottom the many problems with which life in a changing world must inevitably confront him. Emerson, in his *Conduct of Life*, phrased the idea clearly in these words: "Concentration is the secret of strength in all management of human affairs."

If the field of concentration is to be as broad as Richardson has suggested, three-fifths of the student's time should be devoted to it. This means that, on a fifteen-hour program per semester, nine of these hours will be devoted to study within the field which gives a total of thirty-six out of sixty hours for the four semesters. But course requirements are no guaranty of integration within the field. Here again, a comprehensive examination, oral or written, or both, at the end of the senior year, is the best device to stimulate the student to carry forward everything he has learned bearing upon his field of concentration and to use it to advantage in the final test. The preparation of these examinations is one of the major responsibilities of the academic groups responsible for the several fields of concentration the college offers the student at the end of the sophomore year.

We are writing of the liberal college. Distribution, as one

of its function, is primary in the lower biennium, but should be continued in the upper biennium by provision for the student to spend one-fifth of his time pursuing intellectual interests outside of his field of concentration, that is, one course each semester with only a course examination at its completion. Concentration is primary in the upper biennium, but there is a third function which should dominate throughout the four-year period. The liberal college must teach how to live rather than how to make a living. It has often been pointed out that the tragic failures of life are failures of personalities, not failures in technical skill or professional knowledge. The liberal college must develop worthy personalities, and this means its students must develop philosophies of life which will make their living in the world a blessing to themselves and to their associates. Liberal colleges within state institutions will be limited here in terms of some social purpose, but such is not the case with the church-related college. If this church affiliation means anything at all, it means that the college stands for a definite philosophy of life. Its chief endeavor then must be to communicate this philosophy of life to its students. It will realize that its chief instrumentalities for instilling this philosophy of life into its students will be worthy personalities on its administrative and teaching staffs who in their own daily lives display this philosophy in action. It will not be unmindful of the fact that the religious impulses of youth are aroused and held only by active participation in a program of religious action and worship, both public and private. But as a college, it is an intellectual agency. The curriculum, therefore, must present the truths of religious faith to the mind, as well as the truths of philosophy which are to be built into the students' lives: Hence the requirement of formal religious instruction during the first two years, followed by formal training in philosophy during the last two years (the fifth of the student's time) is the reasonable procedure for the Catholic college. Again comprehensive examinations suggest themselves as the proper tests for the assimilation of this truth. But the purpose behind it all is, in one word, "unification." This is the very *raison d'être* of the Catholic college, to instill into its students a purpose in living, to give them a vantage point from which they will "see life steadily and see it whole." And this third function which we call "unification," must be the dominating purpose of the Catholic college throughout the entire period of four years. (See Figure 25, p. 409.)

SELECTION IN THE COLLEGE

We have stated above that the liberal college, if it is to play its part in the preservation and propagation of the intellectual tradition, must deal only with a selected student body as far as high school graduates are concerned. With the great increase in college enrollments, it is now evident that the selective principle must be operative within the college itself. Many "plans" are now in operation to make another selection within the college group from which will come the intellectual leaders of the future. On all sides we hear of "honors courses," "tutorial systems," "praeceptorial systems" and "independent study plans," etc. Catholic colleges have been slow to introduce administrative devices of this type making application of the selective principle on a more rigorous basis. Yet such a procedure has always been characteristic of the Catholic tradition. "In my father's house there are many mansions," is just as true of the intellectual life as it is of the spiritual. Further, as President Hutchins reminded the Catholic group assembled at the meeting of the Midwest Catholic Colleges in Chicago, April 1937, we are the only group in the country that can be said to have an educational tradition that is truly intellectual. Our tradition has been commonly spoken of as the classical tradition. The question is, what are we doing in our colleges today to preserve and propagate this tradition, subject as they are to the everpresent pressure of vocationalism dominant in the American scene. For our larger institutions at least, here is both an opportunity and an obligation. Let us suppose, for example, that one of our large university colleges with an entering freshman class of a thousand students, selected those who had had three or four years of Latin in good high schools and invited them to follow a curriculum in the classical tradition for two years, emphasizing the classical languages and mathematics. Then in the last two years let these students take philosophy as their field of concentration, spending three-fifths of their time going through a course of philosophy that begins at the beginning, passes through the middle, and comes out at the end giving a solid fundamental training in all eight departments. During the remaining two-fifths of their time they would be left free to devote themselves to the arts and sciences fundamental to the life calling they have planned. And let us suppose that the institution selected the very best of its staff to conduct this curriculum both as teachers and advisers to this highly selected group of students; would we not have every reason to believe that this institution would be on its way to have these graduates develop into intellectual leaders in whatever life calling they devoted themselves to, the ministry, medicine, law, teaching, writing, or any other? Unless some such procedure is adopted by our stronger colleges, what hope have we of developing intellectual leaders to meet the problems with which this rapidly changing world is confronting us?

(B) THE UNIVERSITY

When we pass from the college to a consideration of the university level proper, the graduate and professional schools, it is evident that not all is well with this unit of the educational ladder. Three books have appeared in the past decade, all of which are severe critiques of the American university. Flexner's *Universities, American, English and German* (1930), was such a severe indictment of university education as it is carried on in this country that the *Journal of Higher Education* devoted one whole issue to articles by university administrators and teachers attempting to answer the allegations of Flexner and to defend the procedures in vogue in our American institutions. Hutchins', *The Higher Learning in America*, aroused such a storm of protest, that in the summer issue (1937) of *The International Journal of Ethics* six of the eight articles were devoted to Hutchins, both in attack and in defense. Foerster's *The American State University* (1937) will not go unnoticed. No matter how sorry a spectacle the higher learning in America today presents, it has many protagonists and, of course, it is here that the tragedy of the situation is most evident.

What is the purpose of university education? Flexner's statement of this purpose is excellent:

> Whatever allowances we might make for national tradition or temperament, we should see to it somehow that in appropriate ways scholars and scientists would be conscious of four major concerns: the conservation of knowledge and ideas; the interpretation of knowledge and ideas; the search for truth; the training of students who will practise and "carry on." I say, to repeat, "the major concerns" of scholar and scientist. Of course, education has other and important concerns. But I wish to make it plain at the outset that the university is only one of many educational enterprises. It has, in the general educational scheme,

certain specific functions. Other agencies discharge or should discharge other functions.[1]

Inherent in the achievement of these purposes is the training of scholars as research workers and as specialists in the professional fields, of medicine, ministry, and law. Difference of opinion arises as soon as we include among the professions what Hutchins calls the "pseudo-professions:"

> From the university standpoint, at least, a professional discipline to be a professional discipline must have intellectual content, and have it in its own right. All there is to journalism can be learned through a good education and newspaper work. All there is to teaching can be learned through a good education and being a teacher. All there is to public administration can be discovered by getting a good education and being a public servant. As Aristotle said in the *Politics*, "The same education and the same habits will be found to make a good man and a good statesman and king." If the universities can revert to a condition where the number of professional schools and courses is limited to those that have intellectual content in their own right, they will have gone some distance toward disposing of the dilemma of professionalism.[2]

This insistence on intellectual content is in the tradition of Aristotle and St. Thomas as was so admirably stated by Newman. The university is an intellectual agency. As such its specific concern is the development of the intellectual virtues. As Newman says, we are speaking here of the university in its "idea," not as an instrument used by the Church to help the Church achieve its own function. In this conception the one concern of the university is the development of the intellectual virtues within its students. What are the intellectual

[1] Abraham Flexner, *Universities, American, English and German*, Oxford Univ. Press, 1930, pp. 6–7.
[2] Robert Maynard Hutchins, *The Higher Learning in America*, Yale Univ. Press, 1936, p. 56.

virtues?   The classification of Aristotle was adopted by St. Thomas and has never been improved upon.   They fall into two groups: the speculative and the practical.   The speculative are three: (1) *science*, "the ability to demonstrate universal and necessary truths and arrive at new and certain conclusions in the various branches of investigation;" (2) *understanding*, "the power to grasp certain fundamental self-evident truths both theoretical and practical, for example: no effect without a cause; . . . the greater this power of understanding, the wider the range of self-evident principles"; (3) *wisdom*, "the power to put things together and coördinate the data of science and understanding so as to attain to the ultimate explanation of all things and see everything in human life in relation to our last end."

The two virtues of the practical intellect are (1) *art* and (2) *prudence*.   They are distinguished by the "expressive Latin phrases: *recta ratio factibilium* and *recta ordo agibilium*.   In plain English we would say that art is knowing how to do a thing, prudence knowing what to do." [1]

In contrast with these are the moral virtues, commonly called the cardinal virtues, (1) prudence, (2) justice, (3) temperance, and (4) fortitude.   Thus prudence is both an intellectual as well as a moral virtue.   It well illustrates the difference between the two classifications.   Prudence as an intellectual virtue means knowing *what to do* under such and such circumstances.   Prudence as a moral virtue means *doing it*.   Once this distinction is clearly grasped we see the meaning of the statement that the university *as such* is not concerned with the moral virtues.   The teaching situations within a university, the class room, the lecture hall, the library and laboratory, offer little if any opportunity for practice of the moral virtues.   Yet virtue is a habit and as such it develops only

---

[1] Thomas Verner Moore, *Principles of Ethics*, Lippincott, 1935, pp. 54–55.

through voluntary practice. The opportunities for practice which the university situations afford are those resulting in intellectual habits, that is, the intellectual virtues. This brings out the meaning of the statement, "Character is caught; it cannot be taught." The power of inspiring example and the activities outside the class room, the lecture hall, etc., are those which result in the development of the moral virtues.

This distinction between the intellectual and the moral virtues is valuable to delimit the specific function of the university, but it does not solve all the problems of its present situation. The professions are both arts and sciences. Art as an intellectual virtue means "knowing how to do a thing." What things? Only those things the doing of which involves intellectual insight into the situation. Thus the surgeon does not know how to perform a delicate operation unless he has an intimate knowledge of the anatomy and physiology of the organs concerned. Here is intellectual content, and this is the test which determines that teaching the sciences of anatomy and physiology have a proper place in a university medical school. But cannot the same be said for administration in the fields of business, education, etc. Here is Hutchins' answer to those claiming that these callings are among the professions and therefore have a proper place in the university:

> If, for example, . . . (the teacher) seems likely to be a school administrator, and if a school administrator should know the number of janitors per cubic foot that school buildings require, and if a school administrator should not be trusted with a school unless he has this knowledge, then this knowledge should be gained in a technical institute.[1]

This setting up of technical institutes outside the university giving training in those callings without intellectual content,

[1] *Op. cit.*, p. 115.

is Hutchins' recommendation for saving it from the inroads of vocationalism, one of its besetting sins today. (For the place of technical institutes in the Educational Ladder see Figure 23, p. 383.)

The chief weaknesses of the American university in Hutchins' analysis, however, is the confusion and chaos resulting from the excessive departmentalization of knowledge:

> The modern university may be compared with an encyclopedia. The encyclopedia contains many truths. It may consist of nothing else. But its unity can be found only in its alphabetical arrangement. The university is in much the same case. It has departments running from art to zoology; but neither the students nor the professors know what is the relation of one departmental truth to another, or what the relation of departmental truths to those in the domain of another department may be.[1]

The medieval university had a principle of unity, namely, theology. Among the Greeks metaphysics was the ordering discipline. "Without theology or metaphysics," according to Hutchins, "a university cannot exist." [2] Since in the modern world it is futile to seek unification through theology, recourse must be had to metaphysics. How would metaphysics act as an ordering principle?

> It is in the light of metaphysics that the social sciences, dealing with man and man, and the physical sciences dealing with man and nature, take shape and illuminate one another. In metaphysics we are seeking the causes of the things that are. It is the highest science, the first science, and as first, universal. It considers being as being, both what it is and the attributes which belong to it as being.

> The aim of higher education is wisdom. Wisdom is knowledge of principles and causes. Metaphysics deals with the highest

[1] *Op. cit.*, p. 95.
[2] *Op. cit.*, p. 99.

principles and causes.   Therefore metaphysics is the highest wisdom.[1]

Along with the metaphysical sciences Hutchins gives a place in the university to the natural sciences and the social sciences. The departmental system and the professional schools as such would disappear:

> Education for the learned professions would be conducted in the three faculties of metaphysics, social science, and natural science, with prospective clergymen graduating under the faculty of metaphysics, lawyers under that of social science, and doctors and engineers under that of natural science.   Studying under the faculty of metaphysics we should expect to find prospective philosophers, too; under that of the social sciences future administrators, judges, legislators, statesmen, and men of affairs; and under that of natural science those destined for a life of scientific investigation.   Those professional schools which have no intellectual content in their own right would disappear altogether, except as their activities might be thought worthy of preservation in research or technical institutes.[2]

In the light of the fivefold analysis of the curriculum which we have presented (see Figure 17, p. 298) what are we to think of this analysis which is threefold?   There is no inherent conflict between them, as this statement by Hutchins makes plain:

> I have used the word metaphysics to include not only the study of first principles, but also all that follows from it, about the principles of change in the physical world, which is the philosophy of nature, and about the analysis of man and his productions in the fine arts including literature.[3]

Thus the study of literature and the fine arts finds a place in the reorganized university, but under the faculty of metaphysics.

[1] *Op. cit.*, p. 97–98.
[2] *Op. cit.*, p. 111–112.
[3] *Op. cit.*, p. 107.

A CATHOLIC UNIVERSITY

After a period in which the natural sciences have held sway over the life of man with exaggerated importance, and a period in which the techniques of natural science have been carried over without modification into the field of the social sciences, it is certainly refreshing for the Catholic to find the philosophical and theological sciences receive recognition as ordering principles. A Catholic university by its very name places theology at the center of its whole intellectual system. But any theology worthy of the name must have a metaphysical basis. In the outline which we have sketched here, however, this principle of unity is found within the liberal college as the heart of the university. We do not need to destroy what we now have in order to build a rational scheme for the intellectual life. As we have outlined the work of the college, all its students would study theology during their first two years, and some would continue that study during the last two years. All would study the metaphysical sciences during their last two years, and some would continue that study on the graduate level. With both sciences as a foundation, the student is prepared by theology to see life *steadily* and to live it steadfastly; and by his study of philosophy he is prepared to see it *whole*. With students so trained on the undergraduate level the university proper is prepared to play its role in the conservation and interpretation of knowledge and the search for truth.[1]

Nevertheless, this analysis by Hutchins presents a real challenge to Catholic educational institutions. With a principle of order at hand, have our institutions measured up to the opportunity which is presented to them? Have our institutions resisted the inroads of vocationalism and anti-intellectualism

[1] Abraham Flexner, *op. cit.*, p. 6.

so dominant in the American scene? Anyone familiar with American Catholic institutions of higher education cannot find reassuring answers to these questions. Here, then, is both an opportunity and an obligation.

SUGGESTED READINGS

GENERAL

Chapman, J. Crosby, and George S. Counts, *Principles of Education*, Houghton Mifflin, 1924, has four chapters, Problems 19 to 22 inclusive, one on the elementary school, one on the secondary school, one on the college and one on vocational education, the best short presentation in print on this subject from the naturalistic point of view.

Draper, Edgar M. and Alexander C. Roberts, *Principles of American Secondary Education*, Century, 1932, Chapter V, "Articulation of the Educational Units," deals with relations between secondary and elementary education and between secondary and higher education.

I. ELEMENTARY EDUCATION

Of the following books all but the one by Campbell treat elementary education from the point of view of the public school:

Brueckner, Leo J., *The Changing Elementary School*, Ivor Publishing Co., 1940, a report of the Regents' Inquiry into the character and cost of public education in the State of New York.

Campbell, Paul E., *Parish School Administration*, Joseph F. Wagner, 1937, Chapters IV, V, VI and VII, deal with the elementary school curriculum.

Dougherty, James H., Frank H. Gorman, and Claude A. Phillips, *Elementary School Organization and Management*, Macmillan, 1936.

Judd, C. H., *Report of the Commission on the Length of Elementary Education*, Supplementary Education Monograph, No. 34, Univ. of Chicago Press, 1927.

Mann, C. H., *How Schools Use Their Time*, Columbia Univ. Press, 1928.

Otto, Henry J., *Current Practices in the Organization of Elementary Schools*, Northwestern Univ., Contributions to Education, Series No. 5, Evanston, Illinois.

Reavis, W. C., P. R. Pierce, and Stullken, *The Elementary School— Its Organization and Administration*, Univ. of Chicago Press, 1931.

The National Elementary Principal, *Enriching the Curriculum for the Elementary-School Child*, No. 6, Vol. XVIII, Bulletin of the Department of Elementary School Principals, Nat. Ed. Assoc., July, 1939.

2. SECONDARY EDUCATION

Englehart, Fred and Alfred Overn, *Secondary Education, Principles and Practise*, Appleton-Century, 1937, Chapters X to XIX inclusive deal with the separate subjects of the secondary school.

Inglis, Alexander, *Principles of Secondary Education*, Houghton Mifflin, 1918, Chapters XII to XIX inclusive, contains an excellent treatment of the separate subjects in the high school curriculum.

Kandel, I. L., *History of Secondary Education*, Houghton Mifflin, 1930, carries the subtitle, "A Study in the Development of Liberal Education."

Monroe, Walter S., and Oscar F. Weber, *The High School*, Doubleday Doran, 1928, treats the secondary school subjects including Extra-curricular Activities in Chapters VIII to XIV inclusive.

North Central Association, *High School Curriculum Reorganization*, Ann Arbor Press, 1933, presents current theories on the reorganization of the separate subjects.

3. HIGHER EDUCATION

COLLEGE

Boucher, Chauncey Samuel, *The Chicago College Plan*, Univ. of Chicago, 1935, describes the new plan at Chicago University.

Butts, R. Freeman, *The College Charts Its Course*, McGraw-Hill, 1939, subtitle "Historical Conception and Current Proposals."

424 THE PIVOTAL PROBLEMS OF EDUCATION

Kelly, Robert Lincoln, *The Effective College*, Assoc. of American Colleges, 1928, contributions by authorities from representative institutions.

Meiklejohn, Alexander, *The Liberal College*, Marshall-Jones, 1920, is well worth reading.

Nock, Albert J., *The Theory of Education in the United States*, Harcourt Brace, 1932, attacks the theory of education in the American comprehensive high school and college.

Richardson, Leon Burr, *A Study of the Liberal College*, Dartmouth College, 1924, is one of the best books on the liberal college.

Wriston, Henry M., *The Nature of the Liberal College*, Lawrence College Press, 1937, is most stimulating.

UNIVERSITY

Cunningham, W. F., "Administrative Coordination is an American Catholic University," *Catholic Educational Review*, May and June, 1928, deals with the Catholic college as part of a Catholic university.

Flexner, Abraham, *Universities, American, English, German*, Oxford Univ. Press, 1930, is a severe indictment of American higher education. *The Journal of Higher Education* devoted a whole issue to replies to this book by authorities representing the various fields of university education.

Foerster, Norman, *The American State University*, Univ. of N. Car. Press, 1937, defends the Newman interpretation of liberal education.

——, "The Liberal Arts College Curriculum," *North Central Association Quarterly*, July, 1937, attacks four current theories of the curriculum and defends that of the "Great Books" pp. 45–50; the same article is printed in *The American Review*, Summer Numbers, 1937, and as Chapter 4 of *The Future of the Liberal College*, Appleton-Century, 1938.

Gray, William S., (editor), *Current Issues in Higher Education*, Univ. of Chicago Press, 1937, Vol. IX of the "Proceedings of the Institute for Administrative Officers of Higher Institutions, 1937."

Hutchins, Robert Maynard, *The Higher Learning in America*, Yale Univ. Press, 1937, presents a severe criticism of present-day American university education.

Kent, Raymond A., (editor) *Higher Education in America*, Ginn, 1930, Part I, "Divisions of Instruction" Chapters I to XII by different authors, description of all levels from Junior College to Graduate School, Part II, Chapters XIII to XXII, "Organization and Administration."

Kolsching, Walter M. and Elined Prys, (editor), *The University in a Changing World*, Oxford Univ. Press, 1932, has a chapter "The Conception of a Catholic University" by Dietrick von Hildebrand.

Newman, John Henry, *The Idea of a University*, entire.

Russell, John Dale, (editor), *The Outlook for Higher Education*, Univ. of Chicago Press, Vol. XI, "Proceedings of the Institute for Administration Officers of Higher Education, 1939."

The Journal of Higher Education presents current developments in both the collegiate and the university fields.

Thwing, Charles F., *A History of Higher Education in America*, Appleton, 1906.

THREE TECHNIQUES OF TEACHING

We have not been able to follow those who think of the teaching process as encompassed in a single generalization or principle but rather have sought to analyze the varying situations and to suggest the principles which apply in each of them. There is a technique which is particularly applicable when skill is to be achieved or *habits* fixed. While the total social situation may remain the same, the technique is quite different when one stimulates and guides children in the *thinking* process. When *appreciation* is the major consideration, the technique employed will be different from those which are used in habit-forming or in thinking.

Strayer-Frasier-Armentrout, *Principles of Teaching*, American Book Co., 1936, Preface, p. vi.

CHAPTER XIII

THE TECHNIQUE OF TEACHING

Following the curriculum, the second means within the school for the achievement of its objectives presented in Chapter VIII, "The Hierarchy of Educational Objectives," is the teacher. It is the teacher who makes the school. Here, then, if the third of the problems into which we have analyzed the educative process. The selection and education of the teacher is all-important. Before turning to this phase of the problem, however, it will be well first to inquire into the nature of the work the teacher is called upon to do and for which he should be educated. Only when we have an adequate concept of the nature of the teacher's task are we in a position to lay down principles for guidance in the important matter of educating teachers. The work of the teacher brings before us the problem of *method*.

It should be understood at the outset of our study of this problem, that it is impossible in actual classroom procedure to separate method from the materials to be taught. The presentation of any matter in the classroom necessarily involves the use of some method. Nor can method take place in a vacuum. The use of any method necessarily involves using some materials. In fact, this is what method is, the use the teacher makes of teaching materials in order to arouse the student to

427

activity, and, as he works with these materials, to give him the necessary guidance for learning to place. Our separation of method from the curriculum is, then, a logical separation merely made to deepen our understanding of the teaching process. Our aim is to formulate principles of teaching which, clearly apprehended, will guide the teacher in the selection and in the use of the best method to present his subject to the student.

We are using the word "method" here in its broadest connotation, inclusive of all those meanings which it carries when applied to specialized procedures as, for example, the "lecture method," "the project method," etc. Used in this larger sense, method has two definite phases. There is, first of all, that phase of the teacher's work which is concerned with preparing for and actually conducting within the classroom procedures planned to arouse and to guide the learning activities of the pupil. This phase we will call the "technique of teaching." In addition to this there is another phase of the teacher's task which is not concerned so much with the procedures he may employ in carrying on his work of instruction, motivation, and discipline, as it is with creating for the pupil *a situation favorable to learning*. This we will call the "administration of teaching." All phases of school administration, of course, may be said to be concerned in general with creating a situation favorable to learning. The right to determine the education of the child, the financial support of the school and the problem of its control have meaning only in terms of the interests of pupils. We deal here only with those phases of administration with which the teacher is immediately concerned; for example, what provision he makes for meeting individual differences when teaching a group of pupils of variant abilities. This phase of teaching may be planned by an administrative officer, but it is only the teacher who puts the plan into operation, and hence it is part of his "method." In Chapter XIV, "The Administration of Teaching," we will study the various "plans" now being tried out on all levels of the educational ladder to make teaching effective in the American cosmopolitan, comprehensive school. We treat the problem of method, therefore, under these two aspects: first, the technique of teaching; and second, the administration of teaching, meaning by the latter everything teachers do to create a situation favorable to learning.

The technique of teaching also divides into two distinct phases. There is first of all the very important task that teachers perform before they enter the classroom. This preparation for teaching is the *organization* of subject matter. Next there are the teaching procedures themselves actually in operation when the teacher is working with pupils, the *presentation* of subject matter. We now take up the first phase of the technique of teaching.

1. THE ORGANIZATION OF SUBJECT MATTER

If teaching is to be well done, the materials which give it substance must be planned in an orderly way or there will be much waste of time and effort on the part of both pupils and teacher. The term "subject matter" is open to serious objection. It carries the connotation of passive inert material that is to be poured into the pupil like milk into a bottle, to be mentally regurgitated by him in time of tests and examinations. Nothing could be further from what we mean by "subject matter" as the term is used here. Subject matter has meaning for pupil learnings only in terms of the activities of the pupil. Only insofar as subject matter is organized and later presented to pupils in a way that will arouse them to activity and intrigue them to continue active until the learning outcomes have been achieved, has it any part to play in an intelligent technique of teaching.

In the elementary and secondary school the first organization of the curriculum is now commonly effected by governmental authority, either state, or local; and sometimes, particularly on the secondary school level, this organization is handed to the teacher in the form of a printed syllabus. But even when this is the case, this does not mean that responsibility for organizing materials for presentation through teaching has been taken away from the teacher. Printed syllabi may determine the curriculum in the large, but the obligation of breaking down this large mass of material into smaller units, of making out a calendar of the year's or the semester's work, and particularly of determining what small section of this syllabus is to be covered each month or week, or even each day; this obligation can never be taken from the teacher. Nor should it be. The task of immediate preparation, assuming that the teacher is thoroughly familiar with his subject, is primarily one of organization, and it is this day-by-day reorganization, conditioned by the amount of subject matter covered on the previous day, that puts vitality into teaching and prepares the teacher to appear before his class with a definite goal in mind and with procedures determined beforehand that give promise of realizing that goal in terms of pupil learnings. This is the meaning of Morrison's statement: "Always in teaching, organization is the major part of method." [1]

(A) THE UNIT CONCEPT

The major contribution which Morrison made to the technique of teaching in the book just quoted, was the introduction and elaboration of the unit concept as the basis for subject matter organization. What is a unit? We give his definition:

We define a serviceable learning unit as *a comprehensive and significant aspect of the environment, of an organized science, of an art,*

[1] Henry Morrison, *The Practice of Teaching in the Secondary School* (revised edition), 1931, p. 424.

*or of conduct, which being learned results in an adaptation in per-
sonality.*[1]

The key phrase in this definition is "an adaptation in personality." We are familiar with this word "adaptation" from
Chapter III, "The Nature of Man," where we developed the
idea that the three changes which take place in education, as
the development of the individual progresses, are adaptations
fitting the response (behavior) to stimulation which the individual is experiencing (situation). The definition leads to the
distinction between the unit itself, which is a program term
signifying the organization of subject matter into wholes, and
the learning products which are the adaptations. In the
science subjects the adaptations will be meanings or understandings (knowledge); in the appreciation subjects they will
be attitudes; in the arts they will be abilities. (See Figure 6,
" The Outcomes of Learning," pp. 82–83.) The learning product
is, of course an inner change, subjective in the learner, but the
external correlate is the objective thing to be learned. Thus to
quote Morrison again: "The Industrial Revolution is an external interpretation of social and economic evolution, a thing to
be learned. The learning itself is the correlated internal attitude of intelligence and understanding with respect to the
structure of society." [2] Once this distinction is grasped it
brings out the difference between assimilative material organized in the unit and the learning itself:

> The teacher may be developing an appreciation of the beauty of a
> lyric or the truth of a drama or a refined taste for the short story.
> He is, or should be, aiming at a series of individual adaptations.
> If the taste is actually developed, it is a contradiction in terms to
> say that is forgotten. If the beauty or the truth is really seen and
> accepted, the statement itself means that a new attitude is dis-

[1] *Ibid.*, pp. 24–25.
[2] *Ibid.*, p. 24.

covered. Now in the course of this learning, a great deal of read-ing is done and the teacher perhaps talks a great deal as he en-deavors to bring about the changed attitude which he is seeking to effect. In other words, the pupil passes through a body of assimilative experience. Assuming that the new attitude has been acquired, it may very well be that the greater part of the ex-perience itself fades away. The adaptation is revealed by the change which takes place in the character of the reading which the pupil now selects.[1]

Conceived in this way it is evident that a subject running for a half year or even a year cannot have many units. Adaptations so interpreted take time to generate. But this is not impor-tant. Once they are developed they are permanent, except for modifications which later experience may bring about, and it is in this permanence that their value lies.

(B) THE SYLLABUS

The next step in organization after the determination of the learning units is the syllabus. A dictionary definition of a syl-labus is: "an abstract giving the heads, or main subjects of a book, course of study, etc." (*Webster's Collegiate Dictionary*) As the term is used today with reference to the organization of subject matter for teaching, a complete syllabus will include five things:

    I. A statement of the specific aims of the course.
    II. Organization of the materials of the course in large units with references for each unit.
    III. A description of the teaching procedures used in presenting these materials.
    IV. A statement of the learning activities required of students.
    V. Tests on each large unit and final examination on the entire course.

Is such a device necessary or at least highly desirable for teaching all types of courses? The answer to this question is

[1] *Ibid.*, p. 29.

certainly a strong affirmative. It must be remembered, however, that no two syllabi will be exactly alike. A syllabus for a course in beginning foreign language, for example, will be a simple thing compared with a syllabus for a Social Science course for which no text is available. Further, teachers must be free to put their own personalities into their teaching, but definite organization of subject matter before the actual work ʼ teaching begins will insure that freedom rather than be a iction upon it.

ould the making of a syllabus be required of every teacher very course and should copies of these syllabi be on file in e offices of the Heads of Departments? No unqualified answer can be given to this question. There are certain experienced teachers who, for years, have been conducting courses in an efficient manner, without the help a detailed syllabus offers. Further, these experienced teachers are often unsympathetic with the new techniques now being developed for the improvement of instruction, and to require them to go through a form of preparation for teaching with which they are totally unfamiliar would be disturbing to their peace of mind and in all probability, would not materially improve their teaching. But in the case of younger and less experienced teachers, and certainly for all beginning teachers, a detailed syllabus should be required. This syllabus should be the joint product of all instructors teaching the subject, and it should receive the approval of the Head of the Department before being adopted for use in the classroom. The importance that is given to the syllabus as a device for the improvement of instruction on the college level is well brought out in the following quotation:

> Each teacher should be required to prepare, in detail, a syllabus for each course he is paid to give. . . . Adequate references by chapter and page, should be cited. The professor should make sure that such references are on the library shelves and he should

list the call numbers for the use of his students, and as an aid to the librarian.   The constant improvement of the syllabuses should be a major duty of each teacher.   Department heads should supervise this work carefully and should observe class-room instruction so as to suggest improvements.   Before a new course is offered a syllabus should be prepared.   This should be reviewed by the man's own department and by related depart-ments. . . .   Each could contribute pertinent viewpoints from its own special field.   The final result would be more interesting and instructive classroom sessions.[1]

It must be remarked, however, that the possession of a syllabus by any instructor is not in itself the best guarantee that a sub-ject will be taught effectively.   Rather, it is *the construction of a syllabus* by an instructor, either alone or in collaboration with his fellow instructors, which holds out the greatest promise for improving instruction.   It is true that this is an arduous task and is one which is never finished; for every syllabus should be under continual reconstruction by those using it or looking for-ward to using it at some future time.

2. THE THREE TECHNIQUES OF TEACHING

Teaching has meaning only as an aid to learning.   The effec-tive teacher, therefore, must have an adequate understanding of how learning takes place in order that he may guide the proc-ess intelligently.   The "born teacher," if there are any such, has this understanding out of the richness of his experience in dealing with others and through his insight into the nature of the learning process as a result of that experience.   Few, how-ever, are gifted with deep insight of this nature, and even those that are can deepen it by formal study of the process itself. This is the very purpose of Educational Psychology.   Psychol-ogy is the science of human personality.   Educational Psy-chology is the science of human personality *in the act of learning*,

[1] R. S. Uhrbrock, "Is College Leadership Bankrupt," *The Journal of Higher Education*, Jan., 1935; pp. 5–6.

and it is this act of learning which advances mental development. In Chapter V, "Theories of Learning," we called attention to the fact that there is no more controverted question in the whole field of psychology than the problem of learning. Following our review of the present situation, however, we advanced the thesis that though much is controverted with regard to the details of how learning takes place, nevertheless much is known about learning that is of immediate practical value to the teacher who would direct intelligently the learning processes of his pupils. To question this fact would be to question the value of human experience in general. All through the ages, as well as in modern times, the greatest minds of man, Plato, Aristotle and St. Thomas; Locke, Pestolozzi, Herbart, and Froebel; Hamilton and Newman, etc., have all given careful consideration to this problem of learning and teaching, and, happily, we have preserved in their writings much of their thought on this problem. Scientific research in education will continue to refine our knowledge of the learning and teaching process, but a statement of the basic principles need not wait on this development. We have offered such a statement of the basic principles of human learning in Chapter V, Section 2, pp. 135–144, with which the student should now refresh his mind for the particular reason that in our presentation there concerning the learning process, we have anticipated much of what belongs logically in this chapter's treatment of the teaching process. After all, it is all one process. Teaching and learning are the convex and concave aspects of the circle of the pupil's mind. The pupil on the inside is the concave aspect; the teacher from without sees the convex aspect of the circumference of the circle, but it is the same circle. Here we see the real meaning of the statement of Hamilton: "All education is self-education." In self-education the student is both teacher and learner. In our treatment of the teaching process we do not set down any *formal* principles of teaching.   Instead we go back to our definition of education as a threefold process of change (Figure 26, Section B, below.)   Each of these changes into which we have analyzed the educative process leads to the formulation of a principle within the learning process, and these principles in their appli-

FIGURE 26.—THE THREE TECHNIQUES OF TEACHING

Section A.   The Psychological Basis

MENTAL FUNCTIONS	PRINCIPLES OF LEARNING	PHASES OF A LEARNING EXPERIENCE	LEARNING OUTCOMES	
			In General	*In Detail*
Cognition (knowing)	Apperception (reflection) Readiness	Meaning	Knowledge	Facts and meanings
Affection (feeling)	Motivation (interest) Effect	Satisfaction or annoyance	Attitudes	Ideals and appreciations
Conation (doing)	Selfactivity (repetition) Exercise	Tendency to repeat or not to repeat	Abilities	Habits and skills

Section B.   Analysis of the Curriculum

EDUCATION IS CHANGE	TYPES OF SUBJECTS—EXAMPLES			
	3 *Main*	*English*	*Music*	*Others*
From ignorance to knowledge	Science subjects	Grammar (versification)	History of music	Social sciences
From impulses to ideals	Appreciation subjects	Literature (poetry)	Music appreciation	Art appreciation
From capacities to abilities	Arts subjects	Composition (art of writing)	Applied music courses	Physical training

FIGURE 26.—(*continued*)

Section C. Analysis of the Techniques

THE THREE TECHNIQUES	TEACHER FUNCTIONS	TEACHER'S PART	PUPIL'S PART	THE PRODUCT, A MIND
The problem technique	To instruct *instruere* (build in)	Present problems and give leads	Observation and reflective thinking	informed,
The participation technique	To motivate *movere* (put in motion)	Have and communicate the experience	Share and enjoy the experience	cultured,
The practice technique	To discipline *educare* (bring forth)	Guide practice and demand achievment	Distribute practice with self-criticism	disciplined.

cations to the teaching process give us three techniques of teaching. We repeat again: these are *logical distinctions* based on the very nature of the mental process, and as such they are valid. For the intelligent teacher they are great aids in deepening his insight into the work before him. Figure 26, pp. 436–437, analyzes the three techniques of teaching in their relation to the mental process, the learning process, and the curriculum. We will now present a brief treatment of each of these three techniques.

(A) THE PRACTICE TECHNIQUE

In Figure 26, Section A, we identify the outcomes of the learning process as three, knowledge attitudes, and abilities. The forms in which abilities manifest themselves are habits and skills. The word "skills" commonly carries the connotation of motor abilities, neuro-muscular coördinations. "Habit" is more commonly used for mental abilities, habits of thinking, feeling, and willing, etc. The point we wish to emphasize is that the principle of self-activity applies equally on the two levels, on the rational level as well as on the level of sense. (Figure 5, p. 73.) When we put the question, "How does skill come?" it does not take a teacher to give the answer. Every student is aware of it. *Skill comes through practice.* Practice, therefore, is the appropriate label for the hundreds of things teachers do in their efforts to aid pupils develop skill in any ability, whether motor or mental. The principle which is dominant here is that of self-activity. It is most clearly illustrated from the field of motor abilities. Every student knows it would be folly for a football team (or for any team in any sport) which is allowed ten hours for practice through the week (two hours a day, five days a week, one day for the game and one for rest to prevent going stale) to lay off practicing four of these days and take all its ten hours of practice in one day. Skill in any game is not acquired in this way; but, sore muscles, charley horses, and inexpertness; bungling and fumbling. No, we do not acquire motor skills (muscular coördinations) efficiently in such a manner. In psychological terminology, such a procedure violates the law of exercise which demands distribution of practice with alternating periods of rest and relaxation. The law is just as binding in the world of mind as in the world of muscle. Reflective thinking is the supreme human ability. We learn to think in the same way we learn any activity, by practicing that activity. But again this practice in thinking must be distributed over appropriate periods of time with alternating periods of rest, during which the mind is free to follow fancy.

It will be helpful to analyze this teaching situation from the point of view of both teacher and pupil. The teacher's obligation is, first of all, to present and explain a pattern to the pupil guiding his imitation of it. The old word was "model," and the old copy books in penmanship had the model at the top of the page which the pupil was to copy many times on the lines below. Such a model is now looked upon as a static thing far inferior to that produced by the teacher going through the activity itself. Hence the word "pattern." This refers not merely to the product of the activity but to the activity itself as it takes place under the pupil's observation. The second obligation of the teacher is to demand achievement as he guides the practice of the pupil with helpful criticism, using appropriate praise and censure as called for by the pupil's natural ability and application. When we analyze the pupil's part in this learning situation, again two phases are evident. Distributed practice is the *sine qua non* of improvement, but this alone is not sufficient. There must be observation of the pattern with self-criticism under the guidance of the teacher. The two working together are almost certain to bring about improvement unless the task is beyond the capacities of the pupil. (See Figure 26, Section C, p. 437.)

The same factors condition improvement in any mental ability. Students following a course in the Philosophy or Principles of Education in which this treatise is used as a text have a right to demand that it set for them a pattern of philosophizing about education. If it does this, and if the teacher using it vitalizes that pattern by his own philosophizing before them, and if they practice philosophizing over any appreciable period of time under the guidance of an intelligent teacher, taking a critical attitude towards both the pattern set for them and their own efforts to imitate and to improve upon it, there is real prospect that they will experience continued growth in their ability to philosophize about education. With this outcome in prospect they are on the way towards developing a disciplined mind.

(B) THE PROBLEM TECHNIQUE

Anyone familiar with the curriculum of the school concerned with general education knows that the type of subjects dominant within it are the science subjects. In Figure 19, "The Disciplines in School Activities" (p. 330), we have distinguished three groups of sciences dealing with the three worlds in which man lives, the physical sciences (physical world), the humanistic sciences (human world), and the metaphysical sciences (spiritual world). Since all three, however, have the same outcome as their aim, namely, knowledge or an understanding of these three worlds it is to be expected that the teaching techniques appropriate to all three is the same. This is literally the case. Thinking begins only when we are confronted with a problem. For the vast majority of our actions during the day, habit takes care of the situation. But when we find ourselves in a situation for which we have no habit response that is satisfying, then we begin to think out a solution of the problem. Dressing for the child was once a difficult problem. For the college student habit commonly carries through this activity with complete satisfaction. But when the night of the senior ball approaches the situation is radically changed. Here a problem is presented and many and devious are the ways in which students solve it. The same situation is present in all inquiries in the field of the sciences. Study, which here is thinking, goes on only in the effort to solve problems. Hence the appropriate name for the teaching technique in this field is the "problem technique" and it covers all the hundreds of things teachers do to aid students in this activity.

Analysis of the teacher's task here reveals that two activities are dominant. The teacher must, first of all, present problems to students which will challenge their best efforts. In a small way, every question that is asked is the setting of a problem.

Hence the fundamental truth in De Garmo's statement, "The question is the universal instrument of all good teaching." The rhetorical question in a lecture, anticipating no answer, has the same function, namely, to stimulate thinking on the part of listeners in their search for the answer which the skillful lecturer gradually unfolds before them. This unfolding is an illustration of the second phase of this teaching technique, namely, giving leads which point the way to the solution of the problem. If this is not done in any difficult problem, students will blindly flounder around and only too often give up trying. No growth in knowledge results from such a procedure. But with direction from the teacher taking the form of guiding the student towards the solution of the problem, (not in solving it for him,) activity will be stimulated, and through this activity, intelligently guided, growth in knowledge will be the outcome. Analysis of the student's part in problem solving reveals that it also is twofold. There is, first of all, observation of the facts in the situation and second, reflective thinking. The high school physics instructor who has a pitcher of ice water on the desk when the class assembles and asks the question "Why the drops of water on the outside of the pitcher?" will almost certainly be rewarded with spurious explanations. Questions of this kind have their place in starting reflective thinking in the search for the correct explanation. The writer recalls from his high school days how the same instructor who used the ice water pitcher greeted his class one day with a bouquet of flowers on the rostrum. When the class was assembled, he removed the vase which appeared to support the "flowers," in reality an image cast by a concave mirror in the laboratory adjoining. Thus was the class effectively introduced to the unit on light. Not many teachers have ingenuity enough to keep inventing devices of this kind to set problems before students that will capture their interests so effectively. Nor are they necessary for effective teaching. But exploratory tests and other devices will reveal to students how little they know about a subject of study, and with this attitude generated there is real prospect that observation and reflective thinking will be carried on by students with growth in knowledge as the outcome. (See Figure 26, Section C, p. 437.)

(c) THE PARTICIPATION TECHNIQUE

When we inquire into the nature of the technique appropriate to the third type of subjects in the curriculum of general education, appreciation subjects, the problem is much more difficult and less capable of satisfactory analysis. The chemistry instructor seeking relief in the corridor from the disagreeable fumes of the laboratory hears the instructor in literature reading a poem to the class. "What a snap!" he reflects to himself. He thinks of his long hours in the laboratory and the time spent reading students' stupid write-ups of experiments. "And they call that teaching!" is his reflection as he returns to his laboratory. But the question is, what else could an instructor in literature do that would give any better promise of achieving his aim, namely, developing a taste for poetry in the minds of his pupils. Taste is an emotionalized attitude. It arises only when students are led to share the experience of an instructor who has an enthusiasm for poetry, and in sharing that experience, find it pleasurable. This analysis reveals that the effective teacher in this field must, first of all, have this attitude of enthusiasm himself and then he must have the ability of communicating the enthusiasm to students. (Figure 26, Section C, p. 437.)

TWO TECHNIQUES IN TEACHING POETRY APPRECIATION

The writer repeats here, as told to him, the experience of a high school teacher who felt she had achieved some success in this difficult field. One of the several sections of the Poetry class had been assigned to her. It would be a new experience for her. She was desirous of receiving all the help possible so she conferred with the teacher who had taught all the sections for some years previous. This was her technique. First, she had the pupils read the poem the class was studying. Next, they wrote out their understanding of it. Then she interpreted the poem for them revealing their lack of understanding but complimenting the few who had caught the main ideas.

The plan the new teacher proposed to follow was radically different. First, she would read the poem to the class in her best manner, making every appeal possible through rhythm, rhyme, and word picture to aid them in sharing the beauty of the selection. Next she would explain the difficult passages, and when the idea was grasped by the group, she would read it again to present the idea in its original setting. Then she would have them search for expressions of the same idea by other authors, giving specific references to other poems so that their search would not be a blind, fruitless groping. And finally, she would have them express orally or in writing in their own words what they felt they had gotten out of the poem; whether or not they liked it, that is, their appreciation. "But if you begin that way," said the experienced teacher, "you will do all the work." Somewhere, sometime, in one of her Education courses perhaps, there had been impressed upon her the principle, "A pupil learns through his own activities;" and she believed she was faithfully applying this principle in her technique as outlined. The beginning teacher said she didn't mind doing the work provided she accomplished her aim, and that was to develop a liking for poetry in the group as a whole and not merely increase it in those few fortunate individual pupils who brought such a liking to the class the first day it met, due perhaps to living in the environment of a cultured home.

The experienced teacher continued the same teaching procedure she had followed in times past. The class went through the same "activities" which made provision for their "doing the work." And the outcome at the end was the same as before. The class thoroughly hated the course and were resolved never to open a book of poetry again; this, of course, apart from the few individuals who came from homes with rich cultural backgrounds or were gifted with superior ability in this field.

The new teacher persevered in her technique also. The result was that in spite of a mental set against poetry inherited from the class the year previous, the pupils enjoyed the class periods immensely. The teacher, too, sensing the pleasure she was giving to the group, had her own pleasure increased manyfold and everybody was having a good time. Even when "work activities" began, now that they were based on an understanding and a feeling for the beauty of the selections, these periods lost their aspect of drudgery and presented new opportunities for new satisfactions in the feeling of mastery that came to the pupils with the realization that they could write intelligently on the theme expressing their own ideas, as well as sharing in those of the author. The result at the end was that, as a group, no inhibition against poetry had been set up. Some few were enthusiastic about it and there were indications that a fair number would later read poetry for the sheer pleasure of the experience itself. The objective of the course had been realized. Wherein lay the failure of the experienced teacher? Her principle was sound enough. It was in its application that she went awry; her failure to distinguish different types of activities, one type suitable for achieving one objective, another for another. In an appreciation subject, she had employed the problem technique instead of the participation technique.

THREE TYPES OF SUBJECTS AND THREE TEACHING TECHNIQUES

On one occasion after the writer had explained to a class this analysis of the curriculum as made up of three types of subjects, Science, Appreciation, and Arts subjects, and three techniques each appropriate for the achievement of the aim of one of these three groups of subjects, one of the brighter students approached the instructor and said, "Now I know why I hate Shakespeare." The instructor knew, too, but he let the student go on with his story. In their study of Shakespeare they had torn the plays to pieces by analysis, an appropriate technique for science classes, but at no time were they given an opportunity to share in the action of the play by some form of dramatization. Instead of the participation technique, the teacher used the technique appropriate for problem-solving. The tragedy of this situation is that not only are the objectives of the course not realized, but instead positive inhibitions are set up. A dislike is generated that the student may carry all through life. If making this distinction between the techniques may save teachers from committing the error just described, nothing could be more worth while in the formal study of the teaching process.

THE GREAT TEACHER

If the principles of human learning we have formulated in Chapter V with the accompanying techniques of teaching we have been presenting in this chapter, are valid, the Christian teacher would expect that they must have been carried out by the Great Teacher of all times. Nor are we disappointed when we look into this chapter in the history of education. Our Lord's constant use of the question (the problem technique) when teaching His disciples or the multitude is one of the dom-

inant characteristics of His method. "Whom do the people say
that I am?" (Luke IX, 18)   "Which of these three was neighbor
to him that fell among robbers?" (ibid. X, 36)   Questions like
these were constantly on His lips. His use of the simple materials of the everyday life of those He was teaching, the net of
the fisherman, the seed of the farmer, the grote of the house-
keeper, and for all, the birds of the air, the lilies of the field and
the marriage feast—these are illustrations of how He applied
the principle of apperception, leading His listeners on from the
simple experiences of their everyday lives to the sublime truths
He was preparing them for. The parable was, perhaps, His
most effective instrument. The story of the Good Samaritan,
the Prodigal Son, etc., have done more to teach the lessons of
love and mercy to human kind than any other single agency.

In His use of the miracle we see the principle of motivation
(interest) at play. In the multiplication of the loaves as told
in the sixth chapter of St. John, it was not merely a matter of
capturing the interest of those present. The disciples themselves played a prominent part (technique of participation) in
the miracle, distributing the loaves, partaking of them, and
gathering up the fragments "lest they be lost." Thus was created an attitude which carried over to the Last Supper, when
they themselves *took part* in the first sacrament of the Eucharist
and received the commission to repeat it when the Master had
departed: "Do this for a commemoration of me" (Luke XXII,
19).

His use of repetition to drive home His simple lessons is a
good illustration of the practice technique in effective operation. Always was He their model. "Learn of me, because I
am meek, and humble of heart." (Mat. XI, 29) The personal
influence of His presence, His voice, His every mode of life were
constantly molding them to carry on His work. After a period
of apprenticeship He sent them out two by two as missionaries

to the people so that they might have actual experience of the apostleship to which they were called (principle of self-activity). Finally, just before His ascension, He shows the importance He attached to the Teaching function by setting up a teaching Church to carry His message to all men. "Going, therefore, *teach* ye all nations." (Mat. XXVIII, 19.)

Note: for relationships between the techniques and other phases of education, see "The Triangular Distinction in Education," p. 455.

3. THE CYCLE CONCEPT APPLIED TO TEACHING

We have already called attention to the fact that most of the teaching in the school concerned with general education is in the science subjects. The very fact that three of the five fields of knowledge are the three kinds of sciences, the physical, the humanistic and the metaphysical sciences (see Figure 17, p. 298), brings it about that most teaching is through the problem technique, the technique appropriate to science teaching. It will be worthwhile, therefore, to submit this technique to further analysis. We do this by applying the cycle concept to teaching.

THE LIFE CYCLE

In Chapter III, "The Nature of Man," we presented briefly the idea that the cycle concept is applicable to all living things. All life goes on in terms of stimulus, adaption, and response, the response supplying new stimulation with new *adaptions* and reactions following; hence the term "cycle." The concrete presentation of the meaning of this abstract term by a circle is presented in Figure 27, p. 448. The point of view favored in psychology today, whether it be called "functionalism," "dynamism," or Gestalt psychology, or the synthesis of these

FIGURE 27.—THE CYCLE CONCEPT APPLIED TO TEACHING

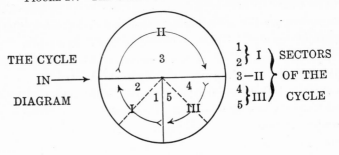

THE LEARNING CYCLE	THE TEACHING CYCLE	THE HERBARTIAN STEPS	THE THOUGHT CYCLE	MILLER'S MOVEMENTS
I. Stimulation	1. Exploration	1. Preparation	1. Problem	I. Problem-Raising M.
	2. Presentation	2. Presentation	2. Definition	
II. Assimilation	3. Assimilation	3. Association	3. Hypothesis	II. Directing-Study M.
III. Reaction	4. Organization	4. Generalization	4. Evaluation	III. Organizing, Unifying M.
	5. Recitation	5. Application	5. Verification	

spoken of as the *organismic point of view* in psychology, stresses the fact that life is inherent in the organism and that the organism acts as a whole in all forms of behavior. Activities arise as a result of an inner felt need, instead of being initiated by external stimulation. We have a typical illustration here of the swing of the pendulum in scientific theory. When the behaviorists were dominant in American psychology, nothing but body was considered. The body was a machine and should be studied as a machine by the objective method alone, the only method of science. In some of the recent publications the body as the physical basis of the psychical functions, seems to have disappeared entirely.[1] The position we have taken in this treatise is that man is a somatopsychic organism, that is, a body-mind organism, and to neglect either part of his dual nature is to fail to understand him. The very meaning of the phrase, *integrating mechanism*, is that through the functioning of the organs that constitute it, the organism acts as an integrated whole. This concept comes to us from the neurologists, but it is a synthesis most helpful in understanding the nature of man. The functional analysis of the three parts of the mechanism into stimulus, adaptation, and response, is just as helpful in understanding behavior. Dynamism stresses that all activities arise within the organism. Some explain the origin of behavior in terms of instincts (Mc-Dougall); others, in terms of impulses (Moore). The cause of all behavior must, of course, be within the living organism itself, but the *occasions* which determine the various forms behavior takes, lie outside the organism in the environment. This is what is meant by the function, stimulation. Environment and organism are always interacting on one another. Adaptation does not mean merely that the organism fits itself to the environment. Rather, in the case of human beings, adaptation (the mental functions) means planning changes in the environment to fit the felt needs of the organism. Human beings build houses instead of living in caves. In fact, the most important of the responses of intelligent man are precisely these, recreating his environment according to his heart's desire. As his environment improves his desires change, and thus the cycle is continuous.

(A) THE LEARNING CYCLE

The phase of behavior which holds the chief interest for the teacher is learning. If all behavior may be thought of as going

[1] See W. D. Commins, *Principles of Educational Psychology*, Ronald Press, 1937.

on in the cycle, stimulus, adaptation, and response, learning as a form of behavior has its own cycle. This is the suggestion of Morrison. The terms he uses to label the three sectors of the learning cycle are stimulation, assimilation, and reaction. (See Figure 27, p. 448.) His illustration of how one passes through the cycle in arriving at an understanding of "that general region of automobile mechanics from which the stimulus comes" (op. cit. page 162) is well worth reading. The teacher who comes to know a subject through teaching it has a similar experience. The trouble with most learning in school is that no occasion is offered the pupil to use the knowledge he has been working over. The teacher, however, through his organization and presentation in the class room, makes vital use of the materials he has been assimilating. He comes to know them thoroughly because he "carries through" into the reaction sector of the cycle. This is the ideal to be aimed at in all learning; *to complete the cycle.*

(b) THE THOUGHT CYCLE

Dewey analyzes an act of thought into five logical steps.[1] Since thinking is the dominant activity in all growth in knowledge, it is easy to see the parallel between this analysis and the learning cycle on the one hand and the teaching cycle on the other as indicated by Figure 27, p. 448. All thinking starts with a problem. The definition of the problem is the next step, followed by various hypotheses as suggested solutions. One hypothesis is selected as the best solution. This Dewey calls "evaluation." The final step is the verification of this solution by actual trial. If verification is not the outcome of this first trial of the solution accepted, the cycle starts over again. Since these steps are merely "logical steps," it is evident that in actual thinking one may pass from one sector

[1] John Dewey, *How We Think*, Heath & Co., 1910, p. 72.

of the cycle back to a previous sector as well as forward to other sectors as analyzed in the diagram. The logical order of the steps is not always the chronological. In simple problems some sectors may be skipped entirely, for example, passing from hypothesis to verification without any delay in evaluation.

(c) THE TEACHING CYCLE

In the Morrison plan the unit concept is the key to the organization of subject matter; the cycle concept is the key to the presentation of subject matter. But Morrison's use of the cycle concept as applied to teaching has certain distinctive features which are definitely his own contribution. (Figure 27, p. 448) The outstanding one is "exploration," as the first sector of the cycle, in which the teacher at the beginning of a new unit, through questions or an exploratory test, finds out to what extent some of the pupils may already be familiar with the unit and therefore may be freed from pursuing it by the assignment of supplementary projects which give them occasion to deepen their knowledge of the field being studied. Exploration may also reveal that some pupils are not ready for the unit on account of deficient "apperceptive masses" basic to the unit, while to the class in general their need for the unit is made evident by their inadequate performance on the test.

Since the word "recitation" has certain connotations linking it with the question-and-answer method, it seems unfortunate that Morrison selected it as the label for the final sector. In Morrison's plan this fifth sector is that in which the pupils bring their study of the unit to completion by floor talks or written papers in which they reveal that the understanding, the aim of the unit, has really been achieved. With this interpretation the first two sectors of the cycle are primarily the teacher's responsibility; exploration, and presentation of the basic aspects of the unit. The last three sectors are primarily the pupil's responsibility with supervised study characterizing the third sector. In organization, the pupil, with the guidance of the teacher, prepares for the fifth sector, recitation, in which he is to reveal that he really has mastered the fundamental understanding peculiar to the unit. The name "application," the fifth of the Herbartian steps, would seem to be a better label than the one selected by Morrison, "recitation," for the activity of this sector.

(D) THE HERBARTIAN STEPS

It is of some interest that Morrison, in his first edition of *The Practice of Teaching in the Secondary School* (1926), makes no mention of the Herbartian steps. Yet anyone familiar with the "five formal steps" could not fail to see the parallelism, once he became acquainted with Morrison's cycle concept. Authors of other texts on the technique of teaching soon called attention to this parallelism. Thus Bossing speaks of the Morrison cycle as "a reconstruction of the Herbartian formal steps."[1] Yet Morrison, in his 1931 edition, says "This five-step procedure is not an application of the Herbartian steps." (p. 256). The opinion of the writer is that the cycle concept has validity because it is a logical analysis of the inductive procedure in problem solving, in much the same way as the steps were meant to be. Bossing expresses a view similar to this in these words:

It should be obvious that in the Herbartian Five Formal Steps the teacher has at hand a problem-solving technique of no mean worth. The fact that it has been made unpopular, through misuse by teachers who have taken over its form without a full

[1] Nelson L. Bossing, *Progressive Methods of Teaching in Secondary Schools*, Houghton Mifflin, 1935, p. 474.

appreciation of its spirit, should not relegate it to the limbo of forgotten methods. Rejuvenated in the light of modern psychological theory and educational thought, the Herbartian five steps can be effectively utilized as a problem-solving method. For example, there is no reason why burden of effort should not be transferred to the shoulders of the student instead of being carried by the teacher. The classroom situation can be so organized that the student assumes direct attack upon the problem under the teacher's direct guidance. The attack may be made, and broadly developed through the steps laid down by Herbart, with the student in the role of chief executor of the attack as general and buck private, and the teacher in the role of technical adviser. There is no reason why the Herbartian formal steps reconstructed to conform to our best educational ideals may not at times be applied to the lecture or recitation methods. (*Ibid.*, pp. 473–474)

The trouble with the Herbartian steps was that they became *formalized*. This means that it was assumed that here was a *form* in which teaching could be cast whereby any teacher could teach any group of pupils any subject in any school. Such an attitude ignores what we have called the variables in a teaching situation (p. 351). Five of these variables are (1) the personality of the teacher, (2) the personalities of the pupils in the class, (3) the subject matter to be taught, (4) the atmosphere of the school in which it is to be taught, and (5) the technique to be used in teaching it. To fix upon one of these five variables, *e.g.*, the technique or method, and expect that the other variables would cease to be variable and hold constant, is a vain wish in any teaching situation. Teachers can never be relieved of the obligation of teaching intelligently, and this means that they must adapt their procedures to the variables in the situations in which they are operating. Hence the important thing in the study of the theory of teaching is to learn principles not devices. Devices are tricks of the trade which may work well in one situation but be absolutely valueless in another. Principles are universal, and if clearly understood and intelligently applied, will give guidance in the selection of procedures in a multitude of situations.

The danger of the foregoing analysis of the techniques of teaching into three, the problem, the participation, and the practice technique, each appropriate for the achievement of one of the outcomes of learning, knowledge, attitudes, and abilities, is that the same fate may befall them that overtook the Herbartian steps, namely, they may become formalized. Nothing more disastrous could happen to a teacher's thinking about the work of teaching. The variables are many in any teaching situation. It is the function of the administration of teaching in the light of the variables actually present in any teaching situation to create an environment in which the teaching techniques may operate effectively. In the following chapter we will make an analysis of this phase of the problem of method.

THE TRIANGULAR DISTINCTION IN EDUCATION

I.	In Psychology,			
	1. Mental Functions	Cognition (knowing)	Affection (feeling)	Conation (doing)
	2. Rational Activities	Intellectual	Emotional	Volitional
	3. Sense Activities	Sensation	Feeling	Impulse
II.	In Philosophy, (norms for)	Logic (the True)	Aesthetics (the Beautiful)	Ethics (the Good)
III.	In Religion	Dogma (faith)	Liturgy (worship)	Moral (works)
	The Catechism (phases)	Know God (instructional)	Love God (devotional)	Serve God (practical)

IV.	In Education			
1.	Changes	From ignorance to knowledge	From impulses to ideals	From capacities to abilities
2.	Latin Labels (translations)	Instruere (build in)	Movere (move)	Educare (bring forth)
3.	Learning Outcomes	Knowledge (facts and meanings)	Attitudes (ideals and appreciations)	Abilities (skills and habits)
4.	Principles of Learning (characteristics) Animal Laws	Apperception (reflection) Readiness	Motivation (interest) Effect	Self-activity (repetition) Exercise
5.	Types of Subjects	Science Subjects	Appreciation Subjects	Arts Subjects
6.	Illustrations from English	Grammar	Literature	Composition
7.	Illustrations from Music	History of Music	Music Appreciation	Applied Music
8.	Illustrations from other fields	Natural Sciences, chemistry	Fine Arts, The Great Masters	Physical Education, swimming
9.	Values (Chapman & Counts)	Utilitarian (content)	Cultural (interest)	Disciplinary (procedure)
10.	Techniques of Teaching	Problem Technique	Participation Technique	Practice Technique
11.	Teacher Functions (problems)	Instruction (materials)	Motivation (motives)	Discipline (method)
12.	Primary Agents	Curriculum	Teacher	Pupil

SUGGESTED READINGS

I. THE ORGANIZATION OF SUBJECT MATTER

Bagley, William C., "Is Subject Matter Obsolete," *Educational Administration and Supervision*, Sept. 1935, XXI, 401–410 asserts against the "activists" that the "abandonment of organized subject-matter is the most indefensible and the most perilous policy ever proposed for American educators."

Keniston, Hayward, Ferdinand Schevill and Arthur P. Scott (editors) *The Humanities Syllabus*, Univ. of Chicago Book Store, 1934, 4th ed.; syllabi of the four "Introductory General Courses" in the Chicago plan are available.

Morrison, Henry, *The Practice of Teaching in the Secondary School*, Univ. Chicago Press, 1931, the whole book stresses organization on the unit plan.

Parker, S. C., *General Methods of Teaching in High Schools*, Ginn, 1920, presents "types of teaching" before the advent of unit organization.

——, *Types of Elementary Teaching and Learning*, Ginn, 1928, presents "types of teaching" based on "types of learning."

Thomas, Frank W., *Principles and Technique of Teaching*, Houghton Mifflin, 1927, Chapter XII is entitled "Organizing Subject-Matter and Planning Instruction."

Uhrbrock, R. S., "Is College Teaching Bankrupt?", *The Journal of Higher Education*, Jan. 1935, discusses the necessity of a syllabus in college teaching.

2. THE THREE TECHNIQUES OF TEACHING

Garrison, Noble Lee, *The Technique and Administration of Teaching*, American Book, 1933, Chap. VI. "What Learning Techniques Should Be Used" and Chap. X. "The Technique of Teaching" discuss the three learning and teaching techniques under these titles (1) "Problem-Solving Technique" (2) "Drill Technique" and (3) "Appreciation Technique."

Holley, Charles Elmer, *High School Teachers Methods*, Garrard Press, Champaign, Ill., 1937, the fifteen Chapters from XI "The Developmental Lesson" to XXV "Using the Laboratory and Library" discuss fifteen different "methods."

Kilpatrick, William H., *Foundation of Method*, Macmillan, 1926, the basic statement of the progressive group.

Strayer, George D., George W. Frasier, and Winfield D. Armentrout, *Principles of Teaching*, American Book, 1936, distinguishes the three techniques, Preface, p. vi.

Thomas, Frank W., *Principles and Technique of Teaching*, Houghton Mifflin, 1927, discusses the three techniques in these three Chapters IX. "The Lesson for Habits and Skills" (Practice) X. "The Lesson for Appreciation" (Participation) and XI. "The Lesson for Mastering Knowledge" (Problem) pp. 149–244.

3. THE CYCLE CONCEPT APPLIED TO TEACHING

Bossing, Nelson L., *Technique of Teaching in Secondary Schools*, Houghton Mifflin, 1935, Chap. XV, "The Problem Method of Teaching," pp. 463–478. In both the deductive procedures one step is omitted, but the Herbartian and Morrison analyses are given as fivefold. See also Chap. XVII, 4, pp. 539–542.

Chapman, J. Crosby and George S. Counts, *Principles of Education*, Houghton Mifflin, 1924, Problem 23, "What Methods Should Control the Conduct of Instruction"—an excellent brief treatment of method; Herbartian Steps, p. 549.

Dewey, John, *How We Think*, Heath, 1910, "five logical steps," p. 72; criticism of Herbartian Steps, pp. 202–213.

Draper, Edgar Marion, *Principles and Techniques of Curriculum Making*, Appleton-Century, 1936, under the title "III. General Methods" discusses "A. Herbartian Steps; B. The Morrison Steps; C. The Miller Steps; D. The Contract Method; E. The Problem-project Method; F. The Socialized Procedure; and G. Supervised Study," pp. 477–503.

Miller, Harry L., *Creative Learning and Teaching*, Scribner's, 1927, Chaps. I and II, frankly admit his "Movements" are an adaption of the Herbartian and Morrison approaches. He uses the "contract" of the Dalton Laboratory Plan for organizing teaching materials but protests against its formalization.

Morrison, Henry, *The Practice of Teaching in the Secondary School*, Univ. Chicago Press, 1931, "Learning Cycle," p. 162; The Teaching Cycle; Chaps. XIV, "Exploration and Presentation"; XV, "Assimilation"; XVI, "Organization and Presentation"; in the 1926 edition Chap. XIV is entitled, "The Teaching Cycle," with the three chapters following presenting the five sectors of the cycle.

Thomas, Frank W., *Principles and Technique of Teaching*, Houghton Mifflin, 1927, Chap. XI, "Mastering Knowledge"; the thought cycle, pp. 221–227; the teaching cycle, pp. 227–240.

THE ADMINISTRATION OF TEACHING

The administration of teaching is the complement of the technique of instruction. Both are always present in any instruction. Either may be very good or may be so poor as to seem lacking to the supervisor. Such variations are natural because of the dual nature of instruction . . .

The administrative activity is the way of carrying on the teaching technique so that a maximum of needed pupil activity may be realized.

Noble Lee Garrison,
The Technique and Administration of Teaching, American Book Co., 1933, pp. 196–198.

458

CHAPTER XIV

THE ADMINISTRATION OF TEACHING

The newer approach now being made to the problem of teaching has resulted in a multiplicity of "methods" such as we listed in Chapter XI, "The Dilemma of Democratic Education," Section 2, "The Search for a Solution" (p. 352). Concerning these "methods" we may make this general statement that they have two aims: first, to vitalize instruction and second, to individualize it. By vitalizing instruction we mean linking it up with the life of the pupil, his interests, his needs, and his abilities. This aim is paramount for example, in the "project method." By individualizing instruction we mean reaching the individual within the group so that he will carry on learning activities that have as their outcome his growth and development. The "contract method" is an illustration of this aim. The two phases into which we have divided the problem of method are definitely related to both aims. The technique of teaching, the subject discussed in the preceding chapter, is primarily concerned with vitalizing instruction. This chapter considers the second phase, the administration of teaching, and it will be concerned primarily with the efforts now being made to individualize instruction, thus creating a classroom situation in which the individual will learn to best advantage.

The administration of teaching divides into three aspects,

the first of which is the administration of the various "plans" that have been introduced during the past two decades with the primary purpose of individualizing instruction, *e.g.*, ability grouping, and the "Dalton Laboratory Plan." The second aspect of the administration of teaching is the perennial problem of discipline. The third is the measurement of pupil achievement through tests and examinations. This last phase involves the teacher's technique also, since tests, particularly objective tests, may be effectively used as teaching devices when through them pupils are made aware of their achievement as well as their failures. In this analysis the whole problem of "method" is presented graphically in the bracket diagram that follows:

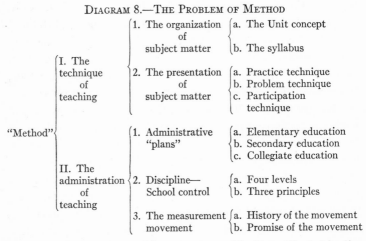

DIAGRAM 8.—THE PROBLEM OF METHOD

"Method"

I. The technique of teaching

1. The organization of subject matter
  a. The Unit concept
  b. The syllabus

2. The presentation of subject matter
  a. Practice technique
  b. Problem technique
  c. Participation technique

II. The administration of teaching

1. Administrative "plans"
  a. Elementary education
  b. Secondary education
  c. Collegiate education

2. Discipline— School control
  a. Four levels
  b. Three principles

3. The measurement movement
  a. History of the movement
  b. Promise of the movement

We now discuss the problems presented in Part II of this diagram, "The administration of teaching."

1. ADMINISTRATIVE "PLANS"

In the history of education the first "Plan of Studies" that exerted wide influence in Western Europe was the *Ratio Stu-*

diorum of the Jesuits first printed in 1586. It "organized classes more carefully than had been done before. It presupposed elementary training in the students. It divided the school into five grades: three in 'grammar,' one called 'humanitas,' and one called 'rhetorica.' The first three aimed chiefly at mastery of Latin; the other two at a study of literature, chiefly with a view to developing the student's powers of expression. In all five, attention was paid to history, geography, ethics, and religion. The *Ratio Studiorum* set down definite subject matter and definite method for each class." [1] Here was both a curriculum and a method. In its administrative procedures the *Ratio* made provision for grading on the level of secondary education. A century later grading was brought down to the elementary level through the introduction of the "simultaneous method" by Saint De la Salle, who founded the Christian Brothers in 1684. Like the *Ratio*, his *Conduct of the Schools* (1720) is both a curriculum and a method. The curriculum was the four R's, reading, 'riting, 'rithmetic, and religion. The method was recitation to the whole class not to the teacher alone, and this was nothing less than a revolution in elementary education, where, up to this time, all instruction had been individual. The practice technique was dominant in the first three of the R's, but the participation technique characterized the teaching of religion through all taking part together in religious exercises. Administrative techniques are presented in minute detail; for example, there is a section entitled "When the Teacher Will Trim the Pens of the Pupils. Time and Manner of Teaching the Pupils to Trim Them." The problem of school discipline constitutes the whole of Part II. "Means of Establishing and Maintaining Order in the Schools."

With the universalization of education through the "simul-

[1] W. Kane, *A History of Education*, Loyola Univ. Press, 1935, p. 271.

taneous method," or class recitation, achieved during the 19th century, the problem of effective instruction today takes on a new aspect. There exists no longer the great need to devise ways and means of bringing education to all the children of all the people. Compulsory school laws have taken care of that everywhere except in isolated districts. Today the problem is how to reach the individual within the great group of pupils that crowd our schools on all levels of general education, elementary, secondary, and collegiate. Here we return to the problem presented in Chapter XI, "The Dilemma of Democratic Education." Can we retain the distinctive characteristic of American education, a single educational ladder (Figure 23, p. 383) which is climbed by all youth, living and learning together, and at the same time make it possible for the individual within the group to have the kind of educational experience that will effectively promote his growth and development? "Plans" to achieve this dual aim are appearing on all levels of the ladder.

On the elementary level the most common device for meeting the different abilities of pupils is called "homogenous grouping." This is the sectioning of pupils on the basis of ability and school achievement. Principal Corning, presents a vivid picture of what may be done in a city school system along this line.[1] In effect within a single system at Trinidad, Colorado, he has set up a triple-track arrangement providing for the slow, the average, and the superior all working up to capacity. For the superior students the curriculum is enriched and their time of completing is shortened. For the slowest group the objective is the mastery of the "minimum essentials." The middle group travels at the same pace as the ordinary school and completes the same curriculum.

Something different is in operation in Winnetka, Illinois.

[1] Hobart M. Corning, *After Testing What?* Scott, Foresman, 1926, entire.

The "Winnetka Plan" provides for individual instruction in the tool subjects during one half of the school day, and makes provision for group instruction during the other half. This plan is significant in that it definitely faces the double problem of promoting group solidarity and providing for individual development in a single school system.[1]

On the secondary school level the plan that has attracted widest attention is known as the "Dalton Laboratory Plan." In this the school rooms are turned into "laboratories," one for each subject, with a teacher who is a specialist in that subject in charge of each room. The ordinary time schedule is done away with, and the pupils work "on contract." Contracts are issued in mimeograph form and the pupils are free to follow their own interests in choosing which subject they will work upon with the common limitation that within the period of a month all the contracts in all the subjects must be completed. Here definite provision is made for individual development, but the common complaint against this new technique is that the social phase of education is slighted. Supporters of the plan in reply to this say group solidarity is promoted by all living together and by working together on common projects. The writer traveling in Europe in the fall of 1927 planned to visit a school in London which had gained recognition as an outstanding example of a school conducted on the Dalton Laboratory Plan but on inquiry he learned that with the death of the individual who had inaugurated the plan within that school, the school had reverted to the traditional type. This is significant. The plan is such a radical departure from traditional methods of conducting schools that its availability for ordinary city school systems is questionable. Its most important contribution without doubt is the "contract"

[1] Carleton Washburn, *Adjusting the School to the Child*, World Book, 1932, entire.

idea, which makes practical differentiated assignments for A, B, C, and D students. But this can be introduced by any teacher within any school without upsetting the existing organization. Considering the plan as a whole from the point of view of educational theory one is reminded here of the words of Nicholas Murray Butler; "No one can be called educated who will not do something that he would rather not do, at the time it ought to be done." The advocates of this plan may boast about the freedom of the school and the abolition of the "lock step" time schedule, but the critics of the system see it rather as an illustration of "soft pedagogy" with excessive emphasis on interest and a violation of the law of habit in the light of what psychology tells us concerning the distribution of practice.

A more significant departure on the secondary school level is perhaps that now in operation in the James Madison High School at Brooklyn, New York. In this school six thousand pupils are classified in three groups, and curricula are planned for the three groups to meet their variant needs and to keep all working up to their capacity. Here again we have provision for individual development and at the same time promotion of group solidarity since all live and learn in the same institution, meeting together from time to time in common activities, of which those that take place in the auditorium would be a good example.

On the college level the same problem is present as on the level of elementary and secondary education with this difference that selection has now become definitely operative. Since the World War, however, the college population has radically changed in character. Originally planned for the selected few, colleges now receive a heterogeneous mass of students who vary greatly in native ability and in their aptitude for college work as it has been traditionally interpreted. The various individual instruction plans, the Harvard Tutorial system, the Princeton Preceptorial system, the Swarthmore Honor Courses, and the Leland Stanford Independent Study Plan are all attempts to make provision for the individual development of the superior student. Dean McConn of Lehigh University holds that this is impossible of realization so long as the potential scholars are a small minority dominated by a much larger group whose interests are not scholarship but "activities" and the social prestige which graduation from college carries with it. He claims that the only way out is to have three separate colleges for the three distinct groups of students which now make up the college population. He suggests first of all a vocational or professional college for the vocationally minded students; second, a scholar's college for those in whom a truly intellectual interest has been aroused and who have the native ability to pursue that interest with profit; and third, a gentleman's college for what he calls the "super-kindergartners." These are those who are to spend four more years continuing their general education protected from the harmful influences of the world, busy for the most part with the so-called "activities" from which will result the most valuable part of their education, but receiving a little incidental instruction through following a curriculum that is definitely graded down to their level. This is segregation indeed. But Dean McConn realizes, as he says in his Prologue that his plan "taken as a whole, is only, at present, a castle in Spain, or perhaps a temple in Attica." He claims, however, in regard to the details of his plan that "every separate stone is real—exists at the present time in the college quarry. There are already, as I shall show, a few institutions which are putting several stones together. Perhaps some day somebody may put them all together and give us really a Real College." [1]

[1] Max McConn, *College or Kindergarten*, New Republic, 1928, p. 11.

Edgar Marion Draper interprets all these plans as a return to the search for a "universal method" which we discussed in Chapter XI, Section 2, "The Search for a Solution" (p. 349).

> In the past many methods of teaching have been developed and fostered by educators in the hope that a plan might be organized which would inevitably result in perfect achievement on the part of all students under the direction of any and all teachers. The Herbartian method, the project method, the problem method, the contract plan, the unit plan, and the activity plan have all been devised for that purpose. Like all schemes for the attainment of perpetual motion, these panaceas of educational method have never been completely successful. All have made contributions to educational practice, but each has failed to develop teaching procedure to a point where it is or ever can be more than one phase of the education of children. There is no such thing in teaching as an absolute and final process or procedure. One is safe in the assumption, however, that the textbook, as content, and the recitation, as teaching procedure, have disappeared almost completely from America's educational program.[1]

We doubt that those who have been responsible for popularizing these "methods" would make any such extravagant claim for them. Nor can we share the optimism of the last sentence in the above quotation concerning the disappearance of the "textbook, as content, and the recitation, as teaching procedure . . . from America's educational program." We are reminded here of Newman's dictum: "Education is a high word; it is the preparation for knowledge, and it is the imparting of knowledge in proportion to that preparation." [2] In this imparting of knowledge, books (not necessarily textbooks) will always remain during the period of general education the chief

---

[1] Edgar Marion Draper, *Principles and Techniques of Curriculum Making,* Appleton-Century, 1936, p. 477.

[2] John Henry Newman, *Idea of a University,* Discourse VI, "Knowledge Viewed in Relation to Learning."

tool of the teacher and they will continue to be abused as long as teachers manifest the common human trait of choosing the easiest way out when confronting an arduous and difficult task. By its very nature most teaching will always remain such a task. The obtuseness of slow learners, the precocity of fast learners, along with the trait of self-display common to all, create situations within the school which call for untiring patience combined with a firmness that is a display of strength, not a defense of weakness. This introduces us to the second phase of the administration of teaching, the perennial problem of discipline.

2. DISCIPLINE—CLASSROOM AND SCHOOL CONTROL

When the administration of teaching is interpreted as including all those things teachers do for the purpose of creating a situation favorable to learning, it is evident that maintaining discipline is one of the major tasks in this field. In the old days discipline was enforced by corporal punishment. The teacher who resorts to such means today is in grave danger of finding himself involved in court proceedings initiated by irate parents. The Rousseauian idea of human nature as essentially good with evil distorting child nature as the result of contact with social institutions (the school among the first) seems to be in complete ascendancy. Whether the labels used are "progressive education" or "the child-centered school" the dominant idea seems to be that the child has the right of way and society must step aside when its interests conflict with those of the individual. Irving Babbitt explains the popularity of this theory as follows:

> Every doctrine of genuine worth is disciplinary and men in the mass do not desire discipline. "Most men," says Aristotle, "would rather live in a disorderly than in a sober manner." But most men do not admit any such preference—that would be crude

and inartistic. They incline rather to substitute for the reality of discipline some art of going through the motions.[1]

Paul Elmer More finds the explanation of the modern attitude towards discipline in the American philosophy, pragmatism:

> The followers of pragmatism, whatever their protestations may be, all agree in taking the flux as the whole of consciousness, and in then staying the reason at this point and rejecting its further function of discretion and combination. . . . Truth is to them whatever persists the longest in the unchecked indiscrete experience of life. Their story, as it is half rational and half institutional, is unstable and elusive. Its result is to dissolve attention and to *discredit discipline*.[2]

In Chapter X, Section 3, "The Disciplines in School Activities" (p. 327), we emphasized the fact that in the realm of study activities the word "discipline" has regained some of its lost prestige. But today we do not speak of "general mental discipline." Rather we use the word in the plural recognizing that there are many "mental disciplines," and that one proper to one field of study, *e.g.*, the discipline of precision in mathematics, may be achieved in another field provided the "essential mode of thought" which characterizes that discipline is carried on in this other field *e.g.*, precision, in philosophical thinking. Is there any likelihood that "moral discipline," the discipline of conduct, will undergo a similar rejuvenation. It would seem that the increase of crime in this country coincident with the adoption by the school of "no discipline" theory, would have an influence in bringing this about. The Federal Bureau of Investigation is placing emphasis in all its published reports on the prevalence of crime among youth. "From 1932

---

[1] Irving Babbitt, *Rousseau and Romanticism*, Houghton Mifflin, 1919, pp. 24–25.
[2] Paul Elmer More, *The Drift of Romanticism*, Houghton Mifflin, 1913, pp. 268–269.

to the middle of 1935, age 19 was the group in which the largest number of arrests occurred." [1] Nineteen is still the 'teen age. It is the age of older adolescents. Can the school escape all responsibility for this deplorable fact that is threatening the very foundation of our moral and civic life? Bagley does not free the school entirely from that responsibility, since it has played so large a part in favoring the changed concept of discipline.

> In sharp contrast to education in most of the civilized countries, an outstanding characteristic of education in the United States is its virtually complete rejection of the disciplinary ideal in the fields both of mind and of morals . . .
> The extreme left wing of the Progressive school not only rejects the ideal of discipline; it would abandon prearranged programs, assigned tasks, and learning activities of all kinds that are imposed from without.[2]

We have been stressing throughout this presentation that "discipline" is a basic concept in the Catholic theory of education. This fact has its theological foundations in the Catholic theory of the nature of man. Again we repeat that the Catholic theory here is not that of the Protestant reformers who brought forth the theory of "total depravity" as a result of the fall of our first parents. If man's nature is totally depraved his every action is sinful. Therefore he can be saved by faith alone (Luther) or he is saved by being among the predestined (Calvin). Not so the Catholic theory. Rather man's nature was wounded by the fall. His intellect was darkened and his will weakened, but offsetting this fact is the redeeming power of Christ's grace which makes it possible for

[1] *Uniform Crime Reports*, Federal Bureau of Investigation Fourth Quarterly Bulletin, 1937, Vol. III, p. 217.
[2] William Chandler Bagley, *Education, Crime and Social Progress*, 1931, Preface pp. vii and ix.

man not merely to regain what was lost but to climb to heights beyond nature and live a life truly supernatural. In this interpretation of the nature of man, discipline is a basic concept. The whole theory and practice of asceticism as presented in Chapter VII, Section 2, "Asceticism and the Supernatural" (p. 248) rests upon it. And since man, a unitary organism, functions as a whole, moral discipline (of the will) as well as mental discipline (of the intellect) are at the very center of the Catholic theory of education.

We must remember, however, that just as in the case of the mental disciplines, the ideal to be aimed at is the development of the ability to carry on self-dependent study whereby the individual reaches his full development in the intellectual life; so too in the moral disciplines, their end and aim is the power of self-control in all the vicissitudes of life. If this outcome is achieved, the moral virtues will characterize the life of the student who has been submitted to this discipline.

With this interpretation of the principle *self-development through self-discipline* the "new freedom" takes on intelligent meaning. The student cannot be expected to develop the power of self-control if he never has an opportunity to practice self-control. From this follows what we called when discussing "Civic Security" in Chapter VI, the principle of *progressive freedom* (p. 218). When the child is sufficiently mature to have any realization of his obligations towards others, toward God, his Father in heaven, and towards his fellows on earth, his brothers in Christ; and as soon as he manifests the ability and the desire to conduct his life in conformity with the laws of God and of society, he should be free to do so. He will grow in this power and he will develop this attitude only insofar as he is free to make his own choices, to feel the sting of regret when they are blunders and gain the respect and confidence of his associates, when they are wise. As he grows older, as his understanding of his obligations deepens and his attitude of respect for others strengthens, he should enjoy a constantly enlarging liberty, until in late adolescence he is practically on his own, subject only to the rules and regulations that society must impose to preserve peace and order in any large community. If by prayer and self-discipline the student spiritualizes his constantly enlarging liberty and brings under control his impulses and his passions, he will enjoy the freedom of which St. Paul speaks, "the freedom wherewith Christ has made us free." [1]

PLANES OF DISCIPLINE

What can the teacher do in his own classroom and in his administrations throughout the school, particularly when he is functioning as the director of any co-curricular activity where freedom is the condition of success, to bring about the realization of the ideal discipline, *liberty under the law?* First of all, the teacher must understand what we may call the "planes" of discipline. There are two of these, the natural and the supernatural, but the natural plane admits of three levels. The lowest level is the level of *compulsion*. Here discipline is imposed from above down. It is external to those who are subject to it. It rules by force and when the force is removed the only residue is a feeling of resentment, not the establishment of habits of proper behavior. The second level we may call *personal* discipline. It is centered in the personality of the one who administers it. Some times it has its origin in respect for that personality, possibly in affection, but there is always a certain admixture of fear; fear lest this person holding the respect or the affection of the one subject to this discipline, be offended. Herein lies its weakness as

[1] Epistle to the Galatians IV, 31.

an educative influence. When the person who exercises this
type of discipline is no longer present to enforce it, its restrain-
ing influence may disappear. The behavior habits which function when he is present may not carry over into life at large
as controls of conduct, and this is the very purpose of discipline
in the educative process. The third level of discipline on the
natural plane we may call *social* discipline. Its basis is respect
for the group, not for one person within the group. For this
reason it is the discipline of democracy. The ideal of democracy is liberty for all but it must be *liberty under the law*, and
the law is the welfare of all. The individual shares in the
communal life. But if he is to share this communal life in a
way that will not infringe on the rights of the community as a
whole, he must exercise self-control. In a dictatorship, control
is imposed from above down. In a democracy the only adequate basis for social control is self-control exercised by the
larger group under intelligent leaders. "The best-governed
people is the least governed,"—if they govern themselves.

The second plane of discipline is the supernatural. This is
the fourth level. It brings God into the picture not merely
as the source of all authority with the right to impose discipline
but also as the source of power to the people, lifting them up
to the plane of the supernatural through the influence of divine
grace. Social discipline is founded in the brotherhood of man.
But supernatural discipline gives real meaning to that brotherhood since it makes all human beings brothers in Christ
through the fatherhood of God. This is the discipline that
should always be the aim of the Christian teacher. It is the new
law that Christ brought to a pagan world. It is founded in his
two commandments "Love God" and "Love your neighbor."
Its fruition is peace and order in the society in which it holds
sway. It is the aim and end of all true education and is
fittingly described by Ruskin in these words:

The entire object of true education is to make people not merely do the right things, but enjoy the right things; not merely industrious, but to love industry; not merely learned, but to love knowledge; not merely pure, but to love purity; not merely just, but to hunger and thirst after justice.

PRINCIPLES OF DISCIPLINE

What principles can be laid down to guide the teacher in his efforts to make such a discipline prevail in the lives of the pupils with whom he is laboring? We will briefly mention three. First, administrative procedures aimed at setting up and maintaining discipline both within the classroom and outside in the recreational activities of the school should be *positive* not negative. The former are constructive, the latter merely restrictive. The teacher's general attitude should be manifested in a challenge, "Let's do this!"; not in frequent prohibitions, "Don't do that!" Pupils will respond wholeheartedly to a challenge if it is within the scope of their abilities and is presented in a way that will capture their interests. Such a challenge may be anything from building a boat to searching out the explanation of the rise of dictatorships in Europe today. Second, a teacher's attack on this problem of discipline should be *indirect*, rather than direct. A suggestion here and there is often more efficacious than a command. A clever teacher can stop abruptly the disturbance caused by two pupils whispering during the presentation of a new unit by himself stopping abruptly, fixing his eyes on the offender, and after a pause saying to him without sarcasm "Pardon, John, you have something you want to contribute to the presentation? No? Well then, I will continue." The approach here is group control through an appeal to the group, but the appeal in indirect. Their rights have been invaded by the disturber and when he is signalled out as one trespassing on their time, it is a stolid individual indeed, who can withstand the social pressure thus brought to bear upon him. The third principle is suggested by such a situation. The teacher should aim to lift his discipline to the *highest level possible*. Seldom if ever should it sink to the bottom level, the level of compulsion. Nor should any teacher be satisfied with maintaining discipline on the personal level. His pupils cannot have him always at hand to be their mentor and guide. Every teacher should strive to raise his discipline to the third level, the social level. Here, conformity comes through loyalty to a principle, the "general welfare," not to a person. The Christian teacher will strive further to supernaturalize this social discipline, thereby raising it to the fourth and highest level. Duty to God is inclusive of respect and consideration for one's fellows, and pupils should be taught to realize that the concrete manifestation of love of God is kindness and consideration for those with whom we are in close contact. Here is a clear statement by the President of the University of Wisconsin, one who, as City Manager of Cincinnati, Ohio, had wide experience in public life. This statement emphasizes the necessity of elevating and maintaining discipline on the social level:

The development of individual personality is of the highest importance, of course, but equally necessary is the *teaching of reverence for personality in others*. Human beings must express human values, and sympathy for other humans is at least as important as sympathy for a forlorn mongrel of the canine family. And our generation *is* good to dogs. . . .

Self-government is *impossible without* some *training in self-discipline*. In our striving during a generation or two for self-expression in the schools we have either neglected or failed to inculcate self-discipline. Perhaps it is the times—for we have lived through blatant times—but we who are in places of public responsibility sense a recklessness and an abandon among adults and youth which show themselves in an utter disregard of the rights of others. This is even more true of the children from the socalled better homes—those, for instance, where there are automobiles to drive. Here is a task in which school and home must join—but certainly it is the business of educators to lead the way.[1]

Newman knew human nature, its strength and its weakness, "the passions and the pride of man." Charles Thwing, formerly President of Western Reserve University says of him: "His interpretations (of the nature of reason as touched by the liberalizing force of education) are among the most moving ever given to the mind of a man to offer to his fellows. . . . His whole conception of the nature and functions, of the purposes and results, of that educational process is pregnant with lasting lessons to the mind and the conscience of man." [2] Here is Newman's protest against the "Compulsion School" of discipline:

Those who have to do with our Colleges give us their experience, that in the case of the young committed to their care, external discipline may change the fashionable excess, but cannot allay the principle of sinning. Stop cigars, they will take to drinking parties; stop drinking, they gamble; stop gambling, and a worse license follows. You do not get rid of vice by human expedients; you can but use them according to circumstance, and in their place, as making the best of a bad matter. You must go to a higher source for renovation of the heart and of the will. You do but play a sort of "hunt the slipper" with the fault of our nature, till you go to Christianity.[3]

[1] C. S. Dykstra, "Whither Education," *North Central Association Quarterly*, October, 1935, p. 187.

[2] Charles Thwing, *Education According to Some Modern Masters*, Platt and Peck, 1916, pp. 248–250.

[3] John Henry Newman, *Discussions and Arguments*, p. 273.

In this interpretation, discipline if it is to bring about the "renovation of the heart and will," cannot be of the compulsion variety. Youth like human beings in general can be led; *they will not be driven*. Neither is the personal appeal, nor the influence of group sanctions, the highest goal that should be in the mind of the Christian teacher. Rather it is the discipline of Christ that is his ideal. *Liberty under the law* but here the law is the law of God. In effect the pupil in the school animated by the spirit of Christ addresses to the teacher the words of the Psalmist:

> Bonitatem, et disciplinam, et scientian doce me: quia mandatis tuis credidi.

> Teach me goodness and discipline and knowledge; for I have believed thy commandments. CXVIII, 66.

If this attitude can be developed in the minds and hearts of pupils, discipline is on the level of the supernatural.

The accusation has been made that only weak personalities choose teaching as their vocational calling. Fearful of competing with adults in the world at large, it is alleged, the weaker spirits choose teaching as a vocation so that they can satisfy their "drive for power" by lording it over children and youth. Whatever truth there may be in this accusation, the discipline problem soon drives out of the profession those who are weak and vacillating. The weak personality may be able to lord it over a child in isolation but to attempt the same procedure over a group of thirty or more children, particularly over a group of adolescents, is fatal. Only strong personalities survive this test of maintaining discipline. The weaker sort may survive for a time, aided and abetted by administrative authority from above, but even while they do, teaching for them is hell on earth and ordinarily they will soon find some other outlet for whatever abilities they may have. But for strong personalities, for those gifted with leadership and a love for knowledge, teaching is a joy. It offers the opportunity to lead the intellectual life free from the competition and the bitter rivalries of the world at large. For them and their pupils school becomes *companionship in the pursuit of knowledge*. For the Christian teacher it becomes companionship with Christ who came that they might have life, and "have it more abundantly." [1]

3. THE MEASUREMENT MOVEMENT

The final phase of the administration of teaching, which we will treat briefly, is the measurement of pupil aptitude, ability, and achievement. It is truly a part of the administration of teaching as we have defined it, "creating a situation favorable to learning," since it is only through measurement that we can determine (1) what promise the pupil gives of continuing his learning and in what direction he should be guided for his own best interests and the interests of society, (aptitudes); (2) what power he possesses in terms of general intelligence and special abilities, (abilities); and (3), what progress he has already made in assimilating the social inheritance whether presented to him through the curriculum in school or learned through life experiences outside of school, (achievements). Great progress has been made in psychological and educational measurement during the first years of this century. In fact Mortimer Adler says that "Psychometrics and, . . . psychoanalysis are the only exceptions to the inductive sterility of psychological research." [2] In Chapter IV, "The Motivation of Human Behavior," Section 2, "The Dominant Human Drives (p. 100)," we have shown that the "complex" intro-

[1] John X, 10.
[2] Mortimer Adler, *What Man Has Made of Man*, Longmans Green, 1937, pp. 89–90.

duced by the psychoanalysts is a development of the traditional interpretation of the poets, philosophers, and theological theorizers of all time, analyzing the motives that move men and women in behavior. So, here, we believe with Adler that the advance made in the field of mental measurements is the most promising development in the whole field of educational theory and practice today. But note what this implies. It means a return of the concept, "mental faculties," supposedly banished forever from educational theory by Herbart. Here is Adler's statement of the about-face that *must* be made by psychology if it accepts the implications of psychometrics:

The formulae of psychometrics,—not only precise, but genuine contributions to knowledge—are, like those of mathematical physics, functional statements. They do not, therefore, solve the aetiological problem. The psychometrician is not concerned with human behavior in the large or with its causes. He is in theory a faculty psychologist—dread name for the doctrine of powers and acts, abilities and performances—and in practice he is a mathematician who tries to make crude measurements approximate rational equations. The amazing thing is the degree to which he has succeeded in this effort. . . . To effect the consummation with clarity and without pretension the philosophical analysis which is faculty psychology must be explicitly recognized as providing the conceptual matrix for the mathematical formulations. I say "without pretension" because by such acknowledgement it will be conceded that psychometrics can add to the traditional account of the essence of human nature only the determination of accidental details. This, after all, is the business of empirical science in any field,—the description of phenomenal relationships. Vd. L. L. Thurstone, *Vectors of Mind*, Chicago, 1935: pp. 44–54 also C. Spearman, *The Abilities of Man*, New York, 1927: pp. 38–39. Spearman more than Thurstone recognizes that psychometrics employs the concepts of faculty analysis, and is thus subordinated to philosophical psychology.[1]

[1] *Ibid.*, pp. 202–203.

Here is Spearman's statement concerning the effect of Herbartiansim on the faculty theory:

> The attacks made long ago by the Herbartians appeared to be irresistible; no serious defense was even attempted. Yet the sole permanent effect of these attacks was only to banish the word 'faculty', leaving the doctrine represented by this word to escape scot-free. As much may be said for the onslaught of Thorndike.[1]

If "faculties" return will the theory of mental discipline have a new birth? Here is a "consummation devoutly to be wished." We will now review briefly the history of the measurement movement and then suggest the promise it holds for helping work out a solution of the major problem confronting American education today.

HISTORY OF THE MEASUREMENT MOVEMENT

Examinations and tests of various kinds are as old as formal education itself. China in 2200 B.C. had a national system of examinations for selecting public officials. The method of Socrates was one of searching examinations. The same may be said of the catechetical method though here the answers became formalized. During the Middle Ages in the guild system, promotion from apprentice, to journeyman, to master, was by examinations. In the teachers' guild the order was, bachelor, licentiate, doctor. The universities of the Middle Ages gave the examination system to our western civilization. The first record of written examinations is at Cambridge University in England in 1702. The first written examination throughout a school system in the United States was the Boston School Committee's examination of the city schools

---

[1] Charles E. Spearman, *The Abilities of Man*, Macmillan, 1927, p. 39.

in 1845. Horace Mann was so enthusiastic about this innovation he published copious extracts from the Committee's
Report in *The Common School Journal*, stressing the superiority of written over oral examinations. The Boston experiment is of historical interest but it had little influence on the
practice of the times. All these examinations were attempts
at measurement but they were crude attempts when compared
with the measurements of the physical sciences.

THE SCIENTIFIC MOVEMENT

The scientific movement entered the field of psychology
with the setting up of the first psychological laboratory by
Wundt in Leipzig, Germany, in 1789. Experiments measuring
reaction-time were among the first carried on. Cattell and
Farrard were studying individual differences at Columbia
University in 1890. The Galton-Pearson movement in Great
Britain in 1895 developed the statistical technique. Thorndike
published his *Theory of Mental and Social Measurements* in
1904. In the same year Binet and Simon in France began
their work with mental defectives which was to revolutionize
measurement in schools for normal children. The chief difficulty was to arrive at a standard or norm since there was no
such thing as zero in performance. Binet solved this problem
by inventing the concept "mental age." Tests were arranged
on a scale of age levels. A child's mental age was the level
which he attained on the scale. Stern in Germany made an
important contribution to the method of calculating test scores:

> Binet had been content to measure subnormality by subtracting
> mental age from chronological age. Stern urged that the absolute
> retardation in years was of less importance than the relative
> retardation; and suggested the use of the Intelligence Quotient
> (IQ), obtained by dividing the mental age by the chronological

age. He showed, moreover, that this quotient is fairly constant, from year to year, for most children.[1]

In 1916 Terman brought out the *Stanford-Revision* of the Binet-Simon scale and the intelligence-test movement was launched in the United States. In the meantime another movement was going forward in the attempt to perfect instruments for the measurement of the results of education, rather than native ability. Rice in 1894 had perfected a Spelling Test but he was ahead of his time and it was rejected by educators. In 1908 Stone brought out his *Arithmetic Test* and, in 1909, Thorndike produced a *Handwriting Scale*, and we may say that with these two begins scientific measurement in education. The measurement movement is thus a culmination of several movements, all converging on the objective of perfecting a technique for the quantitative statement of differences in mental ability or in educational achievement. The tests for mental ability are now commonly called "psychological tests;" those for educational achievement, either "education tests" or simply "achievement tests." The psychological tests are of two main varieties, intelligence tests and aptitude tests. The latter are similar to achievement tests in content but to intelligence tests in function. Their purpose is to predict success or failure in a limited field. Achievement tests are either standardized, *i.e.*, with established norms, or standards, or they are nonstandardized. These latter are tests made by the teacher in his own subject matter field. They have the advantage over the old-type examination in that they give a wider sampling of subject matter and they are scored objectively.

No one holds that the old-type essay examination will disappear from school practice. After all, it measures certain

[1] Gardner Murphy, *An Historical Introduction to Modern Psychology*, Harcourt, Brace, 1929, pp. 349–350.

abilities that cannot be measured by the new type objective tests, namely, the ability to organize and present ideas in written discourse. But with the development of the group intelligence test and achievement tests that can be administered to great numbers at the same time with a saving of time and energy through easy and accurate scoring, education has a new tool to help to solve its problems. The International Business Machine Corporation has now perfected a scoring machine that does mechanically without the possibility of error what before consumed the time of scoring clerks over long periods. Many of these machines are now in operation distributed in educational centers throughout the country.

THE PROMISE OF THE MEASUREMENT MOVEMENT

In Chapter XI, "The Dilemma of Democratic Education," we called attention to the great change that has come about in education from that time in the history of western culture when formal education was for the few, to the present situation wherein all peoples and all nations have accepted the principle of universal education. In this country we have gone beyond the rest of the world in our avowed purpose to bring it about that not only elementary education, training in the fundamentals, shall be for all the children of all the people, but also secondary education wherein the pupil, having attained a certain degree of mastery of the tools, will use those tools in his efforts to make his own that portion of the social inheritance that may best be assimilated through formal school procedures, and in this process of assimilation bring about his own development. This extension of educational opportunity to include secondary education for all is nothing less than revolutionary. The problem it presents is this: granting that in a democracy the content of general education should be substantially the same for all even during the first cycle of secondary education, this content cannot be assimilated by all in the same way due to the great diversity of native ability. In the past, secondary education has been for the most part intellectual in nature, that is, learning through books. Today in this country many of the students in the secondary school have reached their level of intellectual saturation as far as book learning is concerned. Yet these young people must be kept in school. How are they to be taught? They can profit from the training in citizenship which comes as a part of any community living under intelligent leadership, but intensive formal study of an academic curriculum is beyond their powers. What should be the nature of the curriculum, and what should be the method of presentation through which they may derive growth and development. Many adjustments in school procedure are now being made but no one has yet found a completely satisfactory answer to these questions. The problem is succinctly stated by President Hutchins as follows:

> I concede the great difficulty of communicating the kind of education I favor to those who are unable or unwilling to get their education from books. I insist, however, that the education I shall outline is the kind that everybody should have, that the answer to it is not that some people should not have it, but that we should find out how to give it to those whom we do not know how to teach at present. You cannot say my content is wrong because you do not know the method of transmitting it. Let us agree upon content if we can and have faith that the technological genius of America will solve the problem of communication.
>
> Economic conditions require us to provide some kind of education for the young, and for all the young, up to about their twentieth year. Probably one-third of them cannot learn from books. This is no reason why we should not try to work out a better course of study for the other two-thirds. At the same time we should continue our efforts and experiments to find out how

to give a general education to the hand-minded and the functionally illiterate.[1]

President Hutchins' appeal to "the technological genius of America" has meaning for the measurement movement. Measurement by itself will never invent a method "to give a general education to the hand-minded and the functionally illiterate"; nor will it determine the curriculum through which they can achieve a general education. But the measurement movement should play a prominent part in solving both of these problems. The inventive genius of American educators must bring forth the curriculum, and the method of presenting that curriculum to nonacademic minds, but every proposed solution of these problems must be submitted to the crucial test of measured results. Further, in determining those who have the academic type of mind and those who have not, measurement is again the tool of educators. In addition, as aptitude tests are perfected, it should become possible to predict with far greater certainty than we can today, the type of vocational calling in which the individual will achieve greatest success and in which he can reap lasting satisfaction. It may not be possible to put into operation in our economic life the maxim of the Marxists, "To each according to his needs, from each according to his abilities," but nothing less than this must be the aim of democratic education. The measurement movement should be a great aid in helping us achieve this goal.

The philosophy of Supernaturalism takes a definite stand on this problem of education for all. Holding as it does that every human person is an end in himself and that no one (not even the state) has the right to use him as means for the promotion of his own ends, it places upon society the obligation of creating a social environment in which each indi-

[1] Robert Maynard Hutchins, *The Higher Learning in America*, Yale Univ. Press, 1936, p. 61.

vidual will have the opportunity to achieve his end as a human person. In this present day and age, formal education within the school is one of the necessary means for the achievement of that end. The Church in her history has ever protested against the use of individuals as means. She fought vigorously against the pagan institution of slavery and was the influence which raised womankind from the degradation of paganism to be the copartner of man and his equal in sharing human rights. The late Pope, Pius XI and his predecessor Pius X, are striking examples of her democratic spirit. Both ascended from humble origins to the highest office in her power to bestow, The See of Peter, and the way is ever open for others to hold the high offices in her hierarchy provided they are gifted with native ability and develop that ability through a life of industry and high moral integrity. "In my Father's house there are many mansions." [1] This is as true in the social life of any true democracy as it is in the spiritual life in the Kingdom of Christ. There is a place for everyone, if he will only prepare himself to fill it. The measurement movement should be an aid towards helping him find that place, but filling it, once it is found, is his own responsibility.

* * *

If the teacher is to be thoroughly familiar with the two aspects into which we have analyzed the problem of method in these two chapters, XIII, "The Technique of Teaching" preceding, and this chapter, "The Administration of Teaching," it is essential that his education include an intensive study of this important problem. In the next chapter, XV, "The Education of the Teacher," Section 2, "Professional Education," we will analyze the educative process into two phases, the learning process and the teaching process. Study-

[1] John XIV, 2.

ing the learning process in the course commonly called "Education Psychology" the teacher will become familiar with psychological tests.   Studying the teaching process in the courses
Technique of Teaching and his Professional Subject Matter
Courses, for example, The Teaching of the Social Sciences or
The Teaching of Mathematics etc., he will become familiar
with achievement tests in these fields.

SUGGESTED READINGS

GENERAL

Garrison, Noble Lee, *The Technique and Administration of Teaching*,
American Book, Chap. IX, "The Administrative Activity of
Teaching," pp. 197–228.   The treatment here is the nearest
approach in print to that presented in this chapter.

Thomas, Frank W., *Principles and Technique of Teaching*, Houghton Mifflin, 1927, gives a simple presentation of several
"Plans" in Chap. XVII, "Adjustments for Individual Differences."

I. ADMINISTRATIVE "PLANS"

Boucher, Chauncey Samuel, *The Chicago Plan*, Chicago Univ.
Press, 1935, history and description of the reorganization of
the first two college years at the Univ. of Chicago.

Brooks, Robert C., *Reading for Honors at Swarthmore*, Oxford Univ.
Press, 1928.

Burr, M. Y., *A Study of Homogeneous Grouping in Terms of Individual Variations*, Contributions to Education, No. 457,
Teachers College, Columbia University, 1931.

Collins, E., *Project Teaching in the Elementary School*, Century,
1928.

De la Salle, St. Jean-Baptiste, (tr. by De la Fontainerie), *The Conduct of the School*, McGraw-Hill, 1935; the old translation
entitled *Government of the Christian School*, Montreal, 1850,
includes "The Government of the Governor," and also "The
Twelve Virtues of a Good Master."

Dewey, Evelyn, *The Dalton Laboratory Plan*, Dutton, 1922.

Draper, Edgar Marion, *Principles and Techniques of Curriculum Making*, Appleton-Century, 1936, Chaps. X, "Units of Work for Individualized Learning" and XII, "Procedures for Units of Work" are particularly valuable.

Fitzpatrick, Edward A., *St. Ignatius and the Ratio Studiorum*, McGraw-Hill, 1933, Part I, "St. Ignatius and Education," Part II, "Constitution of the Society of Jesus" bearing on the *Ratio*, and Part III, "Ratio Studiorum 1599."

Kelly, Robert Lincoln, *The Effective College*, Assoc. of American Colleges, 1928, Chap. XII, "Sectioning on the Basis of Ability" is by Dean Holt of the United States Military Academy.

Morrison, Henry C., *The Practice of Teaching in the Secondary School*, Univ. Chicago Press, 1926, (rev. ed. 1931), the Morrison Plan.

Parkhurst, H. H., *Education on the Dalton Plan*, Dutton, 1922.

Purdom, T. L., *The Value of Homogenous Grouping*, Warwick and York, 1929.

Ryan, H. H., and P. Coerelius, *Ability Grouping in the Junior High School*, Harcourt Brace, 1927.

Shreve, Francis, *Supervised Study Plan of Teaching*, Johnson Pub., 1927.

Thayer, Vivian Trow, *The Passing of the Recitation*, Heath, 1928, gives the historical background and discusses several of the "Plans," *e.g.*, Chap. XIII, "The Dalton and Winnetka Plans."

Washburne, Carleton W., *Adjusting the School to the Child*, World Book, 1932, the Winnetka Plan.

——, Mabel Vogel and William S. Gray, *Results of Practical Experiments in Fitting Schools to Individuals*, Monograph, *Journal of Educational Research*, 1926, the Winnetka Plan.

2. DISCIPLINE—CLASSROOM AND SCHOOL CONTROL

Bagley, W. C., *School Discipline*, Macmillan, 1914.

——, *Education, Crime and Social Progress*, Macmillan, 1931, Chaps. III, "Discipline and Dogma"; VI. "Through Discipline to Freedom."

Colvin, S. S., *An Introduction to High School Teaching*, Macmillan, 1917, Chaps. IV to VII inclusive.

Harris, P. E., *Changing Conceptions of School Discipline*, Macmillan, 1928, entire.

Holley C. E., *High School Teachers' Methods*, Garrard Press, 1937, Chap. III. "Favorable Conditions for Learning and Teaching—Discipline." pp. 36–68.

Jones, W. H. S., *Disciplina*, Cambridge Univ. Press, 1926, the English point of view.

Jutta, Sister M., *School Discipline and Character*, Bruce, 1930, presents the point of view of Supernaturalism.

Kelly, William A., *Educational Psychology*, Bruce, 1933, Chap. XVIII is entitled "Constructive Discipline," pp. 253–266.

Monroe, W. S., *Directing Learning in the High School*, Doubleday, Page, 1927, Chap. XI. "The Management of Classes," pp. 342–376.

O'Brien, John A. (editor), *Catholics and Scholarship*, Sunday Visitor Press, 1939, Chapter XIII, "Enhancing Catholic Prestige" by Jerome G. Kerwin of Chicago Univ. protests against "the multifarious rules and regulations" of Catholic schools and colleges, p. 161.

Perry, A. C., *Discipline as a School Problem*, Houghton Mifflin, 1915.

Pringle, R. W., *Psychology of High School Discipline*, Heath, 1931.

Wheeler, Raymond H. and Francis T. Perkins, *Principles of Mental Development*, Crowell, 1932, Chap. XXIII, "Discipline."

Wolfe, J. M., *Introduction to the Study of Human Conduct and Character*, Benziger, 1930, entire.

3. MEASUREMENT MOVEMENT

Adler, Mortimer, *What Man Has Made of Man*, Longmans Green, 1937, evaluates the measurement movement under the name "Psychometrics," pp. 89 and 202.

Hawkes, Herbert E., E. F. Lindquist and C. R. Mann, *The Construction and Use of Achievement Examinations*, Houghton Mifflin, 1936.

Jones, Edward Safford, *Comprehensive Examinations in American Colleges*, Macmillan, 1933, entire.

Lang, Albert, *Modern Methods in Written Examination*, Houghton Mifflin, 1930, is excellent for the teacher on all levels.

Madsen, Iver Nelson, *Educational Measurement in the Elementary Grades*, World Book, 1930.

Pressy, S. L., *Psychology and the New Education*, Harpers, 1933, Chap. XII "Methods for the Appraisal and Direction of Learning" is an excellent summary.

Richardson, Russell, Stalnaker and Thurstone, *Manual of Examination Methods*, Univ. of Chicago Bookstore, 1933, explains the technique through which the Univ. of Chicago examinations are constructed, with examples.

Rinsland, Henry Daniel, *Constructing Tests and Grading*, Prentice-Hall, 1938, carries the subtitle "In Elementary and High School Subjects."

Ruch, G. M., *The Objective or New-Type Examination*, Scott, Foresman, 1929.

Ruch, G. M., and G. A. Rice, *Specimen Objective Examinations*, Scott, Foresman, 1930, copies of the best tests submitted in a contest; excellent models.

Ruch, G. M., and George G. Stoddard, *Tests and Measurements in High School Instruction*, Scott, Foresman, 1927.

Spearman, Charles E., *The Abilities of Man*, Macmillan, 1927

Terman, Lewis, *The Measurement of Intelligence*, Houghton Mifflin, 1916.

Tiegs, Earnest W., *Tests and Measurements for Teachers*, Houghton Mifflin Co., 1931, deals with all levels and special fields, *e.g.*, Commercial, Music, etc.

Whipple, Guy Montrose (editor), *Intelligence, Its Nature and Nurture*, Public School Publishing Co., 1940, *Thirty-ninth Year Book of the Nat. Society for the Study of Education*, both sides of the nature-nuture controversy.

Wood, Benjamin, *Measurements in Higher Education*, World Book, 1923.

THE TEACHER MAKES THE SCHOOL

It is not what you study but with whom you study that matters.

Emerson, in a letter to his daughter.

Knowledge may be gained from books but the love of knowledge is transmitted only by personal contact.

Henry Van Dyke.

Perfect schools are the result not so much of good methods as of good teachers, teachers who are thoroughly prepared and well-grounded in the matter they have to teach; who possess the intellectual and moral qualifications required by their important office; who cherish a pure and holy love for the youths confided to them, because they love Jesus Christ and His Church, of which these are the children of predilection; and who have therefore sincerely at heart the true good of family and country.

Pius XI, *The Christian Education of Youth.*

CHAPTER XV

THE EDUCATION OF THE TEACHER

Education is the oldest of the arts; the youngest of the sciences. As an art it has been in evolution ever since parents in prehistoric times made conscious efforts to hand over to their children the knowledge and skills of their primitive culture. As a science its development has been limited to recent times. In the United States Samuel R. Hall opened the first school for training teachers in Vermont in 1823. In 1829 he published his "Lectures on Schoolkeeping," the first American textbook on education.[1] But more than a hundred years before this (1720) St. John de la Salle's *Conduct of the Schools* had been published in Paris. All histories of education give him credit for putting into operation on a large scale the "simultaneous method" at a time when all elementary instruction was individual. But not content with introducing the method of teaching by classes, he established in 1685 at Rheims the first Normal School to train teachers to use this method and thus brought free elementary education to the poor.[2]

During the last half of the 19th century the Normal School replaced the Academy as the teacher-training institution in the United States and before the end of the century completely

[1] Edward W. Knight, *Education in the United States*, Ginn & Co., 1929, p. 316.
[2] Frederick Eby and Charles F. Arrowood, *The Development of Modern Education*, Prentice-Hall, 1934, p. 358.

dominated the training of teachers for the elementary school. Now the Normal Schools are rapidly being converted into Teacher Colleges offering a four-year curriculum and awarding a Bachelor degree at its completion. With this development the Teacher Colleges have entered upon the work of training high school teachers and are now challenging the dominance of the liberal arts college in this field. The Schools of Education of the universities are training both elementary and secondary teachers in great numbers and in addition have taken over preparation of school administrators through graduate work in education.

We are now in a period of transition. No longer is the emphasis on "teacher training." Rather, it is the *education* of the teacher that is now receiving emphasis. This is due to the conviction among leaders in the field of education that the teacher, above anyone else, should be an educated person. Too long has the emphasis been placed on special techniques and particular devices, to the neglect of that larger education that produces the informed, cultured, and disciplined mind. The normal schools are accused of offering a training narrow in scope and anything but liberalizing in its outcome. The most recent attack on this situation, one that goes the whole way, is that presented by President Hutchins.

> The prospective teacher's general education would be identical with that of the lawyer, doctor, and clergyman. With a good education in the liberal arts, which are grammar, rhetoric, logic, and mathematics, he has learned the basic rules of pedagogy. The liberal arts are, after all, the arts of reducing the intellect from mere potentiality to act. And this is what teaching is. The liberal arts train the teacher in how to teach, that is, in how to organize, express, and communicate knowledge. In the university he should learn what to teach. . . .
>
> It is only by educating teachers in this way that we shall ever break the vicious circle to which I have many times referred—the

circle in which the products of a bad system grow up to be the operators and perpetuators of it.[1]

If the advice of President Hutchins were to be followed, all "teacher-training" institutions would be abolished. Does the present situation call for such drastic action? The purpose of this chapter is to make clear that the answer to this question must be a decided negative. The fallacy in President Hutchins' position lies in his failure to distinguish different levels in the development of the learner's mind. If he were speaking only of the university level we would agree with him, but to make the same statement concerning the teacher of the kindergarten and primary grades is preposterous. On the higher levels it is subject matter that is difficult to master. But on the lower levels the chief difficulty to be overcome is gaining an insight into the nature of the child mind. How many university professors would feel themselves adequately prepared for teaching kindergarteners? This is not because they are without sufficient knowledge. They have accumulated such vast stores of knowledge that its very mass would be their greatest handicap. No, knowledge must be adapted to the immature mind of the child if it is to be assimilated by that mind. This is the principle of apperception developed in Chapter V, "Theories of Learning." It introduces the distinction between the logical and psychological organization and presentation of subject matter. By logical organization we mean organization arising out of the nature of the subject matter itself. Thus in the science of physics the several large units, each concerned with one of the forms of physical force, mechanics, heat, light, sound, and electricity, will be presented one after the other. Not that they are not interrelated. In their practical applications they are closely interrelated. In the cinema, for example, electricity, light, and

[1] Robert Maynard Hutchins, *The Higher Learning in America*, Yale Univ. Press, 1938, pp. 114–115.

sound all play important parts in producing the desired effects. But such applications could never have been developed, if these forms of physical force had not been studied separately. This is the way the mature mind functions most effectively. "Divide et impera." The mature mind is prepared to carry on analysis and synthesis, and classification must have its logical basis. But for the immature mind, the mind that is just beginning its development, the point of attack must be the interests aroused through living in a world that James describes as "a big, booming, buzzing confusion." This is what we mean by the psychological organization of subject matter, *i.e.*, organization based on the nature of the mind to which it is to be presented. This means it must be based on interests, abilities, and felt needs. In this distinction, therefore, on the university level logical organization *is* the psychological. The two become one. Not so with the mind of the child. We teach Nature Study in the primary grades beginning with the child's environment though, of course, we enrich that environment through object lessons at every available opportunity. Only when the mind has reached a certain degree of maturity is the same subject matter presented in the logical organization of the sciences, botany and physiology, physics and chemistry, etc. For the psychological organization and presentation of subject matter there is real need for training in method. Even the "born teacher" will profit by such a discipline and his natural ability to present to the child mind the wonders of the world about him, will be rendered the more effective if it takes on the nature of a science and and art, the science and art of education.

From this point of view we see that the problem of method stands in inverse ratio to the problem of subject matter. The higher up the ladder the teacher is working, the more important is his knowledge of subject matter and the less important his knowledge of method. The lower down on the educational ladder a teacher is working, the more important is his knowledge of method and the less important is his mastery of subject matter. On the higher levels *method is the man,* and no matter what eccentricities a university professor may display, this should make no appreciable difference to the university student. Whereas, for the teacher on the primary level, teaching technique is supreme.

Keeping in mind this inverse ratio of the importance of subject matter and method, we see that the period of secondary education is the middle ground. Again we are confronted with the fact that adolescence is the time of educational doubt. To what extent is formal professional training necessary or advisable for the teacher in the secondary school? Because of the difficulty of the problem on this level and because the experience of the writer has been largely in this field, our discussion of the professional education of teachers will be concerned primarily with teachers in the secondary school. But if the principles we present are valid, they will give guidance also for the education of teachers working either on the elementary level or the level of higher education. We will treat the problem under three aspects: (1) the academic education of the teacher; (2) the professional education of the teacher; and (3) the personal influence of the teacher, which means his spiritual education. (See Figure 28, p. 496)

1. ACADEMIC EDUCATION OF THE TEACHER

In the matter of the general academic education of the teacher we find ourselves in complete agreement with President Hutchins when he says: "The prospective teacher's general education would be identical with that of the lawyer, doctor, and clergyman." To these may be added the business man or anyone else privileged to complete his general education in the liberal college. This was the thesis of Chapter IX, "The Phi-

FIGURE 28.—THE EDUCATION OF THE TEACHER

1. Academic Education

A.
The teacher
  should know:

I.
His World—The five fields of knowledge ----------------

1. Natural Sciences
2. Humanistic Sciences
3. Metaphysical
    Sciences
4. Fine Arts
5. Language and
    Literature

II.
His Subject—The subjects which constitute his teaching field.

2. Professional Education

III.
His Object—
(the pupil)

1. The Educative Process
    (objectives)

2. The Learning Process

—Principles or
  Philosophy of
  Education (3 hrs.)
—Educational
  Psychology (3 hrs.)

IV.
How to bring —The
  subject and Teaching
  object Process
  together

1. Theory

"General
Methods"

"Special
Methods"

—Principals and
  Technique of
  Teaching
    (3 hrs.)
—Professional
  Subject Matter
  Courses

2. Appren-
    ticeship

Critical
Evaluation

Practice

—Observation and
  Demonstration
    (3 hrs.)
—Student Teaching
  under Supervision

3. Personal Influence of the Teacher

B.
The teacher
  should be:

An Inspiring
  Personality

1. How personality
    evolves

a. All education is self-education.
b. Need of a model, great teachers.

2. The Master Model,
    Christ.

a. He knew his world; He created it.
b. He knew his subject; Divine Truth.
c. He knew his object, man; He
    redeemed him.
d. He knew how to bring subject and
    object together; His technique.

losophy of the Curriculum," Section 3, "The Five Fields of Knowledge." These five fields, (1) the Natural Sciences, (2) the Humanistic Sciences, (3) the Metaphysical Sciences, (4) the Fine Arts and (5) the Language Arts determine the content of the curriculum on all levels devoted to general education. On the college level they are now commonly organized into five Academic Groups (1) Mathematics and Natural Sciences, (2) History and Humanistic Sciences, (3) Theology (Religion) and Philosophy, (4) Music and Fine Arts and (5) Language and Literature. (See Figure 19, "The Disciplines in School Activities," p. 330.) The very business of the liberal college is to make the student acquainted with all five fields, and, during the last two years, the upper biennium, make him feel particularly at home in one of them, his "field of concentration." Through this transmission of knowledge in these fields he develops his two supreme abilities, the power of thought and the power of expression. If such growth and development is not the experience of the prospective teacher as an outcome of his academic education, he is prepared neither for teaching nor for life in a cultured community.

But the prospective teacher has another obligation in the matter of academic education. In addition to this general academic education which he, in common with all cultured people, should possess, the teacher must have special competence in certain subjects which constitute his teaching field. The needs here are strikingly different for teachers of elementary, secondary, and higher education.

The teacher in the elementary school, particularly if teaching in the lower grades, must to a certain extent be familiar with all five fields of knowledge if he is to play his part in satisfactorily passing on to the child his social heritage. The danger here is superficiality. At the other extreme is the teacher on the level of higher education. His teaching field may be so narrow and his intense interest in pursuing his researches so engrossing that he loses all contact with life about him. Not only civic and social interests but even intellectual interests outside his own field, may disappear from his life. When this happens he is well on the way towards becoming an uneducated specialist. General education is not finished with the completion of college. It is coterminous with life. More than ever today we live in a changing world. To lose all interest in these changes; to be perfectly oblivious that they are going on—even though pursuing "scholarship" in one small field—is not the proper life for one whose calling demands that he be an inspiration to youth. Intense specialization has special dangers for anyone in the teaching profession.

The teacher in the secondary school is confronted with both these dangers. On the one hand, if he is working in the small high school inadequately staffed, not only will he be overloaded with administrative duties, particularly those involved in guiding the co-curricular activities, but in addition he may be asked to teach any subject in the whole gamut of curricular offerings from astronomy to zoology. Here again the danger is superficiality. With his activities divided among several fields, the only defense for a teacher interested in his own growth and development is to capitalize his leisure time (insofar as he has any) and concentrate on one or more intellectual hobbies the pursuit of which, if it does not make him an expert in that field, will at least bring intellectual satisfactions to enrich his life, if not his purse, and keep him active in a way that will ward off the danger of intellectual stalemate leading to decay. It is reported that the Dean of the College of Johns Hopkins University never received a college degree but through the pursuit of an intellectual hobby, geology, made himself such an expert in the field that he could not be denied recognition. On the other hand, the teacher in the huge high school enrolling students by the thousands, such as are characteristic of the large metropolitan centers, is in danger of narrow specialization. He will be crowded with classes but as a result of departmentalization these will ordinarily be limited to one field, mathematics, litera-ture, or one of the sciences, and the monotony of frequent repe-tition of the same teaching materials may bring ennui to his spirit and kill all zest for teaching. Here again outside inter-ests, intellectual and social, are the only safeguard. In Nicho-las Murray Butler's phrase, teaching demands "broad minds sharpened to a point" but the sharpening process should not be carried to the point where breadth of interests is sacrificed to developing expertness in one field.

The teacher, then, above all others, should realize the truth of the saying that *all education is self-education*. He should be a living exemplar of the principle that a student learns through *his own activities*. If this principle is operative throughout his life, in his reading, in careful observation, and reflective think-ing thereon, he will become familiar with the five fields of knowledge in a way that no college experience of four years could ever bring to any student however brilliant.

The teacher in the tax-supported schools, because of their nonsectarian basis, will seldom have an opportunity to com-municate to students by direct instruction one of these five fields, the metaphysical sciences (philosophy and religion). But as Rev. John Cavanaugh, C.S.C., President of the Uni-versity of Notre Dame, said some years ago, addressing a meet-ing called by the Indiana State Department to discuss the prob-lem of religious education in the public school, "If we can't put religion into the curriculum of the public school, let us put it into the teachers." Since example is the great teacher in the matter of forming life attitudes, a public school with a staff of teachers demonstrating in their lives, both within and without the school, the social and moral virtues, will be a powerful influence for the development of these same virtues in the lives of the pupils with whom they live and labor. The constantly increasing number of Catholic teachers in the tax-supported schools have a positive obligation to let the light of truly Catholic lives "shine before men." [1] The Catholic school, even though it devotes a certain portion of the school day to formal instruction in religion, cannot be complacent in this regard. Knowledge is not virtue. The late Holy Father, Pius XI, in his encylical *The Christian Education of Youth* has laid strong emphasis on this phase of general education in these words:

> The mere fact that a school gives some religious instruction (often extremely stinted), does not bring it into accord with the rights of the Church and of the Christian family, or make it a fit place for Catholic students. To be this, it is necessary that all the teaching and the whole organization of the school, and its teachers, syllabi and textbooks in every branch, be regulated by *the Christian spirit*, under the direction and maternal supervision of the Church; so that religion may be in very truth the foundation and crown of the youth's entire training; and this in every grade of school, not only the elementary, but the intermediate and the higher institutions of learning as well.

2. PROFESSIONAL EDUCATION OF TEACHERS

Turning now to the professional education of teachers, it is heartening to record that there is a decided change of emphasis that holds hope for the future. In the past the aim of prospective teachers in training and the activities of "teacher-training" institutions were centered on the acquisition of what has been labelled "the magic tricks of the teaching trade." Now it is recognized that a bag full of tricks is no proper preparation for one entering the profession of teaching. The variables in the teaching situation (analysed in Chapter XI, Section 2, "The Search for a Solution," p. 351) render sterile prepa-

[1] Matthew V, 16.

ration for teaching that is limited to tricks and devices. A device employed by one teacher in one situation may work perfectly, whereas the same device in the hands of another teacher, or of the same teacher in another situation, may be worse than useless. What students preparing for teaching must learn are *principles* not devices. Principles are abstract in nature but universal in application. Since they are abstract they are difficult to comprehend. Here is the proper sphere of devices in the education of teachers. They illustrate principles. They give meaning to the abstract generalizations which principles are. But the student must realize that if he truly understands a principle, he ought to be able to select or, if necessary, invent a device that will put the principle into operation. Principles here are of two varieties, those descriptive of the learning process and those dealing with the teaching process, the two phases of the educative process. (See Figure 28, "The Education of the Teacher," p. 496.)

But this fact of the primary importance of general education over special training as preparation for teaching has not yet won general recognition by those responsible for teacher-training programs. Some years ago (1936) a large city teachers college, accredited as a junior college by one of the regional accrediting associations but conducting a four-year program and awarding a Bachelor degree, made application to be accredited as a four-year college. The curriculum they presented was overloaded with "special methods" courses to the neglect of courses recognized as part of a program of general education on the college level. After the application had been rejected, one of the members of the accrediting board (president of a liberal arts college engaged in teacher training) made the remark: "What would happen to this country in a generation if all elementary school teachers were prepared for teaching by a curriculum such as that!"

Unhappily it cannot be said that state departments of education have given intelligent leadership in this problem. All recognize now that the training period for the elementary school teachers of the future will be four years beyond the high school leading to the Bachelor degree. But what will be the content of that four years of collegiate study? The absurdities to which prescriptions can go in answer to this question is made evident by one of the regulations issued in 1937 by a state department inaugurating a four-year training period for elementary school teachers:

> Not more than eight quarter hours or five semester hours of credit may be earned in any subject-matter field *not regularly taught in the public schools* or listed in the required courses of the above curriculum.

How could the collegiate training of Catholic school teachers planning to qualify for elementary school licenses in the same way as public school teachers, meet this requirement? Is religion, or better, theology, one of the metaphysical sciences, to be limited to five semester hours? And what about philosophy? Ordinarily the Catholic liberal college includes in its four-year curriculum twelve hours of philosophy in the upper two years with general psychology and logic as a basis in the first two years. Shall we have "Health and Physical Education" supplant "Philosophy and Theology" as the fifth field of knowledge in general education, as is suggested in a late publication of the National Education Association? [1] Be it said to the credit of the officers of this state department, when a Catholic college submitted its four-year curriculum for elementary school teachers containing eight semester hours of theology

[1] Educational Policies Commission, *The Structure and Administration of Education in American Democracy*, National Education Association, 1938, pp. 12 and 16.

(religion) in the lower biennium, and twelve hours of philosophy in the upper biennium, it was approved "as a special case."

The chief responsibility for this overemphasis on professional subjects must however, be laid at the door of the Departments of Education in Teacher Colleges and Schools of Education in the universities. Multiplication of courses, with padding and repetition of subject matter has gone on to the great discredit of the profession. When one listens to the contributions of these "experts" in the field of education on the programs of their "learned societies," the basic cause for the sterility of their leadership is revealed at once. They themselves are not educated men even though they may be highly trained in "scientific techniques." The one reassuring sign appearing on the horizon is the study now being undertaken by The American Council on Education. A subvention has been secured from one of the foundations. The title of the study is "The Education of the Teacher" not his "training." If this title is truly indicative of the spirit in which the study will be carried on, there is real hope that its report will have a salutary influence in curbing the overemphasis of teacher colleges, schools of education, and state departments on courses in education.

SECONDARY SCHOOL TEACHERS

In the field of training teachers for the secondary school there has occurred this same overemphasis on professional training to the neglect of academic education in its two phases, general education and the teaching field. Professional training is commonly limited to the last two years of college. State department requirements for a certificate in many cases run well over twenty semester hours. On a fifteen-hour basis for each of the four semesters of these two years, this means that more than one third of the student's time is devoted to professional training, twenty hours plus, out of sixty hours for the four semesters. Accrediting associations like the North Central have been content with fifteen hours of education, which is one fourth of the student's time. We believe it should be cut down to twelve hours as a maximum, or one fifth of the student's time. That we are not alone in this recommendation is evidenced by the report of the American Association of University Professors entitled, "Committee on Required Courses in Education." In their inquiry the specific question raised was, "Does the present professional training actually improve secondary school teachers to a degree commensurate with the high requirements that prevail?" On the basis of its findings the Committee states:

a. There is no reliable evidence that professional requirements have resulted in an improvement in secondary instruction at all commensurate with the amount of the requirements.
b. A considerable lowering in the requirements would result in economy, and would not lessen the effectiveness of instruction in the high school.
c. A maximum of twelve semester hours is ample to cover that part of professional training which can be regarded as essential for the beginning teacher who has a bachelor's degree from a standard college or university, and who qualifies for teaching an academic subject. The training should involve practice teaching and methods, the methods course being closely integrated with the practice teaching. Courses in psychology or educational psychology, when these are required, should be counted toward the requirement.[1]

Except for the inclusion of general psychology, this coincides with the analysis we present in Figure 28, "The Education of the Teacher," 2, "Professional Education," p. 496. This analysis recommends one three-hour course for each semester of the

[1] *Bulletin*, American Association of University Professors, March, 1933, Report of Committee Q., p. 199.

last two years of college. The first semester of the junior year would be concerned with the objectives of education and with the curriculum as a means for the achievement of those objectives, "Principles" or "Philosophy of Education;" the second semester, with how pupils learn, "Educational Psychology." The whole of the senior year would be devoted to a study of the teaching process, the first semester to theory, "Technique of Teaching" and "Professional Subject Matter Courses," *e.g.*, "The Teaching of the Social Sciences," and the second semester to practice, a period of apprenticeship including demonstration, observation, and "Student Teaching" under critical but sympathetic supervision. It is the almost universal testimony of students in training that they learn more from this period of apprenticeship than from all the other courses combined. This is the typical student reaction, to overvalue practice and underestimate the value of the study of principles concerned with the learning process and the teaching process, but further experience with maturity will restore the balance, at least, for the more intelligent.

This period of training for secondary school teachers, is now being extended to a "five-year plan" adding one year to the four of college. Here again the tendency is to overemphasize the professional aspect. In the fall of 1937 the writer attended a meeting called by a state department which had recently inaugurated a five-year plan for secondary school teachers. All institutions in the state engaged in teacher training were invited to send representatives. In spite of protests on the part of some of the college representatives, the plan as approved called for thirty semester hours during the last three years to be devoted to professional training. This again is one third of the entire time. An addition of two courses of three semester hours each (total six semester hours) added to the twelve hours of the old four-year plan recommended above should be a maximum, keeping the ratio in the last three years to one fifth (eighteen in ninety hours) instead of one third (thirty in ninety hours). One of the representatives present at this meeting, a professor of education, remarked afterwards that this was too much time devoted to education subjects but he added significantly, "This is our bread and butter!"

PROFESSIONAL TRAINING FOR TEACHERS IN COLLEGE

Apart from the junior college situation, which is now recognized as the upper limit of secondary education, there is little likelihood that any agency will attempt to impose professional educational requirements in this field. Nor should this be done. Students in college, at least in the four-year liberal college, should have attained that degree of maturity which makes the logical organization and presentation of subject matter the proper technique on this level. Nevertheless, there is no doubt that many beginning college teachers would be better prepared for their work if they spent some time studying the college problem and the proper place of their own teaching subject in the college curriculum, as well as the best technique for its presentation. The recommendations of The Commission on the Enlistment and Training of College Teachers of the Association of American Colleges in this matter are sensible and sane. We give them in part as published in the *Bulletin* of the Association.

> Since the college teacher has not merely the responsibility of knowing but has also the responsibility of conveying his knowledge and of stimulating other minds, we suggest that carefully considered effort be made—as is already done in many cases—to give to each graduate student intending to engage in college teaching an adequate training in methods of teaching as applied to particular departments of knowledge in which the student is working. We suggest further, in this connection, that so far as possible opportunity be provided for graduate students to watch the teaching of successful college teachers; and that insofar as

graduate students are themselves employed as instructors or assistants such employment be supervised and be regarded as part of their own educational experience.

Since the college enterprise is a single enterprise in which every college teacher should bear his part, and since every college teacher should have a good general understanding of the enterprise as a whole, we suggest that each Graduate School offer to students intending to engage in college teaching an adequate and varied course on the American College. Such a course should deal in particular with progressive instructional and curricular movements; and should include some account of the main types of departmental and general administrative service. We do not suggest that such a course be made a requirement; but we do suggest that each department be urged to accept such a course toward the meeting of its own quantitative requirements.

While we believe that significant experience in the field of research should be given to every prospective college teacher, we believe that the Graduate School in general now tends to stress unduly the relative importance of such experience for students intending to engage in college teaching; and we therefore suggest that for such students there be an optional quantitative relaxation of the research requirement in favor of some additional mastery of subject matter or other educational resources. Such relaxation might take the form of the assignment of presumably smaller and shorter thesis problems.[1]

So much for what the teacher should know. We now consider what the teacher should be in terms of the qualities that should characterize his personality.

3. PERSONAL INFLUENCE OF THE TEACHER

Even if the academic education of the teacher-to-be has been effectively carried forward in the fields of knowledge and along with it his professional education in the purposes of the school and the procedures appropriate for achieving those purposes,

[1] *Bulletin*, Association of American Colleges, Vol. XV, No. 3, Nov. 1929, p. 342.

his education is not thereby completed. In fact a third phase of the teacher's education, a phase not necessarily involved in either academic or professional education, remains unmentioned. And this third phase is by all means the most important of the three. We search in vain for an appropriate word with which to label it but this does not deny the fact that it is the most impressive reality in the whole experience of the pupil-teacher relationship. We commonly speak of this characteristic as the teacher's *personality*. The connotation of the word "personality" includes that entire congeries of traits, both physical and mental that marks off each person from every other person. The personality of the teacher includes therefore his academic learning and his professional skill but it goes far beyond these. The student soon learns this and when recommending courses to his fellow students he places the emphasis where it rightly belongs when he says, "It's the teacher that makes the course."

How does this thing we call "personality" evolve? What brings about the development of a personality that makes an effective teacher? There are two influences here which are paramount. The first is the part we ourselves play in the formation of our own personalities. Many great educators have stressed the fact that all education is self-education. Hamilton phrases it: "Self-activity is the indispensible condition of improvement. Education is only education, that is, accomplishes its purpose, only by affording objects and supplying incitements to this spontaneous exertion. *Strictly speaking, every one must educate himself*." Bishop Spalding returns again and again to this same theme, and Cardinal Newman in his great classic, *The Idea of a University*, gives a description of a faulty system of education that might have been written of American education with its emphasis on the mechanics of school keeping. These are his words:

Knowledge is something more than a sort of passive reception of scraps and details; it is a something, and it does a something, which never will issue from the most strenuous efforts of a set of teachers, with no mutual sympathies and no inter-communion, of a set of examiners with no opinions which they dare profess, and with no common principles, who are teaching or questioning a set of youths who do not know them, and do not know each other, on a large number of subjects, different in kind, and connected by no wide philosophy, three times a week, or three times a year, or once in three years, in chill lecture rooms or on a pompous anniversary.

Of such education in the following paragraph he says:

Self-education in any shape, in the most restricted sense, is preferable to a system of teaching which, professing so much, really does so little for the mind.[1]

If this process of self-education is so important in the acquisition of knowledge and the development of skills, what shall we say about its importance in the development of attitudes and ideals which more than any other single thing determine what we call "personality." Here it is of paramount importance. In our philosophy of Supernaturalism, God's grace is ever at our disposal as a help in overcoming the defects of personality, but fundamentally the responsibility for this striving for perfection rests first of all upon ourselves.

Besides the supernatural help of God's grace, however, we have need of a natural help if our efforts in this endeavor are to meet with success. Self-activity alone does not necessarily advance us towards perfection. Our activities may be leading us in the wrong direction. We need a worthy model to imitate if our activities are to lead us towards our goal of self-perfection. This is what we mean by the personal influence of the teacher.

[1] John Henry Newman, *Idea of a University*, Discourse VI, "Knowledge Viewed in Relation to Learning."

Anyone who has been privileged to come under the influence of a truly great teacher knows what this has meant in his own life. Looking back the writer can say that he has been privileged to sit at the feet of three teachers who were truly inspiring, one in the elementary school, one in the high school, and one in the university. Here was a great privilege twice repeated.

But even though a beginning teacher has been so unfortunate as never to have come under the influence of a truly inspiring teacher, this does not mean that he is without a model to imitate. There is one teacher who is the model for all; one whom the histories of education describe as "The Great Teacher," Jesus Christ.[1] He had all of the qualifications analyzed in Figure 28, p. 496. He knew His *world* since He was the creator of that world. He knew His *subject*, Divine Truth, since He is the author of all truth, both natural and divine. He knew his *object*, man, since He had created man and then came on earth to save man from himself. And finally He knew *how* to bring His subject and object together, divine truth illuminating the mind of man. This is the most difficult of all teaching since these two by nature are so far apart. This is how He proceeded. He began with the simple and proceeded to the complex. When speaking to tillers of the soil, He told the parables of the sower, the lost sheep, the wicked husbandman, and the laborers in the vineyard; when speaking to fisherman, the kingdom of heaven was likened to a net cast into the sea; for all, He used the analogies of the lilies of the fields, the birds of the air, and the mustard seed. Here is the principle of *apperception* applied in its fullest meaning, proceeding from the known to the unknown. He prepared his listeners for the great truths they were about to receive. The miracle of the multiplication of the loaves in the 6th chapter of St. John, preceded the promise of the Eucharist; the miracle of giving sight to the

[1] Philip R. Curoe, *History of Education*, Globe Book Co., 1921, p. 46.

man born blind preceded the pronouncement that his sins were forgiven. Here is the principle of *motivation*. The disciples distributed the loaves and fishes among the multitude, and gathered up the fragments "lest they be lost;" they took part with Him in the last supper and there received the commission to share the life giving bread of the Eucharist with the faithful when the Master no longer would be with them, "Do this in commemoration of me." Here is the *technique of participation*. He kept his disciples close to Himself during the whole of his public life as a period of apprenticeship and when they were ready, He sent them out two by two to extend His work returning to Him with the story of their successes and their failures to receive His commendations and His criticisms. Here is the *practice technique* putting into operation the principle of *self-activity*. Always and everywhere He used the question, the universal instrument of all good teaching, introducing thereby the sublime truths He would have them consider. "What think you of Christ: Whose son is he?" [1] At the conclusion of the parable of the Good Samaritan with the priest and the Levite who passed by and the Samaritan who bound up the wounds of the man assaulted by robbers, He drove home the lesson with the question: "Which of these three . . . was neighbor to him that fell among robbers?" [2] Here is the *problem technique* operating in all its effectiveness.

But this analysis of the teaching technique of Jesus translated into the technical terms of the presentday science of education does not bring out the real effectiveness of His teaching. There was something else about Him more impressive than any mere technique, a something else we call the personal influence of the teacher. Jesus lived intimately with his disciples. In every way He was their model and their inspira-

[1] Matthew XXII, 42.
[2] Luke X, 36.

tion. Here is the supreme contribution the great teacher makes to the growth and development of the pupil. This continued contact of mind with mind that teaching makes possible is the factor that leaves the most enduring impression upon the pupil. As Emerson put it in a letter to his daughter, "It is not what you study but with whom you study, that matters."

THE REWARDS OF TEACHING

We have discussed the education of the teacher under the three headings: (1) academic education, (2) professional education, and (3) what for want of a better term we may call his "spiritual" education meaning by that the confluence of those forces which play a part in the development of his personality, chief among which we have listed his own personal endeavors. It remains now to say a word about the rewards of teaching, referring by that term to those returns which are spiritual in nature rather than monetary or promotional. That they are real no one who has any natural aptitude for teaching and who has had opportunity to demonstrate that aptitude by work in the class room under favorable circumstances, ever for one moment doubts. Here is the testimony of one who for more than a quarter of a century followed this life calling. William Lyon Phelps thus expresses himself:

> I do not know that I could make entirely clear to an outsider the pleasure I have in teaching. I had rather earn my living by teaching than in any other way. In my mind, teaching is not merely a lifework, a profession, an occupation, a struggle; it is a passion. I love to teach. I love to teach as a painter loves to paint, as a singer loves to sing, as a strong man rejoices to run a race. Teaching is an art—an art so great and so difficult to master that a man or woman can spend a long life at it, without realizing much more than his limitations and mistakes and his

distance from the ideal. There never has been in the world's history a period when it was more worthwhile to be a teacher than in the twentieth century; for there was never an age when such vast multitudes were eager for an education or when the necessity of a liberal education was so generally recognized. It would seem as though the whole world were trying to lift itself to a higher plane of thought.[1]

When we recall the monotony of daily and hourly appointments, and the drudgery of reading and correcting written assignments, we may not be prone to rhapsodize on the pleasures of teaching as Phelps has done in this beautiful tribute to the calling. But the rewards are real nevertheless. And they are available to the teacher who with adequate preparation throws himself wholeheartedly into the work. To reap these rewards at their highest, the teacher must realize the full meaning of the words of St. John the Baptist who, when appealed to by his own disciples, grown jealous of the favor Our Lord was winning in the eyes of the multitude, made this pronouncement: "He must increase, but I must decrease." (John VI, 30) And so with the teacher. When he begins his ministrations there is a wide gap in knowledge and ability between him and his pupils, but if his teaching is effective this gap gradually grows narrower, often closing entirely. In some instances the pupil surpasses the teacher in the very field in which he began learning under his tutelage. But this outcome is the glory of teaching. Here it has truly been effective. The pupil must increase, but the teacher must decrease the distance that separates him from the pupil and if possible spur on the pupil to surpass his own acquirements.

This brings us face to face with the paradox that was continually on the lips of our Lord: 'He that will save his life, shall lose it; and he that shall lose his life for my sake, shall find it.'

[1] William Lyon Phelps, *Autobiography with Letters*, Oxford Univ. Press, 1939, p. 307.

(Mat. XVI, 25) So the ideal teacher loses his life in promoting the life of the pupil. If his academic and professional education have been effective his knowledge and his abilities pass over and become the possession of the pupil. But more than this. If his spiritual education has done its work, his life ideals, his standards of conduct, and his sense of values pass over to the pupil. These are possessions that far outweigh in value those others, since these are the factors which determine the spiritual education of the pupil. This means they determine the kind of person he is to be. Anyone who plays such a part in determining the life destinies of youth committed to his care need look no farther for satisfactions that will amply compensate for all the labor expended.

THE SELECTION OF TEACHERS

One might think that if the ideal education of the teacher which we have sketched in the foregoing is applied at all, the selection of candidates for the profession of teaching will be adequately provided for. That this ideal is far from realization was brought home to the American public with the publication of Bulletin Number Twenty Nine of The Carnegie Foundation for the Advancement of Teaching. The revelations brought forth by this study of high school and college students in Pennsylvania with regard to the type of students electing teaching as their future vocational calling are nothing less than shocking, and there is no reason to believe that these conditions are peculiar to Pennsylvania. Here are some of the findings:

Comparative Achievement of Teachers and Other Groups. The results concern two large groups of prospective teachers about to graduate from college—1,422 out of a total of 4,412 students tested in 1928, and 1,410 out of a total of 2,830 tested in 1932. In both tests the teachers' average was below the average total score for the entire group and was below all other group averages except those of the business, art, agriculture, and secretarial candidates. In the second test, the artists scored above the teachers.[1]

But when a comparison is made between students about to leave college and pupils finishing high school the revelations are still more startling. Here is the interpretation of Chart E p. 40, in this report:

> *Many Pupils Surpass Candidates for Teaching.* The median score of the teachers is 626. Above this are the scores of 12 per cent of the high school seniors; 22 per cent of them have scores above 25 per cent of the teachers. Seven per cent of the prospective teachers make lower scores than 36 per cent of the high school pupils. Thirteen per cent of the high-school participants score higher than 44 per cent of the college group.
>
> The true situation is probably somewhat worse than this, for the teacher group includes an undetermined number who expect to go forward to graduate work immediately and to teach in college or to engage in research. Although not necessarily of exceptional quality, these are probably above the mean of the distribution. If they were omitted, the average of those expecting to teach in high school would doubtless be lower.
>
> *Low Scores of Prospective Teachers in Science and Vocabulary.* The scores just described are total scores in a highly varied test including many kinds of knowledge. The lower insert on Chart E restricts the comparison to a knowledge of words. In a 100-word vocabulary test, high-school seniors are again matched with persons four years ahead of them, persons especially trained to teach high-school pupils. In spite of the limitation of this measure to verbal tools supposed to be familiar to every teacher, these two distributions overlap to such an extent as to bring students of both kinds into every score group but the lowest. Thirty per cent of the teacher group know fewer than 50 words of the test, while 29 per cent of the high-school pupils recognize 50 or more words. Nearly 18 per cent of the younger group just leaving high school have better vocabularies according to this test than

[1] William S. Learned and Ben D. Wood, *The Student and His Knowledge,* Bulletin Number Twenty Nine, The Carnegie Foundation for the Advancement of Teaching, 1938, pp. 38–39.

48 per cent of the older group on the point of leaving college "prepared" to teach. . . .

There can be no question that the tests disclose a condition which, if made the basis of a pupil-teacher relationship, would render healthy learning difficult if not impossible for many pupils.[1]

This is not a reassuring picture of the type of candidate entering the teaching profession in the public schools. One wonders whether the situation is any better among those preparing to teach in Catholic schools. There is one thing, however, that is strongly in their favor. As members of religious communities for the most part, teaching for them is a life calling not a stopgap until marriage looms or a more remunerative vocational opportunity opens up. But there is one situation in the Catholic system which leaves much room for improvement. This is increased opportunity for lay men and women to devote themselves to teaching as a life calling, with assurance of permanency and salaries that make economic security a reality. This is particularly a need in the field of college and university teaching.

SUGGESTED READINGS

Bagley, W. C., and J. A. Keith, *An Introduction to Teaching*, Macmillan, 1924, Chap. XI, analyses the personal qualities affecting a teacher's success.

Burton, William H., *Introduction to Education*, Appleton-Century, 1934, Chap. XXVII, "The Rewards of Educational Workers" and XXIX, "The Desirable Training and Personality for Educational Workers."

Chapman, J. Crosby and George S. Counts, *Principles of Education*, Houghton Mifflin, 1924, Problem 24, "To Whom Should Society Delegate the Educational Function?"

De la Salle, Saint Jean Baptiste, (tr. and intro. by De la Fontainerie), *Conduct of the Schools*, McGraw-Hill, 1935.

[1] *Ibid.*, pp. 41–43.

——, *Government of the Christian Schools*, Lovell and Gibson, Montreal, 1850, an old edition, includes the third part "The Government of the Governor," pp. 130–153 and also "The Twelve Virtues of a Good Master," pp. 1–52.

Holley, Charles Elmer, *High School Teachers Methods*, Garrard Press, 1937, Chap. XXVII. "Problems of Teacher Adjustment" gives a list of 26 points, "considered important by pupils in their teachers' personalities" pp. 454–455, followed by a "Rating Scale," p. 457.

Horn, John Louis, *The American Public School*, Century, 1926, Chap. XV. "Public Education as a Life Career," discusses the profession from the point of view of teacher and administrator.

James, William, *Talks to Teachers on Psychology*, Henry Holt, 1939, James, the philosopher, and his inspiring lectures for teachers reprinted after forty years with an "Introduction by John Dewey and William H. Kilpatrick."

Kirsch, Rev. Felix, *The Catholic Teacher's Companion*, Benziger Bros., 1924.

McKenny, Charles, *The Personality of the Teacher*, Row Peterson, 1910.

Morgan, George, "Can Teaching be Taught?," *The Commonweal*, July 16, 1936, an excellent discussion of this problem stressing the value of a period of apprenticeship, pp. 209–211.

Palmer, George Herbart, *The Ideal Teacher*, Houghton Mifflin, 1910, a monograph of 31 pages that should be read by every teacher interested in self-improvement.

Pottier, Rev. H., *Twelve Virtues of a Good Teacher*, Benziger Bros.

Schmitz, Sylvester, *The Adjustment of Teacher Training to Modern Educational Needs*, Abbey Student Press, Atchison, Kans., 1927, Part II is entitled "A Constructive Policy for the Professional Preparation of Teachers for Catholic Elementary and Secondary Schools," pp. 91–264.

Shields, Thomas E., *Philosophy of Education*, Catholic Ed. Press, 1917, Chap. XXIII. "The Teacher and His Training," discusses this problem from the point of view of Catholic education.

Thomas, Frank W., *Principles and Technique of Teaching*, Houghton Mifflin, 1927, Chap. XIX, "Personality and Personal Factors in Teaching," pp. 386–401.

GOVERNMENT AND RELIGIOUS EDUCATION

Religion, morality, and knowledge, being necessary to good government and the happiness of mankind, schools and the means of education shall forever be encouraged.

Northwest Ordinance of 1787

Let us with caution indulge the supposition, that morality can be maintained without religion. Whatever may be conceded to the influence of refined education on minds of peculiar structure, reason and experience both forbid us to expect, that national morality can prevail in exclusion of religious principle. . . . Of all dispositions and habits which lead to political prosperity, Religion and Morality are indispensable supports. In vain would man claim the tribute of patriotism who should labor to subvert these great pillars of human happiness, these firmest props of the duties of Men and Citizens.

George Washington, Farewell Address.

Our doctrine of equality and liberty, of humanity and charity, comes from our belief in the brotherhood of man through the fatherhood of God. The whole foundation of enlightened civilization, in government, in society, and in business, rests on religion. Unless our people are thoroughly instructed in its great truths, they are not fitted either to understand our institutions or provide them with adequate support. For our . . . schools to be neglectful of their responsibilities in this direction is to turn their graduates loose with simply an increased capacity to prey upon each other. Such a dereliction of duty would put in jeopardy the whole fabric of society.

Calvin Coolidge, address delivered at Phillips Academy, Massachusetts, while President of the United States

CHAPTER XVI

RIGHTS AND DUTIES IN EDUCATION

In the analysis which we have made of the pivotal problems of education, the fourth and last problem is "The Institution." This problem includes those activities commonly treated today under the term "administration." Since many of the phases of this problem are far removed from the considerations with which the philosopher of education commonly concerns himself, our task is to consider only those phases of deeper import and not attempt an evaluation of the many administrative techniques now being developed. These phases are two, both indicated by the title of this chapter: first, the right to determine the education of the child; and second, the duty to make that education a reality through intelligent planning and adequate support. The first of these problems, the right to educate, is settled in terms of moral considerations and the legal decisions made concerning it. The second, the duty of supporting education is much more intricate. Here ways and means change from time to time, and differ from country to country. Our purpose will be to suggest ways and means appropriate for ensuring adequate education for all in this country today. But by "adequate education" we mean education that has religion for its foundation. Supernaturalists will be satisfied with nothing less than this.

1. THE RIGHT TO EDUCATE

The general principle here may be stated: an individual, or a society, destined by nature for the achievement of a worthy end, has a right to the means necessary for the achievement of that end. It follows from this that the individual human being destined by nature for the advancement of his own perfection, has a right to education, even formal education within the school, since in civilized society, such education is necessary for the achievement of his natural end. But the immature child cannot exercise this right for himself. Therefore, those charged with the responsibility of his upbringing must exercise it for him. By natural right therefore, this responsibility and this duty rest in the first instance with parents. When parents fail to exercise this right, the responsibility passes to the state, the organization of individuals in society which has for its end promoting the general welfare. Certainly in a democracy some formal education of all individual citizens is necessary for the well-being of the state. From this fact arises the justice of compulsory school laws demanding that all citizens complete a minimum period of formal education either in organized institutions or under private tutors.

THE THREE SOCIETIES

But this is not a complete statement of the problem. Besides the family and the state which have rights in the education of children, there is a third society which has rights here. The rights of this third society are not merely natural; they are supernatural, since this third society by its very nature is supernatural. It is the Church. The late Holy Father, Pius XI, in his encyclical *The Christian Education of Youth*, has given a clear and authoritative statement of the relative rights of these three societies in the following words:

There are three necessary societies distinct from one another and yet harmoniously combined by God, into which man is born: two, namely the family and civil society, belong to the natural order. The third society, into which man is born when through baptism he receives the divine life of grace, is the Church: a society of the supernatural order and of universal extent; a perfect society, because it has in itself all the means required for its own end, which is the eternal salvation of mankind; hence it is supreme in its own domain. Consequently, education which is concerned with man as a whole, individually and socially, in the order of nature and in the order of grace, necessarily belongs to all these three societies, in due proportion, corresponding, according to the disposition of Divine Providence, to the coördination of their respective ends.

In its practical application this doctrine means that the supernatural right of the Church is made effective through the exercise of the natural rights of parents, under the guidance of the Church. This is the problem discussed in works presenting the ethics of Aris-thomistic philosophy.[1] The priority of the rights of the parent is established over those of the state on the principle that the family itself is prior to the state. The end of the state is the protection and welfare of individuals and families. If all states were destroyed through universal anarchy, individuals and families would still exist and they would bring forth a new state to safeguard their well-being. Hence the rights of the state in the education of children are secondary to those of the parents.[2]

This doctrine is denied today by all totalitarian states. In Chapter II we have quoted *The Political Doctrine of Fascism* by Alfredo Rocco who states clearly: "For Fascism, society is the end, the individual is the means and its whole life consists

---

[1] e.g., Charles C. Miltner, *The Elements of Ethics*, Chapter XV, "The Educational Problem."

[2] Thomas Verner Moore, *Principles of Ethics*, Lippincott, 1935, "State's Right Secondary to Family's Right," p. 256.

in using individuals for its social ends." [1]   This is the very op-
posite of the "inalienable rights" of the American constitution.
Nevertheless the attempt was made in the state of Oregon in
1922 to deprive parents of their natural right to determine the
education of their children. A law was passed which compelled
parents to send children between the ages of eight and sixteen
to public schools. The issue was brought to the United States
supreme court and on June 1st, 1925, Justice McReynolds delivered the following decision:

> We think it entirely plain that the Act of 1922 unreasonably
> interferes with the liberty of parents and guardians to direct the
> upbringing and education of children under their control. As
> often heretofore pointed out, rights guaranteed by the Constitu-
> tion may not be abridged by legislation which has no reasonable
> relation to some purpose within the competency of the state.
> The fundamental theory of liberty upon which all governments
> in this Union repose excludes any general power of the state to
> standardize its children by forcing them to accept instruction
> from public teachers only. The child is not the mere creature of
> the state; those who nurture him and direct his destiny have the
> right coupled with the high duty, to recognize and prepare him
> for additional obligations. [2]

Thus it seems settled for all time in this country that "the child
is not the mere creature of the state" and that with parents
rests the right to determine his education. But rights and
duties are correlative terms. [3] The right guaranteed by the
constitution and clarified by the decision of Justice McReynolds imposes on parents a "high duty." To resolve the relative
duties of parents and state in regard to the education of children is a much more intricate problem. An adequate insight

[1] See complete quotation, p. 30.
[2] *Oregon School Cases*, Belvedere Press, Baltimore, 1925, transcript of Record,
Supreme Court of the United States, Oct. term, 1924, No. 583, p. 942.
[3] See Figure 14, "Rights and Duties in Three Societies," p. 176.

into this problem demands that we review briefly the development of education in this country during the past three hundred years.

2. DUTIES OF PARENTS AND STATE IN EDUCATION

It might seem at first sight that since in the large the interests of parents and society for the welfare of children are identical, there would be little occasion for conflict to arise in planning an educational program to advance those interests. Such, however, has not been the case. There is general agreement concerning the necessity of thorough training in the elements, "the three R's," reading, 'riting and 'rithmetic, but when it is the question of the fourth "R," religion, the situation is entirely different. Even if all were agreed that the child is entitled to all five phases of what Butler calls the "spiritual inheritance" of the race and that the religious inheritance is one of those five; even if it were recognized that "without them all, he cannot become a truly educated or a truly cultivated man," [1] nevertheless, the question immediately arises, "which religion shall be taught?"

THE SECULARIZATION OF AMERICAN EDUCATION

A glance back through the three centuries during which this country has reached its present state of development reveals that in the beginning all education was fundamentally religious. This statement is true not merely of the education given by the early Catholic missionaries to the Indians, notably in the southwest (an education which played no part in the development of the American system), but also of the beginnings in New England. The first legislation was passed in Massachusetts in 1642 charging the town selectmen to see that parents provided for the education of their children in reading,

[1] For complete quotation, see p. 280.

suitable employment, the chief laws of the colony and the *principles of religion*. The Old Deluder Satan Act (1647) said to be "the most important law in American educational history" receives its name from the fact that it required every town of fifty householders to appoint a master "to teach all such children as shall resort to him to read and write" so that knowledge of the scriptures would not be denied them by "that old deluder Satan." [1]   All schools established as a result of this law were definitely Protestant in purpose and in control. The first Academy established by Franklin in Philadelphia in 1751 was to be nonsectarian in control but the curriculum included the study of "morality and religion." During the first half of the 19th century, although most schools were established by religious denominations, they commonly had some share in the public funds. But sectarianism was rife at this time and the fight for funds to support denominational schools served to embitter the issue. Horace Mann, the leader of the "Great Awakening" in Massachusetts in the late 30's, at first a Calvinist, later a Unitarian, advocated the reading of the Bible in the schools without comment. When, however, the controversy between the advocates of church- and state-controlled schools arose, he became the apostle of the secularized public school, with the word "public" interpreted as meaning tax-supported and state-controlled. [2]

THE BISHOP HUGHES CONTROVERSY

In New York City public funds for denominational schools was the accepted procedure. St. Peter's School, in 1806, requested and received a share of the public funds and other Catholic schools were established later on the same basis. The

---

[1] Edgar M. Draper and Alexander C. Roberts, *Principles of American Secondary Education*, Century, 1932, p. 30.

[2] T. Brosnahan, "The Education Fact," *Cath. Quarterly Review*, Vol. 30, p. 515.

largest organization was the "Public School Society" which though regarded as nondenominational was chartered to teach "the sublime truths of religion and morality contained in the Holy Scriptures." [1] All its schools were definitely Protestant. In 1824 the legislature empowered the City Council to name the institutions that were to receive funds. In doing this, the Council cut off the Catholic schools as well as other denominational schools leaving only the orphan asylums a share in the public funds. As a result, most of the money set aside for school purposes went to the Public School Society. In 1840 Governor Seward recommended to the legislature the establishment of schools in which the pupils would be taught by teachers of the same race and faith. Encouraged by this, Catholics in New York City, joined by the Scotch Presbyterians and the Hebrew Congregation petitioned the City Council for a share in the school funds. This petition was rejected. Bishop Hughes then personally took charge of the fight. On the basis of simple justice, since the taxes of Catholics were paid into the school funds, he requested a share in these funds, at the same time stipulating that the Catholic schools "should be under the same policy and regulations as those of the Public School Society; the same hours, the same order, the same exercises, even the same inspection," guaranteeing that "nothing against the creed of any other denomination shall be introduced." [2] But politics had entered the situation and the petition was overwhelmingly defeated. Next the fight was carried to the State Capital at Albany. Action was delayed until after the elections. Feeling became very bitter and the "No-popery" cry rang throughout the state. Governor Seward again brought the matter before the Legislature in 1842. But

[1] Burns & Kohlbrenner, *History of Catholic Education in the United States*, Benziger Bros., 1937, p. 158.
[2] John Hughes, *Complete Works*, Vol. I, p. 200.

the Legislature ended the controversy by creating a Board of Education for New York City, at the same time decreeing that no funds were to be given to any school in which "any religious sectarian doctrine or tenet should be taught, inculcated, or practised."

Bishop Hughes beaten in the fight for a share of the public school funds adopted a new policy. If the state would not meet its obligation to help parents establish schools to which they could in conscience send their children, the Church would carry this burden alone. "Let parochial schools be established and maintained everywhere." he declared; "The day has come in which the school is more necessary than the church." In 1884 the 3rd Plenary Council of Baltimore in effect extended this principle to the whole United States by decreeing that "I. Near each church, where it does not exist, a parochial school is to be erected within two years from the promulgation of this Council," and "IV. All Catholic parents are bound to send their children to the parochial schools." [1] Nevertheless, in spite of the great sacrifices of Catholic parents in carrying the burden of double taxation for both parochial and public schools and in spite of the enthusiasm and energy of pastors expended in building parochial schools, it is estimated that today hardly more than half the Catholic children of the country are in Catholic schools.

THE SOCIAL VALUE OF RELIGION

Today after one hundred years of secularized education in the "public" schools, a change is slowly taking place in the mind of the American people. The great increase in juvenile crime in this country is one factor making the American people inquire whether education in the secularized school is all that

[1] Burns & Kohlbrenner, *History of Catholic Education in the United States*, pp. 143–144.

it should be.   A committee of the U. S. Senate under the chair-manship of Senator Royal S. Copeland of New York investi-gating crime and racketeering found that the cost of crime in the nation is approximately thirteen billion dollars annually, that this staggering sum represents one-fourth of our national income, and that it is more than three times our total expendi-ture for education.   The committee also found that the average age of criminals in America is 23 years, that the largest age group is 19 years, and the next largest 18 years.   These age groups clearly indicate that crime in America today is com-mitted largely by comparatively young people.   "Any effort, therefore, by the duly constituted authorities of government and social welfare to reduce crime must be made in behalf of the young people of the nation, many of whom are now in our public schools, or have recently left public school instruction." [1] This movement is typical of what is happening in public school systems throughout the country.   But the question is, how ef-fective can these programs of character education be, if the reli-gious basis on which they should rest, belief in God and a sacred obligation to keep His law, is denied them?

Even if the church and home should do a good job in bring-ing the religious inheritance to children, are not the minis-trations of the secularized school in which this religious in-heritance is denied them having an effect upon the work of the church and home that is the negation of all they are attempting to do?   In the mind of youth the school is teaching him every-thing necessary for the good life.   If religion is not a part of that teaching, religion cannot be important for life.   The effect upon the mind of youth of such teaching can only be disastrous. This social value of religion as one of the foundations for build-

[1] Mimeographed report entitled "The Washington Experiment in Character Education" by Frank W. Ballou, Supt. of Schools, Washington, D. C., read and distributed at the Coöperative Test Service Conference in New York City, Nov. 1st, 1934.

ing the qualities of good citizenship has always been part of the American tradition. The quotations introducing this chapter (p. 518) from the Northwest Ordinance of 1787, from Washington's Farewell Address, and from an address by President Coolidge all bear this out. The statement by President Coolidge is particularly forceful:

> The whole foundation of enlightened civilization, in government, in society, and in business, rests on religion. Our doctrine of equality and liberty, of humanity and charity, comes from our belief in the brotherhood of man through the fatherhood of God. Unless our people are thoroughly instructed in its great truths, they are not fitted either to understand our institutions or provide them with adequate support. For . . . schools to be neglectful of their responsibilities in this direction is to turn their graduates loose with simply an increased capacity to prey upon each other. Such a dereliction of duty would put in jeopardy the whole fabric of society.

This obligation to teach the "great truths" rests upon *all* schools. Since by its very nature the secularized school cannot do so, that is all the more reason why the state should make available its resources to bring into existence other schools in which youth through the ministrations of religious education will be "fitted to understand our institutions." Other countries have faced the same difficulty squarely and have worked out solutions that are giving results far beyond anything our secularized school can ever hope to accomplish. In Canada, England, and Holland and other countries, tax-supported schools are religious schools. Nicholas Murray Butler has often called attention to the fact that the institution not directly under public administration and control is a public institution in the best sense of the term in that *it renders a great public service*. This is the meaning of the term when used to designate the famous English Public Schools, all privately controlled. Dr. George Johnson has used the term "public" in this way referring to the Catholic school as the "privately administered public school." [1] It is public in that it renders a great public service instilling into its pupils the only foundation for true patriotism which is religion. The secularized school of which Horace Mann became the apostle was a stupid and un-American way to meet the problem. We see now that it was about as intelligent as another enthusiasm of his, discovering vocational capacity through phrenology. We now present briefly how other countries have been working out solutions of this problem.

3. STATE SCHOOLS TRANSMITTING THE RELIGIOUS INHERITANCE

We need not leave this continent to see how this is being done. Canada, our neighbor to the north, furnishes a striking illustration of tax-supported schools, that is, "public" schools that make definite provision for passing on to pupils their religious inheritance. In the province of Quebec this is done with justice to all. Since 1869 a Board of Commissioners is elected by law in every school municipality for Catholics only or for Protestants only, depending upon the religious affiliations of the majority of the inhabitants. But any number of the taxpayers may dissent and form a separate board of trustees. The "separate" schools in Quebec, therefore, may be either Protestant or Catholic. Since, however, 85 per cent of the inhabitants are Catholic the vast majority of the public schools are Catholic. "Separate" schools receive towards their support the taxes of the dissentient minority, and teach the religious formularies of their respective denominations. "Otherwise, the courses of study, examination requirements, qualification of teachers, etc., are the same for both public and

[1] See complete quotation, p. 542.

separate schools." [1]   Thus in large cities like Montreal it is not unusual to find a Catholic school on one side of the street and a Protestant school on the other, but all are "public" schools in the sense that they are tax-supported. In addition, they contribute a distinct public service by making religion an integral part of their education.

Provision is made in the other provinces also for "separate" schools but not with the same degree of fairness as is done in Quebec. The source of school funds is a special tax assessed against property in the municipality in which the schools are situated. Today the great source of income is the properties of corporations and publicly owned utilities. In Quebec taxes from these sources are paid into a neutral fund and divided between the two types of schools in proportion to school attendance. This has not been the practice in Ontario. If an incorporated company could establish that a specific proportion of its stock was owned by Catholics it might allot a corresponding proportion of its taxes to the support of Catholic "separate" schools. Otherwise all its taxes went to the support of the "public" schools. Catholics had no share in the levy made on publicly owned utilities. To what an extent this has worked unfairly against Catholic "separate" schools is shown by this statement:

> In Ottawa, for example, where the Protestant and Catholic school population is about equal, out of a total assessment against companies and publicly owned utilities of 45,500,000, 44,000,000 are assessed for the support of public schools and only 1,500,000 for separate schools purposes. Were the two rates equal, therefore, the separate schools would have to educate the same number of pupils as the public schools, with about one-fifth of the revenue. This being impossible the separate school board has been obliged to fix a rate of 14.80 mills, as compared with the public school rate of 7.44, leading weak-kneed Catholics,

[1] Peter Sandiford, *Comparative Education*, Dutton, 1918, p. 358.

who care more for their pockets than for their principles, to transfer their support to the public schools and thus still further increase the inequality.   In Toronto, to cite another example,
though the separate schools, as compared with the public schools,
stand 1 to 6 in service, they stand only 1 to 91 in taxes received.[1]

United by the injustice of this situation the Catholic switched
allegiance from the Conservative party to the Liberals and
brought pressure on the government to change the law.   They
were partially successful in this in 1937.   The new legislation
does not change the situation as regards publicly owned utilities but it does change it in the case of corporations.   Companies are now divided into those in which it is deemed possible
to ascertain the wishes of the shareholders and those in which
this is thought to be impossible.   In the case of the latter defined as those whose head offices are situated, and more than
50 per cent of whose shares are held, outside of the province,
or those whose presidents certify that the shareholders are too
scattered for him to ascertain their wishes, "the school taxes
are to be divided between schools in the municipality where
the taxes are payable.   If the companies affected act fairly,
particularly those in class B, the gain in revenue to the Catholic schools should be very substantial.   For example, it is cal-
culated that this will amount in Ottawa to $70,000, and in
Toronto to $170,000 per annum." [2]

ENGLISH TAX-SUPPORTED RELIGIOUS SCHOOLS

Public support for schools belonging to religious denominations in England dates back to lesislation passed in 1902.
Since that time there are two types of public elementary
schools.   One type, the Council schools, are called "provided"
schools because the school building is provided by the local

[1] W. L. Scott, "Ontario Schools," *Commonweal*, June 12, 1936, pp. 180–181.
[2] *Ibid.*, p. 181.

Council as well as maintained thereby. The other type, voluntary schools, are called "nonprovided" because the local educational authority, the Council, does not provide the school building. This may be done by any religious denomination with the approval of the Council. When that approval has been received, however, and the building furnished, the Council maintains the school, renting it from the owners at a charge sufficient to cover the cost of reasonable "wear and tear." The voluntary or "nonprovided" schools are governed by a board of six managers, four of whom are appointed by the trustees of the religious body owning the school and two by the Local Educational Authority that is, the County, City, or Borough Council. To these managers is given the appointment and dismissal of teachers, subject to a veto by the Local Educational Authority.[1] The distribution of the two types of schools in England and Wales for March 31, 1931 with their enrollments is given in the following table:

TABLE III.—PROVIDED AND NONPROVIDED SCHOOLS IN ENGLAND[2]

SCHOOLS	TYPE	NUMBER	AVERAGE ENROLLMENT
Provided	Council	9,698	3,696,360
Nonprovided (voluntary)	1. Church of England	9,598	1,403,765
	2. Wesleyan	113	20,866
	3. Catholic	1,188	376,782
	4. Jewish	13	5,291
	5. Others	257	32,077
Total		20,867	5,535,141

From this table it is evident that the "nonprovided" schools outnumber the provided (11,149 to 9,698), but their enroll-

[1] S. J. Gosling, "The State and Religious Education—The English Way,' *Catholic Educational Review*, June, 1935, pp. 321–331.

[2] Adapted from Kandel's *Comparative Education*, p. 364.

ment is much less (1,842,412 to 3,696,360). This is accounted for by the fact that the majority of the Church of England schools are small schools in rural districts. It is a question how long the "nonprovided schools" will be in the majority. Sandiford states it thus: "School buildings do not last forever and no church seems rich enough to pay for the erection of a costly modern school building. The rate of transference of voluntary schools from the control of a religious denomination to that of a publicly elected nondenominational council is fairly rapid at present and will probably be accelerated in the future." [1] The one exception to this transfer from "nonprovided" to "provided" schools is the case of the Catholic schools, which are continuing to increase.

The "provided" or Council schools, however, are not secularized to the same degree that the American public school is. Though "no religious catechism or religious formulary which is distinctive of any particular denomination is to be taught," religious instruction is given in all schools. Kandel lists four elements in this religious instruction: (1) Bible reading without comment, (2) the Apostle's Creed, (3) the Lord's Prayer, and (4) the Ten Commandments. [2] Usually the first period of the day from 9:00 to 9:30 is set aside for this religious instruction but the period is often curtailed through the taking of attendance, etc. In the "nonprovided" schools, religion forms an integral part of the curriculum and the management has a voice in the selection of teachers, particularly with regard to their qualifications to teach religion.

Secondary education in England stands in sharp contrast with that of the United States in that almost all secondary schools charge fees. Provision is made for public support of schools controlled by religious denominations by the "Grant"

[1] *Op. cit.*, pp. 198–199.
[2] *Op. cit.*, p. 363.

list. To be placed on this list a school must submit to inspection and meet certain definite standards. Once it is placed on the list, it is granted a share in the national funds available for this purpose. One other condition must be complied with, namely, offering each year special places (the term that has replaced "free places") to the amount of at least 25 per cent of the previous year's enrollment. These special places are awarded on the basis of competitive examinations but only those children are eligible whose parents' income is £3 to £4 per week, subject to changes that may be made in view of the fees charged by schools and special circumstances in particular areas. In 1922–23 sixty-seven Catholic schools were on the "Grant List" enrolling 17,782 pupils; only fourteen of which were for boys with fifty-three for girls.[1]

HOLLAND'S RELIGIOUS PUBLIC SCHOOLS

In contrast with this situation in England where denominational schools are laboring under a severe financial handicap, two countries have led the way in making available public funds for the support of schools to which parents with deep religious convictions can send their children without violating their consciences, Scotland with its Education Act of 1918 and the Netherlands in 1920. The details of the arrangement in Holland are now available in English [2] and we will give a brief description of it here.

Holland achieved its independence in 1648 through the Peace of Munster. But for 200 years Catholics were not free to have their own schools. The Education Act of 1848 placed the Catholics of Holland in the same position that Catholics now hold in the United States, *i.e.*, they could establish denomina-

---

[1] Draper and Roberts, *op. cit.*, p. 84.

[2] Dr. Verhoeven, *The Netherlands Solution of the Education Question*, Roman Catholic Central Bureau of Education at the Hague, 1938.

tional schools without governmental licensing and control but also without any share in public funds. The Dutch Catholics were not satisfied with this victory. Recognizing the intrinsic unfairness of this situation on democratic principles and the impossibility of the financial resources of parents competing with those of the state, they demanded absolute "Pecuniary Parity of Position." The issue was fought out at times with bitterness but always in the democratic way, through the appeal to reason. Victory was finally won in 1917 by the revision of Article 192 of the Netherlands constitution, the article which deals with education. In its revised form this article is known as Article 200 and it lays down the principles which the Act of 1920 put into operation, granting absolute parity of position to private and public schools alike in the distribution of school funds. The outstanding feature of this victory was that it was not won by Catholics fighting alone, but by a coalition of Catholics and Protestants forming the Right in Parliament. With rare good sense both groups saw that a nation given over to purely secular education was an open invitation to the various "isms" leading inevitably to state totalitarianism. As a result public schools today in Holland are Protestant, Catholic, or Liberal. How does the law operate that makes this possible?

1. *The School Plant.* The private managers of a corporate Institution or Association wishing to establish a school must deposit in the public treasury a guarantee of 15 per cent of the total estimated cost of construction and must establish the fact that the number of prospective pupils equals the minimum fixed by law. The municipality satisfies itself that all conditions fixed by law as regards hygiene, safety, and equipment, etc., have been complied with. When the school is in operation the municipality pays interest on the fund deposited and after twenty years returns the entire amount. If the number of pupils registered falls below three fourths of the fixed amount, the cash guarantee is re-

tained by the municipality and in certain cases it takes over ownership of the property.

2. *Maintenance.* Expenditures for light, heat, cleaning, and wear and tear are all paid for out of public tax money. Improvements in equipment and materials are shared equally by all schools.

3. *Curriculum.* Government-appointed school inspectors have control over instruction in the secular subjects of all schools but "the law guarantees full liberty concerning the creeds upon which any private school bases its teaching." [1] The only restriction is that no creed shall be such as "to disseminate tenets incompatible with morals or to incite to disobedience to the laws of the country." [2]

4. *Teachers.* The number of teachers is fixed by law in proportion to the number of pupils. All teachers in all schools must meet the same qualifications and all receive the same salaries. The manager of a private school is free in selecting teachers. He pays them directly and is reimbursed by the government. If a teacher is dismissed he may appeal to a board on which all parties are equally represented.

5. *Extent.* These provisions operate in all types of schools, elementary, secondary, and teacher-training institutions.[3]

From this brief presentation one can well understand that Catholics and Protestants alike are well satisfied with the situation. Schools controlled by Christian bodies have increased over 100 per cent during the twenty years that the law has been in operation. In 1935–36 there were 2,680 Catholic schools in Holland each standing next to the parish church. "Nearly half a million Catholic children are there receiving elementary instruction by 13,370 teachers (3,914 religious and 9,456 lay-teachers." [4] The reassuring thing about the permanency of the situation is that the law has not resulted, as was

[1] *Ibid.*, p. 34.

[2] *Ibid.*, p. 35.

[3] Adapted from Thomas J. Quigley, "A Lesson in Democracy," *Catholic Educational Review*, June, 1939, pp. 365–379.

[4] Dr. Verhoeven, *The Netherlands Solution of the Education Question*, Roman Catholic Central Bureau of Education, The Hague, Holland, 1938, p. 57.

feared, in an undue multiplication of small schools by many groups.

4. REGAINING PUBLIC SUPPORT FOR TRANSMITTING THE RELIGIOUS INHERITANCE

In the United States the depression of 1930 and the years following brought home to the Catholic public and to the bishops of the country the magnitude of the task they had undertaken in pledging themselves to the principle "every Catholic child in a Catholic school." In several small communities where the parish found it impossible to continue the parochial school, the building was rented to the public authorities for a nominal sum and the school continued with the payment of teachers' salaries out of public funds. Since these salaries were less than one third of those paid to teachers in the public schools, this meant a considerable saving for the community which otherwise would have had to erect another building with the employment of additional teachers at the usual salaries. Today with financial conditions materially improved over 1930 and the years immediately following, the conviction is growing among Catholics that state aid to help finance their school system is not only a right of Catholic taxpayers; it is their duty to demand it. As we quoted Sandiford above, writing of conditions in England with regard to the denominational, that is, the so called "nonprovided" schools, "School buildings do not last forever." [1] With only half our children in Catholic schools today, it is evidently impossible to continue this building program unaided, when already it is becoming increasingly difficult to keep our present schools and equipment in condition comparable with that of the tax-supported schools, to say nothing of doubling the number of school buildings to take care of the remaining half of the Cath-

[1] *Op. cit.*, see quotation above, p. 533.

olic children now in public schools.   As Thomas J. Quigley says of the United States in an article describing the arrangement for denominational schools in Holland: "State aid is our only salvation." [1]

We have briefly described above how three of the leading democracies of the world, Canada, England, and Holland are making provision out of public funds for schools in which the religious inheritance is passed on to pupils.   This is the best means that democracy can use to insure its own continuance. In Chapter II, "The Four Philosophies of Education," we have called attention to the fact that the countries outstanding today in their attack on religion, Germany and Russia, are the two where the doctrine of the inalienable rights of man has been repudiated and totalitarianism is the official philosophy of state.   In the quotations introducing this Chapter (p. 518) we have quoted American sources beginning with the Northwest Ordinance of 1787, emphasizing the fact that religious belief and practise is the only guarantee of stable government in a democracy.   The argument may be briefly stated thus: Democracy rests upon the doctrine of man's inalienable rights; every right a man possesses carries with it the duty of respecting those same rights possessed by his fellow citizens; duties, to be effective in the lives of the great generality of men, must have a sanction, *i.e.*, a universally accepted principle demanding performance of those duties; the one principle that has been successful in making this demand and thereby making democracy possible is "The Fatherhood of God and the Brotherhood of Man," the very core of the Christian religion.   "He that loveth his neighbor hath fulfilled the law." [2] This principle must be planted in the minds and hearts of youth

[1] Thomas J. Quigley, "A Lesson in Democracy," *Catholic Educational Review*, June, 1939, p. 366.
[2] Romans XIII, 8.

RIGHTS AND DUTIES IN EDUCATION   539

if it is to control their conduct; such indoctrination (if we may call it that) is effective only in schools teaching religion. The force of this argument seems to be gradually dawning upon the minds of Americans. We have a striking illustration of this in the *Report of the Special Committee on Economical and Efficient Education* of the New York State Chamber of Commerce. Here is one statement in the report: "Accordingly we place *First* on our list of things necessary to produce 'The Schools New York State Wants' a *Deep, True, Religious Understanding and Viewpoint.*" [1] That such a religious understanding and viewpoint be inculcated without teaching the belief and practice of some "particular church," is impossible. This, at least, is the conviction of Catholics, and the Catholic school system is their method of meeting the situation.

Turning now to the task of bringing it about that denominations wishing to conduct their own schools share in the school funds to which they have contributed through taxation, we must realize that there is a long fight ahead. It means re-educating the American public to recognize the justice of these claims. Here we are confronted with vested interests that will fight every foot of the way. It was one outside the Catholic Church who declared recently: "*Organized education is one of the largest rackets in this country, and the teachers' colleges, especially the influential ones . . . are the gangs which control what goes on,* in ways that do not always meet the eye and would not stand inspection. To call education a *racket* is, of course, to speak metaphorically, but the comparison has point. Reforming education will have to use racket-busting techniques or it will not succeed." [2] An illustration of a technique in the public school systems of several states that takes on the

---

[1] *Commonweal*, August 25, 1939, p. 405.

[2] Mortimer J. Adler, "The Crisis in Contemporary Education," *The Social Frontier*, February, 1939, p. 145.

nature of a racket is this: the allotment of state funds to school municipalities is made on the basis of total school enrollment; in this total enrollment is included the enrollment of the parochial schools as well as that of the public schools; not one cent of this money goes to the parochial schools which, in some cities where this practice is in operation, furnish almost half of the total enrollment.

The systems giving public support to religious schools in vogue in Canada, England, and Holland in all probability do not suggest a way out of this difficulty for religious denominations in the United States.   Here we are confronted with a great multiplicity of religious sects in sharp contrast with Holland where Catholics and Calvinists united on a common program of reform.   The separate tax funds of Canada would strike the American mind as too complicated and too open to abuse, and the "nonprovided" schools of England are not what we should strive for.   But there is one way that suggests a possible solution if the voters of any community can be won over to it.   American public school systems have now developed elaborate accounting systems.   Municipalities figure to a fraction of a cent how much it costs to educate a child for a year.   If a denominational school were to receive for each pupil it educates a substantial portion of the *per capita* cost of educating a child in the public schools of its city it could operate successfully even to the extent of keeping the building and equipment in good condition.   Of course this would mean that the school must undergo inspection by the public authorities before it would be entitled to share in public funds.   But should we not welcome such inspection?   We claim that our schools, in addition to teaching the religious inheritance, are as efficient in teaching the secular branches as the public schools.   Such inspection would be an added stimulus to bring this about in any school that did not measure up to standard.

This, at least, is the way it has worked among Catholic colleges holding membership in the voluntary associations. It is recognized by the Catholic colleges of the Middle West that the greatest single influence in improving the training of their faculties has been the North Central Association of College and Secondary Schools.

If what happened in Ohio, when an attempt was made by the Catholics of the state to share in a school emergency fund set up by the state to keep schools open during the depths of the depression, is any indication of what would happen in a city where denominational schools demanded a share in the school funds on a *per capita* basis as suggested above, we can see that it is going to be no easy task to have such a measure adopted in any community. Immediately in Ohio the cry "separation of Church and State" was raised. It was organized and led by sectarian ministers, though one would think they could see that the secularized school has been one of the big influences in depleting their churches. The Protestants in Holland saw this clearly and uniting with Catholics took steps to remedy the situation. In this country, besides Catholics, only the Episcopalians and Lutherans with some few other isolated cases have maintained elementary schools in which their religious formularies are taught. Many of these disappeared during the depression and from all indications they will be slow to revive. Dr. George Johnson made a fitting reply to this objection of union of church and state when Catholics in New York state demanded the use of school busses for Catholic children going to parochial schools.

> Catholics do not forget for one moment that the refusal of the State to permit them to use the money they contribute through taxes for education to provide for their children a schooling that accords with the dictates of their conscience, is a limitation imposed on their religious freedom. . . .

Today the State is putting certain advantages at the disposal of children, such as transportation to and from school, medical care, free textbooks, recreational facilities, school lunches, and opportunities for vocational training that belong to all the children of the United States just because they are children, and should not be denied to certain children simply because they do not happen to be enrolled in state-supported schools. . . . There would be as much logic in forbidding the Catholic child the use of tax-provided streets and sidewalks on his way to school as in depriving him of tax-provided bus transportation or tax-provided school lunches. To conjure up the bugaboo of union of Church and State in this connection is nothing more than a cowardly refusal to face the facts and to meet them in an American way.

In reality the same could be said of the failure to date of the American people to face the controversy concerning *public support of the privately administered public school*, for such in effect is what the Catholic school is in the United States. We estimate that one-half of the Catholic children of the United States are in tax-supported schools. . . . The State compels them to go to school and the State does not supply them with the kind of schools that accord with the dictates of their conscience. The State is ready to spend millions of dollars to teach them how to weave baskets, to play in rhythmic orchestras, to learn trades, to acquire professional training, in a word to receive the kind and the degree of education for which they seem fitted, and yet not one penny is available for the one thing necessary—for that education in religion which is the only ultimate safeguard for the institutions of liberty and democracy.[1]

The tax situation is going to be as difficult an obstacle to overcome as religious bigotry. Public support of the "privately administered public school" (which now in the United States generally means the Catholic school) would relieve Catholics of the double taxation they are now carrying in supporting both the public and the Catholic school, but it would raise the tax burden for the community as a whole and

[1] George Johnson, "The Catholic School and American Democracy," *Catholic Educational Review*, May, 1936, pp. 260–261.

with the continued increase in taxes which has been going on during the past decade, this will be no easy obstacle to surmount.

STATE CONSTITUTIONS AND THE RELIGIOUS INHERITANCE

A still more difficult obstacle to overcome is the fact that many state constitutions forbid the appropriation of public funds for the support of denominational schools. Burton Confrey gives a summary of this situation in these words:

> Arkansas, Iowa, Maine, Maryland, North Carolina, Rhode Island, Vermont, and West Virginia are the only states without constitutional provisions against appropriating public funds for denominational schools. Article VIII, Section 2, of the Connecticut Constitution (1818) is characteristic: "No law shall ever be made authorizing said school fund to be diverted to any other use than the encouragement and support of public and common schools." [1]

It would seem from this that the fight for a share in public funds for denominational schools should be begun in Rhode Island since the Catholic population there today is dominant. With success achieved in one state the movement would receive a great impetus to spread to others as conditions proved favorable.

At present there is little sentiment for attempting to change the state constitutions. Many of them were written when religious bigotry was at its height in this country, and, although this situation has changed radically for the better, it would be unwise to do anything which might arouse antireligious movements like the Know-nothing Party of the 1850's, the American Protective Association (A.P.A.) movement of the 1890's, or the Ku Klux Klan of the 1920's. If we cannot expect to change

[1] Burton Confrey, *Secularism in American Education*, Catholic Univ., 1931, p. 129.

the state constitutions, is there any way in which it may become possible for members of denominations to have returned to them at least part of the money they are now paying to support schools to which they cannot in conscience send their children? The Federal government is now demonstrating a way out of this difficulty. Of the $50,000,000 N.Y.A. allotment in 1935, $20,000,000 was for student aid. Students may attend any private or church college at their own selection and when they have been certified by the institutions as in attendance, they receive checks from the Federal fund to help pay their tuition. In the same way it is suggested that states could pay to parents a portion of what it would cost to educate their children in the public schools and thus aid them to educate their children in schools of their own choosing. An arrangement could be worked out "by which parents would receive a voucher which they could give to the school of their choice for the education of their children. This check or draft of the State could be cashed only by some school." [1]

The recent *Report of the Advisory Committee* of the President recommends that (1) health and welfare service, (2) aid for reading materials, (3) transportation and (4) scholarships be made available to privately controlled schools.[2] Whether or not this suggestion is the way out of the difficulty, it is evident that many thoughtful men and women are beginning to see that a way must be found. It must have been something of a shock to the professors of education attending the lectures of Sir Michael Sadler delivered at Columbia University in 1930 when he said:

> Sooner or later in all countries, governments will have to find a synthesis which will give a place in the national system both to

[1] Richard J. Gabel, *Public Funds for Church and Private Schools*, Murray and Heister, Washington, D. C., 1937, p. 763.
[2] Floyd W. Reeves (chairman), *Report of the Advisory Committee*, Government Printing Office, Washington, D. C., pp. 54, 86, 198.

Catholic and to secular schools, and to that great variety of types of schools which lie between those sharp extremes. Here, I am well aware, the view which I submit to you is in direct opposition to that now prevailing, possibly for good and sufficient reasons, in the United States, and in those countries in which the political philosophy of American education has most widely prevailed. But it is not counter to the judgment of many American educators who live in countries in which schools conducted upon a specifically religious basis are not shut out from a share in subsidies derived from public funds.[1]

As these "many American educators" of whom Sir Michael speaks, return to the United States, their influence should be helpful in developing a more favorable attitude towards denominational schools in this country.   There is a constantly growing mass of evidence today indicating that this development is already in process.   Take, for example, this statement by Dr. F. E. Johnson of the Federal Council of the Churches of America: "Protestants are coming to see that Catholics are right in holding that religion and education cannot be separated without injury to both."   He considers the traditional Protestant position on this point "inept and outmoded" and believes that the stand he takes "is gaining ground in Protestant thinking." [2]   Another sign is the growth in membership of the National Conference of Church-Related Colleges organized a few years ago.   The National Conference has a paid Executive Secretary with offices in Washington, D. C.; it holds annual meetings and sponsors regional meetings of state and regional conferences of Church-Related Colleges, the programs of which emphasize the idea that religion is an integral part of higher education, with both Protestant and Catholic college representatives appearing on the programs.   This coöperation of

[1] Sir Michael Sadler, *The Outlook in Secondary Education*, Bureau of Publications, Teachers College, Columbia Univ., 1930, p. 23.
[2] F. E. Johnson, "Religion in the Public Schools," *Religion: A Digest*, a quarterly published at Arlington, Va., Autumn Number, 1939.

Church-Related colleges shows what might be done if all truly religious-minded educators would adopt the same attitude with regard to the necessity of church-related elementary and secondary schools. How *not* to proceed in this campaign of re-education is well illustrated by this pronouncement reported in the 1939 press as delivered in Trinity Church, Manhattan, by Dr. Bernard I. Bell of the Protestant Episcopal Church:

> Our schools should not merely teach religion as a subject, but rather teach every single subject with a God-ward point of view. Let those schools be subject to State supervision, that there may be insurance within them of trained teachers and sound method. Let the State keep them up to the mark. And finally—this is very important—let the State pay for them. Why not? They will be doing the State's educational work for her, doing it better than Godless schools ever can. There is nothing startling or unprecedented about the State's paying for religious schools. In England it is done—not only for schools conducted by the Church of England, but for Roman Catholic schools, Protestant schools, Jewish schools. And the constitution of the New Ireland, adopted in 1937, provides that there shall be State aid for schools conducted by the religious bodies, and no discrimination between the denominations. Why not in America, too? Let the secularized schools be kept going, of course, for the children of such parents as have too little understanding to desire a religious education for their boys and girls; but no longer let us condemn to a Godless training the children of the more percipient majority. It will not do to go on year after year with most of our children lost to God. Come weal, come woe, we Christians must secure the reintroduction of God into American education.

Years ago it was not unusual for Catholics when becoming vocal on this subject to label the public schools "Godless." But name calling never won an argument; it merely antagonizes an adversary. We must face the fact that the American public school has become the religion of the great multitude of unchurched people in this country and nothing is gained by offending them.

As a matter of fact there is probably very little antireligious teaching in the American public elementary and secondary schools. It is in the secularized universities where antireligious teaching is first encountered by the graduates of public high schools. For the most part the men and women administering and teaching in our public schools are favorably disposed to religion. Many school systems (as Pittsburgh has recently done, 1939) have now made provision for religious instruction by members of religious sects that are willing and able to supply teachers, placing these courses on the same credit basis as other courses in the school. Further, if we believe that the most potent influence in forming youth's life ideals are the personalities with whom they come in daily contact, rather than the formal teaching in a classroom, we must believe that public schools systems with God-fearing and God-loving men and women on their staffs (many of whom are Catholics) are implanting these same ideals in the hearts and minds of youth to whom they minister. This is anything but "Godless" education. Nevertheless, leaving religion out of the curriculum cannot help but have a deleterious effect on the mind of youth. How this comes about is pointed out by Dr. Ernest Johnson, Professor of Education at Teachers College, Columbia, whom the 1939 press reported as saying:

Even the controversial issues that are agitating adult minds, it is now contended by leading educators, should be faced in the schools to the extent that children are prepared to understand them. But this process stops abruptly at the door of the church. Politics, yes. Industry, yes. Race questions, yes. Religion, no! The inescapable result is that boys and girls come to regard religion as the one matter in contemporary life that is unimportant and not requiring serious thought. The only reason why the whole nation does not go completely secular in a single generation is that other cultural influences, such as the Church and the home, slow down the secularization process. But it is only a slowing down.

If this "slowing down" of the secularization process is to be stopped and transformed into a speeding up of religious influence in the minds of youth, we agree with Dr. Bell that this can only be done in schools that "not merely teach religion as a subject, but rather teach every single subject with a God-ward point of view." This is the very meaning of the Catholic school system and since we now see that State aid is necessary to preserve and improve it, we must continue the campaign to convince our fellow citizens of the justice of our claims for a share in the taxes which we contribute to school funds.

We have now completed insofar as that is possible within a single volume our philosophical investigation introducing the student to the main aspects of the pivotal problems of education. Two principles have been our guides throughout the whole inquiry; the principle of permanence—man's nature is everconstant—and the principle of change—the nature of society is ever changing. Both points of view must be kept constantly in mind if we are to work out satisfactory solutions of these four problems, in words of Sir Graham Balfour, "(1) to enable the right pupils (2) to receive the right education (3) from the right teachers, (4) under conditions which will enable the pupils best to profit by their training."

SUGGESTED READINGS

I. & 2. RIGHTS AND DUTIES IN EDUCATION

Burns, James A., *Principles, Origin and Establishment of the Catholic School System*, Benziger, 1912, Chapter IX., "Bishop Hughes and the School System," pp. 359–377.

Cronin, Michael, *The Science of Ethics*, Benziger, 1922, Vol. II, "Special Ethics," "The Rights of the State in regard to Education," pp. 486–491.

Hill, A. A., *Ethics, General and Special*, Macmillan, 1920, Thesis XI, pp. 342–358.

Miltner, Charles, *Elements of Ethics*, Macmillan, revised 1939, Chapter II, "Rights," III, "Duties," pp. 161–186, and XVI, "The Educational Problem," pp. 305–315.

Oregon School Cases, "Transcript of Record,"—No. 583, Belvedere Press, Baltimore, 1925, Justice McReynolds' Decision, pp. 937–943.

3. STATE SCHOOLS TRANSMITTING THE RELIGIOUS INHERITANCE

Anonymous, "The Scottish Educating System," *Clergy Review*, Sept., 1937, by a "teacher who spent three years in Scotland," pp. 321–329.

Coler, Bird S., "Can We Improve Education?" *Commonweal*, April 2, 1937, pp. 628–630 suggests payment by the state to parents for the education of their children "on the unit basis, a fair allotment for each child for each subject."

Confrey, Burton, *Secularism in American Education—Its History*, Catholic Univ., 1931, Chapter III, "Constitutional Provisions, Statutes, and Legal Decisions Relating to the Secularization of the Public Schools in the United States," pp. 47–125.

Gabel, Richard J., *Public Funds for Church and Private Schools*, Murray and Heister, Washington, D. C., 1937, Chapter XVIII, "State Constitutional and Statutory Provisions and Judicial Decisions (1865–1936)," pp. 537–569.

Kandel, I. L., *Comparative Education*, Houghton Mifflin, 1933, for "provided" and "nonprovided" schools in England and "religious instruction" therein, see index.

Quigley, Thomas J., *Catholic Educational Review*, June, 1939, a brief presentation of Holland's provision for tax-supported religious schools.

Reeves, Floyd W. (Chairman), *Report of the Advisory Committee*, Government Printing Office, Washington, D. C., 1938, recommends that (1) health and welfare service, (2) aid for reading materials, (3) transportation and (4) scholarships be made available to privately controlled schools, pp. 54, 86, 198.

Shields, Thomas, *The Philosophy of Education*, Cath. Ed. Press, 1917, Chapter XX, "State School Systems," and XXI. "The Catholic School System," from the point of view of a supernaturalist.

THE FOURFOLD DEVELOPMENT OF MAN

The greatest service we can do a human being

is to give him a
right education
(1) physical,
(2) intellectual,
(3) moral (social)
(4) and religious. . . .

that no child of God
may live with
(1) an enfeebled body, or
(2) a darkened mind, or
(3) a callous heart, or
(4) a perverted conscience.

John Lancaster Spalding, *Religion,
Agnosticism and Education*, pp. 151–152.

CATHOLIC EDUCATION VERSUS NATURALISM

It must never be forgotten that the subject of Christian education is man whole and entire, soul united to body in unity of nature, with all his faculties natural and supernatural, such as right reason and revelation show him to be; man, therefore, fallen from his original estate, but redeemed by Christ and restored to the supernatural condition of adopted son of God . . .

Hence every form of pedagogic naturalism which in any way excludes or weakens supernatural Christian formation in the teaching of youth, is false. Every method of education founded, wholly or in part, on the denial or forgetfulness of original sin and of grace, and relying on the sole powers of human nature, is unsound.

Pius XI, *The Christian Education of Youth.*

•

CHAPTER XVII

THE PHILOSOPHY OF CATHOLIC EDUCATION

We have now considered in some detail the four phases of the educative process that must be included in any treatment that merits the appelation "philosophical"; the problem of ends (pupil nature and needs) and the three means within the school for the achievement of these ends, (1). the curriculum, (2). the teacher and (3). the institution. It now remains for us to summarize briefly the point of view we have been stressing throughout this presentation, the philosophy of Supernaturalism as interpreted by the Catholic Chruch divinely commissioned to carry forward the work of Christian education: "Going therefore, teach ye all nations." (Math. XXVIII, 19.)

1. THE FOURFOLD DEVELOPMENT OF MAN

Education concerns the whole man, a body-mind organism, living in a material environment (the physical universe), a social environment (fellowman) and, for the humanist as we have defined him as well as for the supernaturalist, an environment which is spiritual (God's providence). In this larger meaning of the term "education," the school is by no means the only educative agency. Every experience the individual lives through is educative if he passes through it with mind awake. If he sees the mistakes he made in any experience and in the light of that knowledge learns how to avoid those mistakes, he is better prepared to meet similar experiences with the prospect of more adequate adjustment in those problematic situations with which life will inevitably confront him.   There are, in addition to the school three important agencies which, in a very special way, have educational functions to perform.

(A) PHYSICAL DEVELOPMENT

There is first of all the home.   The child begins his life in the home.   Commonly, he spends his entire childhood and the greater part of the period of adolescence under the same influence.   The physical development of the child is determined primarily by heredity, and this factor is settled at birth in the family.   With the advance of medical science, the health-conserving agencies are playing a larger and larger part in safeguarding, promoting, and when lost, restoring health.   But all these influences together can never equal the factor of heredity in determining the health that any individual enjoys through life.

(B) SOCIAL DEVELOPMENT

The second agency that early plays a part in the development of the individual is the community.   Here the factor of environment is supreme.   The home, of course, is the first environment that influences the development of the child, but early in life the neighborhood begins to exert its influence. This influence first comes through play groups, but as the individual grows older, the larger community of which he forms a part, whether urban or rural, and later government in all its forms, local, state and national, all play their part in influencing the development of the individual.   As adolescence passes into maturity, vocational calling becomes an outstanding influence. Professional men, the doctor, the lawyer, the clergyman, all have their distinctive traits that mark them as a group. So too with those who labor with their hands, the farmer and the factory worker. Leisure time also plays its part. The congeries of traits we call "personality" is to a great extent determined by the influences which the community in all its forms brings to bear on the developing individual beginning with birth and continuing all through life, since to be alive is to be undergoing the process of change.

(c) RELIGIOUS DEVELOPMENT

The third agency which plays a part in determining the kind of individual the child develops into—is an influence that operates in the realm of the spirit, the Church. Here is the distinctive feature that marks off the philosophy of Supernaturalism from all other philosophies giving naturalistic answers, to the threefold inquiry into the origin, nature, and destiny of man. With regard to origin, Supernaturalism says that man came from God (the fact of creation); with regard to nature, he is made to the image and likeness of God ("And God created man to his own image." Gen. I, 27.); and in destiny, man's chief object in life is to return to God from whom he came. The Church is ever at hand all through life to guide him and, through the administration of the sacraments, strengthen him in living a life above the natural. In this way only can he attain the supernatural destiny to which he is called, life with God hereafter.

(d) MENTAL DEVELOPMENT

The school, as the formal agency of education, has a most important part to play in all phases of this development. In the matter of physical development (health) too often in the past have the ministrations of the school been harmful rather than helpful. But with the advance of knowledge in the fields

554   THE PIVOTAL PROBLEMS OF EDUCATION

of physical and mental hygiene all this has been radically changed for the better. The school today often substituting for the failure of the home, develops within its pupils health knowledge, health habits, and health attitudes that should play a great part in reducing the incidence of sickness and prolonging life. The striking difference in this field between a Catholic school informed by the philosophy of Supernaturalism and a school conducting a purely naturalistic program will be in the matter of attitudes. For the naturalist, loss of health is the greatest calamity that can befall an individual. Not so, for the supernaturalist. Rather, it is the loss of health of soul, not health of body, which is the great calamity of life. Sin not sickness is the great evil. In fact, often it is a siege of sickness that awakens the sinner to the evils of a misspent life and puts him again on the road of virtue which alone can lead him to his true destiny, life with God. Developing this attitude in the mind of the pupil is one of the great contributions the Catholic school should make in forming the true Christian.

Similarly in the social development of the pupil, the school has an important part to play. From the family and the play group of the neighborhood the child passes into the larger school group, the kindergarten or the primary grade. As he grows older this school group continually increases in size, and the part the individual pupil plays in its activities grows in importance. Characterized by teacher control in the early years the social life of the school gradually comes more and more under the control of the students themselves, until, during the later years devoted to general education, the function of the school administrator is primarily that of guidance. The one thing youths lack in directing their social life is experience, and this must be substituted for by the experience of those responsible for the administration of the school as a community of scholars. The ideal to be aimed at is *companionship in the pur-*

suit of knowledge. Students privileged to pass their years of later adolescences in such a community have the best promise of developing the personality traits of kindness, courtesy, and coöperation which characterize the ideal citizen.

Again, in the religious development of its pupils the school is an important factor. Through the curriculum the ideal Catholic school gives the pupil a knowledge of his faith of deepening intensity as the pupil climbs the educational ladder, so that at the end of his period of general education one may be confident that he *knows* his faith and, if necessary, is prepared to defend it against assault and misinterpretations. Through the reception of the sacraments and participation in common worship, the community of scholars that is the school, shares in the effects of divine grace. They feel themselves lifted up to a level of devotion and deep appreciation of their faith, and it may truthfully be said of them—they *love* it. Finally throughout the social life of the school—through the example of inspiring teachers, through personal guidance and disciplinary regulations drawn up for their welfare, and through a system of rewards and punishment truly social in nature—they receive training in the moral virtues. In any community with a feeling of solidarity the severest punishment for an antisocial offense is exclusion from that community. The school should be slow to use this severe penalty but it is the most effective of all penalties and in extreme situations must be applied. The ideal to be striven for is that a discipline superimposed from above down in the early years is gradually transformed into a discipline self-imposed from within out. Virtues are habits. Every habit is set in action by some stimulus. In the case of the moral virtues this stimulus must be from within the individual in the form of attitudes that will put these habits into action in those situations which call for them. When this is achieved, then students *live* their faith.

THE SPECIFIC FUNCTION OF THE SCHOOL

The school will play a part in all these phases of pupil development, but the question arises, is there not one area in which it is supreme? Is there not *one specific function* for which the school, as one of the great social agencies, is to be held accountable? The Church throughout its history has carried on many educational functions, even using the term "education" in its narrower significance. For centuries the monasteries carried on whatever schooling there was for the great mass of mankind in Western Europe. There agriculture was developed as a science and an art and taught to the tillers of the soil. There and there alone was the lamp of learning kept burning when the dark cloud of the barbaric invasions settled over Europe in the fifth century and following. During the Middle Ages the universities owed their origin and development to the Church as the patron of learning. Many of her greatest saints like Albertus Magnus and Thomas Aquinas were the intellectual lights of this period and they taught within the universities. But no one would claim that mental development, the education of students in the liberal arts and sciences, or in the practical arts such as agriculture, is the specific function of the Church. Rather is it the religious development of mankind for which it was divinely commissioned and in all its activities this must take precedence.

Similarly, the school has one specific function for which it has been brought into being by society and this is the mental development of youth privileged to share its ministrations. With Newman we may call this "intellectual education" but since all knowledge begins in the senses, the word "intellectual" when used in this phrase has a wide connotation embracing the whole of our mental life. In this sense the school is an intellectual agency. This does not mean the school ignores the body. Just the contrary. Man as a somatopsychic organism functions as a whole in all life activities, and this is particularly true in that life activity which is the school's particular concern, learning. But in the philosophy we are presenting the thing that makes man man, is mind. The distinctions implied in speaking of physical, mental, social and religious development are *logical* distinctions made for clarifying thought so that with clear thinking behind it the practical procedures of the school may be carried on intelligently. With these distinctions clearly in mind, we say that the specific function of the school on all levels of general education is the making of minds. It is an intellectual agency. Cloudy thinking among American educators during the past several decades has brought forth what is called the "residual theory" of the school. The school is to take care of the "residue" after it has been determined what functions are adequately provided for by the other social agencies. With the breakdown of the American home through divorce and the urbanization of our population; with the community failing to do its part in developing within its members those qualities of character that are the test of responsible citizenship; and with the church ceasing to play a dominant role in the life of individuals and the community as it did in the founding of the nation and throughout its early history, the claim is now made that the school must take over all of these functions. Courses in cooking are introduced on the lower levels and in "Choosing a Mate" on the higher levels, as if this is the way to restore the American home to its former status. So many so-called "practical" courses have been introduced, that rare indeed is a school found now where a few first-line subjects are studied intensely and continuously over a number of years. Yet such study is the only procedure that insures mastery of the fundamentals in the early years and mastery of that part of the social inheritance adapted to assimilation through formal study in the later years. "Enrichment of the curriculum" has brought about impoverishment of the student with debilitation of the best in the American educational tradition. And all this we can lay at the door of those administrators who have unintelligently advocated this "residual theory."

We realize that this emphasis on the school as an intellectual agency may easily lead to a misunderstanding of our position. This was the experience of Newman. In spite of the clarity with which he presented his thesis in the great educational classic *The Idea of a University* [1] the distinction which he makes between the "instrumental" function of the university and its one "essential" function has not been grasped by many of his readers. Our contention here is that this same distinction applies on all levels of the educational ladder devoted to general education. The school is not a hospital or health center, though it will not be indifferent to the health of its students; it is not a parish church, though it will not neglect their moral and spiritual formation; it is not the home, though it acknowledges that it stands in *loco parentis* and will not neglect giving its students training in the social amenities of community living; it is not a country club, though it will recognize its obligation to furnish recreational facilities for its students under sympathetic supervision; it is not a training school for gladiators, though when dealing with later adolescents it may have an extensive athletic program of intramural and intercollegiate athletics; and finally, it is not a community center as that term is ordinarily understood, though school life will furnish many opportunities for the practice of the social virtues of loyalty and coöperation. The school will do all of these things, but if intelligently administered it will recognize that these are

[1] See quotation, page 163, in Chapter VI, "The Universal Human Needs," Section 1, "The School."

instrumental functions; efforts on its part to help other agencies, the hospital, the home, the church, etc., achieve their functions. But again, if intelligently administered, it will never let the performance of any one or all of these functions interfere with the effective performance of its own *essential* function, intellectual education.

The insistence with which Newman returns again and again to this point has led one writer to label Newman's idea "the philosophy of severance"[1] Yet separation of the intellectual and religious elements in education was farthest from Newman's mind. True enough, in his great work on the university he does not treat of religious training. But the title of the book explains why. He is treating of the university in its "bare idea," not as an "instrument of the Church" helping the Church achieve its functions. If we wish to know Newman's attitude with regard to how the university should combine these two functions, we must go to his sermons, notably the first sermon delivered before the newly founded university, entitled "Intellect, the Instrument of Religious Training," which we have quoted at length in Chapter VII, "The Fourth Factor in Man Making" (pp. 260–261). In that sermon he says:

> It will not satisfy me, what satisfies so many, to have two independent systems, intellectual and religious, going at once side by side, by a sort of division of labour, and accidentally brought together. It will not satisfy me, if religion is here, and science there, and young men converse with science all day, and lodge with religion in the evening. It is not touching the evil, to which these remarks have been directed, if the young men eat and drink and sleep in one place, and think in another; I want the *same roof* to contain *both the intellectual and moral discipline . . . I want the intellectual layman to be religious, and the devout ecclesiastic to be intellectual.*[2]

[1] T. Corcoran, S.J., "Liberal Education and Moral Aims," *Thought*, June, 1926.

[2] *Sermons on Various Occasions.*

FIGURE 29.—STATEMENT OF PURPOSE

The Catholic School

concerned with general education whether elementary school, high school or liberal college of arts and sciences, has as its aim the education of youth in a manner that will promote

The Fourfold Development of Man.

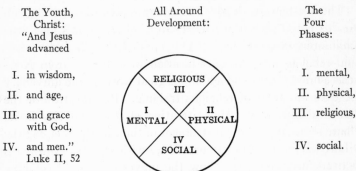

The Youth, Christ: "And Jesus advanced	All Around Development:	The Four Phases:
I. in wisdom,		I. mental,
II. and age,		II. physical,
III. and grace with God,		III. religious,
IV. and men." Luke II, 52		IV. social.

I. The Catholic school recognizes that its *specific function* is the preservation and propagation of the intellectual tradition of Catholic culture and that the means to this end is the development in students of the intellectual virtues that they may "advance in wisdom."

II. But it realizes that an educational program truly Catholic gives due attention to their physical development (health)

IV. and to their social development as good neighbors in community living and as loyal citizens of the state.

III. Finally, the Catholic school as a social agency serving the Church, gives special attention to the religious development of its students
  (1.) through instruction truly intellectual that they may *know* their faith,
  (2.) through participation in divine worship that they may *love* it,
  (3.) and through training in the moral virtues that they may *live* it.

St. Luke in his statement concerning the youth, Christ, suggests the analysis we have made here of the school's three instrumental functions on the one hand, and its one specific function on the other: "And Jesus advanced in wisdom, and age, and grace with God and men." (See Figure 29, "Statement of Purpose," p. 560.) Wisdom is one of the intellectual virtues as analyzed by St. Thomas following Aristotle, with knowledge and understanding as the other two in the speculative order. Prudence, knowing what to do, and art, knowing how to do it, are the two in the practical order.[1] It is, of course, the liberal arts and sciences the school is chiefly concerned with. Their development is particularly the work of the school. The instructional activities of the classroom, lecture hall, library, and laboratory are those that develop the intellectual virtues. In school as in life we must place first things first. This means the specific function of the school must take precedence over all supplementary instrumental functions. No matter how important they may be in life, *e.g.*, the moral virtues, they cannot be first in the school, for the simple reason that the instructional activities of the school are aimed at the development of the intellectual virtues. Insofar as the school is successful in this endeavor its students will "advance in wisdom," and with their growth in knowledge and understanding basic to wisdom, the school has made its primary contribution to the other three phases of development, physical, social and religious. We have emphasized this point in Figure 29, "Statement of Purpose," underlining the word "*specific*" in statement I. "The Catholic school recognizes that its *specific* function is the preservation and propagation of the intellectual tradition of Catholic culture" (p. 560).

2. THE EDUCATIVE PROCESS IN CATHOLIC EDUCATION

A careful scrutiny of the analysis of Catholic education we have just presented under the title "The Fourfold Development of Man" reveals that this is simply another way of view-

[1] St. Thomas Aquinas, *Summa Theologica*, 1, 2, Q. LVII.

ing the objectives of Christian Education analyzed in Part I,
"Ends in Education," and summarized in Chapter VIII, "The
Hierarchy of Educational Objectives." (Figure 16, p. 273.)
Mental Development covers the first level of the Hierarchy,
the teacher's level, the objective "Education," which runs

FIGURE 30.—THE FOURFOLD DEVELOPMENT AND THE SEVEN
OBJECTIVES OF THE HIERARCHY

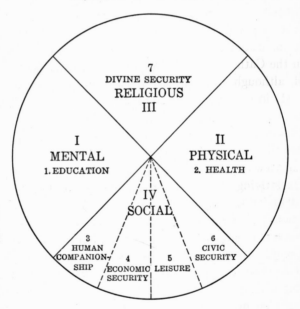

through the two upper levels of the sociologist and the philosopher. Of the six remaining objectives on the sociologist's level
"Health" and "Divine Security" are identical with Physical
Development and Religious Development. The other four,
"Human Companionship," "Economic Security," "Leisure"
and "Civic Security" are phases of social development. (Figure 30.) Finally, the realization of this fourfold develop-

ment in any adequate degree is foundation for the hope of achieving the two objectives of the philosopher's level, Christain perfection in this life and eternal salvation in the next, the ultimate objectives of Catholic education.

Following this analysis of the ends of education as interpreted by Catholic education, it is to be expected that we would now turn to the means that make formal education possible. The whole of "Part II. Means in Education" is such an analysis; it presents the three instrumentalities that make the educative process possible: (1) the curriculum, (2) the teacher, and (3) the institution as a whole. But these three means function within the Catholic school in the same way as they do in any school, although, of course, there are vital differences in all three, (1) in content, (2) in the type of teacher directing the process, and (3) in the atmosphere that characterize the institution in which the process takes place.

When, however, we look at "means" in education from the point of view of the process itself as it takes place in the pupil, we see a striking contrast between education initiated and conducted under the guidance of a naturalistic philosophy and education that is truly Catholic in both purpose and procedures. This was our point of view in Chapter II, "The Four Philosophies of Education," Section 4, "Supernaturalism, pp. 49–53 (Figure 1, p. 32). We will now continue that analysis carrying it forward in more detail as a fitting summary of the point of view presented in this statement of the philosophy of Catholic education.

On the level of brute creation, instinct is the dominant characteristic of animal life; on the human level, reason is supreme; but for the Catholic, the final arbiter in all problems with which life is continually confronting us is not instinct; nor is it reason; it is *faith*. St. Augustine's "Credo ut intelligam," "I believe that I may understand," is an expression of this attitude towards the riddles of the universe. Reason alone could never give the great philosophers of all time, Plato, Aristotle, etc., any concept of the promise that revelation brings to the Christian, the beatific vision of God hereafter. Nor could it bring a conscious realization of the supernatural life to be lived here and now.

In the same way does faith bring to the Catholic an insight into the process of education that makes the realization of these ultimate objectives possible, an insight denied to the unbelieving. For the Catholic seeking an understanding of the nature of man which will explain his behavior in all its contradictions, the depths of degradation to which he falls and the heights of sanctity to which he climbs, the doctrine of *original sin* on the one hand and that of *divine grace* on the other are the solutions of these mysteries. In regard to the first Pascal has well stated the attitude of the Catholic:

> It is an astonishing thing that the mystery most removed from our knowledge, that of original sin, should be something without which we cannot have knowledge of ourselves. For it is certain that nothing so shocks our reason as saying that the sin of the first man rendered those culpable, who, being so distinct from the source, seem incapable of participation in it. . . . Certainly nothing shocks us more rudely than this doctrine, and yet without this mystery, the most incomprehensible of all, we are incomprehensible to ourselves.[1]

When we inquire, "What are the educational implications of this doctrine of original sin?", we can state the answer in this brief phrase *the necessity of discipline*. Here is the sharp contrast in educational procedures that characterize an education truly Catholic in contrast with the naturalistic theories

[1] Quoted by Matthias Laros, *Confirmation in the Modern World*, Sheed & Ward, 1938, pp. 165–166.

parading today under such high sounding names as "progressive education," in which the true concept of liberty, that is, *liberty under the law*, is confounded with a liberty that runs to license.

When we analyze the concept "discipline," intelligently interpreted, we see that it admits of two varieties, both of which must characterize the "bringing forth" of the child (*educare*, to bring forth) if the process is to be education. In the first place chronologically, there is a discipline that must be superimposed. Even the ultramoderns admit this in the case of the infant. Habits of feeding, sleeping, etc., and other vital activities intimately associated with the customs of the society in which the infant is to take his place one day as an adult, must be imposed upon him. Similarly during childhood and adolescence the same process must be continued. In school this is the very meaning of the curriculum, a series of selected activities that are graded to meet the developing capacities of youth, through the learning of which he becomes capable of taking his place in civilized society. Even the adult does not escape from this discipline from without. It touches him in the many forms that we call "social control," *e.g.*, custom and law.

But early in the life of the child this discipline which we may call "social discipline" imposed, as it is, by society, must be replaced in any system of education intelligently administered, by a discipline which is self-imposed. In the school these two aspects of mental discipline, the social and the individual (which is self-discipline) are in inverse ratio as the child matures and mounts higher and higher on the educational ladder until, on the university level, the student is on his own and a high degree of self-discipline is his only safeguard against wasted hours and dissipated opportunities.

In life in general when wounded human nature is contending against what Newman calls "those giants, the passions and the pride of man," the question arises whether human nature alone can win the battle. Here is where faith once more brings insight to the Catholic along with assurance that victory is possible. Redemption by Christ means help to reestablish our fallen human nature. "My grace is sufficient for thee" were the assuring words to St. Paul. And grace means that we have it within our power not merely to conquer the animal within us but to rise above it and lead a life truly supernatural, that is, a life above nature. But the price of this help we call "grace" is effort on our part to overcome the disordered inclinations within us. God helps those who help themselves.

In the intellectual life many are the mysteries that confront us. Here again the Catholic has an advantage. The grace of divine faith illumines his intellect, and his belief enables him to understand, where the unbeliever finds nothing but discouragement and despair. In the *Divine Comedy*, Virgil, symbolizing reason, could lead Dante only so far. Then it remained for Beatrice, symbolizing revelation, to lead him on. In Virgil's words: "So far as reason sees here, I can tell thee; from beyond that point, ever await Beatrice, for 'tis a matter of faith." [1] St. Thomas received his greatest help in writing his masterpiece, the *Summa*, at the foot of the crucifix. Through the influence of divine grace we are made "adopted sons of God" in St. Paul's words, and through this adoption as members of the mystical Body we share the life of Christ, Our Brother, a life that is above nature because it is with God. As Pope Pius XI has expressed it in his *The Christian Education of Youth:*

> The true Christian, product of Christian Education, is the supernatural man who thinks, judges, and acts constantly and consistently in accordance with right reason illumined by the supernatural light of the example and teaching of Christ.

[1] *Purgatorio*, Canto XVIII, 46.

That the channels of grace might always be open to the faithful, Christ established His Church. And in its establishment He made it a teaching institution. "Going therefore teach ye all nations." [1] In the light of this fact we are prepared now to formulate our definition of Catholic education. It is:

> the process of growth and development whereby the natural man baptized in Christ, *under the guidance of the teaching Church* (1) assimilates a body of knowledge derived from human effort and divine revelation, (2) makes his life ideal the person of Jesus Christ, and (3) develops the ability, with the aid of divine grace, to use that knowledge in pursuit of this ideal.

It is education so defined and so interpreted that must ever be the concern of the Catholic school for all pupils at all levels of maturity, in all countries, at all times. To the Catholic school throughout the world, therefore, we address the words of the Psalmist:

> Specie tua et pulchritudine tua, intende, prospere procede, et regna.
> With thy comeliness and thy beauty, set out, proceed prosperously, and reign. [2]

SUGGESTED READINGS

Adam, Karl, *The Spirit of Catholicism* (tr. by Dom. Justin McCann), Macmillan, 1930, rev. ed. 1935, Chap. XII "The Educative Action of the Church," stresses the teaching function of the Church.

Brubacher, John S., *Modern Philosophies of Education*, McGraw-Hill, 1939, presents "scholasticism" as the basis for the dualistic essentialism of the Catholic; see Index for Supernaturalism.

[1] Matthew XXVIII, 19.
[2] Psalm XL, 5.

568 THE PIVOTAL PROBLEMS OF EDUCATION

Deman, Thomas, O.P., "Christian Humanism," *Blackfriars*, Aug. 1938, a good discussion of "the decisive difference between philosophy and faith," pp. 555–570.

Kelly, William A., "Needed: A Directive Philosophy of Education," *Thought*, June, 1938, pp. 197–205, a critique of "progressive education" presenting the Catholic philosophy of education as "the only philosophy which is truly directive amid perplexing conditions."

Marique, P.S., *The Philosophy of Christian Education*, Prentice-Hall, 1939, an elementary statement of Supernaturalism by a Catholic.

Newman, John Henry, *Discussions and Arguments*, "The Tamworth Reading Room," pp. 270–274, Section 3, is entitled "Secular Knowledge not a Direct Means of Moral Improvement."

——, *Sermons on Various Occasions*, Sermon I. "Intellect, the Instrument of Religious Training."

Proceedings of the American Catholic Philosophical Association, 1937, the first seven addresses are all on some phase of the philosophy of education, e. g., "The Essential Features of the Philosophy of Education of St. Thomas" by Robert J. Slavin, pp. 22–37.

Van, Gerald, *On Being Human*, Sheed & Ward, 1934, presents the thesis that Supernaturalism is the perfection of Humanism on the principle, *gratia perficit naturam*, grace perfects nature, p. 18.

APPENDIX

LIST OF BOOKS RECOMMENDED FOR USE WITH THIS TEXT

The books starred (*) are recommended as particularly worthwhile. Two or more copies of these books (depending on the size of the class) should be available for reference and circulation in the libraries of institutions using this text.

Advisory Committee on Education, *Report of the Committee*, U. S. Government Printing Office, Washington, 1938.

Allers, Rudolph, *The New Psychologies*, Sheed & Ward, New York, 1932.

* ——, *The Psychology of Character*, Sheed & Ward, New York, 1932.

Aristotle (tr. by Welldon), *Politics*, London, 1908.

——, *Ethics*, any edition.

Babbit, Irving, *Literature and the American College*, Houghton Mifflin, Boston, 1908.

* Bagley, William C., *Education, Crime, and Social Progress*, Macmillan, New York, 1931.

——, *The Educative Process*, Macmillan, New York, 1920.

* Bode, Boyd H., *Conflicting Psychologies of Learning*, Heath, Boston, 1929.

——, *Modern Educational Theories*, Macmillan, New York, 1927.

* Bossing, Nelson L., *Progressive Methods of Teaching in Secondary Schools*, Houghton Mifflin, Boston, 1935.

Breed, Frederick S., *Education and the New Realism*, Macmillan, New York, 1939.

Brubacher, John S., *Modern Philosophies of Education*, McGraw-Hill, New York, 1939.

* Burns, J. A., and B. J. Kohlbrenner, *A History of Catholic Education in the United States*, Benziger, New York, 1937.

Butler, Nicholas Murray, *The Meaning of Education*, Scribner's, New York, 1915.

* Chapman, J. Crosby and George S. Counts, *Principles of Education*, Houghton Mifflin, Boston, 1924.

Curoe, Philip R., *History of Education*, Globe, New York, 1921.

* De Hovre, Franz (tr. by Edward B. Jordan), *Philosophy and Education*, Benziger, New York, 1931.

* ——, *Catholicism in Education*, Benziger, New York, 1934.

De la Salle, Saint Jean Baptiste (tr. by F. Fontainerie), *The Conduct of the Schools*, McGraw-Hill, New York, 1935.

* Dewey, John, *Democracy and Education*, Macmillan, New York, 1917.

Douglass, Audrey A., *Secondary Education*, Houghton Mifflin, Boston, 1927.

* Draper, Edgar M., and Alexander C. Roberts, *Principles of American Secondary Education*, Century, New York, 1932.

Finney, Ross L., *A Sociological Philosophy of Education*, Macmillan, New York, 1928.

* Fitzpatrick, Edward A., *Readings in the Philosophy of Education*, Appleton-Century, New York, 1936.

Flexner, Abraham, *Universities, American, English, German*, Oxford Univ. Press, New York, 1930.

* Foerster, Norman, *Humanism and America*, Farrar and Rinehart, New York, 1930.

——, *The American State University*, University of North Carolina Press, Chapel Hill, 1937.

Gates, Arthur I., *Psychology for Students of Education*, Macmillan, 1924.

Higginson, Glenn De Vere, *Fields of Psychology*, Holt, New York, 1931.

Holley, Charles Elmer, *High School Teacher's Methods*, Garrard, Champaign, Ill., 1937.

Horne, Herman Harrell, *Idealism in Education*, Macmillan, New York, 1910.

* ——, *The Democratic Philosophy of Education*, Macmillan, New York, 1933.

* Hutchins, Robert Maynard, *The Higher Learning in America*, Yale University Press, New Haven, 1936.

* Inglis, Alexander, *Principles of Secondary Education*, Houghton Mifflin, Boston, 1918.

* Kandel, I. L., *Comparative Education*, Houghton Mifflin, Boston, 1933.

* Kane, W., *A History of Education*, Loyola University Press, Chicago, 1935.

* Kilpatrick, William H., *Source Book in the Philosophy of Education*, Macmillan, New York, 1934.

Kuehner, Quincy A., *A Philosophy of Education*, Prentice-Hall, New York, 1935.

Leighton, Joseph A., *Social Philosophies in Conflict*, Appleton-Century, 1937.

Marique, P. S., *The Philosophy of Christian Education*, Prentice-Hall, New York, 1939.

McGucken, William J., *The Catholic Way in Education*, Bruce, Milwaukee, 1934.

* Miltner, Charles C., *The Elements of Ethics*, Macmillan, New York, 1925 (revised 1939).

Monroe, Walter S., *Directing Learning in the High School*, Doubleday, Page, Garden City, 1927.

——, James C. DeVoss and George W. Reagan, *Educational Psychology*, Doubleday, Doran, Garden City, 1930.

Moore, Thomas Verner, *Cognitive Psychology*, Lippincott, Philadelphia, 1939.

* ——, *Dynamic Psychology*, Lippincott, Philadelphia, 1924.

* Morrison, Henry C., *The Practice of Teaching in the Secondary School*, University of Chicago Press, Chicago, 1926 (revised 1931).

Murphy, Gardner, *Historical Introduction to Modern Psychology*, Harcourt, Brace, New York, 1929.

* Newman, John Henry, *Idea of a University*, 1852, any edition.

——, *Discussions and Arguments*, any edition.

* ——, *Sermons on Various Occasions*, Sermon I.

Nock, Albert Jay, *The Theory of Education in the United States*, Harcourt, Brace, New York, 1932.

* Plato, *The Republic*, any edition.

——, *The Laws*, any edition.

Ragsdale, Clarence Edwin, *Modern Psychologies and Education*, Macmillan, New York, 1932.

* Shields, Thomas Edward, *Philosophy of Education*, The Catholic Education Press, Washington, 1917.

Skinner, Charles E., (editor), *Educational Psychology*, Prentice-Hall, New York, 1936.

Smith, Walter Robinson, *Principles of Educational Sociology*, Houghton Mifflin, Boston, 1928.

Spalding, J. L., *Education and the Higher Life*, McClurg, Chicago, 1890.

——, *Means and Ends of Education*, McClurg, Chicago, 1897.

——, *Religion, Agnosticism and Education*, McClurg, Chicago, 1902.

* Thomas, Frank W., *Principles and Technique of Teaching*, Houghton Mifflin, Boston, 1927.

* Warren, Howard C., *Human Psychology*, Houghton Mifflin, Boston, 1919.

Washburne, Carleton W., *Adjusting the School to the Child*, World Book, Yonkers, 1932.

* Woodworth, Robert S., *Contemporary Schools of Psychology*, Ronald Press, New York, 1931.

AUTHOR INDEX

Adler, Mortimer, 43, 131, 132, 477–8, 539
Adler, Sigmund, 103, 104
Albertus Magnus, 556
Allers, Rudolph, 186
Aquinas, Thomas, 13, 14, 31, 45, 53, 60, 136, 313, 417, 435, 556, 561–6
Aristotle, 13, 14, 18, 31, 45, 60, 208, 240, 288, 313, 316, 417, 435, 467, 561–4, 566–8–9
Armentrout, 426
Arnold, Matthew, 291, 307–8, 333, 370
Arrowood, Charles, 370, 491
Augustine, Saint, 31, 52, 276, 563

Babbitt, Irving, 18, 27, 31, 43, 400, 467
Bagley, William Chandler, 18, 82, 469
Balfour, Sir Graham, vii, 548
Ballou, Frank W., 527
Baucher, Chauncey Samuel, 299
Bell, Bernard Iddings, 251–2, 546
Benson, Robert Hugh, 245
Bentham, Jeremy, 215–6
Berkely, Bishop, 84
Berkely, Governor, 159
Bellarmine, Robert, 209–10
Binet, Alfred, 480
Blow, Susan, 351
Bode, Boyd H., 129
Bossing, Nelson L., 82, 452–3
Brosnahan, T., 524
Bryce, James, 223–5
Buddha, 45, 101–2–9
Buhler, K., 186
Burns, James, 400, 525–6
Butler, Nicholas Murray, 18, 280, 298, 304, 372, 407, 464, 499, 528

Calvin, John, 50, 240–1, 469
Castiello, Jaime, 134–5
Cattell, J. M., 480
Cavanaugh, John, 499
Chapman, J. Crosby, 18, 98, 156, 169, 302–6, 310, 321, 340–9, 370–4
Chesterton, Gilbert K., 49
Christ, Jesus, 14, 50, 52, 173, 179, 218, 240–3, 271, 445–7, 469, 472, 510, 560
Coady, Moses, 199
Coffey, P., 12
Comenius, 18, 314–15–16, 331, 347, 370
Commins, W. D., 449
Compton, Arthur H., 52
Confrey, Burton, 543
Colvin, Stephen Sheldon, 266
Confucius, 45, 211
Coolidge, Calvin, 363, 518–28
Copeland, Royal S., 527
Corcoran, T., 559
Corning, Hobart M., 462
Counts, George S., 18, 98, 114, 156, 169, 302, 306–10–17–18–21, 340–9, 370–4
Croce, 28
Curoe, Philip R. V., 342–3, 367, 510

Dante, 60, 101–2, 566
Darwin, Charles, 33
Daugherty, Carroll, 193
Dawson, Christopher, 27, 223
Descartes, 84, 131
Dewey, John, 2, 18, 37–9, 141, 269, 450
Dillon, William T., 219
Douglas, Aubrey A., 82
Draper, Edgar M., 366, 385, 524–34

573

SUBJECT INDEX

197